THE ARCHAEOLOGY OF ETHNOGENESIS

THE ARCHAEOLOGY
OF ETHNOGENESIS

Race and Sexuality in Colonial San Francisco

Barbara L. Voss

University of California Press   Berkeley Los Angeles London

University of California Press, one of the most distinguished
university presses in the United States, enriches lives around
the world by advancing scholarship in the humanities, social
sciences, and natural sciences. Its activities are supported by
the UC Press Foundation and by philanthropic contributions
from individuals and institutions. For more information, visit
www.ucpress.edu.

University of California Press
Berkeley and Los Angeles, California

University of California Press, Ltd.
London, England

Library of Congress Cataloging-in-Publication Data

Voss, Barbara L., 1967–.
    The archaeology of ethnogenesis : race and sexuality in
colonial San Francisco / Barbara L. Voss.
        p.   cm.
    Includes bibliographical references and index.
    ISBN: 978-0-520-24492-4 (cloth : alk. paper)
    1. Ethnology—California—Presidio of San Francisco.   2. Sex
role—California—Presidio of San Francisco.   3. Ethnicity—
California—Presidio of San Francisco.   4. Excavations
(Archaeology)—California—Presidio of San Francisco.
5. Social archaeology—California—Presidio of San Francisco.   6. Presidio of San Francisco (Calif.)—History.
7. Presidio of San Francisco (Calif.)—Race relations.
8. Presidio of San Francisco (Calif.)—Social life and customs.
9. California—History—To 1846.   I. Title.

F868.S156V67   2008
305.309794'6109034—dc22   2007011566

Cartography of maps 1–12 developed by Landis Bennett.

Manufactured in the United States of America

17   16   15   14   13   12   11   10   09   08
10   9   8   7   6   5   4   3   2   1

This book is printed on Natures Book, which contains 50%
post-consumer waste and meets the minimum requirements
of ANSI/NISO Z39.48–1992 (R 1997) (Permanence of Paper).

To Deb
for everything

CONTENTS

ILLUSTRATIONS

Figures

Maps

TABLES

Appendix Tables

ACKNOWLEDGMENTS

This book is based on research conducted from 1992 to 2005 at the Presidio of San Francisco, formerly a U.S. Army post and today a National Historic Park that is part of the Golden Gate National Recreation Area. Archaeological research is necessarily a group effort, the product of the shared expertise and hard work of many. I am glad to have this opportunity to express my gratitude to those whose intellectual generosity, collaborative spirit, and overall kindness have greatly contributed to this work.

My first thanks go to Sannie Kenton Osborn of the Presidio Trust and Leo Barker of the National Park Service, who led the search for archaeological remains of El Presidio de San Francisco in the late 1980s and early 1990s, and whose foresight and dedication have ensured the preservation of this important archaeological landscape. Today, they lead the Presidio Archaeology Center, a federal facility that directs all archaeological research at the park and curates the Presidio's archaeological collections. Sannie and Leo welcomed my research interest in the site, invited me to participate in and develop field and laboratory research programs, provided financial and logistical support for the work reported here, and at every step of the way shared their knowledge and experience. I am honored to have them as mentors and colleagues and friends.

Presidio Trust and National Park Service staff contributed immensely to this project. The current and former staff of the Presidio Archaeology Center—Hans Barnaal, Eric Blind, Liz Clevenger, Rose Healy, Chris Lee, Stacey Maung, Jenn McCann, and Megan Wilkinson—deserve special mention for their day-to-day involvement. At the Presidio Trust, Randy Delehanty, Jody Sanford, Ron Sonenshine, Allison Stone, and Cherilyn Widell continually amazed me with their willingness to do whatever they could to support archaeological research. At the National Park Service, special thanks go to Brett Bankie, Ric Borjes, Fatima Colindres, Will Elder, Steven Haller, Diane Nicholsen, and Paul Scolari, who have been instrumental in interpreting the Presidio's history and archaeology for the public. Staff, residents, and volunteers at the Presidio welcomed our research teams to the park, graciously tolerated the disruptions of their routines, and furthered this project in innumerable ways. My thanks to all of you.

My research at the Presidio has been enabled and nurtured by my professional affiliations. I began work at the Presidio of San Francisco in 1992, as a staff archaeologist in the Cultural Resources Group at Woodward-Clyde Consultants. I will always be grateful to Vance Benté for sharing his passion for Spanish-colonial archaeology with me, and to Sally Morgan, Brian Hatoff, Laura Melton, and Karen Boyd for being such good mentors and colleagues.

From 1996 to 2002, I continued my research as a graduate student in the Department of Anthropology at the University of California, Berkeley. There, the Archaeological Research Facility and the Designated Emphasis in Women, Gender, and Sexuality program provided warm and stimulating interdisciplinary communities. This study is especially indebted to Kent Lightfoot, whose research at Colony Ross has fostered new paradigms for the archaeology of colonial settlements. His innovative scholarship is matched only by his thoughtfulness and great sense of humor. Meg Conkey's unceasing commitment to feminist practice in archaeological research continues to inspire me. Margaret Chowning, Rosemary Joyce, Ed Luby, Ruth Tringham, Laurie Wilkie, and Caren Kaplan each played a particularly important role in shaping my development as a researcher and a scholar, as did my fellow graduate students, especially Steve Archer, Kira Blaisdell-Sloan, El Casella, Bonnie Clark, Kathleen Hull, Nette Martinez, Anna Naruta, Erica Radewagen, Amy Ramsay, Rob Schmidt, Steve Silliman, Cheryl Smith-Lintner, Kath Sterling, and Kathy Twiss.

Since 2001, I have continued research at the Presidio as a faculty member at Stanford University. The Department of Cultural and Social Anthropology is a wonderful environment in which to think and work, and I thank each of my colleagues here. Fellow archaeologists Ian Hodder, Lynn Meskell, and Mike Wilcox were the source of many provocative discussions that helped me to clarify the focus of this book. Graduate students Stacey Camp, Liz Clevenger, and Bryn Williams must be thanked not only for their contributions to recent field and laboratory projects at the Presidio but also for many stimulating conversations about theory, method, and practice in historical archaeology. Finally, Stanford's programs in Archaeology, Feminist Studies, Urban Studies, and Comparative Studies of Race and Ethnicity have provided important interdisciplinary venues for further development of this project.

All of us who conduct archaeological research at El Presidio de San Francisco are indebted to the documentary research program conducted under the leadership of National Park Service archaeologists and historians. Gordon Chappell, Leo Barker, John Langellier, and Daniel Rosen have produced a collection of historical source materials (Chappell 1976) and a Historic Resources Study (Langellier and Rosen 1992). Additionally, Leo Barker (2007) obtained a microfilm library of historical documents from the Archivo General de la Nación in Mexico; this valuable collection was later amended with additional microfilms donated by Francis Weber and Catherine Rudolph of the Santa Barbara Presidio History Center. Veronica Dado, an intern with the International Council on Monuments and Sites, has been translating and transcribing these microfilmed archives (Dado 2003, 2004, 2006). I am also indebted to Randy Milliken's studies of Native Californian ethnohistory (Milliken 1995; Milliken, Shoup, and Ortiz 2005) and to William Marvin Mason's demographic studies of Alta California's colonial population (Mason 1998). Far more than simply providing "historical context" for archaeological research, these documentary research programs have transformed historical understandings of Spanish colonization of Alta California.

Over the years, many scholars have encouraged my research interests and shared their knowledge and expertise, among them Rebecca Allen, Rosemarie Beebe, Judy Bense, Victor Buchli, Al Camarillo, Anita Cohen-Williams, Barbara Corff, Julia Costello, Kathleen Deagan, Rob Edwards, Paul Farnsworth, Larry Felton, Bunny Fontana, Lee Foster, Andy Galvan, Joan Gero, Roberta Gilchrist, Sarah Ginn, Roberta Greenwood, Martin Hall, Sandy Hollimon, Bob Hoover, Roberta Jewett, Jakki Kehl, Roger Kelly, John Langellier, Linda Longoria, Diana Loren, Ron May, Reuben Mendoza, Jeanne McDonnell, Randy Milliken, Paul Mullins, Gary Pahl, Breck Parkman, Liz Perry, Adrian Praetzellis, Mary Praetzellis, Nan Rothschild, Pat Rubertone, Gayle Rubin, Bob Senkewicz, Russ Skowronek, Charr Simpson-Smith, Marie Louise Stig Sørensen, David Hurst Thomas, Kathleen Ungvarsky, Francis Weber, Jack Williams, Alison Wylie, and Linda Yamane.

None of this would have been possible without the talent and labor of the many staff members, consultants, students, and volunteers who worked alongside me on these field and lab research projects. They are thanked by name elsewhere (Voss 2002:xxi-xxii; Voss et al. 2004:8–9; Voss et al. 2005:8–9) and are to be commended for enduring hot sun and cold fog, for their careful and meticulous work, and especially for sharing their enthusiasm and curiosity. I would also like to thank members of the public who visited field and laboratory investigations at the Presidio, especially the many Ohlone and Californio descendants who have talked with me about their family and community history. Their questions, insights, and comments were always thought-provoking and helped me to define the key issues discussed in this book.

I would like to acknowledge several specialists whose expertise was essential: Hans Barnaal (mapping specialist); El Casella and Heather Blind (laboratory managers); Amy Ramsay, Karis Eklund, and Bea Cox (public interpretation); Nancy Valente, Ken Gobalet, Kalie Harden, and Laura Melton (zooarchaeology); Virginia Popper (archaeobotany); Kathleen Hull, Steven Shackley, and Jennifer Coats (lithics); and Jack Meyer (geoarchaeology). Kendra Carlisle, Emily Erler, Molly Fierer-Donaldson, and Rika Hirata also deserve special recognition for their involvement in the 2000−2001 ceramics analysis project. Nicole von Germaten, Kath Sterling, and Cashman Kerr Prince assisted with translations of Spanish, French, and Latin texts, respectively.

During the writing of this book in 2005−2006, Blake Edgar steadily guided me through manuscript development, preparation, and submission; his keen editorial sense greatly improved the book. Blake's assistant, Matthew Winfield, was especially helpful regarding the art program. The skillful editorial attention of Rose Vekony and Mary Renaud was greatly appreciated. Bryn Williams's adroit library research skills proved invaluable, as did Natalia Cooper's editorial assistance. Several colleagues generously reviewed part or all of earlier drafts of this book, including Hans Barnaal, Leo Barker, Eric Blind, Liz Clevenger, Deborah Cohler, Kathleen Coll, Veronica Dado, Rob Edwards, Ian Hodder, Kathleen Hull, Kent Lightfoot, Sannie Kenton Osborn, Virginia Popper, Charr Simpson-Smith, and Cheryl Smith-Lintner. Randy McGuire and Mary Beaudry also provided particularly insightful commentary on the completed manuscript. For all improvements, these readers deserve full credit; any remaining shortcomings exist despite their good efforts.

The artifacts photographed for this book are curated at the Presidio Archaeology Center, and I would like to thank the staff there for facilitating the publication of images of these archaeological finds. The maps, diagrams, charts, and graphs in this book were drafted by cartographer and graphic designer Landis Bennett, who also converted the artifact photographs into print-ready images. Landis's careful attention to detail and thoughtful visual aesthetic made working on the book's art program a pleasure. Randy Milliken graciously allowed us to develop maps 2 and 3 from his earlier works and generously reviewed our map adaptations, providing updated tribal community locations based on his current research. Maps 6, 7, 8, and 9 were adapted in part from primary mapping sources developed by Hans Barnaal. The staff at the Bancroft Library and their agent, Susan Snyder, were especially helpful in locating historical maps and images of the Presidio and arranging permission for publication. John Langellier and Ilona Katzew also aided in tracking down other hard-to-find historical images. Trini Rico translated correspondence with archives and museums in Spain.

Many organizations and institutions provided funding for this research and for the writing of this book. My graduate studies during 1996–2001 were supported by a National Science Foundation graduate fellowship, a William and Flora Hewlett Foundation fellowship, and a Career Development Grant from the American Association of University Women. During 1997–2001, the National Park Service and the Presidio Trust provided funding and in-kind support for field and laboratory research. The Vice Chancellor for Research Fund at the University of California, Berkeley, and a Berkeley Humanities Research grant supplied funding for zooarchaeological and archaeobotanical analysis. Field and laboratory research during 2003–2005 was funded by the Presidio Trust as well as by several Stanford University programs including Urban Studies, Feminist Studies, the Office of Technology Licensing Research Incentive Fund, the Vice Provost for Undergraduate Education, and the Iris F. Litt, MD, Fund of the Institute for Research on Women and Gender. Stanford University's junior faculty leave program provided relief from regular duties during the 2005–2006 academic year, allowing me to complete the book manuscript.

Most important of all is encouragement from family and friends. My parents, Ray and Lois Voss, deserve special mention for encouraging my early interest in archaeology. Along with family members, Karen Boyd, Bernie Burk, Mike Byrne, Jana Cerny, Ann Mei Chang, Hale Fulton, Carrie Graham-Lee, Kathleen Hull, Kate Jessup, Malu Lujan, John Magee, Tom Martin, Linda Rose McRoy, Jerilyn Mendoza, Adriana Schoenberg, and Wickie Stamps have each been a source of support and inspiration.

Last—but certainly not least—this book is dedicated to my life partner, Deb Cohler, who has graciously tolerated the many disruptions that archaeological research can cause. More important, Deb has been an intellectual mentor, always challenging me to be more rigorous in my approach and holding me accountable for my interpretations of the past. She helped me believe that this project was both possible and worthwhile. Her love and good humor have meant more than I can say.

Ethnogenesis refers to the birthing of new cultural identities. The emergence of a new ethnic identity or the reconfiguration of an existing one is not simply a question of terminology. Moments of ethnogenesis signal the workings of historical and cultural shifts that make previous kinds of identification less relevant, giving rise to new forms of identity.

Studying ethnogenesis, as it happens today and as it has unfolded in the past, provides a means to trace the changing contours of social life. At its core, the investigation of ethnogenesis reveals the politics of social difference. Identities simultaneously provide ontological security (we know who we are) and are flashpoints in social conflict ("Don't call me that!"). We can thus conceptualize ethnicity as a cultural dialogue rather than as something fixed and essential: "an unarticulated negotiation between what you call yourself and what other people are willing to call you back" (Hitt 2005:40). The politics of identities point to relationships of authority and coercion—the power to name oneself is, for example, quite different from the power to assign a name to others.

This book presents an archaeological and historical study of ethnogenesis among colonial settlers in San Francisco, California, during its years as a Spanish *presidio*, or military outpost (1776–1821). The settlers were a diverse group of families who had been recruited primarily from the present-day Mexican states of Sonora, Sinaloa, Baja California, and Baja California Sur. Most settlers had some combination of Mexican Indian, African, and European ancestry. Under Spanish-colonial law, the settlers were classified according to the *sistema de castas*, an elaborate racial code in which lighter skin generally corresponded with higher social rank.

Many people at El Presidio de San Francisco and in other parts of the Spanish Americas actively manipulated the sistema de castas to improve their social standing—for example, by reporting a higher-ranking *casta*, or racial status, on their military enlistment or marriage papers than the one they had been assigned at birth. But in California at the end of the eighteenth century, the colonial settlers went a step further and rejected the sistema de castas altogether. One priest in charge of recording casta information in census records lamented that "such enumeration was in vain since the inhabitants of the district considered themselves Spaniards" (Miranda 1988:271). The colonial residents started to describe themselves as *gente de razón* (literally, people of reason), *hijos* and *hijas del país* (sons and daughters of the land), and, increasingly, *Californios* and *Californianas* (Californians). The new Californio ethnic identity simultaneously referenced the region in which the colonial settlers lived and emphasized Spanish ancestry at the expense of indigenous and African identities. The settlers continued to refer to themselves as "Californios" throughout the region's years as a Mexican province (1822–1846) and as a new U.S. state (from 1850 to the present). Although the term faded from common use in the twentieth century, many modern descendants of California's Spanish colonists still proudly call themselves "Los Californianos" and maintain a pedigreed heritage organization that commemorates the historical contributions of their ancestors (fig. 1).

The case of colonial ethnogenesis at El Presidio de San Francisco is significant in its own right: as the first colonial settlement in what has come to be one of the world's major metropolitan areas, the actions of its residents have had broad historical ramifications. But the significance of this study derives in equal measure from this settlement's commonalities with other colonial outposts throughout the world. Too often, archaeologists and historians emphasize a firm divide between European colonizers and indigenous victims of colonization, treating the categories of "colonist" and "native" as static groupings. The case of El Presidio de San Francisco—in which colonized peoples were relocated to serve as colonizers—is typical of the frontier settlements of many prehistoric and historical empires. The investigation of colonial ethnogenesis in San Francisco documents how a pluralistic community of displaced families reinvented itself as a unified colonizing force, a phenomenon that has occurred countless times in frontier colonial settlements across history and throughout the globe.

Four core themes shape this study of ethnogenesis: colonization, material practice, overdetermination, and sexuality.

Colonization is the appropriation of a previously autonomous region and its transformation into a dependency under the control of a remote entity. Colo-

FIGURE 1.   Los Californianos commemorating Presidio Pasados. This annual
event marks the anniversary of the founding of El Presidio de San Francisco.
The location—the Presidio's Main Post—is also the archaeological site of the
historical Presidio quadrangle (see fig. 10). The building in the background is
the Officers' Club, which contains the only extant adobe walls of the Spanish-
colonial settlement (see fig. 11).

nization transformed California from a region populated by scores of independent native communities into a province of Spain's American empire. El Presidio de San Francisco was a military instrument of Spain's seizure of California, and its residents provided the military force behind the "spiritual" conquest
orchestrated by Catholic missionaries.

Acts of colonization cause profound ruptures in the cultures of both colonizer and colonized. Though the indigenous populations displaced by or entangled with colonial institutions are the most severely affected, the colonists
themselves are also irrevocably transformed by their own displacement and by
their encounters with local indigenous people. In Spanish-colonial California,
this period of rapid political and cultural change dramatically shifted the limits and possibilities of the lives of both groups. Cultural disruption and physical deprivation forced innovation. Old ways of doing things took on new meanings. Colonial encounters produced conditions under which social identities
had to be refashioned in response to intercultural contact. The study of ethnogenesis at El Presidio de San Francisco thus reveals the changing fault lines of
both colonial and indigenous societies.

This study is unusual among recent archaeological investigations of colonization in its focus on the colonizers themselves. Since the 1980s, archaeologists have tended to emphasize indigenous responses to the effects of European colonization in the Americas. This important change in our discipline marked a shift from viewing indigenous peoples as passive victims of colonial regimes to considering the ways that native communities actively worked to maximize their chances of survival and ensure the continuation of their cultures. This study's focus on colonial ethnogenesis is not intended to divert attention from the experiences of indigenous populations. Rather, it seeks to shed light on the ways that the military settlers manipulated identity categories to consolidate their position as colonizers. Such critical investigations of colonial life remind us that the outcome of colonial projects was never certain and that colonial control was never complete.

The second theme of this study is material practice, which encompasses the physical activities that humans engage in every moment of the day: moving, eating, working, playing. In social theory, material practice (what people do) is often contrasted with discourse (what people say), but this distinction is permeable: even the words you are reading right now are printed on a physical medium and were composed through finger strokes on a keyboard. However, a focus on the ways that material practices participate in ethnogenesis can provide a very different perspective than that afforded by historical documents alone.

In the historical context of El Presidio de San Francisco, attention to the role of material practice in the maintenance and transformation of identity is critical. Few of the colonists were literate, and the documents they left behind generally present the perspectives of a small number of priests and high-ranking military officers. Such documents can be read creatively to ferret out the "hidden" voices of rank-and-file soldiers, colonial women and children, and Native Californians, but the result is constrained by the source itself. Unlike these documentary records, however, archaeological research reveals the traces left behind by the full population of the Presidio, regardless of literacy, rank, race, gender, or age.

Even more important, social subjects are entangled with the materiality of the world. Where people live, how food is cooked, the clothes people wear, the objects they use in daily life: these genres of material practice are silent tools used in the reworking of social identity. Because of the durability and persistence of material culture, it can function to stabilize social identities that are otherwise quite volatile. The meanings of places and things are never fixed, however, and objects can be taken up for various purposes by different users. Studying material practice allows us to investigate the ways that identities are often simultaneously ambiguous yet surprisingly enduring.

The third theme that shapes this book is the concept of overdetermination. "Overdetermination" is a term that many social theorists associate with poststructuralism, where it is used to argue that social phenomena are too complex to be explained with mechanistic, cause-and-effect models. This poststructuralist usage draws heavily on earlier psychological and mathematical uses of the term. Sigmund Freud, for example, employed the word "overdetermination" to describe cases in which a given symptom, such as hysteria, was the manifestation of multiple traumas, no single one of which could be isolated as the "cause" of the illness. Similarly, in mathematics, a system of equations is "overdetermined" when it has more equations than unknowns; in general, such systems cannot be precisely solved. In other words, overdetermination is a theory of irreducibility, in which a given phenomenon is conceptualized as an effect produced by a potentially infinite number of other contributing and interacting phenomena.

This book applies the concept of overdetermination to social identities generally and to ethnicity specifically. Archaeology has adopted a static approach to the study of identities for too long, viewing social identities as stable categories rather than ongoing social processes. Additionally, archaeologists tend to compartmentalize the study of identities by isolating specific aspects of identity such as gender or class or race, without considering how these practices of identification are interconnected. For example, in Spanish-colonial California, the term *soldado* (soldier) at face value indicated a person's military occupation. But in practice it meant much more, connoting gender, age, nationality, colonial status, rank, class, future economic prospects, and physical ability in ways that cannot be disentangled.

If social identities are overdetermined, then changes in those identities—such as the phenomenon of ethnogenesis—cannot be traced back to a single root cause. The research presented here is not aimed at discovering the "cause" of ethnogenesis but rather at using archaeological evidence, historical documents, and oral history to trace the webs of social discourse and material practices that participated in the emergence and consolidation of Californio identity.

The fourth theme is sexuality and the closely related concept of gender. If social identities are overdetermined, then it must follow that the emergence of a new ethnic category such as Californio is about more than a sense of regional pride. In particular, sexuality is just as central to the formation and maintenance of ethnic identities as race, nationality, and citizenship. Because ethnicity is produced in complicated ways through references to common ancestry (real or perceived), ethnicity is invariably involved in the politics of sexuality and reproduction. Anti-miscegenation laws and anxieties about "marrying out" both use the trope of ethnic integrity to justify controls on sexual and romantic behaviors. Simultaneously, sexual desires and sexual violence circulate through-out and across what Joane Nagel (2003) terms "ethnosexual frontiers." Fur-ther, the operation of gendered and sexualized power is often camouflaged in terms of national or ethnic belonging or conflict, often through concerns about the sexual honor and respectability of the community. Consequently, gender and sexual identities are commonly used to legitimate or discount social claims of ethnic belonging. Lest we trivialize this cultural dialogue of acceptance and exclusion, we must recall that a person's social and often physical survival de-pends on performing identities that are recognizable and intelligible to others. Rejection, ostracism, exile, neglect, imprisonment, and violence are common consequences of being "too different." The dance of ethnogenesis, of shifting identities, is a perilous one.

Becoming Californio was as much about sexuality and gender as it was about race and regionalism. The findings of archaeological investigations and read-ings of historical documents indicate that Californio identity was constructed partly through relations of differential masculinity that were materially produced through labor practices and architecture. This identity also emerged from sev-eral decades of routinized household practices that emphasized the common-alities between colonists and materially exaggerated their differences from Na-tive Californians. From foodways to ceramics to clothing to architecture, the material habits of daily life conditioned and transformed the ways that colonists at El Presidio de San Francisco perceived their own identities and those of Na-tive Californians.

The first chapter of this book establishes the conceptual groundwork for this investigation, interrogating, in turn, theoretical and methodological issues in-volved in studies of identity, ethnicity, sexuality, and ethnogenesis. The re-maining chapters are organized into two parts. Part 1, "Historical and Archae-ological Contexts," begins by introducing Spanish-colonial San Francisco, including its colonial institutions and the historical events that affected the lives of the people who lived there (chapter 2). Chapter 3 presents the findings of demographic research on both the colonial and indigenous populations of the Presidio and also discusses the historically specific formulation of racial, gen-dered, and sexual identities in eighteenth-century New Spain. Chapter 4 con-tinues this examination of colonial identities by presenting the documentary evidence for Californio ethnogenesis and assessing the prevalent historical ex-planations of this new identity's emergence. Chapter 5 turns to archaeology, providing an overview of the field and laboratory research that forms the em-pirical basis for this study.

Part 2, "Spatial and Material Practices," interrogates the ways in which the production and consumption of places, objects, and foods participated in the emergence of Californio identity at the Presidio. This section might be conceptualized as a funnel in which the spatial and temporal scale of analysis begins broadly, with landscape (chapter 6) and architecture (chapter 7), and then gradually narrows to examine increasingly smaller-scale material practices such as ceramic manufacture and use (chapter 8), foodways (chapter 9), and clothing (chapter 10). The text progressively reconstructs the production of social identities through material routines that were practiced at the community, household, and individual levels. This provides an ever-increasing intimacy with the colonial subjects whose lives are represented in the archaeological record of the Presidio.

The conclusion considers the articulations between these different aspects of material practice and offers a synthetic interpretation of the ways in which places and objects participated in shaping colonial ethnogenesis. It also outlines the broader implications of these findings for archaeologies of identity and colonization. This final section closes with a discussion of how present-day Californio descendants are negotiating their ambiguous status as a near-invisible minority group of mixed racial and ethnic heritage.

Overall, the study's findings are paradoxical. The colonial settlers' repudiation of the sistema de castas—a colonial doctrine of racial inequality—can be understood as an act of resistance by relocated colonized peoples who refused to be defined by their parentage or by the color of their skin. That this transition from casta to Californio was accomplished in part from the bottom up, from the material practices of daily life, testifies to the power of the everyday in transforming social reality. Yet simultaneously, the Californio ethnicity that replaced the sistema de castas was created and sustained through practices of cultural homogeneity, through hierarchical distinction from California's native peoples, and through a heightened emphasis on masculinity as a marker of social distinction. The case study of El Presidio de San Francisco is significant because it maps a process through which one marginalized sector of society advanced by exercising power over other marginalized peoples. And, perhaps more important, it demonstrates that colonial military power was enacted not only through overt acts of military aggression but also through the mundane routines of daily life.

"Found any gold yet?" the driver called out from the UPS truck passing by the excavation site. I've come to recognize these catch phrases about buried treasure and dinosaur bones for what they are: not evidence of the public's ignorance about archaeology, but a tentative opening gambit in a conversation between strangers.

"Not yet," I called back, trying to sound welcoming. "But we are finding some interesting things. Want to come take a look?"

In the Presidio of San Francisco, an urban park that is part of the Golden Gate National Recreation Area, public participation and interpretation are core components of our archaeological research (fig. 2). Since 1997, I have partnered with the Presidio Archaeology Center to bring university field schools to the Presidio to study the remains of the Spanish-colonial settlement for which the park is named. We excavate along well-traveled streets and jogging paths, in parking lots and the narrow yards surrounding decommissioned military housing (now rented out to civilian tenants). During a typical six-week excavation, our field school commonly receives more than two thousand visitors, some of whom volunteer in our field lab, becoming members of the research team. Our public program rests on two core concepts: an open site and a conversational approach. There are no barriers that keep visitors from entering the research area; they are free to come into our workspace and observe in whatever manner they prefer. Interactions between archaeologists and visitors follow the flow of normal conversations: the visitors' questions direct the content and tone of

FIGURE 2. Archaeologist Bea Cox shows park visitors a recently recovered artifact.

the discussion, and the archaeologists share what we are doing that day and what we have found. Rather than giving a prepared speech, we focus instead on each visitor's interests as well as our own.

The content and length of these conversations vary widely. Some people are interested in the park's history; others ask about the archaeological process. Many have information they'd like to share with us about their own historical research, their genealogy and heritage, or their experiences with archaeology. We—the archaeologists—are often the object of fascination: who are we, how did we get permission to dig here, how much schooling do we have, do we get paid, do we like what we do?

For me, the most challenging interactions are those that turn to the topic of historical identity. Such conversations often start with the query, "So, who lived here?" or, more commonly, "Are you excavating Indians?" These straightforward questions have complicated answers. Yes, Native Californians lived here, both before colonization and also in sizeable numbers during the Spanish-colonial and Mexican eras. If the person seems particularly interested in indigenous history, I might mention how the colonial military brought workers here from throughout central California, so that in addition to the Ohlone Indians (the local tribe), there were Coast Miwok, Bay Miwok, Patwin, Yokuts, Salinans, and others at El Presidio de San Francisco.

And, I add, there were the colonists themselves. For some people, the term "colonist" is sufficient, but others will ask, "The Spanish, right?" Spanish by nationality, I answer, but from villages in what today is northern Mexico. Some are perplexed: "So, they were Mexicans?" You might say that—a mixed population, people primarily of Mexican Indian and African ancestry. The term "African" always gets people's attention. "Were they slaves?" Not here, I respond, fumbling through a description of the large population of free black people in eighteenth-century northern Mexico, some of whom were recruited as colonists to California. And Mexican Indians? If I'm feeling expansive, I'll trot out the historical anecdote recorded by one foreign (European) visitor to the early settlement, who reported that indigenous Mexican languages were spoken at the Presidio as much as Spanish was.

At some point in these conversations, I usually begin to feel uneasy. It is important to dispel California's myth of Spanish conquistadors and put Mexican Indians, African Mexicans, and Native Californians at the center of California's Spanish-colonial and Mexican history. Yet only two decades after arriving here in Alta California, the colonists, themselves formerly colonized peoples, ceased to think of themselves in these racial terms. Abandoning the sistema de castas, Spain's colonial race laws, they embraced a shared colonial identity: Californio.

In these conversations about historical identities at the Presidio—with site visitors, at public lectures, in the classroom, with colleagues at the Presidio Archaeology Center, at academic conferences—I frequently find myself either without words or frustrated by the limitations of the words I do have. Social scientists have long demonstrated that the notion of "race" has no scientific basis,[1] so why do I persist in describing some of the people whose lives I study as "African" four centuries after they were taken from that continent, and two centuries after they rejected that designation? When a descendant of the colonial population pulls out a well-worn map to show me which villages in Spain his ancestors came from, how do I reconcile that conversation with the historical documents I've read that list his great-great-great-great-great grandparents as mulatos and indios from mining towns in Sonora, Mexico?

The only discernable "truth" about historical identities in Spanish-colonial and Mexican Alta California is that they were constantly changing. Other researchers have reached similar conclusions: "We were struck," write Brian Haley and Larry Wilcoxon (2005:433, 442) of their genealogical research on colonial families in Santa Barbara, "by how abundant and well documented identity changes in particular family lines were. . . . They cross supposedly impermeable boundaries. . . . Their social history demonstrates and explains identity's continuous reformulation." Such transformations lead us to ask how or why it is that certain forms of social identification came to be meaningful and accepted in particular moments, both historically and in the present day.

Colonization is one historical phenomenon that generates conditions under which existing patterns of social identification lose their relevance and new social identities emerge, both with consent and by force. From the fifteenth century onward, European colonial powers moved and relocated colonized peoples from one part of the globe to another in the service of the military, economic, and religious goals of their empires. The case of El Presidio de San Francisco, while rich in its specific historical context, is also relevant to considerations of global empire, diaspora, indigeneity, and colonial identification.

The importance of archaeological research on ethnogenesis is thus found not only in abstract theories of social life but also in these specific historical contexts. Archaeologists have often treated identities as stable categories (gender, ethnicity, race, class, or age) that can be used to sort people and the artifacts they leave behind into groups for comparative analysis. We have been less attentive to the permeability and mutability of these categories. We have been more concerned with how we can assign an artifact to a specific racial, ethnic, or gender group than with understanding the role of material culture and everyday routines as resources that people use to both stabilize and transform their identities. For archaeology to be able to contribute to a better understanding of the macro-historical phenomena that shape peoples' lives—colonization, imperialism, the expansion of capitalism, labor regimes, consumerism, intercultural exchange—we must discover ways to talk about social identities that embrace change as well as stability, permeability as well as boundedness, fluidity as well as fixity, and social agency as well as social structure.

As an archaeological and historical investigation of ethnogenesis among military settlers who lived at El Presidio de San Francisco, this book presents the findings of over thirteen years of field and laboratory studies as well as archival and historical research. Most of the book focuses on this rich body of evidence and my interpretations of it. To begin, however, this chapter establishes a conceptual foundation for the study, first discussing epistemological and theoretical tensions in archaeological research on identities and then tracing the historical specificity and interdependence of specific tropes of identity (ethnicity, race, nation, class, gender, sexuality). The last section turns to the book's specific subject, ethnogenesis, examining the relationship between my own use of this concept and its use by other scholars.

Social Identity: Similarity, Alterity, and the In-Between

By taking identity as its central focus, this study enters a contested field. Not only do anthropologists and archaeologists fiercely debate what constitutes a particular identity, but there are also epistemological and political implications of taking "identity" as an object of knowledge. The research presented here examines the formulation and transformation of identities in what has come to be known as the post-Columbian "modern world" (after Martin Hall [2000]), in which identity practices were dramatically reconfigured through the intertwined development of European nationalism, imperialist expansion, global capitalism, and the Enlightenment cult of the rational, self-interested individual. "This kind of self-consistent person," Katherine Verdery (1994:37) writes, "who 'has' an 'identity' is a product of a specific historical process: the process of modern nation-state formation." She argues that "the idea that to *have* 'identities' is normal" is an outgrowth of the "ever-greater efforts by state-makers to keep track of, manage, and control their 'populations.'" The constellations of identifications and social categories that adhere in present-day social life are indeed a partial legacy of statism, colonialism, capitalism, and individualism: such terms and categories were and continue to be met with, altered by, and woven into other practices of social identification and differentiation.

To study identity is to embrace paradox. As Stuart Hall observes, the recent explosion in scholarship on identities is conjoined with critiques and deconstructions of such inquiries, with a particular rejection of the notion of an integral, originary, and unified subject who "has" an identity. Despite the acknowledged limitations of the concept of identity, it has yet to be supplanted by new concepts that are better to think with. Identity is, then, "an idea which cannot be thought in the old way, but without which certain key questions cannot be thought at all" (Hall 1996:2). Indeed, the core question of this study—how was a heterogeneous population of colonized subjects transformed into a unified (although not uniform) colonizing force?—is unaskable without reference to the relations of sameness and difference that connote some form of social identity. It was through subject positions such as race, gender, sexuality, generation, institutional location, and geopolitical locale that such persons were able to forge claims to subjectivity and survival in their new situations as colonizing agents of the Spanish crown (after Bhabha 2004:2).

I understand identity as the means through which social subjects are constructed into relationships of taxonomic similarity and difference in comparison with other subjects. Consequently, identity is multiscalar. It is simultaneously personal and collective, generated through internal experiences and imposed from external disciplining practices and institutionalized structures. Identity is generative, not passive, which is why we might wish to talk of identification rather than identity. Practices of identification follow and (re)produce the contours of power in social life. The desire to better understand how power is operationalized has perhaps inspired and sustained the current florescence of research on identities and personhood, not only in archaeology but also throughout the social sciences and the humanities.

Identities are suspended within the tensions between similarity and alterity, or sameness and difference. To identify is to establish a relationship of similarity between one thing or person and another, and self-reflexively to position oneself in such an affinity with others. In this sense, practices of identification call attention to perceived similarities and, in doing so, achieve an erasure or elision of other kinds of variability. These erasures of variations pose an internal threat to the stability of identities, requiring continual "work" (in the sense of the multifaceted deployment of social power) to maintain the coherence of relations of similarity. Much of this identity work occurs through attention to other relations of difference (alterity, exclusion, separation, othering), what is widely termed the "constitutive outside" that "forms the corona of difference through which identities are enunciated" (Meskell 2002:280).[2] What any hypothetical "we" may have in common, our identification with each other, may have as much to do with our perception of shared difference from a real or imagined "other" as with any intrinsic similarity among ourselves. Practices of identification must thus be understood as continually operating within that "difference which must be acknowledged, but also sameness which must be conceded" (Young 1995:92).

Studies of identity have increasingly interrogated this tension between alterity and similarity, drawing attention to the ambiguity and lack of closure that such tension brings to social identities. There has been a particular effort to trouble the binaries that lend the appearance of stability to categories of identity and otherness (for example, colonizer/colonized, white/black, or man/woman) along with related power-laden dichotomies that buttress such divisions (such as culture/nature, orient/occident, and so on).[3] Homi Bhabha calls special attention to hybridity, to the "'in between' spaces [that] provide the terrain for elaborating strategies of selfhood—singular or communal—that initiate new signs of identity, and innovative sites of collaboration, and contestation" (2004:2), while Gloria Anzaldua (1987) highlights the transformative potential of geographic and conceptual borderlands, and Stuart Hall exhorts us to develop "a new cultural politics which engages rather than suppresses difference" (1989:29). Others point out how hybridity and other markers of ambivalence (such as borderlands or "third spaces") have been used to regulate and control social subjects rather than to liberate them (Chatan 2003; Meskell

2002; Mitchell 1997; Verdery 1994; Young 1995). The reactionary potential of hybridities and frontiers has considerable relevance to this study, for the military settlers who founded and lived at El Presidio de San Francisco inhabited such middle spaces of identity and location. Exploring the ways in which these ambiguously situated subjects navigated the politics of identity and empire contributes an important perspective to ongoing dialogues about the potentialities and limitations of life "in between."

By examining a historically known instance of ethnogenesis, this study also contributes to the movement away from conceptualizing identity as something stable, categorical, and inherent to bounded groups and individuals. However, models of personhood and community that emphasize the partitive, situational, and contingent aspects of social identity should not be misread to suggest that identity is an "anything-goes" dimension of social practice. Although socially constructed, identities operate as "social facts" (Durkheim 1982). They become embedded in the organizational structures, histories, and procedures of institutions and other social collectivities. Consequently, identities come to have objective effects on the lives of social subjects. Even before birth, modern subjects are interpolated into particular modes of identification (race, gender, nation, kinship, and so on). Ongoing disciplines of identification are embedded within social interactions because identities are relational and depend on recognition and legitimation.

The challenge is to interrogate the interplay between the coercive and voluntary aspects of identity practices, and to do so with attention to specific historical contexts. This is especially important in studies of what Gavin Lucas has aptly named the "trinity" of race, class, and gender. Often mistakenly viewed as stable and universal aspects of social life, these categories of persons must be understood as "historical formations specific to the period being discussed" that "are not so much categories of analysis, but subjects of analysis" (Lucas 2006:181, 185). One of the explicit aims of this book is to denaturalize and de-essentialize aspects of identity that are often experienced as fixed and stable. Tracing the shifting permutations of race, ethnicity, gender, and status in colonial San Francisco exposes the historical contingency not only of any given person's "identity" but also of the underlying postulates through which social identities are constructed.

Fluidity and Fixity

How can studies of historical identity navigate the tension between the fluidity and fixity of social identities? This study participates in the current moment's fascination with the malleability of identities. From transnationalism, ethnogenesis, creolization, hybridity, and passings of all sorts to queerness, transgenderings, and transsexualities, there is an abiding interest in those who have crossed and are crossing social boundaries. Identities are "plural and changing" (Casella and Fowler 2005:2), "never unified and, in late modern times, increasingly fragmented and fractured; never singular but multiply constructed across different, often intersecting and antagonistic, discourses, practices, and positions" (Hall 1996:4). This deconstruction of identities corresponds to a shift from taking individuals or predefined groups as primary units of analysis to understanding that personhood and community are similarly partitive, permeable, contingent, dispersed, and situational (Fowler 2004; Mauss 1990; Ramamurthy 2003; Strathern 1990).

In one sense, this interest in the disunification of identity can be understood as an appropriate corrective to those approaches that have viewed identity as stable categories determined by macro-scale phenomena. I suspect, however, that this curiosity about identity transformation and transgression is more than a reaction to the shortcomings of past research. Could it be related to a certain perplexity about the apparent durability of certain kinds of identity categories that were once expected to become less relevant (or even disappear) in the wake of feminism, civil rights, globalization, and economic development? For most, gender, race, nationality, and class are experienced as "facts in the field" that must be navigated with care. Identities are "fixed" through social, institutional, and governmental practices that are often beyond the effective reach of individual agency. That those who cross such boundaries are frequently subject to harassment, persecution, and violence exposes the ways in which power is deployed to stabilize hierarchies of social difference.

It is thus worth returning to the interface between structure and agency in practices of identification. Some specific examples point to useful directions. Laurie Wilkie, writing of African Americans living at the Oakley Plantation of Louisiana before and after the abolition of slavery, considers "how imposed identities were adopted and maintained by these families both as coping mechanisms and as a means of empowerment" (2000:xv). Gerald Sider, tracing the effects of first Spanish, then British, and finally U.S. colonization of the American Southeast, notes how Native Americans claimed "forms of differentiation [that] were imposed 'from above' . . . as part of processes of asserting their own interests and of resisting—and colluding with, evading, and accommodating to—domination" (1994:112). Of indigenous responses to the Spanish conquest of the Americas, Michel de Certeau writes that "they [the Indians] subverted them [colonial regimes] not by rejecting or altering them, but by using them with respect to ends and references foreign to the system they had no choice but to accept. They were other within the very colonization that outwardly assimilated them" (1984:xiii).

New identity groupings and categories continue to emerge, including the Californios. But what are the conditions that enable new practices of identity to appear? How do some emergent identities become stabilized, institutionalized, and imbued with historical traditions that belie their recent formation (Anderson 1993; Hill 1996; Hobsbawm and Ranger 1983)? While such phenomena are multiscalar, the examples just listed suggest that interfaces between the local and the global, and between personhood or community and institutions of power, are particularly potent sites where identities are simultaneously imposed, negotiated, and transformed. It is by attending to the "microphysics of power" (de Certeau 1984:xvi) within the ongoing negotiation of governmentality and discipline (Foucault 1975, 1978) that we are most likely to obtain glimpses of the ongoing play between fixity and fluidity in the articulation of social identities.

Practice and Performance

Theoretical pluralism is an epistemological asset for archaeology generally and for the study of past identities especially (Longino 1990; Wylie 1992b, 1996a). Social theories provide models for analyzing and interpreting observed archaeological phenomena; they aid archaeologists in conceptualizing and coping with our research findings. As Victor Buchli notes, "there is a tendency to envision these conceptual tools as actually representing what is going on rather than simply a provisional means of coming to terms with what has been experienced" (2000:186). Theoretical pluralism reinforces the contingency of any social theory by calling forward multiple perspectives on the past. My own approach is informed by feminist and queer theory and engendered archaeologies in conjunction with historical materialism, critical race theory, postcolonial studies, and culture contact archaeology. My understanding of identities is especially indebted to Michel Foucault's (1975, 1978, 1980) historicization of identity and to poststructuralist theories of social iteration that locate the articulation of identities in repetitive practices and performances (Bourdieu 1977, 1980; Butler 1990, 1993a; de Certeau 1984; Giddens 1984).

Theories of social iteration model the historical production of identities through the recursive relationship between structure and agency. In this context, structures are understood not as external forces or ideas but rather as the products and media of social agency. Structures simultaneously enable certain forms of social action and constrain others and thus might be conceptualized as a metaphor for the workings of top-down power in social life. Yet structures are produced through the agency of social subjects (what might be considered bottom-up power) and so are not separate from the workings of everyday life. Agency, Anthony Giddens (1984:14) writes, is the capacity to "make a difference" in the sense that alternative historical consequences could have resulted had a social subject followed another course of action. Theories of social iteration provide a model for conceptualizing this back-and-forth relationship between the endless stream of on-the-ground actions involved in daily life and the ways that social subjects participate in the production of the very structures that enable and constrain their lives. In this way, theories of social iteration emphasize the historicity of culture. Social identities are not external or prior to the situations and interactions in which they appear, but are continually enacted, reproduced, and transformed in social life.

Pierre Bourdieu conceptualizes this relationship between agency and structure as the interplay between practice and habitus, the latter likened to a conductorless orchestra (1977:72) whose members play their instruments according to durably installed, generative principles of regulated improvisation. Habitus guides but does not determine the routines of daily life, which themselves participate in the ongoing formation and transformation of the habitus. Because habitus also conditions perception, social subjects experience the objective conditions of their lives through the subjective practical knowledge obtained through practice. In demonstrating how habitus and practice are mutually constituted, Bourdieu's analyses turn particularly to the material activities of daily life: the patterned use of space and time; sequences of repeated actions; the selection, production, and use of material culture; the preparation, presentation, and consumption of food; the selection and wearing of clothing. It is perhaps no surprise that his model of practice and habitus has been widely adopted by archaeologists, for many of the bodies of evidence recovered in archaeological investigations consist of material residues that accumulated as by-products of such quotidian practices and routines.

One of Bourdieu's many contributions to the study of social identities is his landmark research (1984) on class distinctions and taste in 1960s France. The study sought to understand how habitus, in the form of cultivated dispositions, was revealed in the consumption of cultural goods. Bourdieu proposes that "taste" is the practical knowledge through which social subjects exercise preferences among the universe of stylistic possibilities. In exercising taste, social subjects assert and reproduce their own position in the social order, for their preferences are shaped by the objective conditions of social stratification and the relations of production as well as the subjective experiences of practice. "Taste classifies, and it classifies the classifier. Social subjects, classified by their classifications, distinguish themselves by the distinctions they make" (Bourdieu 1984:6). This model of the relationship between taste and status focuses attention on the production and deployment of "cultural capital" (noneconomic assets, such as education, that are resources in the ongoing negotiation of social life). As the role of habitus and practice in the expression of taste has been extended beyond class distinctions to include race and ethnicity (Bentley 1987; Yelvington 1991), archaeologists have become better able to investigate the ways that consumption practices participate in the reproduction and, at times, the transformation of the social order.[4]

While Bourdieu's theories of practice and habitus (and related models of taste, cultural capital, and practical knowledge) are widely used in archaeological research, another theory of social iteration—Judith Butler's theory of gender performance—is less commonly deployed (Voss 2000b).[5] Whereas Bourdieu interrogates the production and reproduction of culture broadly and ethnicity and class specifically, Butler deconstructs the categories of gender, sex, and sexuality, arguing that these are mutually produced through a heterosexual matrix that requires a division of persons into two gender categories and simultaneously legitimizes sexual desires for the opposite gender. Through this matrix, those with nonnormative gender identities and those whose sexual desires and practices deviate from heterosexuality are simultaneously constructed as abject others. The heterosexual matrix is sustained by defining itself against those practices and identities that it stigmatizes, thus relying on the abject for its own existence (Butler 1993a, 1993b, 1999).

Butler also questions the distinction between biological and cultural aspects of sexuality and gender. The line between what is "cultural" or "natural" about gender and sexuality is highly contested and debated. Butler argues that what is perceived as "natural" is delineated and fixed through cultural practices and that it is more productive to see the distinction between natural and cultural as a disciplining practice that seeks to establish certain aspects of identity as irreducible and unchangeable (1999:7–12). "There is," Butler notes, "an insistent materiality of the body, but . . . it never makes itself known or legible outside of the cultural articulation in which it appears" (quoted in Breen and Blumenfeld 2001:12).

Like Bourdieu, Butler turns to models of iteration (in this case, of social performances) to account for the historical production and instability of gendered and sexual identities that have the appearance of being essential and stable. This appearance of continuity, she posits, is an illusion created by an endless series of mimetic repetitions, much as a film projector creates an illusion of continuity by flashing a rapid sequence of still images on a screen. Thus, "there is no gender identity behind the expressions of gender; that identity is performatively constituted by the very 'expressions' that are said to be its results" (Butler 1999:33). These gendered and sexual performances are not volitional but rather are "a set of repeated acts within a highly rigid regulatory frame" (43). It is within the gaps between these repetitions that Butler identifies potential for agency, as subjects may be able to subtly transform these mimetic performances through subversive practices like mimicry, satire, drag, exaggeration, and so on (1993a:121–140; 1999:173–177). Just as Bourdieu envisions that social subjects may transform habitus through improvisation within repetitive practices, Butler asserts that "to operate within the matrix of power is not the same as to replicate uncritically relations of domination. It offers the possibility of a repetition of the law which is not its consolidation, but its displacement" (1999:40).

Butler's and Bourdieu's theories of the iterative production of social identity are both complementary and contradictory. Bourdieu centers his analysis on ethnographic cultures and on internal divisions within such cultures, especially class but also ethnicity and race; Butler, while clearly attentive to such hierarchies, is primarily concerned with the production and reproduction of gendered and sexualized subjects, especially those whose appearances, dispositions, and practices are rendered abject through normative discourses and laws. Further, Bourdieu's emphasis on material practices (what people do) is complemented by Butler's focus on discourse and representation. Together, their research provides conceptual resources that enable a more integrated approach to social identity.

This is not to deny the very real epistemological differences in their studies, however. Bourdieu's post-Marxist stance emphasizes the ways that power is deployed through capital (economic, cultural, political) in an empirically knowable, although subjectively experienced, world. Butler, in contrast, engages heavily with Foucault, psychoanalytic theory, and poststructuralist methodologies of discourse analysis that deconstruct the ontological stability of the material world. Their divergent methodologies produce what historian Lisa Duggan (1995) has termed "the discipline problem": broken pots, faunal remains, collapsed structures, burials, soil residues, and other evidentiary sources in archaeology rarely resemble the literary works or films that are privileged in Butler's performance theory; nor has Bourdieu's practice theory been widely adopted outside the social sciences. However, this common dichotomy between discourse and practice, though heuristically useful, is another binary that warrants deconstruction and refusal; more pragmatically, historical archaeology's promiscuous engagements with objects, images, and texts (Voss 2007) require a theoretical pluralism that can account for both materiality and representation.

Theories of social iteration have been most widely critiqued for emphasizing the reproduction and persistence of hegemonic structures of power rather than articulating clear programs for achieving social change (Ortner 1996:1–20). Bourdieu's improvisations, as well as Butler's parody, mimicry, gaps, and passings, afford a somewhat narrow scope for intervention by social subjects who are themselves produced within these very structures. This study of ethnogenesis provides an opportunity to stretch such theories into examinations of changefulness and to consider whether modifications in practices and performances of social identity, such as the appearance of Californios, are indeed transformative or alternatively might reproduce the social order within which they emerged.

Power and Position

Power, Foucault writes, forms "a dense web that passes through apparatuses and institutions" (1978:96). This understanding of power as diffuse and distributed provides a vantage point from which to consider how agency is positional, that is, how subjects experience different capabilities and constraints through their locations in various social structures and institutions (Foucault 1975, 1978). Giddens differentiates, for example, between the capabilities held by agents and institutions, yet emphasizes that subordinates always have some capability to influence their superiors (1984:5–16). De Certeau (1984:xviii–xx, 35–37) similarly offers the metaphors of strategy and tactic. Strategies involve relationships of force that are possible for subjects who can act from a place of power. From this place (both metaphorical and physical), they can command space, resources, and authority, which enable a deliberateness and forethought in the exercise of agency. Tactics, in contrast, are the realm of the disenfranchised and dispossessed, those who have no base from which to prepare or strategize and who must seize the opportunities of the moment: "the ingenious ways in which the weak make use of the strong, [and] thus lend a political dimension to everyday practices" (de Certeau 1984:xvii).

The importance of positionality in social negotiations of identity is further illustrated by Gerald Sider. Culture, he notes, is often described as a web, perhaps most famously by Clifford Geertz (1977:5): "Believing . . . that man is an animal suspended in webs of significance he himself has spun, I take culture to be those webs." Sider calls attention to

> a small but crucial point: suspended on the spider's web are two kinds of creatures, often with two different fates, the spider and its prey. Moreover, the spider spun its web not just for itself but "for," as it were, its prey, who may or may not have known what it "meant" to alight upon it, at least when it first landed. Webs of significance are spun in the real and changing world *and are often spun for different, not similar others*: spiders rarely get caught in other spider's webs. (1994:115)

Writing of identity changes in North America during and after colonization, Sider continues the metaphor to observe that the fly, the moth, and the bug lose distinction and simply become prey to the spider, just as differentiations among enslaved Africans and African Americans are collapsed by the racial category "black" and Native American tribal affiliations erased by the term "Indian" (1994:117; see also Jackson 1999). Identities are not a location of shared culture; they are sites "where people struggle to create different and ongoing conceptual and material histories within and against the same general history" (Sider 1994:116).

Materialization

Foucault, Weber (1978), Geertz, and Sider's webs of power and culture provide still one more point of consideration, namely, that relationships between predator and prey are mediated through the materiality of the strands of the web itself, which vary not only in their thicknesses and adhesiveness and interconnections but also, through their anchor points, in their articulations with other substances and surfaces. There is an entanglement (after Thomas 1991) among social subjects and the materiality of the world. While transformations of social identity are often examined as changes in discourses of belonging and alterity (for example, Anderson 1993; Hobsbawm and Ranger 1983), there is much to be gained from an approach that takes materiality as central to the ongoing negotiation of social life. In this vein, I follow the theoretical slippage articulated by Arjun Appadurai:

> Even if our own approach to things is conditioned necessarily by the view that things have no meanings apart from those that human transactions, attributions, and motivations endow them with, the anthropological problem is that this formal truth does not illuminate the concrete, historical circulation of things. For that we have to follow the things themselves, for their meanings are inscribed in their forms, their uses, their trajectories. . . . Thus, even though from a *theoretical* point of view human actors encode things with significance, from a *methodological* point of view it is the things-in-motion that illuminate their human and social context. (1986:5)

From an archaeological perspective, this "methodological fetishism" (Appadurai 1986:5) takes on even greater significance as archaeological research often traces the diachronic continuities and changes that occur over time. The materiality of earlier practices can have durable (though not deterministic) effects on subsequent practices, perhaps most dramatically illustrated by the construction of buildings and structures whose persistence continues to alter patterns of movement over decades or even millennia. Likewise, concerted efforts to erase the material traces of past practices (such as "redevelopment" projects writ large or small, discussed further in chapter 7) may signal dramatic moments of social change. This book will take methodological license to examine how material practices and objects participated in colonial ethnogenesis, with the disclaimer, of course, that this refers not to the animation of the inanimate but rather to the entanglements that bind people, things, and places together.

Materiality functions on a dual register: it is the substance that serves as a resource in practices and performances that transform or trouble social identities, yet materiality is also deployed to "fix" identities and institutionalize otherwise volatile social constructions into social facts. Perhaps the most apparent of these material strategies is the naturalization of social identities and hierarchies through reference to imputed traits of the physiological body (Yanagisako and Delaney 1995):

> Oh, now and then you will hear grown-ups say, "Can the Ethiopian change his skin or the Leopard his spots?" I don't think even grown-ups would keep on saying such a silly thing if the Leopard and the Ethiopian hadn't done it once—do you? But they will never do it again, Best Beloved. They are quite contented as they are. (Kipling 1996:28)

The projection of identity onto the body ought not to be dismissed as "just so stories," for such dispositions can come to materialize the very effects that they purport to describe. If, for example, ideas of frail femininity discourage girls from physical exertion, they will indeed become "the weaker sex" (which once again illustrates the interdigitation of materiality and discourse). Poverty and wealth, and the strains related to various labors, whether menial or clerical, also produce bodies marked by their circumstances. Further, physical characteristics do not need to be empirically "real" to be mobilized in service of social hierarchies, as demonstrated, for example, by nineteenth-century European studies of craniometry. Social identities are never completely apart from the bodies, however constructed and fashioned, of the social subjects to which they refer.

Objects, from the unmovable walls of buildings to the smallest portable charms, also participate in the materialization of identity through their association with persons and groups and the leaky distinctions (Haraway 1997) between bodies and technologies. "Objects—buildings, dress, foods—are called on to prove that volatile and contingent social identities are stable and intrinsic" (Upton 1996:4). Colonial regimes often attempt to establish a "tight connection between status and its material signifiers" (Hall 2000:72), although such connections should not be misunderstood as a singular relationship akin to a mathematical equation (Hodder 1982; Miller 1987; Spector 1993). The powerful role played by material culture in the ongoing negotiation of social identities is in fact a result of its dual properties. The meanings of things are never fixed, and hence objects can be taken up for different purposes by different users; but the materiality of objects provides a durability and persistence quite different than the ephemeral qualities of speech, dance, or music—which are also stabilized through recourse to physical media (such as writing or recording). In this study of identity transformations, it is particularly important to ask how material practices such as bodily movement, architecture, household objects, food, dress, and adornment served as resources that shifted the terms of identification.

Overdetermination

There has been a tendency to balkanize the study of identities by isolating specific aspects of identity without considering the ways that social identities are experienced holistically. Owing in great part to the insights of women of color and Third World feminist activists and scholars, recent decades have seen a notable increase in calls for a theoretical and analytical reintegration of identity categories, especially race, class, and gender.[6] As Anne McClintock (1995:5) notes, identities are increasingly understood as categorical distinctions that "come into existence *in and through* each other. . . . I do not mean to imply that these domains are reducible to, or identical with, each other; instead they exist in intimate, reciprocal, and contradictory relations." Such relations among practices of identification are variably conceptualized as enunciations, articulations, intersectionality, modulations, ethnosexual frontiers, mutual constitutions, and enmeshments.[7] This perspective foregrounds the perplexities of subjectivity: "Many identities vie for importance in daily life" (Staats 1996:163).

In the growing understanding of social identities as mutually constituted and enmeshed, little attention has been paid to exactly how power—of all kinds—participates in these articulations. Ann Stoler provides one such instance in her analysis of white endogamy in colonial Indonesia: "Ratios of men to women *followed* from how sexuality was managed and how racial categories were produced rather than the other way around" (2002:2). This statement suggests that a diachronic perspective may yield important insights into the historical articulations of various forms of differencing (after Verdery 1994). There is also a need to attend to the synchronic enmeshment of identities: "identity names . . . possess phenomenal power—inherent in their nature as single-word signifiers of complex and heterogeneous significations—to mask both the multidimensionality and the very nature of the identities they denote" (Larson 1996:545).

It is here that the concept of overdetermination proves particularly useful as an analytical tool. I visualize social identities as having social properties analogous to the physical attributes of icebergs: what is enunciated on the surface of social discourse is only a small fraction of the identification, which obtains its mass and momentum from its vastly larger, submerged components. The introduction mentioned the example of the Spanish-colonial occupational term "soldado" and its unspoken, but nonetheless ever-present, production through gender (male), age (adult, but not elderly), physique (able-bodied), nationality (Spanish), colonial status (not indigenous and usually not African), rank (ordinary, nonelite), level of respectability (honorable), class (unlanded, of modest means), and economic prospects (future landowner). Most implications of being a soldado lurk beneath the surface of the designation, and, because these are shadowed, they are less susceptible to overt examination. Like the naturalization and objectification of identities that occur through materiality, overdetermination is one of the ways that volatile identities come to appear inevitable and intractable.

In that sense, using the concept of overdetermination risks a certain slippage, in that the contributing components to a specific configuration of identities might give the mistaken impression that such identities *are* closed and complete rather than always in production through practices and performances. Here again the historicity of Butler's and Bourdieu's theories of iteration—the gaps and uncertain pauses in which the possibility of failed or skewed repetitions are present—provides a means to hold open the contingency of social identity. To return to the metaphor of the iceberg, we might consider the gradual remodelings of surface and substance, the sudden fragmentations and reassemblings, which result from changing encounters with warmth or chill and from abrasions and even collisions.

Methodologically, overdetermination encourages us to continually peer into the depths of identification practices while simultaneously taking note of subtle (and not so subtle) changes in readily apparent identity practices. In the case of Californio ethnogenesis, overdetermination draws attention to the immense significance of a change from racially based identification practices to identities referencing a regionalized ethnicity. What other transformations in social life were occurring during this period so that older forms of identification lost relevancy and others became salient? How were the "subsurface" components of racialized identities reconfigured in order to enable and stabilize Californio identity?

Interrogating Ethnicity

Ethnicity became an important means of social differencing in Spanish-colonial San Francisco. What, then, is ethnicity? Although I concur with Fraser Neiman

(1999:139) that "attempts to offer strict definitions [of ethnicity] are likely to generate more heat than light," it is nonetheless important to examine how this category has been understood, both the category itself and its relation to other practices of identification.

Culture Concept to Boundary Maintenance to Primordial Bonds

In 1969, Norwegian anthropologist Fredrick Barth published a slim edited volume titled *Ethnic Groups and Boundaries: The Social Organization of Cultural Difference.* More than any other work, this book caused a fundamental shift in how social scientists approach the study of ethnicity. Before the 1960s, ethnic groups were generally viewed as static reflections of shared cultural norms such as language, traditions, ancestry, and territory. Ethnicities were viewed as inherently inward-looking and tradition-bound, which lent support to political arguments that ethnic affiliations were barriers to modernization and progress. In archaeology, this approach to ethnicity was explicitly formulated in the concept of "archaeological culture": a set of co-occurring artifacts and stylistic traits thought to "correlate with particular peoples, ethnic groups, tribes, and/or races" (Jones 1997:15).[8]

Barth's *Ethnic Groups and Boundaries* (1969) powerfully inverted conventional views of ethnicity. Societies, he argued, are inherently polyethnic. Ethnic groups develop not in isolation but through intense, ongoing interaction. What defines an ethnic group, then, is not the cultural "stuff" shared among its members, but differentiation between "us" and "them." Such ethnic boundaries are inherently permeable and constantly in negotiation. Cultural traits, language, territory, and ancestry may be utilized as resources during these ongoing negotiations, but "only those which the actors themselves regard as significant" (Barth 1969:14) are employed in this way. Because ethnicities are defined through external boundaries, ethnic groups are internally heterogeneous, so much so that even within a single family, each member has a different relationship to the ethnic identity (Barth 1994).

Barth's view of ethnic groups as self-defining, subjective social entities was hailed as the first postmodern approach to identity, one that continues to reverberate in postcolonial scholarship.[9] An emphasis on ethnic boundaries also slowly displaced the archaeological culture concept, sometimes resulting in dramatic reinterpretations of the archaeological record.[10] Sympathetic critiques called for greater attention to power dynamics in ethnic boundary definition: Barth's emphasis on self-definition slights the ways in which ethnic ascription by outsiders places firm constraints on the mutability of ethnic boundaries.[11]

The reformulation of ethnicity as something defined through intergroup negotiation rather than intragroup cohesion sparked a substantive debate about the relationship between subjectivity, culture, and ethnicity. Barth's model is now understood as an *instrumentalist* approach in which ethnicity is viewed as a means to an end, especially to secure and protect economic and political interests (Barth 1969; Cohen 1974). Instrumentalist models provide little means of distinguishing ethnicities from other social collectivities (for example, religions, political parties, or trade guilds) and fail to account for the profound emotional strength of some ethnic attachments. The response to these weaknesses has been a resurgence of interest in intragroup cohesion and the development of *primordialist* theories of ethnicity, which draw on psychoanalytical theories of a universal human need for connection and belonging. In this view, ethnicity is viewed less as a strategic alliance and more as an involuntary attachment ascribed at birth and reinforced by shared experiences throughout the life course.

Debates between primordialist and instrumentalist approaches to ethnicity have filled the pages of social science journals for decades without conclusive resolution. There is, however, a loose consensus that ethnicity, as a form of "consciousness of difference" (Vermeulen and Govers 1994:4), is distinct from other forms of social identity in that it references some combination of cultural difference and ideologies of shared ancestry, history, and tradition. But history is never "the objective source and cause of ethnicity" because ethnicity involves "a struggle to appropriate the past" (Barth 1994:13). Ethnicity thus consists of overlapping sets of loyalties and obligations that operate at multiple scales, "a *series* of nesting dichotomizations of inclusiveness and exclusiveness" (Cohen 1978:387). This interpretive gap between primordialist and instrumentalist models is a productive theoretical tension that points to the importance of the exercise of power in negotiating social identity. Neither primordialism nor instrumentalism can account for the persistence of ethnic distinctions in certain historical moments and their rapid transformation in others, nor does either model explain how "new" ethnicities—ones that might arise even in the course of a single lifetime—can generate emotional attachment, intragroup affinity, and intergroup antagonism. The study of ethnogenesis adds a temporal component to theories of ethnicity that have for too long looked primarily to synchronic social interactions.

Race and Nation, Class and Citizen: Whither Ethnicity?

If ethnicity is forged through perceptions of common heritage or ancestry and through cultural difference from others, how is it different from race and nationality, which commonly reference the same components? Even class, often defined strictly in terms of economic status or relationship to the means of production, has been amply demonstrated to be a vehicle of cultural transmission and differentiation (for example, Bourdieu 1984). For every "rule" that draws strict distinctions between ethnicity, race, class, citizenship, and nation, a historical or ethnographic exception can be found to prove that the situation is far more complex. The interdigitation of these forms of social identity has led some scholars to mistakenly conclude that ethnicity, race, and nationality—and, to a lesser degree, class and citizenship—are one and the same. Most commonly, ethnicity is posited as the overarching concept with race, nationality, and class viewed as different "flavors" of ethnicity (as examples, see Ericksen 1993; Nagel 2003; Sollors 1986).

I strongly disagree with this approach. As Benedict Anderson notes, all communities are imagined, but they are distinguished "by the style in which they are imagined" (1993:6). Since identities are overdetermined, the overlap between race, ethnicity, nationality, class, and citizenship can be interpreted as an indication that they are each strongly implicated in the production of the others. Collapsing together different forms of social identification has the effect of obscuring the specific power relations involved in the production and maintenance of social hierarchies (Hall 1989). In historical archaeology, privileging ethnicity has contributed to a view of modern history in which racism and poverty are increasingly made invisible.[12]

Unquestionably, race and ethnicity are "deeply enmeshed" (Verdery 1994:46). Both became prominent during the nineteenth-century expansion of scientific classifications of humans. In that context, race was used as a synonym for certain national, cultural, and linguistic groups and tended to emphasize hereditary physical traits. This latter aspect increased in importance with the growing influence of Darwinian evolutionary theory in the late nineteenth and early twentieth centuries. By the 1950s, ethnicity and race, once interchangeable, had acquired separate meanings, with ethnicity referring to perceived cultural difference and race to perceived physical difference. Today, most physical and social scientists consider race to be culturally constructed. This perception and the development of critical race theory has blurred the conceptual boundary between race and ethnicity.

Currently, race is generally understood as distinct from ethnicity in that racialization naturalizes social difference through reference to bodily attributes—notably skin color, but also hair, facial features, and physique—and racial distinctions generally rest on arguments of congenital inferiority or superiority. Race thus builds on the assumption that personhood is determined by hereditary characteristics that differ systematically according to perceived physical criteria (Ericksen 1993). Racialization sediments many forms of social identification—such as ethnicity, class, nation, and religion—by projecting cultural difference and social hierarchy onto the bodies of social subjects. Even though race is a cultural construct, it assumes importance as a social fact because of racism.

Nation and nationality are also easily conflated with race and ethnicity, in part because of the legacy of nineteenth-century Romantic nationalism, which idealized the homogeneous nation-state (Hall 1989; Jones 1997:43; Shennan 1989). As imagined communities, nations are sustained through myths of iso-morphic boundaries (linguistic, territorial, political, cultural, ethnic, racial, and religious) (Anderson 1993). Ethnicization is thus central to the formation and reproduction of nation-states. On the one hand, "claims to statehood or polit-ical autonomy [are] most often rooted in assertions of cultural distinctiveness, a unique history, and ethnic or racial purity" (Nagel 2000:110). On the other hand, ethnic types are also developed through the efforts of governments to manage their national subjects (Verdery 1994:37). But ethnicities also work against nationalities and nationalisms when groups assert ethnic solidarities to claim rights and recognition within or across national boundaries (Calhoun 1993:211). Nationality and nationalism, then, must be seen as a particular form of social identity differentiated by its association with or aspiration to the mod-ern territorial state and the political apparatus of governmentality (Calhoun 1993; Ericksen 1993; Kohl 1998; Pels 1997).

Class identities primarily reference economic relationships. LouAnn Wurst (1999:7) identifies three ways of conceptualizing class in historical archaeol-ogy: as an economic category, such as "middle class"; as a relative ranking of individuals according to social or economic position; and as the formation of social relations related to the means of production. In all instances, class must be understood as situational and historically constituted. Like ethnicity and na-tionality, class is a "culture bearing unit" (Williams 1992:609). Bourdieu, in par-ticular, demonstrates that classes are reproduced through many of the attrib-utes generally associated with ethnicity: shared cultural practices or dispositions, maintenance of group boundaries, and a feeling of tradition or common past along with a sense of shared future interests (1984).

The complex interrelationship between class, race, ethnicity, and national-ity can be understood in part through what Charles Orser (2004) terms "class-racism"—the way that elites graft notions of inherent inferiority onto nonelites. Poverty is often discussed in racial or ethnic terms, attributing its cause to the inherent qualities of the poor themselves rather than to the structures of power and economic systems that direct the distribution of resources in a society. Au-drey Horning (1999), for example, describes the imposition of an Appalachian "folk" ethnicity on rural mountain dwellers in the eastern United States as a means of justifying the seizure of their lands. Because race and ethnicity are often used as codes for class-based distinctions, it is doubly important to attend to the specific relationships between class and identity. Additionally, ethnic and racial groups are internally stratified by class, and classes are internally divided by race and ethnicity.

Ethnic, racial, national, and class-based identity terms are polysemic. Each mobilizes and references another in its deployment and interpretation. Thus a single identity term can shift in meaning from context to context and over time. As Prema Kurien (1994) and Pier Larson (1996) demonstrate, many ethnonyms were once religious, political, linguistic, or social groupings whose meanings changed with historical events. Identity names are thus imprecise, evoking a "constellation of meanings" (Larson 1996:558) through the multiplicity of past usages. Ethnogenesis is a concept that is especially useful in tracing these changes, for as "new" ethnicities emerge, they are frequently constructed with names and meanings recycled from previous usages.

Sex, Gender, and Sexuality

Sex, gender, and sexuality are often treated as private, interpersonal, and even familial identities. By contrast, ethnicity, race, nationality, and class have been conventionally viewed as more public, political, or economic identities. Feminist politics and scholarship have challenged this false binary by exposing such distinctions as part of the naturalization of gender (Ortner and Whitehead 1981; Rubin 1975; Yanagisako and Delaney 1995) and by demonstrating the gendering and sexualization of public life (Enloe 1990). Consequently, during the past two decades, new scholarship has emerged that examines the articulations between sex, gender, and sexuality and ethnicity, race, nationality, and class. In particular, we can delineate two areas in which gender and sexuality are intrinsically tied to the production of ethnicity: one concerns how ethnicities reference shared ancestry, and the other deals with how ethnicity is mobilized to define and police gendered and sexual behaviors and identities.

It is important to first define sex, gender, and sexuality and their relationship to each other. In standard English, the word "sex" has ambiguous meanings: being male or female, the act of coitus, eroticism, and reproduction. These varied definitions reveal some of the ways in which Anglophone cultures imbricate coitus, genitalia, and gender. "Having sex" is both an activity and a state of being (Voss and Schmidt 2000:2). In feminist scholarship, "sex" is increasingly used to refer specifically to biological differences between males and females, whereas "gender" refers to culturally constructed ideas of masculine and feminine identities (Rubin 1975). This analytical distinction between biological sex and cultural gender has been especially important in denaturalizing sex roles, for if gender is culturally constructed, then it has a history (Scott 1986).

In late nineteenth-century Europe and its settler colonies (the United States, Canada, and Australia), sexuality was discursively separated from sex and gender through the scientizing discipline of sexology (Bland and Doan 1998a, 1998b; Foucault 1978; Rubin 1984). Although the research goals and practices of sexologists were diverse, they shared the premises that sexuality was an enduring determinant of a person's character and identity and that people could be classified according to these sexual dispositions. Sexual acts and practices, along with some nonsexual preferences, habits, and behaviors, were interpreted as symptomatic expressions of durable underlying sexual dispositions. Most sexual identity terms used today (for example, "pedophile," "transvestite," "heterosexual," and "homosexual") are an enduring legacy of sexology. This legacy has considerable implications for archaeological and historical research: the categorization of sexuality as a distinct aspect of social relations and the premise that sexuality is a central component of social identity may both be historical products of Western modernity. What we think of as "sexuality" may have been organized quite differently in the past.[13]

More recently, feminist scholars have challenged the separation between sex, gender, and sexuality; what is natural (sex) and what is cultural (gender) is not always clear, nor are sexual identities and acts always separable from sex and gender.[14] Butler's conceptualization of the heterosexual matrix, described earlier in this chapter, is perhaps the most prominent intervention of this kind. Without diminishing the conceptual utility of the heterosexual matrix, archaeologists and historians must be cautious not to dehistoricize what Butler intended as a comment on late twentieth-century and early twenty-first-century identities in North America. Indeed, there is a historical question to be investigated regarding what other configurations of disciplinary matrices have regulated sexual and gendered identities in other times and places (Voss 2005b).

Ethnicity, race, and nationality share a "sexual substructure" (Nagel 2000:109) through reference to actual or perceived shared ancestry, heredity, and kinship. "The myth (or reality) of 'common origin' plays [a central role] in the construction of most ethnic and national collectivities" (Yuval-Davis 1996:17), binding ethnicity and nationality firmly to the social production of sex, gender, and sexuality. Consequently, "ethnic boundaries are also sexual boundaries—erotic intersections where people make intimate connections across ethnic, racial, or national borders" (Nagel 2000:113).

Ancestry is the outcome of social and biological reproduction, connected both materially and symbolically to sexual activity. In the most narrow and clinical sense, this implicates heterosexual coitus, conception, and birth. The resulting kinship networks are similarly understood in part through sexual prohibitions among members (that is, the incest taboo). Kinship, of course, is not always biological or heterosexual (Butler 2004; Spillers 1987; Weber 1978:389; Weston 1995; Yanagisako 1983); but in reproduction of all sorts, what is at stake is the ontological status of the child—its belongings and exclusions. As Nira Yuval-Davis (1996:17) notes, the most secure path to membership in a social collectivity is "being born into it." Consequently, "the child figures in the debate as the dense site for the transfer and reproduction of culture, where 'culture' carries with it implicit norms of racial purity and domination" (Butler 2004:110).

The gendered and sexual implications of concerns about the intergenerational perpetuation of ethnic, racial, or national collectives can be loosely organized into three intersecting categories. First, intragroup pressures to contribute to the biological and cultural perpetuation of the group condition a subject's reproductive positions and obligations to his or her ethnic and national collectivities (Yuval-Davis 1996). For example, the eugenics movement in nineteenth-century Britain emphasized that middle- and upper-class white women had a duty to increase and improve the English "race" not only through physical reproduction but also by adopting new standards of sanitation, medical care, and education. "The birth rate then was a matter of national importance: population was power" (Davin 1978:10). This latter sentiment is echoed in present-day debates about comparative birthrates among Israeli and Palestinian populations—what is in shorthand referred to as the "battle of the bedroom" (Americans for Peace Now 2005; Sabbagh 1998). As discussed in chapters 2 and 3, similar concerns about reproductive capabilities were at the forefront of the Spanish military's recruitment policies for its colonization of Alta California.

Second, concerns about racial, ethnic, and national integrity are operationalized through prohibitions against racial miscegenation and anxieties about marrying out (Nagel 2003; Young 1995). Barriers to interethnic, interracial, and international sexual relationships are enforced through legal measures (until 1967, at least forty of the fifty U.S. states prohibited interracial marriage), through extralegal social sanctions, and through the cultural production of desire (Young 1995). Third, such sexual crossings can be alternatively promoted (for example, through the celebration of so-called hybrid vigor), perpetrated (as in cases of interethnic sexual violence), and instilled through representations and practices that eroticize the ethnic or racial "other."[15] Such factors led Max Weber (1978:385) to observe that sexual repulsion or attraction is often expressed in ethnic terms.

The interconnection between sexuality, gender, and ethnicity is particularly pertinent in considerations of ethnogenesis. Early nineteenth-century uses of the term attributed new ethnicities to offspring from intermarriages who could not claim membership in either of their parents' ethnic or racial groups. This attention to the emergence of creole, hybrid, and mixed-race communities continues in current research on the subject (for example, Albers 1996; Bilby 1996; Devine 2004; Pérez 2000).

Membership in and the threat of expulsion from ethnic, racial, and national collectivities are also deployed to police and control gender and sexuality. Ethnically correct masculine and feminine behavior "constitutes gender regimes that often lie at the core of ethnic cultures" (Nagel 2000:113), often articulated through concerns about the sexual honor and respectability of the community (a prominent factor in this study, as discussed in chapters 3 and 4). Well-studied examples include the mobilization of African American womanhood to further the improvement and respectability of the race during Reconstruction in the United States: "motherhood and its associated domestic sphere were things to be done correctly—not just for the sake of children, but also for the good of the race" (Wilkie 2003:80; see also Carby 1987; Collins 2000; Davis 1981). More recently, controversies about the *hijab* (veiling) among Muslim women reverberate within concerns about religious observance, ethnic and national pride, and resistance to Western imperialism (El Guindi 1999; Mohanty 1997; Shirazi 2001). Symbols of ethnic pride can figure prominently in contests of masculine authority and power among men of the same ethnicity (Harrison 2002; Hodder 1982; Larick 1991). Persecution of sexual others can also be deployed in the consolidation of nationalism, as in the homosexual panics of Nazi Germany and U.S. McCarthyism (Nagel 2000; Rubin 1984). Consequently, investigations of ethnogenesis must attend to the entanglements of ethnic belonging and ethnic othering with race, nation, class, gender, and sexuality.

Ethnogenesis

This book's focus on ethnogenesis draws attention to the ongoing transformations of social identities. Ethnogenesis should not be confused with the Biblical image of something new being created out of nothing: the word's second root, "genesis," refers to *genus*—a race, a species, a grouping based on shared lineage. Ethnogenesis occurs through significations and practices that reference the past and anticipate the future. It is the unpredictable outcome of practical strategies and tactics and of cultural creativity, rather than a predicable process driven by external stimuli. In this, ethnogenesis joins theories of culture contact, creolization, transculturation, and hybridity in providing conceptual alternatives to the unilinear models of assimilation and acculturation that formerly dominated research on culture change.

This section traces the origins of the concept of ethnogenesis and briefly outlines its different uses in studies of cultural change.[16] This study is most closely aligned with an intellectual tradition of ethnogenesis research that examines the interrelationships between colonization, governmentality, and racism and their effects on social identity. However, within this body of scholarly work, ethnogenesis is increasingly conceptualized as a form of subaltern resistance to oppression. It is, however, equally important for studies of ethnogenesis to consider how new forms of ethnic identification can be used to assert power over others and to consolidate institutionalized forms of domination.

The concept of ethnogenesis was formulated in the mid-1800s as a response to Biblically inspired theories of racial history and racial degradation. The racial history perspective argued that migration and interbreeding had eroded the purity of divinely created races and that these mixtures were inferior to the originals. Most infamously, some authors argued that Germany represented the purest strain of the Aryan race and that the populations of France, England, and other nations had been degraded through interbreeding with indigenous Celtic and Slavic peoples. In contrast, nineteenth-century theories of ethnogenesis refused the ideology of racial purity by positing that all modern nations arose from ongoing cultural interactions and waves of migration. Each new ethnic form superseded its predecessors, making old forms obsolete; this ongoing process was viewed as a source of cultural improvement and civilization rather than degradation (Moore 2004:3046). It is no coincidence that both racial history and the study of ethnogenesis emerged out of the anxieties that surrounded European national identities during a period when colonization and the rapid expansion of world capitalism intensified encounters between peoples once thought to be separate and apart.

Although the concept of ethnogenesis developed as a progressive alternative to historical theories of pure races, it was rapidly pressed into service on behalf of nationalist rhetoric and state control of ethnic groups within national borders. Most nineteenth-century studies of ethnogenesis sought to identify the historical ethnic antecedents of modern nations; such "cultural cores," they claimed, had the greatest influence on national character and language. Following this approach, a scholar might proclaim that France, for example, is primarily a Roman nation or, alternatively, a Celtic one (Moore 2004:3046). Ethnogenesis first entered archaeological research through its articulation with the archaeological culture concept and V. Gordon Childe's interest in the effects of diffusion and migration (perhaps best exemplified by his monograph The Aryans [1926], which traced a prehistoric lineage between Britain and India).[17] In the early Soviet Union, ethnogenesis was further adapted as a methodology that could solve the "problem" of ethnic diversity within socialist states.[18] Studies of ethnogenesis in the Soviet Union were instrumental in state efforts to manage cultural heterogeneity within national borders. Ironically, both nationalist and Soviet approaches to ethnogenesis worked to "fix" and delimit ethnic groups and their histories, more closely resembling theories of racial purity than the original concept of ethnogenesis as a continual flow of cultural and identity transformation.

These earlier concepts of ethnogenesis were resurrected in North America in the 1960s and 1970s through historical, sociological, and anthropological research on the ongoing transformation of contemporary racial, ethnic, and tribal identities within contemporary society. Two articles were particularly instrumental in articulating this new approach: Lester Singer's "Ethnogenesis and Negro Americans Today" (1962), and William Sturtevant's "Creek into Seminole" (1971). Both Singer and Sturtevant challenged the common premise that minority identities—in this case, African Americans and Native Americans—were defined solely by racial attributes or common ancestry. Instead, at a time when ethnic and racial differences were considered a divisive and disruptive threat to the U.S. melting pot, Singer and Sturtevant demonstrated that contemporary ethnic identities were produced *internally* through the same historical events involved in nation building, governance, and economic development.

Significantly, both writers emphasized that ethnogenesis is a continuous phenomenon, traceable in the past and ongoing in the present. Singer pointed to the then-recent emergence of the civil rights movement as a new benchmark in American Negro ethnogenesis, and Sturtevant explored the effects of Bureau of Indian Affairs policies, Christian evangelism, economic development, and tourism on the transformation of Seminole identity and the relationships between Seminole society and non-Indians. Unlike the national origins research of earlier ethnogenesis studies, which focused on linguistic continuity and cultural tradition, the approach pioneered by Singer and Sturtevant considered imperialism, the state, military conflict, and economic systems to be central forces in the transformation and reproduction of ethnic identities.

The groundbreaking work of Singer and Sturtevant set the foundation for several decades of scholarship aimed at reconstructing the historical development of ethnic groups and tribes that had been previously viewed as "people without history" (Wolf 1982). Research within this field has generally centered on three themes. First, some scholars extend Singer's studies of the ethnogenesis of racialized minority groups in the United States and elsewhere.[19] These studies examine how shared experiences of racial discrimination and economic marginalization forge a sense of commonality and "a new politics of resistance, amongst groups and communities with, in fact, very different histories, traditions, and ethnic identities" (Hall 1989:27). The second, and perhaps the largest cluster, of ethnogenesis studies have followed Sturtevant's lead by researching the transformation of Native American tribal identities through European colonization and nation-state formation in both North and South America.[20]

The third theme in ethnogenesis research focuses on the formation and persistence of so-called neoteric ethnicities, such as maroon societies of runaway slaves, pan-Indian (nontribal) communities, and polyracial ethnicities such as Black Seminoles or Canadian Metís. Although these social groups are viewed as having no direct antecedents, they nonetheless present the full complement of traditions, myths, kinship systems, religious beliefs, and shared cultural practices that are often viewed as signs of authentic ethnic continuity.[21] Studies of these groups demonstrate not only that "the creation of ethnicities can be a fluid and rapid process" (Horning 1999:132) but also that diverse groups of unrelated peoples can rapidly forge a sense of "primordial ties and loyalties" that are as strong as those "associated with an ancient or immemorial past" (Bilby 1996:137). The ethnogenesis of neoteric communities demonstrates that even under the worst circumstances, people determined to survive may do so by reinventing culture if necessary (Anderson 1999). The research on Californio ethnogenesis presented in this book is most closely aligned with the study of neoteric identities, but it differs in taking colonial, rather than colonized, populations as its object of study.

The most important intellectual legacy of Singer and Sturtevant may be that their own research and the many studies they inspired have put to rest debates about "cultural authenticity" by demonstrating that ethnic identities are in a continual process of interaction and transformation. Ethnogenesis studies have also provided a methodological bridge between local and global scales of historical analysis (Matsuda 2004:4854), one that refuses the dichotomy "between a complex and transcontinentally active core and a static, locally bounded periphery" (Tsing 1994:282). Finally, ethnogenetic research refuses "the racialist policy" (Whitten 1996b:410) that has previously separated studies of indigenous history from research on the African diaspora.

During the past decade, researchers have increasingly argued that ethnogenesis is a form of subaltern resistance to external domination: "people's cultural and political struggles to exist as well as their historical consciousness of these struggles" (Hill 1996:2). Along these lines, ethnogenesis is viewed as a creative means of survival among people with few options: to resist domination, oppressed peoples must "set themselves against their own history and their own experiences, must also claim the new against the old" (Sider 1994:118). Through ethnogenesis, "native peoples are active players, not only in their own cultural survival, but in the forging of the larger colonial world" (Powers 1995:5). Ethnogenesis has become a powerful metaphor for the creativity of oppressed and marginalized peoples birthing a new cultural space for themselves amidst their desperate struggle to survive.

Ethnogenesis might be one way in which the subaltern can "speak" (Spivak 1988), even as the forces of history and systems of domination seek to exploit or destroy them. Yet conceptualizing ethnogenesis as inherently connected with political resistance and liberation ignores the reality that new forms of ethnic identification can also be used to assert power over others and to consolidate institutional forms of domination. As John Metz (1999) and Alison Bell (2005) emphatically demonstrate, ethnogenesis in British-colonial North America also took place among immigrants of European descent, who forged commonalities across differences of religion and national origin to assert a "white" identity. Stuart Hall (1989, 1996) similarly calls attention to recent assertions of British ethnicities that have been marshaled in support of racist and anti-immigrant legislation. Further, colonization led to factionalism among subjugated indigenous and diasporic populations. Such factions, which often were expressed in terms of ethnic identities, produced and were shaped by internecine struggles over trade and military alliances with colonial powers and involvement in the slave trade (Hill 1996; Sider 1994).

In other words, the claims for survival made by colonized peoples often simultaneously required asserting dominance over other colonized groups. The research presented in this book exemplifies this phenomenon: the people who came to call themselves Californios were themselves colonized peoples who were enrolled as agents of colonial expansion. If we celebrate ethnogenesis as a strategy of liberation and cultural survival, we must equally take into account its possible role as a means of achieving domination and control. What is required is, first, an understanding of power that moves beyond simple binaries of oppression and resistance; and, second, a more rigorous multiscalar methodology that can articulate the connections between micro-level social practices of identification, meso-level representations of collective identities, and the macro-level effects of statism, governmentality, and institutions. The following chapters use the concept of ethnogenesis to illuminate the workings and effects of colonization and to simultaneously intervene in earlier theories of ethnogenesis that have sidestepped an understanding of how neoteric social identities can be deployed in the exertion of power over others.

PART 1   HISTORICAL AND
ARCHAEOLOGICAL
CONTEXTS

On July 26, 1776, a caravan of 193 men, women, and children arrived at a small plateau at the northern edge of the San Francisco peninsula. Defined on its east and west by two valleys containing spring-fed creeks, the plateau was somewhat sheltered by a bank of hills rising sharply to the south. The site commanded an impressive view of the San Francisco Bay and of the Yelamu Ohlone village of Petlenuc,[1] which stood on the bayshore only a few minutes' walk to the north.

The expedition of military settlers had been traveling together for nine months. Some families had been in transit much longer, having first journeyed from their home villages to the expedition's gathering point at the Presidio of Tubac, in present-day southern Arizona. The most arduous part of the journey was the five-month trek from Tubac to the Presidio of Monterey (map 1). The travelers faced constant pressure to continue moving forward, on horseback and on foot, in order to pass through the Sonoran and Colorado deserts during the cooler winter months. This timing was necessary not only for the safety of the human members of the expedition but also so that their livestock—hundreds of horses and mules and nearly a thousand head of cattle—would have adequate pasturage along the way. Thirst and hunger were not infrequent. Further, the expedition feared being attacked by the native communities whose lands they were traversing. But the military settlers' encounters with indigenous peoples were peaceful, perhaps because it was clear that the colonists were just passing through. In fact, the travelers rarely stopped to rest, and when they did,

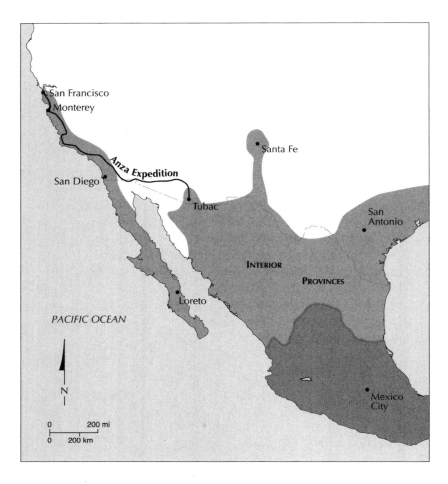

MAP 1. New Spain, ca. 1776, including the Interior Provinces and the route of the Anza expedition. The lighter shaded area indicates the approximate limit of actual colonial settlement. Adapted from Mason 1998:19.

it was for only one or two days, primarily when a woman was giving birth. By the time the party reached El Presidio de Monterey on March 10, 1776, it had gained four infant settlers and lost one adult woman in childbirth.

Most of the settlers rested in Monterey for three months, to recover from the journey and pasture their livestock. Meanwhile, the expedition's leader, Juan Bautista de Anza, formed a scouting party composed of his second-in-command, José Joaquín Moraga; Franciscan priest Pedro Font; eleven soldiers; and seven servants. On March 23, 1776, they left Monterey and traveled north to the San

Francisco peninsula. Because their primary goal was to choose sites for the Presidio and mission, they traveled widely throughout the area to identify the locations of Native Californian villages and to find sources of timber, firewood, pasturage, and water.

By this point, Native Californians in the San Francisco Bay area were increasingly familiar with the Spanish-colonial soldiers and priests. Between 1769 and 1775, Bay area tribes had encountered four land-based colonial exploration parties: the 1769 Portolá expedition, the 1770 and 1772 Fages parties, and the 1774 Rivera expedition.[2] In 1775, the *San Carlos* had anchored in the bay for forty-four days, while preparing a maritime chart of the region's waterways. During their stay, the crew of the *San Carlos* visited several local villages, some of which prepared feasts for the strange newcomers. To reciprocate, the sailors offered gifts and invited some villagers aboard ship. In addition to these early direct encounters, native peoples living around the San Francisco Bay were undoubtedly aware of the 1770 establishment of the Presidio of Monterey and Mission San Carlos in the areas immediately south.

Consequently, when Anza's scouting party entered the region in March 1776, news of its arrival spread quickly. Some local people sought out the colonial explorers, offering gifts of firewood, food, and water. Others brandished weapons and threatened the colonists but stopped short of directly attacking them. When visiting indigenous communities, the explorers usually distributed gifts of glass beads and cloth and often received gifts of food in return. At times, these early exchanges revealed points of similarity between local villagers and the newcomers. Soldiers described native food in familiar terms—cakes of acorn flour and deer meat resembled *tamales*, and gruels of ground seeds were similar to the corn-based *atole* (porridge) that was a staple of the colonial diet. Yet at other times, the cultural differences appeared insurmountable, especially regarding spiritual matters. The colonists' Catholic prayers and rituals were as incomprehensible to the Native Californians as the Indians' dances and songs were to the colonists (Milliken 1995:52–59).

Eventually, the expedition reached the Yelamu district (see map 3), which encompassed the northern tip of the San Francisco peninsula. Covered with sand dunes and grasslands interrupted by small creeks, this was the most arid and windswept part of the San Francisco Bay area. It was also the least populated, with only three communities, totaling approximately 150 to 200 people (Milliken 1995:62; Milliken, Shoup, and Ortiz 2005). The scouting party surveyed the region and selected sites for the new mission and Presidio. They returned to Monterey on April 8. Anza and Font departed for Mexico, leaving Lieutenant Moraga in command of the planned Presidio (table 1) and Franciscan priests Francisco Palóu and Pedro Cambon in charge of the effort to establish the mission.

TABLE 1.   Commanders of El Presidio de San Francisco, 1776–1846

Commander	Term of Service
José Joaquín Moraga	July 1776–July 1785
Diego González	July 1785–February 1787
Hermenegildo Sal (acting)	February 1787–June 1787
José Darío Argüello	June 1787–August 1806
Hemenegildo Sal (acting in Argüello's absences)	1791–1794; 1795–1796
José Pérez Fernández (acting in Argüello's absence)	1794–1795
Pedro de Alberni (Catalonian Volunteers)	1796–1801
Manuel Rodríguez	1806–1813 (never present)
Luis Antonio Argüello	August 1806–March 1830
Ignacio Martínez (acting in Argüello's absences)	1822–1827; 1828–1831
José Antonio Sánchez (acting in Argüello's absences)	1829–1831
Mariano Guadalupe Vallejo	September 1831–1834 (thereafter commander of both Sonoma and San Francisco)
(Acting in Vallejo's absences)	1835–1846
Dámaso Rodríguez	
Francisco Sánchez	
Juan Prado Mesa	
Santiago Hernández (caretaker)	1841
Joaquín Peña (caretaker)	1844

SOURCE: Adapted from Langellier and Rosen 1996:189–190, app. A.

On June 17, 1776, the settlers and their livestock left Monterey, arriving in San Francisco ten days later. They brought with them thirteen young Native Californian servants from the Monterey region, who also acted as interpreters (Milliken 1995:62). Palóu writes that the Native Californians they met along the way were surprised to see people of both sexes and all ages, since all of the earlier colonial exploration parties had been composed entirely of adult men (1926:119–120). For the first month, the settlers camped in a valley near the Yelamu village of Chutchui, the site where Mission San Francisco de Asís would be established. They were awaiting the supply ship *San Carlos*, which had been delayed long past its planned arrival date. Weeks passed with no word. On July 26, aware that the settlers needed to shelter themselves before winter arrived, Moraga moved most of the expedition to the site chosen for the new Presidio. The two priests remained at the mission site along with six soldiers who served as the mission *escolta* (guard).

It is difficult to imagine what it was like for the members of the Anza expedition to leave their homes and families and friends, travel through uncharted lands, and establish new lives in the most remote, isolated frontier of the Spanish-colonial empire. Records of the recruitment drive for the expedition provide glimpses of their motivations and aspirations. Anza recruited most of the military settlers from Culiacán, in Sinaloa, and Fuerte, in Sonora, because these towns were impoverished by crop failures and by ongoing battles between the colonial military and an intertribal alliance of local indigenous communities. The people living in this war-torn region, Anza wrote, were "best suited for the purpose and most easy to obtain without being missed," for they were "submerged in the greatest poverty and misery" (Bouvier 2001:59). In other words, in the eyes of the colonial government, the members of the expedition were expendable, desperate, and susceptible to promises of future opportunity.

Anza recruited married couples with proven fertility; the families averaged four children per couple (Castañeda 1992:34). They were promised rewards that would lift them and their children out of poverty: livestock, clothing, supplies for the journey ahead, advance pay for the first two years of service, and free rations for the first five years. There was also the nebulous but tantalizing promise of land to be granted in reward for service to the colonial government. In exchange, the recruits pledged the next twenty years of their lives to colonial military service in Alta California.

Arriving on this windy and fog-shrouded promontory overlooking the mouth of the San Francisco Bay, the settlers had finally reached their new home. They began to construct rudimentary shelters. Some soldiers also accompanied Father Palóu in his visits to Yelamu villages, where he distributed presents of beads and cloth and encouraged the Yelamu to visit the new mission settlement (Milliken 1995:63). But on August 12, the villages in the Yelamu district were attacked and burned by the Ssalson, an Ohlone tribe based just south of the Yelamu. With several Yelamu wounded and some dead, and their homes destroyed, the survivors fled across the San Francisco Bay in tule boats to take refuge among the Huimen of present-day Marin County and the Huchiun of present-day Alameda County. As a result, the area selected for the new Presidio and mission settlements was quickly depopulated without any military action on the part of the colonial settlers.[3]

A few days after the Ssalson attack, the delayed *San Carlos* finally entered the bay, bringing badly needed supplies. From that point forward, construction of the Presidio proceeded in earnest. Moraga and the ship's pilot, José de Cañizares, laid out the formal quadrangle of the fort. The soldiers and their families continued work on their own dwellings, while the ship's crew began to build the warehouse, the chapel, and the *comandancia* (the military and administrative headquarters, which also served as the commanding officer's residence).

A month later, on September 17, the military settlers, mission priests, and sailors celebrated a high mass and the formal dedication of El Presidio de San Francisco. The settlement would guard the mouth of the San Francisco Bay, one of the world's best natural harbors and a strategic resource that Spain could not afford to let fall into the hands of another European empire. The colonial settlers would also provide military muscle to the messianic project of Christianizing the area's indigenous peoples and suppressing native rebellions against colonial rule. Most of all, the settlers' days would be occupied with the basics of survival: creating shelter and obtaining sustenance in an unfamiliar land. From the beginning, the military settlers knew that they would never return to their former homes in what today is northwest Mexico. Their decisions to emigrate to the northernmost edge of the Spanish empire irrevocably changed their lives and those of their descendants.

Between 1776 and 1834, at least four generations of military settlers called El Presidio de San Francisco their home. They departed for weeks and even months on military expeditions into California's interior and served tours of guard duty for several years at nearby missions. Some were appointed as colonial officials in civilian pueblos. Most, however, returned to the Presidio when a particular assignment ended. As the center of colonial life in the San Francisco Bay area, the Presidio was the crucible within which colonial identities were melded and formed. It was here that the settlers rejected the racially charged casta terms that had been their primary form of identification and forged new, shared identities as gente de razón, hijos del país, and Californios.

This chapter presents the historical background and the political and cultural context for this study of colonial ethnogenesis. It begins by describing the indigenous cultural landscape that the military settlers entered in 1776. Because of how Native Californian communities were internally organized, California was colonized not through a single battle or treaty but through decades of colonial entanglement involving military battles, voluntary and coerced labor programs, and religious proselytizing. The colonists were profoundly transformed by their ongoing interactions with the Native Californians whose homeland they had invaded and appropriated and among whom they were always a small minority. Colonial ethnogenesis can be understood only within this context of intercultural interaction, exploitation, and violence.

The chapter next delves into the institutions that together constituted the colonial province of Alta California. In some other European colonies (and during the later U.S. expansion into western North America), government policies and practices encouraged individual settlers and private companies to pioneer as explorers, prospectors, farmers, land speculators, or entrepreneurs. In contrast, Spanish-colonial Alta California was a rigidly organized society. Military presidios and religious missions dominated colonial life; colonists were not even allowed to travel unescorted without a written pass from the appropriate commanding officer or priest. Only three civilian settlements were established in the entire province, and these were also tightly regulated by the colonial government. As military recruits, the settlers were shaped by these institutional practices, even as they themselves were responsible for implementing and enforcing colonial rules and regulations. Their options were constrained by the government ordinances, military regulations, and religious doctrines that structured every aspect of their daily lives. Nonetheless, within these institutions, the military settlers forged new cultural paths, and their successes in developing new forms of social identification indicate their ability to manipulate policy and procedure to their own ends.

This chapter also situates colonial San Francisco within the context of broader regional and international events. Throughout its colonial history, San Francisco presented a historical paradox. It was profoundly isolated, so much so that news of Mexican independence in 1821 did not reach the settlement until more than a year after Spain had withdrawn from North America. Yet San Francisco was also deeply integrated into the institutional networks of the colonial empire and the economic networks of the emerging capitalist world market. Remote events, such as the Yuma revolt and distant wars among European powers, had profound effects on the colonists' lives and on the historical trajectory of Spanish colonization in Alta California.

Indigenous Landscapes

The founding of Mission San Francisco de Asís (today known as Mission Dolores) and El Presidio de San Francisco occurred in the midst of a complex indigenous landscape that colonial priests, officers, and military settlers could scarcely comprehend.[4] The native cultures of the central California coast were unlike any that Spain had previously encountered in the Americas. The structural differences between the state-level organization of Spanish-colonial institutions and the weblike political networks of the San Francisco Bay region's native peoples profoundly shaped the trajectory of colonization. Spain appropriated Alta California through slow incremental expansion involving decades of colonial entanglement. By the 1810s, at the twilight of Spain's empire in North America, the military settlers and missionaries had managed to secure only a narrow coastal strip of land as colonized territory.

The Native Californians who lived around the San Francisco Bay are today generally referred to by language group: Ohlone (Costanoan),[5] Patwin, Wappo, Bay Miwok, Coast Miwok, Eastern Miwok, Pomo, and Yokuts (map 2). Anthropologists usually describe these historical communities as "complex hunter-gatherers": largely sedentary peoples who lived not by agriculture but by gathering plants and shellfish, by hunting game, and by fishing. In central California's relatively mild Mediterranean climate, indigenous communities had developed sophisticated environmental management strategies that maximized wild food yields. Rather than domesticating individual species, they domesticated entire habitats, using controlled burning, erosion control, plant and seed distribution, game management, and selective gathering to maximize the likelihood of sustained, reliable harvests (Blackburn and Anderson 1993). To guard against short-term fluctuations in resource yields, villages stored considerable quantities of dried meats, acorns, and edible seeds in granaries and storage pits; these surpluses were also used to sponsor regional feasts and in intervillage trade.

Native Californians of the central coast lived in small autonomous districts, each measuring eight to twelve miles across, which usually encompassed lands surrounding one or more watersheds running from the mountain crests to bay and ocean shores. This arrangement allowed each community to harvest resources from the full range of ecological niches created by changes in elevation, moisture, and temperature. At the time of Spanish colonization, the San Francisco Bay area was organized into more than sixty of these autonomous districts, whose residents each spoke their own distinctive language or dialect (map 3). Each district was further organized into two to four village communities, which could include anywhere from forty to three hundred people. For example, the Yelamu Ohlone, who lived in an area roughly corresponding to present-day San Francisco, generally resided in three village groups. Petlenuc was a small village on or nearby the bayshore of the Presidio. Another village group lived along Mission Creek, moving seasonally from Sitlintac on the bayshore to Chutchui two or three miles inland. A third group moved between Amuctac and Tubsinte, two village sites in the south-central area of San Fran-

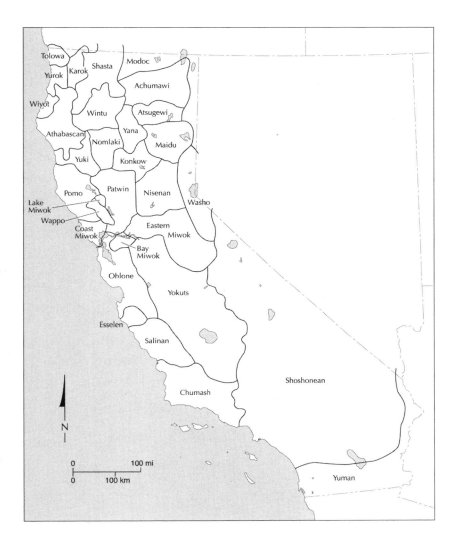

MAP 2.   Native Californian language group areas. Today, many language group names have come to be used as tribal names. Adapted from Milliken 1995:25.

cisco (Milliken, Shoup, and Ortiz 2005:177). This largely sedentary residential pattern, along with intensive management of the environment, supported what may have been one of the highest indigenous population densities in North America (Milliken 1995:19; Milliken, Shoup and Ortiz 2005:72–73).

    The political organization of Bay Area native communities is difficult to

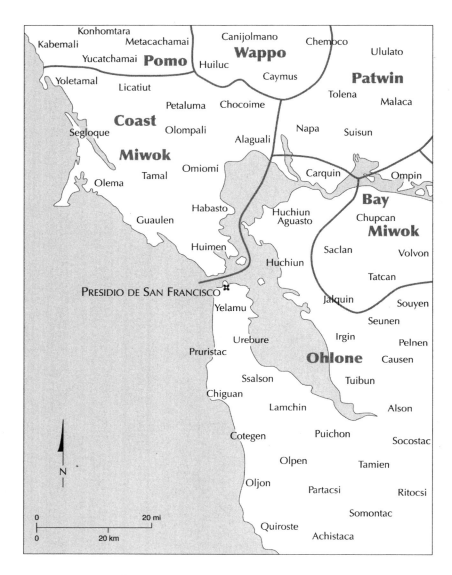

MAP 3.   Native Californian districts in the San Francisco Bay area. Each district usually contained one to three permanent villages. Adapted from Milliken 1995:229 and information provided by Randall Milliken in December 2006.

describe in conventional terms. Each district was composed of several interrelated extended families, and its daily affairs were guided by a head-person and by spiritual doctors, moiety leaders, craft specialists, elders, and others who showed talent or insight into particular matters. Researchers are divided regarding the degree to which these leaders constituted a hereditary elite, with some arguing that there was little possibility for social mobility among community members. Others suggest that the family unit, under the leadership of its elders, was the primary center of authority; from this perspective, community leaders coordinated group activities but had little real power or status.[6]

The small size and political autonomy of these village districts, in comparison with other North American indigenous tribes, initially led anthropologists such as Alfred Kroeber (1925, 1955) to conclude that native communities of the San Francisco Bay area were insular, bounded entities. More recent scholarship emphasizes that the political autonomy and territorial integrity of village districts were complemented by a complex web of regional ties formed through intermarriage, military alliances, long-distance trade networks, craft guilds, extended kinship groups, and moiety associations and other religious affiliations (Field et al. 1992; Lightfoot 2005; Milliken 1995; Milliken, Shoup, and Ortiz 2005; Yamane 2002). These bonds intertwined districts with each other but did not bring the region under any form of central leadership.

To the missionaries and the military settlers who arrived in the San Francisco Bay area in the 1770s, the gathering and hunting economy of the region's native peoples and their lack of centralized leadership were antithetical to the colonial view of a proper civilized lifestyle. Settlers found Native Californians' appearance even more offensive, since most indigenous dress displayed rather than concealed the body. The colonists were also simultaneously fascinated and repulsed by some indigenous sexual practices, which included not only monogamous heterosexual marriage but also polygamy, premarital sex, same-sex sexuality, and transgendered practices (Voss 2000a, 2000b). The perceived savagery of the regions' inhabitants provided religious justification for initiating the colonial policy of *reducción* (literally, reduction), through which native peoples were removed from their home villages and aggregated at missions for religious conversion. Further, colonial officials prohibited seasonal burning and allowed their livestock to graze the grassy hills, destroying wild seed crops and introducing exotic weeds that disrupted local ecosystems. Within a few years of the arrival of the Anza party, hunger led many Native Californians to enter the missions out of desperation, to raid colonial settlements, to hire themselves out to colonial settlers as laborers, or to relocate to uncolonized regions to the east and north.

Because each village and district was relatively autonomous, the region's native peoples made no unified response to the arrival of the Anza expedition. Randall Milliken (1995:225) writes that "tribal groups in Central California were never able to forge enduring regional military alliances to oppose the Europeans precisely because they did not consider themselves to be a single people." Instead, individuals, families, and villages adopted a range of strategies. Initial reactions to the colonial settlements included fear, curiosity, hostility, and friendliness. Some people demonstrated considerable generosity to the colonists, although we will never know whether the gifts of food and firewood were offered in a spirit of hospitality or in hopes of appeasing the strangers. Others sought alliances with the colonial military, hoping to gain advantages in disputes with neighboring villages. Many people took a wait-and-see attitude, keeping their distance while monitoring the situation. Some families hedged their bets by sending one or two relatives to live at the missions while the majority remained in their home villages; others fled the region entirely. The impacts of colonization rippled eastward and northward from the coastal area as refugees swelled the population of inland villages and brought with them livestock, horses, new kinds of material culture, and diseases.

Direct violence between the colonial military and San Francisco indigenous people did not occur until more than six months after the Presidio and mission were founded. We know of this first armed conflict from the memoirs of Father Palóu (1926:135–138), head priest of Mission San Francisco de Asís. Palóu wrote that in the fall of 1776, some Yelamu men and boys began to return periodically to the lagoon near the mission to hunt ducks. Perhaps they were also trying to assess whether it would be possible to return to their homeland. These visits were relatively uneventful, with the Yelamu sometimes presenting the missionaries with some of the ducks and receiving gifts of glass beads and food in return.

But in early December, Palóu began to experience these visits as hostile threats. He wrote that the Yelamu men "began to disgrace themselves, now by thefts, now by firing an arrow close to the corporal of the guard, and again by trying to kiss the wife of a soldier, as well as by threatening to fire an arrow at a neophyte from the mission of Carmelo who was at this mission" (1926:135). Sergeant Juan Grijalva, the second highest ranking officer at the Presidio, was at the mission when the man who had threatened to fire an arrow at the Mission Carmel neophyte—a neofito, as Native Californians who were newly converted to Christianity were called—returned to the area. Grijalva had the man arrested and flogged. Two Yelamu men who were hunting in the lagoon heard the man's cries and ran toward the mission to try to rescue him, "making ready to shoot arrows at the soldiers, who fired two gunshots only to frighten them" (136). The two Yelamu men fled to their campsite at the bayshore.

The next day, Grijalva returned from the Presidio with additional soldiers. It seems from Palóu's account that Grijalva was determined to make an example of the two men who had challenged colonial authority by attempting to protect their companion. Grijalva and his troops found a group of Yelamu men camping on the beach and asked which of them had fired arrows at the mission. According to Palóu, some of the Yelamu pointed out two of their group, although these men denied the accusation. Grijalva dismounted his horse; the two accused men fled with several soldiers in pursuit. The rest of the Yelamu began to shoot arrows at the soldiers, wounding one man and a horse, "although," Palóu noted, "they were not seriously hurt" (1926:137).

Grijalva ordered his troops to open fire, and they quickly shot two of the Yelamu men, killing one and severely wounding another. At this, the Yelamu surrendered, throwing their bows and arrows on the ground. Grijalva lowered his musket to the ground to signal acceptance of the truce. Meanwhile, Grijalva's soldiers captured the two men who had run away when accused of trying to rescue the imprisoned Yelamu man. Grijalva ordered the two men whipped, and he used signs to tell them that he would kill them if they ever threatened the mission again.

We are left to speculate about how the Yelamu viewed these events. Were the "thefts" that Palóu alluded to an attempt to claim compensation for the colonists' use of Yelamu lands and resources? Did the Yelamu man who attempted to kiss the unnamed colonial woman do so in hopes of forging an alliance through intermarriage? Were the Yelamu who shot arrows at the mission hoping that the colonists would flee the area, just as the Yelamu had done in response to Ssalson aggression? Regardless, at the close of 1776, three Yelamu men had been captured and flogged, a fourth had been shot in the leg, and a fifth killed by musket fire.

If the Yelamu had once envisioned a peaceful return to their homelands, they soon realized that it would be accomplished only through subordination to the new colonial military and religious order. In spring 1777, a small number of Yelamu young men and boys entered Mission San Francisco de Asís and began training in Christian catechism. The first three were baptized on June 24, 1777. By the end of 1777, twenty-eight additional Yelamu had accepted baptism and become members of the mission community (Milliken 1995:68–69; Milliken, Shoup, and Ortiz 2005:81–91).

In only one year, the Yelamu district was transformed from a network of interconnected native communities to a landscape dominated by colonial institutions. As colonial influence expanded, the process was repeated time and time again in indigenous communities throughout the San Francisco Bay region. By 1793, no native villages remained on the San Francisco peninsula; and by 1810, all but the northernmost extent of the San Francisco Bay area had been emptied (Milliken 1995:1; Milliken, Shoup, and Ortiz 2005:81–91).

Colonial Institutions

The colonization of Alta California was a deliberately organized enterprise, one that was centrally planned and directed by high-ranking officers in New Spain's colonial military. The decision to expand into Alta California was made in 1767, at the end of the Seven Years' War, which brought increased French, British, Dutch, and Russian activity to the Pacific coast. It soon became clear that Spain needed to physically occupy the territory, or it would lose its claim to possession. Once foreign interests forced Spain's hand, the colonial government was quick to act. In 1768, Visitador-General José de Gálvez established a shipyard and naval depot at San Blas, a port located just north of present-day Puerto Vallarta, to organize and supply maritime shipments to the new colony. He also ordered the construction of a new military headquarters across the Sea of Cortéz in Baja California so that Alta California could be reached by land.[7]

Colonization of the new province began in 1769, with the establishment of the San Diego mission and presidio, shortly followed by the 1770 founding of El Presidio de Monterey and its associated mission, San Carlos de Borromeo. In the mid-1770s, Anza forged an overland trail that connected Alta California with the province of Sonora. In 1776, El Presidio de San Francisco was the first settlement established via this new trail, followed by El Presidio de Santa Bárbara in 1782. Each of these military settlements was the headquarters of a presidio district that shared the settlement's name (map 4). El Presidio de Monterey held the added distinction of being the capital of the province and consequently the residence of the governor, usually a Spaniard appointed to the position by the viceroy of New Spain.

Within each district, colonization followed the tripartite settlement system that had been developed during the previous two centuries of Spanish-colonial expansion in North America (Costello and Hornbeck 1989; Weber 1992). The presidios were the first settlements to be established. In addition to providing military defense, they were the seat of government for each district and oversaw the administrative, judicial, and economic organization of the region. Shortly afterward, religious missions were founded to aggregate and Christianize indigenous peoples. Finally, civilian pueblos were formed to supply agricultural

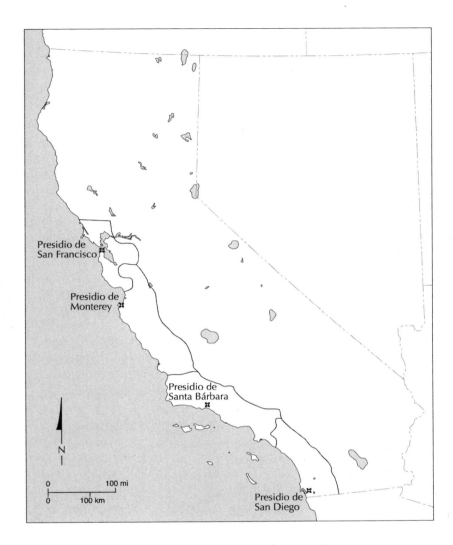

MAP 4. Alta California presidio districts. Adapted from Costello and Hornbeck 1989:311.

products and craft goods to the military outposts. Most of the military settlers who made up Alta California's colonial population were involved in all three institutions. Many viewed the presidios as their primary residence but also served tours of duty at the missions and pueblos. Understanding this regional network of colonial institutions provides a necessary context for interpreting the archaeological site of El Presidio de San Francisco (map 5).

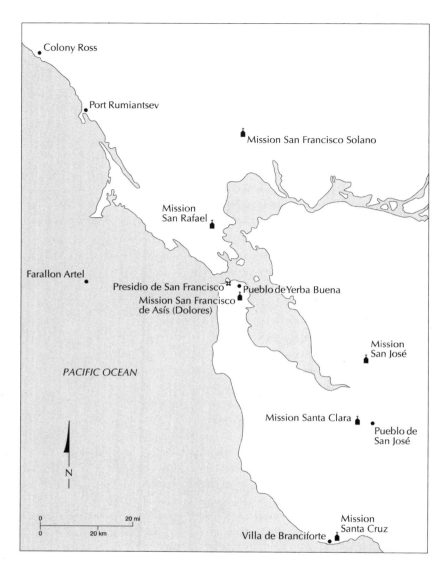

Colony Ross

Port Rumiantsev

Mission San Francisco Solano

Mission San Rafael

Farallon Artel

Presidio de San Francisco

Pueblo de Yerba Buena

Mission San Francisco de Asís (Dolores)

Mission San José

PACIFIC OCEAN

N

Mission Santa Clara

Pueblo de San José

0   20 mi
0   20 km

Mission Santa Cruz

Villa de Branciforte

MAP 5.   Major Spanish-colonial and Russian-colonial settlements,
1776–1845, San Francisco Bay region.

El Presidio de San Francisco

Presidios were frontier military institutions that developed through centuries of Spanish military encounters with non-Christian peoples, first during Spain's imperial expansion into North Africa in the early 1500s, and subsequently in the New World during territorial expansion following the 1521 conquest of the Aztec empire. The Latin term *presidium* refers to a garrisoned place that is "set before" to create a defense perimeter, an enclave of civilization in a savage land (Moorhead 1975:3; Naylor and Polzer 1986:16). By the 1600s, presidios had become the dominant military institution in the northwest frontier region of New Spain, an area that came to be known as the Provincias Internas, or Interior Provinces. (These provinces encompassed the territory now held by the Mexican states of Coahuila, Chihuahua, Durango, Sonora, Sinaloa, Baja California, and Baja California Sur as well as the U.S. states of Louisiana, Texas, New Mexico, Arizona, and California.) Because presidios were designed to secure and defend Spain's claim on territory that was occupied primarily by indigenous populations, the development of the forts was influenced more by the conditions of frontier engagement than by contemporary European theories of warfare (Bense 2004; Moorhead 1975; Thomas 1941). In the eighteenth century, the administration of military operations in the Interior Provinces was separated from the rest of the colonial military, and special regulations were issued to govern the presidios' operations.[8]

Unlike other frontier presidios, the four in Alta California were intended to secure the new province from both indigenous resistance and maritime attacks by other European powers. Consequently, they were positioned at strategic points along the coastline, especially to guard natural harbors that might be attractive to passing ships (Whitehead 1983). All presidios were governed by the 1772 Reglamento (regulations), which specified the architecture of the fortifications, the composition of the presidio company, the economic system through which goods were distributed and accounted for, and the uniforms, equipment, and livestock that each soldier was required to maintain for his own use (Brinkerhoff and Faulk 1965). (These regulations are discussed at greater length in subsequent chapters.)

As the administrative, judicial, residential, and economic centers of the districts, Alta California's presidios were villages as well as defensive fortifications. The nucleus of each presidio was its main quadrangle, a compound of buildings around a central rectangular plaza. The quadrangle housed most of the colonists living in each district and also included a guardhouse, a comandancia, a jail, a chapel, storehouses, and craft workshops such as carpentry and blacksmith shops. Presidio quadrangles were compact settlements, usually covering only two to six acres. As chapters 6 and 7 discuss, the 1772 Reglamento ordered the fortification of the quadrangle with thick exterior walls, ramparts, and bastions, but these defenses were not always present at El Presidio de San Francisco and at other presidios in Alta California.

Each presidio quadrangle lay in the center of the royal presidio reserve, a large tract of land set aside for the exclusive use of the presidio company. The lands and natural resources on the reserve were developed to support the settlement. Archaeological investigations in the hinterlands surrounding El Presidio de San Francisco's main quadrangle have uncovered evidence of substantial waterworks, perhaps intended to supply water to the quadrangle and to irrigate the colony's fields (Voss et al. 2005). San Francisco's presidio reserve also had a wharf, located on the bayshore immediately north of the main quadrangle. In the 1790s, under growing fears of foreign invasion, two additional fortifications were constructed along the bayshore: El Castillo de San Joaquín, positioned immediately above the narrow mouth of the bay; and La Batería de San José, located about a mile and a half east of the main quadrangle.

With supply ships arriving only once a year at best, each presidio community was expected to produce most of its own foodstuffs and did so by raising livestock and cultivating crops. In addition to the pastures and cultivated fields on its reserve, each presidio company controlled a large expanse of grazing land called *ranchos del rey* (royal ranchlands). San Francisco's ranch was located south of the Presidio in the San Bruno Mountains, in what is today San Mateo County. The colonists also relied on the local landscape for raw materials used in construction and craft production. At El Presidio de San Francisco, clay for making adobe bricks, roof tiles, and household ceramics was harvested from large borrow pits surrounding the main quadrangle. Stone for building foundations was quarried from bedrock outcrops only a short distance away. Other resources were harder to obtain: the nearest source of limestone for producing mortar and plaster was more than six leagues (about twenty miles) to the south. Harvesting timber for construction and gathering firewood rapidly deforested the presidio reserve itself; only a few years after the Presidio was established, the military settlers had to venture to the south and even across the bay to obtain lumber (the Marin County suburb of Corte Madera—literally, cut wood—retains its name from Spanish-colonial timber harvests). Hence, while the presidio quadrangle was the center of colonial life in each presidio district, the military settlers' use of the surrounding landscape extended far beyond the walls of the compound.

Missions

Gálvez envisioned California as a military colony, but he lacked the funds and personnel necessary to subdue Alta California's native populations while simultaneously guarding against incursions by other European powers (Campbell 1977). Reluctantly, Gálvez decided to involve Franciscan missionaries because they were "the only group experienced in managing Indians at low cost" (Weber 1992:242). Hence the expeditions that established Alta California's colonial settlements were jointly headed by military officers and priests—in the case of El Presidio de San Francisco, Anza and Font. Consequently, Alta California's colonial administration was forged through an uneasy alliance between military tactics and messianic fervor. This tension continued throughout the colonial era, especially after 1790, when missions began to dominate Alta California's economy. Political debates about the role of religion in colonial government were accompanied by power struggles between church and military regarding the right to control Native Californian labor and the lands reserved for native peoples under colonial policy.

Missions were the most numerous colonial institutions in Alta California, and the most populous. In the end, twenty-one missions were established alongside Alta California's four presidios and three civilian settlements. Each mission housed two priests, a small guard of four to eight presidio soldiers (and, at times, their families), and anywhere from five hundred to twenty-five hundred Native Californians who had been relocated from their home villages and baptized in the Christian faith. In comparison, the largest colonial settlements never exceeded three hundred in total population.[9]

Six of the twenty-one missions lay within the San Francisco Presidio district. Mission San Francisco de Asís was founded in 1776, concurrently with the Presidio, and Mission Santa Clara was established the following year. By the 1790s, nearly all Native Californians on the San Francisco peninsula had either entered the missions or fled the region; in that decade, the mission effort expanded to the south and east, with the opening of Mission Santa Cruz in 1791 and Mission San José in 1797. After the Russian-American Company founded Colony Ross on the Sonoma County coast in 1812, the Spanish-colonial government responded by setting up two new missions north of El Presidio de San Francisco: San Rafael in 1817 and San Francisco Solano in 1823. Like the presidios, each mission was a broad complex of interconnected facilities: religious buildings, residential neighborhoods, craft workshops, corrals, pastures, aqueduct systems, and agricultural fields (Costello and Hornbeck 1989). Most missions also maintained one or more asistencias, which functioned primarily as agricultural outposts, similar to the presidios' ranchos del rey.

The missions are the most studied and the most controversial of Spain's colonial institutions in Alta California.[10] At the core of these debates is the degree to which native peoples were coerced to join and remain at the missions and their subsequent treatment as neophytes. Because of the high mortality rates among neophytes, the missions were not self-reproducing and depended on continuously recruiting new members to sustain themselves.

For the San Francisco Bay area, Milliken's research (1995:29) indicates that in the 1770s and 1780s, most Native Californians entering missions did so voluntarily but under difficult circumstances. The first converts were young, often orphaned, individuals who likely were attracted by the priests' apparent spiritual power and unusual material technology. Further, indigenous communities on the San Francisco peninsula rapidly underwent population stress as they lost members from new diseases, and their hunting and gathering economy was disrupted by environmental degradation. Increasingly, new converts came to the missions out of desperation, devastated by the recent deaths of their loved ones and weak from lack of food. Entering the mission system was a permanent and irrevocable decision, something that most Native Californians probably did not understand when they agreed to be baptized. Baptized Native Californians were classified as neophytes to the faith and had the legal and spiritual status of children. Missionaries viewed baptism as irreversible; physical confinement and corporal punishment of the worldly body were considered preferable to allowing a soul to be spiritually condemned (Guest 1996).

Presidio soldiers were stationed at the missions as escoltas, charged with enforcing discipline, preventing escapes, and suppressing rebellions among the largely captive population of neophytes. Colonial women, usually wives of the escolta soldiers, worked in the missions as dormitory matrons, labor supervisors, and religious instructors (Castañeda 1992, 1998). Colonists were also called upon to stand as compadres (godparents) for newly baptized converts at the missions; in Spanish-colonial society, these bonds of compadrazgo could be as durable and intimate as familial kinship roles (Haas 1995; Newell 2004).

From the 1790s onward, the process of recruiting new converts became increasingly militarized. By that time, most Native Californians in the San Francisco Bay area who were amenable to mission life had already accepted baptism. Native villages outside the missions became intertribal fugitive communities that provided safe haven for mission runaways; with native food systems disrupted, these communities increasingly survived by raiding colonial settlements. Further, between 1790 and 1810, a series of epidemics caused thousands of deaths among the Native Californians living at the missions. Both the missionaries and the military settlers were anxious to replace this lost population, because the colonists had become dependent on foodstuffs and craft goods produced by neophyte labor.

Presidio soldiers engaged in countless punitive campaigns to subdue Native Californians who had not entered the missions. In the 1790s, military action targeted villages throughout the land south of the San Francisco peninsula and in the hills on the east and north sides of the bay (Milliken 1995:190–191). In the early 1800s, battle lines shifted farther east as military expeditions traversed the Diablo Range, the Altamont Hills, and the San Joaquín Valley. To supplement the small numbers of colonial troops, the military recruited and trained mission Indian Auxiliary companies to fight alongside the soldiers. Native Californians captured during these military campaigns were forcibly marched to colonial strongholds; native women and children were usually sent directly to missions, while adult men were taken to the Presidio to serve a term of forced labor. These military campaigns devastated indigenous communities throughout central California. Native Californians were truly caught "between crucifix and lance" (Sandos 1998). "No one," Milliken (1995:191) writes, "could stay where they were and remain unaffected."

Pueblos and Villas

With the presidios serving as the military and administrative centers of the districts and the religious missions controlling indigenous land and labor, civilian settlements were few and did not gain prominence until after the 1834 secularization of the missions. Although residents of civilian settlements were under less surveillance than those living at missions and presidios, pueblos and villas were also tightly regulated. Laws dictating the planning and establishment of colonial towns in the Spanish Americas had been in effect since 1573 and were enforced until the end of colonial rule. These edicts stipulated the organization of town governance and the allocation of lands, including specific provisions for plazas, house lots, farming lots, government and church allocations, and grazing commons (Jones 1979:6–11).

El Pueblo de San José de Guadalupe, founded in 1777, was established by five civilian families and nine soldiers "with some knowledge of farming" (Langellier and Rosen 1996:38) who had been living at El Presidio de San Francisco since their arrival with the Anza party. The Pueblo of San José was intended to supply the Presidio with grains, beans, and fresh produce. Its population grew slowly through the addition of the families of retired and invalided soldiers but remained fewer than one hundred fifty people throughout the Spanish-colonial era (Hornbeck and Fuller 1983:50–51).

The Villa de Branciforte, founded in 1797, was the second civilian settlement in the San Francisco district. Located in what is now Santa Cruz, it was a chartered villa intended to serve as a center of local manufacture, with its citizens forming a militia that would lend support to the Presidio. Initially, the new settlement was populated by about a hundred destitute paupers and convicts from Guadalajara and Guanajuanto who were transported to Alta California by ship. The colonial government hoped that retired soldiers from the San Francisco and

Monterey presidios would move to the villa, but most chose to live near the presidios or in the more established Pueblo of San José. The population of the villa never rose much above a hundred until the growth of the hide and tallow trade in the 1830s transformed the settlement into a minor regional port (Langellier and Rosen 1996:88–90; Reader 1997).

Yerba Buena, located in the present-day North Beach area of San Francisco, was established after Mexican independence. The settlement began as a small village populated by foreign traders involved in the hide and tallow trade and was officially chartered in 1837. Some military families maintained residences there along with their homes at El Presidio de San Francisco, only a few miles away (Langellier and Rosen 1996:167). Yerba Buena rapidly grew to be the major center of trade and commerce in central California, and the population increased steadily to nearly five hundred people by the end of Mexican rule in California. In 1847, upon the U.S. annexation of California, the mission, Presidio, and pueblo were merged together into the City of San Francisco.

From the beginning, the military settlers garrisoned at El Presidio de San Francisco were intimately involved with these civilian settlements. Many soldiers served in the civilian towns as guards and as *comisionados* (an appointed military position combining the duties of mayor, magistrate, and city manager), and they were expected to populate the pueblos and villas when they retired from military service. Especially after the expansion of ranching in the 1830s and 1840s, military families often had concurrent residences at the Presidio, at the Pueblo of Yerba Buena or San José, at the family rancho, and sometimes in or near the mission where they worshipped.

The institutions that Spain deployed in its northward colonial expansion structured the lives of both colonists and Native Californians, albeit in very different ways. From 1776 until the end of Spanish colonial rule in 1821, most people in the San Francisco Bay area lived within a matrix of rules and regulations formed through military ordinances and religious doctrines. The spatial organization of their communities, their movements, the architecture of their homes, the work they performed, the objects they used, the food they ate, the clothes they wore—all of these aspects of daily life were informed by secular and sacred directives. In this sense, the San Francisco Bay area—and, indeed, all of Alta California—was strikingly different from many mercantile and agrarian zones of colonization elsewhere in North America. The common perception of the frontier as a lawless place, advanced by rugged and self-reliant individuals living outside of government and society, could not be further from the daily realities of social life in Spanish-colonial California. The military settlers who lived at El Presidio de San Francisco were tightly bound to their government, their church, their commanding officers, and to each other through a dense web of legal obligations, religious observances, and social ties. While institutionalization shaped all aspects of daily life, it also enabled certain pathways of action. It was through these institutional channels that Alta California settlers, viewed as expendable by the government that recruited them, claimed land and resources to ensure their own survival.

Emphasizing the institutions that made up Spanish-colonial Alta California does not deny the very real agency that allowed the military colonists to influence the trajectories of their own lives. Indeed, the settlers exercised this capability from the start when they elected to leave their homelands and venture into new occupations, with new people, in a new place. The ethnogenesis of Californio identity is yet another indication of the settlers' ability to forge new and unanticipated historical pathways. Understanding these institutions foregrounds the ways in which the colonists' tactics and strategies (de Certeau 1984) were always deployed within and through institutional structures of power and practice.

Isolation and Entanglement: Province to Republic to State

Alta California is often portrayed as one of the most isolated regions of the Spanish-colonial empire in North America; El Presidio de San Francisco, its northernmost outpost, was the most remote corner of this far-flung frontier. Some historians have even attributed the emergence of Californio identity to this isolation, arguing that distance from the rest of New Spain fostered cultural drift and an inward-looking tendency among Alta California's colonial settlers. While their geographic isolation was tangible, historic events drew Alta California into international contests for empire and the development of global capitalism. The Presidio was located on the front lines of international politics during the age of European expansion into western North America. Additionally, as just outlined, the Presidio was connected to the other institutions of colonization throughout the province. The emergence of Californio identity must be understood within this complex interplay between the global, the regional, and the local.

The Closing of the Anza Trail

Colonial administrators and military strategists anticipated that the Anza Trail, from Sonora to San Francisco, would open a new realm of commerce in the Interior Provinces. They envisioned that the trail would guide caravans of landless peasants to new farmsteads in Alta California, developing the new province into an agricultural stronghold of the empire. Mule trains would bring foodstuffs from Alta California to the arid deserts and mining districts of Sonora and

Sinaloa and would return to Alta California loaded with cloth, pottery, metal objects, and other commercial goods from the manufactories of central New Spain.

The overland route depended on agreements that Juan Bautista de Anza had reached with Yuma (Quechan) tribal members, who had allowed him to establish a mission and travelers' waystation near the junction of the Colorado and Gila rivers in return for promises of trade and military protection. However, colonial administrators never fulfilled Anza's promises to the Yuma. Instead, travelers and missionaries abused the Yuma, demanding food and pasturing their livestock without permission on Yuma lands. In 1781, Olleyquotequiebe, a Yuma leader, led a revolt against the colonial settlement. The uprising permanently closed the trail and ended all plans for further emigration and trade between Sonora and Alta California (Bancroft 1886a:256–271; Forbes 1965; Weber 1992:256–258).

The closure of the Anza Trail had a profound influence on the development of Alta California. Perhaps the chief effect was demographic: until the 1830s, more than 80 percent of the colonial population consisted of those who had migrated before 1782 and their descendants (Mason 1998:44). A second effect was territorial: with no new groups of colonists arriving in the province, Spain's control never extended far beyond the four presidio districts established along the coastline from San Diego to San Francisco. The isolation of the province also contributed to the economic dominance of Alta California's missions; with royal support limited to a single supply ship each year, the presidios became dependent on the missions for agricultural supplies (Campbell 1977:63; Weber 1992:264).

The decade following the closure of the Anza Trail was marked by deprivation and shortages (Langellier and Rosen 1996:35–42). In 1785, the Spanish-colonial military sent Captain Nicolás Soler to Alta California to inspect its presidios. Soler found the conditions at San Francisco deplorable and reported that the understaffed and ill-equipped Presidio would be useless in defending the San Francisco Bay against foreign incursion. He advised that El Presidio de San Francisco should be closed and its personnel transferred to El Presidio de Santa Bárbara, which was also understaffed. Soler's recommendation was denied at the request of local missionaries, who argued that they needed the protection of the Presidio soldiers (Bancroft 1886a:394). Although El Presidio de San Francisco was allowed to remain open, it did not receive any increase in royal support and continued to decline throughout the remainder of the 1780s.

Fears of Foreign Invasion

In the 1790s, El Presidio de San Francisco's role in Spanish foreign defense took center stage. Spain lost claim to the Pacific Northwest in the Nootka Convention of 1790. Concerned that Russian and British imperialist ventures in North America would soon expand to Alta California, Spain's military strategists focused new attention on El Presidio de San Francisco (Cutter 1990:42–43; Fireman 1977:113; Langellier and Rosen 1996:56).

Their fears of foreign invasion were not unfounded. Ships of unknown nationality frequently appeared outside the mouth of the San Francisco Bay, presumably to assess the Spanish defenses or to engage in smuggling or poaching (Langellier and Rosen 1996:64). In 1792, French and British explorers, including George Vancouver and the H.M.S. *Discovery*, visited El Presidio de San Francisco. Ostensibly, these expeditions were undertaking scientific studies, but Vancouver also itemized the many shortcomings of the Presidio's defenses and speculated on the ease with which the bay might be taken (Vancouver 1984). Reports by Spanish military inspectors dispatched to the province in the early 1790s mirrored Vancouver's accounts (Fireman 1977:93–139; Servín 1970). The Presidio's weaknesses were corroborated by a damning report submitted in 1792 by its acting commander, Hermenegildo Sal (1976), which described in great detail the poor condition of the Presidio's buildings and the inadequacy of its defenses.

With the threat of foreign invasion looming, in 1793 Alta California governor José Joaquín de Arrillaga diverted funds to construct an earthenworks battery, El Castillo de San Joaquín, at the mouth of San Francisco Bay. The viceroy of New Spain also dispatched cadres of military engineers, master craftsworkers, and members of a special infantry unit, the Catalonian Volunteers, to Alta California to strengthen the local troops. A company of artillerymen and gunners was also assigned to the Presidio for the express purpose of staffing El Castillo de San Joaquín (Fireman 1977; Langellier and Rosen 1996:77; Schuetz-Miller 1994:18–19).

The outbreak of war between Spain and Great Britain in 1797 ended this period of expansion. A second defenseworks, La Batería de San José, was rapidly constructed along the bayshore to the east of the Presidio. However, the damp fog and winter storms eroded both the *castillo* and the *batería* earthworks, so that by 1799 both were essentially useless. The Catalonian Volunteers and the artillerymen and gunners were recalled to other posts (Langellier and Rosen 1996:100–102).

By the end of the eighteenth century, conditions at the Presidio were little better than those described in 1792. Absorbed in its war with Britain, the Spanish crown reduced its expenditures on its American colonies. Among Native Californians, resistance was increasing, in response to the 1797 founding of Mission San José; and the hostile interactions between indigenous resistance groups and the Presidio soldiers began to take the form of battles lasting several days, in contrast to the shorter skirmishes of earlier years. As the nineteenth century began, the soldiers of El Presidio de San Francisco turned away from the problems of foreign defense to engage in protracted punitive campaigns against unbaptized and runaway Indians (Phillips 1993).

The Hidalgo Revolt, Russian Incursions, and Mexican Independence

The Hidalgo Revolt of 1810 marked the beginning of the eleven-year Mexican War for Independence. Alta California saw almost no military action connected with this war; the only incident occurred in 1818, when Argentinean insurgent Hipólito Bouchard led an attack on El Presidio de Monterey, looting and then burning the Monterey Presidio and destroying its cannons.[11] In response, the Spanish-colonial military dispatched soldiers from the San Blas infantry to Alta California's presidios; San Francisco received forty foot soldiers, most of whom left the settlement shortly after Mexican independence. Otherwise, the effects of the war were largely economic: insurgents captured supplies and equipment destined for Alta California; San Francisco's soldiers received little pay; and the Presidio had to rely even more heavily on missions and illicit foreign trade for food and other necessary goods.

In the midst of this renewed isolation, El Presidio de San Francisco became the front line of territorial defense against Russian incursions into Alta California.[12] As early as 1803, ships affiliated with the mercantile Russian-American Company had sailed along the Alta California coast, establishing a seasonal camp at Bodega Bay for hunting fur-bearing sea mammals such as otters. In 1812, Russia established Colony Ross, a permanent, year-round base for its operations in California waters, which was located only sixty miles north of El Presidio de San Francisco. Unequipped to battle the Russian settlers, Commander Luis Antonio Argüello instead sent official requests warning the Russian-American Company to stand down and withdraw from Alta California. He also ordered his troops to harass the Native Alaskan kayakers who had been pressed into service by the Russians to hunt marine mammals.

Despite these official diplomatic tensions and small-scale hostilities, the Russian colony was an economic and social boon to the Presidio colonists. The two settlements became trading partners, and it was not unusual for officers of both settlements to host parties for each other.[13] Amid this friendly relationship, the Presidio responded to Russian territorial incursion with new colonial expansion north of San Francisco. Mission San Rafael and Mission San Francisco Solano were founded in an attempt to keep Native Californians in the northern regions of the bay from developing alliances with the Russian settlement.

On February 24, 1821, Agustín de Iturbide declared Mexico's independence, ending Spain's imperial holdings in North America. It is perhaps a mark of the deterioration of the frontier's infrastructure that the news of independence did not arrive in Alta California until more than a year later, on April 11, 1822 (Fink 1972:53; Weber 1992:301). After twelve years of self-sufficiency and growing interactions with foreign merchants, the community of military settlers at El Presidio de San Francisco found little economic relief in the establishment of the Mexican Republic. However, Alta California's growing self-rule, which had been a de facto effect of the eleven-year insurgency, was formalized under the new federalist policies of the Mexican Republic. Additionally, Mexican economic liberalization lifted prohibitions against foreign trade. Alta California legally entered the capitalist world market, trading hides and tallow for European-manufactured goods. During the next two decades, the grandchildren and great-grandchildren of the members of the Anza expedition left service as colonial soldiers to find new opportunities in ranching and commodity trading.

From Mexican Province to American State

This study's focus on San Francisco's forty-five years as a Spanish-colonial outpost (1776–1821) is deliberate: after Mexican independence, the military declined in importance, and the Presidio eventually ceased to be the center of colonial life in the San Francisco district. This change was spurred both by economic necessities and economic opportunities. The Mexican government increased the practice of giving land grants to retired and active soldiers and their families. With soldiers' salaries often in arrears, many seized the opportunity to leave the military and establish ranchos of their own, most raising cattle for the hide and tallow trade. This shift was accelerated by the 1834 secularization of Alta California's missions, which increased the amount of agricultural land available to former soldiers and their families. Secularization also reduced most of the missions' Native Californian residents to landless paupers, and the rancheros (ranch owners) quickly rounded up many of them as laborers in their agricultural enterprises (Costello 1989b; Costello and Hornbeck 1989; Frierman 1992; Greenwood 1989; Silliman 2004a, 2004b). El Presidio de San Francisco's importance declined; travelers visiting the Presidio in the 1830s often described it as a nearly deserted "formless pile of half-ruined dwellings" (Kotzebue 1830:86; see also Beechey 1941; Robinson 1970).

The decline of the Presidio's military importance was cemented by a strategic realignment of defensive forces: Mexico had recognized that the primary threat to Alta California was no longer from foreign maritime attack but from land-based Russian and U.S. territorial expansion. In the early 1830s, Mission Santa Cruz and the Villa de Branciforte were reassigned to the Monterey presidio district so that San Francisco's troops could further dedicate their resources to stemming Russian incursions. In 1834, San Francisco commander Mariano G. Vallejo transferred most of El Presidio de San Francisco's troops to the Sonoma Barracks, a military facility adjacent to Mission San Francisco Solano (Davis 1889; Langellier and Rosen 1996:165).

Mexican governance of Alta California lasted only twenty-five years. Beginning in the 1830s, the United States had viewed Alta California as a key component in its strategy of manifest destiny. After Mexico refused U.S. offers to purchase the property, the U.S. Army developed a plan to take Alta California by force. U.S. Army officer John C. Frémont arrived in Alta California in 1845 with a band of civilian "explorers." In cooperation with some Californios, he fomented the Bear Flag Revolt, which declared Alta California's independence from Mexico in June 1846. On July 1, Frémont and his crew took control of El Presidio de San Francisco, disabling the Presidio's cannons and raising the U.S. flag over the main quadrangle. U.S. forces entered the San Francisco Bay area a few days later and garrisoned their troops in the Presidio's adobe buildings. They were joined by the New York Volunteers in 1847 (Langellier and Rosen 1996:175–182). The Presidio became a U.S. Army post and remained so until it was transferred to the National Park Service in 1994 under the Base Realignment and Closure Act.

Between 1846 and 1848, battles throughout Alta California between loyalists and U.S. troops and sympathizers eroded Mexican governance of the province. The Treaty of Guadalupe Hidalgo ceding Alta California to the United States was ratified in 1848; a constitutional convention for the new state was convened in 1849; and California became a state in 1850 (Harlow 1982). Concurrent with this transition in governance, the famed 1849 discovery of gold at Sutter's Mill drew an avalanche of settlers and immigrants seeking quick wealth in the mines or employment by farmers, ranchers, railroads, or timber companies. In 1845, the nonnative population of California numbered 5,600 people; within only five years, by 1850, it had surged to 93,000, and it reached 380,000 in 1860 (Hornbeck and Fuller 1983:51, 68).

Both Native Californians and Californios were rapidly outnumbered by the newcomers. Rancheros lost their landholdings to squatters or through costly court cases. Native Californians, who, with the exception of coastal tribes, had retained control of their tribal territories throughout the Spanish and Mexican periods, were also displaced. Landless, stripped of political influence, and stigmatized by U.S. racial politics, by the 1860s most Native Californians and Californios ended up working as agricultural laborers and in other low-pay and low-status occupations.[14] Though Californio identity had been forged through the military settlers' role as an occupying colonial force, within less than half a century, they themselves were disenfranchised and displaced through the U.S. conquest of the very lands that the Californios had come to identify as their *patria* and birthright.

.   .   .

In the years between the Anza expedition's overland journey and the dawn of Mexican independence, the small community of military settlers at El Presidio de San Francisco was instrumental in establishing a network of colonial institutions that exerted control over indigenous peoples and their lands. They also deterred other European powers from claiming the harbor. Even Russian expansion into Alta California was confined to northern regions, stopping short of directly challenging the Presidio's military control of the bay and surrounding lands.

The Presidio soldiers and their families were transformed through their entanglements with Native Californians, with colonial institutions, and with Russian and other European explorers and merchants. Once members of colonized populations, they emerged as colonial agents of the Spanish crown. This book considers how material practices participated in the military settlers' transition from colonized to colonizer. In particular, it examines how the settlers came to develop a shared identity that reinforced their new status as colonizers yet simultaneously challenged the race-based regulations and practices of the colonial institutions within which they lived and worked. However, before turning to the findings of archaeological investigations, it is important to look more closely at the demographic composition of the colonial and indigenous populations that resided at El Presidio de San Francisco and the documentary records of the colonists' repudiation of the sistema de castas in favor of a shared identity. These aspects of San Francisco's history are taken up in chapters 3 and 4, with chapter 5 introducing the archaeological investigations.

3 FROM CASTA TO CALIFORNIO, I

Who Lived at El Presidio de San Francisco?

The artist's reconstruction shown in figure 3 depicts El Presidio de San Francisco as it may have appeared in 1792. National Park Service interpreters and illustrators created this image in 1996, basing their depiction of the site on historical and archaeological research. The image was developed through a long review process involving NPS historians, archaeologists, and interpretive staff. At that time, I was working at the Presidio of San Francisco as an archaeological consultant and was invited to sit in on some of the review sessions. Most discussions in which I participated focused on whether or not the site's architecture was being accurately depicted. The human figures seen in the picture were added later in the process; perhaps they were included for scale, to convey the height of the buildings and the overall size of the settlement.

In this image, the Presidio looks nearly deserted. The social world represented by the drawing is almost entirely adult, colonial, and male. There are three huddled figures in the far right corner of the quadrangle's plaza, perhaps women, who appear to be scraping animal skins staked to the ground.[1] However, the most populous groups at the settlement—children and Native Californians—are completely absent.

As Stephanie Moser and Clive Gamble (1997) demonstrate, images like this one powerfully express underlying postulates of archaeological research. Far from being trivial "eye candy" used to lighten up dull text, pictorial reconstructions are interpretations of archaeological and historical evidence. The interpretive content of such images is often passed over, without critical com-

FIGURE 3.   Artist's conception of El Presidio de San Francisco as it may have
appeared in 1792. National Park Service, Golden Gate National Recreation Area.

ment, because it presents visual rather than narrative arguments. But this image demonstrates how important it is for archaeologists to be explicit about how
we conceptualize the historical communities that we study.

Who, in fact, lived and worked at El Presidio de San Francisco? This seems
like a simple question, but the answers are not straightforward. The written
colonial record is fragmentary; those records that do exist systematically document certain segments of the population in detail while entirely neglecting
others. Despite these limitations, documentary sources provide valuable insights
into the composition of this pluralistic settlement and convey a social world
that was substantially more complex than the one represented in figure 3.

Using these sources, this chapter both estimates and analyzes the colonial
and Native Californian populations who lived at the Presidio, including age,
gender, and the composition of household groups. As in other parts of New
Spain, the sistema de castas classified colonial subjects according to perceived
degrees of African, Mexican Indian, and Iberian heritage. Census data reveals
that Presidio settlers manipulated these racial categories through individual actions that may have been the first steps toward the emergence of a shared Californio identity. Also of importance were the sexual and gendered ideologies
that structured social life in Alta California. Far from being restricted to the sexed
classification of individuals, the politics of gender and sexuality permeated every
aspect of colonial life. Together, these discussions of who lived at the Presidio
foreground the historical production and transformation of social identity.

Estimating the Population
of El Presidio de San Francisco

In Alta California, the number of colonial settlers was never large: approximately 500 during the first decade of colonization, reaching roughly 3,000 by the end of Spanish colonial rule. They were dispersed in small presidio and pueblo settlements and in mission *escoltas* spread out along more than 550 miles of coastline. In comparison, the indigenous population of Alta California was an estimated 300,000 people at the time of colonization, 21,000 of whom eventually came to reside in the coastal missions.[2] Colonial and indigenous populations were documented through separate processes. Military censuses, enlistment papers, troop rosters, and other records document the arrivals and departures of colonial settlers, both military and civilian. Because of short-term deployments, the number of colonists at El Presidio de San Francisco fluctuated; but the core population was constant, consisting of the founding members of the Anza expedition and their descendants. It is considerably more difficult to reconstruct the profile of Native Californians who lived and worked at the Presidio, as records of indigenous populations were maintained only by missionaries.[3] However, military records provide tantalizing glimpses into the characteristics of this group. With notable exceptions, the indigenous population at the Presidio consisted primarily of adult men recruited or impressed into service as laborers working in agriculture, craft production, and building construction.

Colonial Population, Troop Strength, and Civilian Personnel

I have been able to locate reliable colonial population estimates for only nine of the settlement's seventy years (fig. 4), with an unfortunate gap between 1796 and 1830. These data show that during the Presidio's years as an active military garrison (1776–1835), its population ranged from a little over 100 to a little over 200. The community was composed of a diverse mix of households (forty-eight households in 1776, thirty-eight in 1782, and forty-one in 1790), including married couples with children, married couples without children, widowed parents, single men, and households shared by adult siblings (fig. 5). However, multigenerational and extended family households were not common. Children formed the vast majority of the colonial population, and there were nearly as many adult women in the settlement as adult men (fig. 6).

Most colonial adult men were military personnel. I was able to develop estimates of total troop strength for forty-five of the settlement's seventy years (fig. 7). It is important to distinguish between the Presidio's total troop strength and the actual number of military personnel assigned to duty at the settlement. Usually only 25 to 50 percent of available personnel were on duty at the Pre-

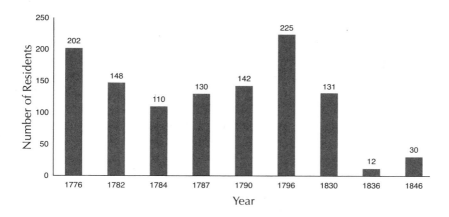

FIGURE 4. Colonial population of El Presidio de San Francisco, 1776–1846. The drop in population between 1776 and 1782 reflects the transfer of some troops and their families to Mission San Francisco de Asís, Mission Santa Clara, and the Pueblo de San José. The 1796 population spike was caused by the short-term deployment of an artillery company and a detachment of the Catalonian Volunteers to the Presidio. In 1834, most of the Presidio's troops were transferred to the Sonoma Barracks, after which only a small number of military families resided permanently at the Presidio (Bancroft 1886a:472, 693; Bancroft 1886c:702; Barker, Whatford, and Benté 1997; Davis 1889:569–570; Federal Writers' Project 1976:50; Forbes 1983:178–183; Langellier and Rosen 1996:166, 191–197; Mason 1998:142).

sidio itself, the rest serving as guards in missions and pueblos, traveling on expeditions into the interior of the province, or escorting priests, officers, and mail carriers on their journeys between colonial settlements. Such off-site assignments could last anywhere from a few days or weeks to several years. During shorter deployments, a soldier's family usually continued living at El Presidio de San Francisco. During longer assignments, the family usually transferred with the soldier to his site of duty. For example, in 1776, 6 soldiers and their families transferred to Mission San Francisco de Asís; 9 soldiers, presumably also with their families, left the Presidio to establish the Pueblo of San José in 1777; still more moved to Mission Santa Clara when it was established in the same year (Langellier and Rosen 1996:37–28; Milliken 1995:63). These deployments undoubtedly accounted for the sharp drop in the Presidio's colonial population between 1776 (202 residents) and 1784 (110 residents), shown in figure 4.

During the first twenty years, from 1776 to 1795, the San Francisco troops numbered about 30 to 40 officers and soldiers, with 10 to 20 on duty at the

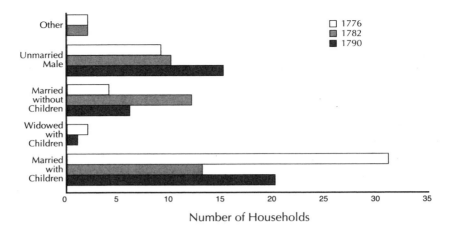

FIGURE 5. Colonial household composition at El Presidio de San Francisco
(Forbes 1983:178–183; Langellier and Rosen 1996:191–193; Mason
1998:100–104).

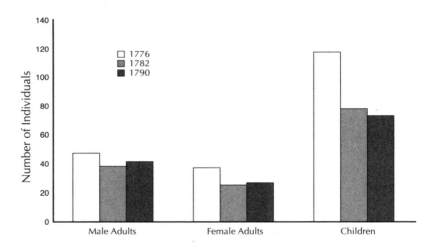

FIGURE 6. Colonial population of El Presidio de San Francisco, by age and
sex. The category of children includes all descendants listed within a given
household and could include unmarried adolescent or young adult dependents, as their precise age was rarely listed in census records. Children are
classed together because their sex was not always apparent (Forbes 1983:178–
183; Langellier and Rosen 1996:191–193; Mason 1998:100–104).

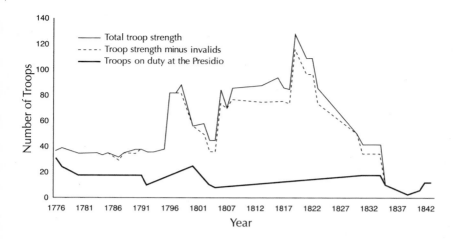

FIGURE 7. Colonial troop strength at El Presidio de San Francisco, 1776–1842. The upper solid line indicates the number of troops under the garrison's command, including those stationed at missions and pueblos and those listed as invalids. The middle dashed line indicates the effective number of troops by subtracting the number of invalids. The lower heavy solid line indicates the number of troops actually assigned to duty at the Presidio itself (Bancroft 1886a:472, 693; Bancroft 1886b:133, 255, 585; Federal Writers' Project 1976:50; Langellier and Rosen 1996:38, 43, 48, 57, 59, 64, 69, 74, 94, 105–106, 110–111, 141–142, 191–197; Mahr 1932:359; Mason 1998:100–104; Menzies 1924:265).

Presidio itself. They were all *soldados de cuera* (leather jacket soldiers), cavalry trained to fight with the lance, who specialized in combat with native insurgents. In 1796, the military personnel assigned to the Presidio increased through two deployments. Twenty-six members of the Catalonian Volunteers were assigned to the Presidio as part of the Spanish government's attempts to reinforce Alta California's defenses against foreign invasion. Unlike the soldados de cuera recruited for the Anza expedition, the Catalonian Volunteers were riflemen and infantry trained in European-style battle techniques (Langellier and Rosen 1996:77–79; Sánchez 1990). Most of the Catalonian Volunteers assigned to the Presidio were married; they were encouraged to bring their wives and children with them (Fireman 1977:120; Langellier and Rosen 1996:79). Later that year, a detachment of 18 artillerymen and gunners was dispatched from San Blas to staff the newly constructed Castillo de San Joaquín (Langellier and Rosen 1996:78). Both the Catalonian Volunteers and the artillerymen remained under separate command from the Presidio company. Combined, the three companies totaled 82 military personnel. The population of the Presidio settlement reached a height of 225 people during this year (Bancroft 1886a:693).

The Catalonian Volunteers and the artillerymen remained at El Presidio de San Francisco for only about five years; nearly all of them were gone by 1803. In 1804, Commander José Darío Argüello wrote that he had only 8 active soldiers under his command; the remainder had been assigned to escolta duties or removed from active duty on invalid status (Langellier and Rosen 1996:111). In 1805, he received permission to recruit new soldiers from the civilians living at the Pueblo of San José; and by the following year, the troop strength returned to between 70 and 80 personnel (Bancroft 1886b:30, 133, 197; Langellier and Rosen 1996:114, 194–197). The increase was absorbed by providing detachments of guards for the new settlements of Mission San José and the Villa de Branciforte.

The next significant addition to Presidio troops occurred after Hipólito Bouchard's 1818 attack on Monterey. To bolster California's defenses, the colonial administration of New Spain dispatched 40 foot soldiers from the San Blas infantry to the Presidio. Given the shortage of troops during these last years of the struggle for Mexican independence, many members of the San Blas infantry company had been recruited from jails or kidnapped by press gangs. Many of these recruits had little or no military experience and were soon released from service or deserted. By 1823, only 14 members of the San Blas infantry still served at the Presidio (Bancroft 1886b:255; Langellier and Rosen 1996:141–142). After Mexican independence, the number of military personnel at the Presidio dwindled from attrition. By 1831, troop strength had decreased to about 35 active personnel, and the overall colonial population of the Presidio had fallen to 131 people (Bancroft 1886c:700–701; Barker, Whatford, and Benté 1997).

Over the years, the Presidio also housed nonmilitary personnel. Crews from visiting ships periodically resided at the Presidio settlement. More than 30 laborers from the ship *San Carlos* helped construct the first buildings of the settlement between August and October of 1776 (Milliken 1995:64). Other civilian construction teams included a group of 6 laborers in 1793 from the ship *Aranzazú* and about 30 from the ship *Concepción* in 1797 (Langellier and Rosen 1996:70). Schoolmasters and craftsworkers also lived at the Presidio from time to time (Langellier and Rosen 1996:48, 87; Schuetz-Miller 1994). Finally, the Presidio served as a jail for civilian colonists convicted of serious crimes and sentenced to imprisonment, corporal punishment, and/or hard labor (Bancroft 1886b:591–594; Langellier and Rosen 1996:124, 128). Throughout these military and civilian deployments, the Presidio's colonial population retained a stable core of the soldiers and their families who had been recruited for the Anza expedition and their descendants.

Native Californians at the Presidio

While it is challenging to trace the Presidio's colonial population, it is nearly impossible to identify the Native Californians who lived and worked there. Both the 1782 and the 1790 censuses list only four as residents of the Presidio: Carlos, a civilian employee originally from San Diego; Agustín, originally from Mission San Vicente in Baja California; Nicolás, a prisoner transferred to San Francisco from Mission San Gabriel; and Margarita, the wife of retired soldier Manuel Buitrón (Forbes 1983: 179; Mason 1998: 104). In sum, few Native Californians—and apparently none of local origin—were considered Presidio residents by the colonial census takers.

Other colonial records, however, attest to the constant presence of Native Californians in the Presidio community. Most came to the Presidio as members of labor gangs, although there were exceptions to this general rule. Some resided in the community as the household servants or sexual partners of colonists. But marriage between colonists and Native Californians was rare: between 1776 and 1834, only six such marriages were performed at Mission San Francisco de Asís (Milliken, Shoup, and Ortiz 2005: 128–129). A few colonial families adopted Native Californian orphans.[4] But most interactions between military settlers and Native Californians revolved around labor. Some native workers came to the Presidio to work for wages or goods; others were members of mission work parties laboring under contracts between Presidio officers and mission priests; many served terms of forced labor as prisoners of war. They worked primarily on construction projects, agriculture, and craft production.

The number of Native Californian laborers at the Presidio increased over time throughout the colonial era. There are few direct records documenting their employment during the first decade of colonial settlement, but a series of edicts issued by Commander José Joaquín Moraga in 1782 imply that labor relations were central to the colonization effort. Following the Yuma Uprising of 1781, Moraga became uneasy about the threat that local Native Californians might pose to the colonial settlements:

> Although the Indians . . . are well-disposed and for now give no indication of disquiet, we should consider them enemies, all the more because we are surrounded by a great number of pagans. At any hour they could turn ugly, come to realize what they could do as a united group, and direct their will against our work.

Moraga prohibited any soldiers, settlers, or missionaries from traveling to the Indian villages without permission and spelled out procedures for labor negotiations:

When any person needs some pagans for their work on the more laborious pueblo projects, he will first give notice to the corporal [of the local military escort] who will arrange it, either accompanying him himself, or sending along a good soldier to request them through the captain of their *ranchería*. In no case are they to be brought in by force. Those who want to come are to be paid according to the work that they have done, so that they will return to their villages content.

In an attempt to curb sexual abuse of Native Californian women and to discourage concubinage, Moraga also issued this order:

If it is necessary to employ the Indian women to mill grain or do other chores, they are to do it outside the doorway, in plain view, without being permitted to go inside (as has been done until now), inasmuch as this kind of familiarity leads to grievances against both populations. (Moraga quoted in Milliken 1995:75–76)

Native Californians who still resided in their tribal villages may have decided to work at the Presidio for many reasons related to their own survival as well as that of their communities. The foremost benefit was the wages earned, usually paid in a food ration of meat and corn, with cloth blankets or garments distributed as a hiring bonus (Bancroft 1886a:614). Villages also entered into labor agreements with the Presidio as a way of gaining military protection against intervillage conflicts, which intensified during the political chaos caused by colonization. Additionally, village leaders were undoubtedly afraid that refusing a request for labor would antagonize colonial officers and expose their community to reprisals.

Negotiated labor agreements between Native Californian villages and the Presidio increased during the 1790s. Most such agreements were with villages in the southern reaches of the San Francisco Bay region: in 1793, unbaptized native people from the Santa Clara area worked on the first construction of the castillo; and in 1794 and 1796, the Presidio's commanders recruited laborers from the San José region (Langellier and Rosen 1996:61, 70–71; Milliken 1995:122).

The records of these labor arrangements give some insights into the negotiations that were occurring between leaders of native villages and the Presidio soldiers. In March 1794, Sergeant Pedro Amador's labor recruiting trip to the San José region was not fully successful; he reported that he was unable to find more than twenty-two laborers, despite offering both a blanket and a shirt as a hiring bonus. Of these laborers, "two of the freely hired villagers ran away after three days. The other twenty ran away after having worked for fifteen days, leaving their shirts and blankets behind" (Milliken 1995:122). Acting Commander Hermenegildo Sal then ordered Amador to find some Indians who were more willing to work; this second recruitment effort brought thirty-three hired laborers to the Presidio in April 1794. Sal wrote that the laborers were being treated well, and he expressed confidence that they would speak well of their work experience when they returned to their villages (Milliken 1995:123). Sal continued to build relationships with San José area villages in the following years, paying workers for their travel time to the Presidio and offering village leaders gifts for their assistance in recruiting laborers (Bancroft 1886a:614). Despite material incentives, however, many Native Californians were reluctant to work at the Presidio because it meant leaving their home villages for an extended period of time. In 1797, one village captain offered to provide laborers for an agricultural project near the Pueblo of San José "if only they would be excused from supplying workers at the presidios. While they have been away on these projects their women and seed crops have been harmed by other pagans" (Milliken 1995:150).

In addition to negotiating with tribal leaders to hire labor parties, the colonial military officers entered into agreements with the missionaries to provide laborers to the Presidio. Missions San Francisco de Asís and Santa Clara provided workers for the castillo construction projects in 1793 and 1794, and again for the construction of new quadrangle buildings in 1815 and 1819 (Langellier and Rosen 1996:70–71, 131, 142; Milliken 1995:122–123). Mission laborers came to the Presidio during the years 1795–1800 for apprenticeships to master artisans, who had been sent to Alta California to teach their crafts to settlers and neophytes (Schuetz-Miller 1994). Priests also used labor assignments at the Presidio as punishment "for stubbornness or other infractions against the padres" (Langellier and Rosen 1996:71). All payments for neophyte labor were made directly to the missionaries (Bancroft 1886a:614).

Although contract laborers and mission labor gangs were often recruited for large construction projects, many of the Presidio's routine labor needs were fulfilled by prisoners of war. Table 2 lists documented instances when Native Californians were captured and brought to the Presidio for punishment. Because such events were not systematically recorded, this listing likely represents only a fraction of such cases. During the 1780s, most captives were arrested for killing or harassing livestock; often, the cattle and horses were grazing on the seed meadows that provided staple foods in the Native Californian diet. In the 1790s, military campaigns against Native Californians shifted toward an emphasis on recapturing runaways from missions, punishing villages that harbored

TABLE 2. Historical accounts of captive native labor at El Presidio de San Francisco

Date	Military Campaign	Number of Captives	Sentence
1782	Capture of Indians who had killed cattle and horses near El Presidio de San Francisco	Not recorded	8–10 days of incarceration and labor and 20–25 lashes (Milliken 1995:72)
1783 (January)	Capture of Indians who had killed livestock south of Mission Santa Clara	2	15–20 days of labor under guard; flogging every third day (Langellier and Rosen 1996:46; Milliken 1995:74)
1786	Arrest of Mission San Franciscan Indians for killing soldiers' cattle	Not recorded	Imprisoned and flogged (Bancroft 1886a:472)
1790	Capture of 10 Matalan men who had tried to kill a mare near the Pueblo de San José	10	Labor at the Presidio (Milliken 1995:99)
1794 (February)	Capture of leaders of a resistance faction	2	Labor at the Presidio; transferred to Monterey in April 1796 (Milliken 1995:119–120)
1794 (March)	Capture of 4 Christian and 4 non-Christian Indians who stole horses and cattle	8	Labor at the Presidio (Milliken 1995:121)
1795 (February)	Round up runaways from Mission Santa Clara	Not recorded	Whippings and a month of labor at the Presidio in shackles (Langellier and Rosen 1996:75)
1796 (January)	Arrest of Christian Indians involved in the death of mares and cows	4	Labor at the Presidio (Milliken 1995:148–150)
1796	Transfer of two Indian prisoners from another presidio	2	Work without wages, short rations, "and giving them sacks for cover" (Governor Borica quoted by Milliken 1995:149)
1797 (July)	Fight with escapees from Mission San José and their allies; 83 Christians, 9 "pagans" captured; women and children taken to the mission	4 Christians and 9 non-Christians	Two to twelve months of hard labor in irons, short rations, and 25–75 lashes (Langellier and Rosen 1996:96; Milliken 1995:159–160)

TABLE 2   (continued)

Date	Military Campaign	Number of Captives	Sentence
Ca. 1790s	Raid on Apalmes ranchería	50 "more or less"	Labor at the Presidio on public works projects (Mora-Torres 2005:35)
1804 (October)	Punitive expedition against village refusing conversion; women and children turned over to missionaries	32	Labor at the Presidio through at least 1805 (Langellier and Rosen 1996:111–112; Milliken 1995:185)
1805 (Spring)	Punitive expedition against Indians of the San José region who refused conversion	30	Labor at the Presidio (Bancroft 1886b:35; Langellier and Rosen 1996:112)
1805 (June)	Punitive expedition against Indians of the Livermore region who refused conversion; women and children turned over to missionaries	Not recorded; all adult male prisoners	Labor at the Presidio (Langellier and Rosen 1996:113)
1805 (June)	Expedition into the hills between Santa Clara and San José to capture unconverted Indians	9	Labor at the Presidio (Langellier and Rosen 1996:113; Mora-Torres 2005:43)
1809	Capture of Alaskan Indians from the Russian-American Company who were hunting sea otters and fur seals	Not recorded	Labor at the Presidio (Langellier and Rosen 1996:124)
1810	Capture of Alaskan and/or Californian Indian fur hunters near San José	3	Labor at the Presidio (Langellier and Rosen 1996:126)
1818	Punitive campaign against Indians in the Calaveras/Stockton area	50	Labor at the Presidio constructing quadrangle walls (Mora-Torres 2005:43–45)
1819 (October)	Punitive campaign against Indians in the San Joaquín Valley	16	Labor at the Presidio making adobe bricks (Langellier and Rosen 1996:140)
1826	Punitive expedition against Cosomne; women and children turned over to missionaries	Not recorded	Labor at the Presidio (Phillips 1993:72)

runaways, and suppressing insurgent movements led by both baptized and unbaptized Native Californians. Unbaptized Native Californian men captured during these battles were brought to the Presidio to work as laborers, while women and children were sent to a mission for Christian instruction. This pattern escalated between 1800 and 1820, including punitive expeditions against villages that had refused conversion. Guarding the imprisoned Native Californians and overseeing their work appear to have been the main duties assigned to soldiers on duty at the Presidio (Langellier and Rosen 1996:71, 105–106).

Through participation in Indian Auxiliary companies, baptized Native Californians increasingly served as partners in these military campaigns. Members of Indian Auxiliaries lived at the missions but came to the Presidio to train and drill. Indian Auxiliary troops soon numbered in the hundreds, and in the 1810s and 1820s they participated in every major campaign against Native Californian communities that had refused conversion (Bancroft 1886a:175; Langellier and Rosen 1996:128, 131; Milliken 1995; Phillips 1993:72).

Although we lack sufficient archival or archaeological evidence to estimate the population of Native Californians at the Presidio, the written record suggests that their presence increased over time.[5] From the 1780s on, at least five to twenty captives, compensated laborers, and mission neophytes were present at the settlement at any given time. In the 1790s and 1800s, the number of native laborers at the Presidio could have been as many as seventy to one hundred people, accounting for as much as a third to a half of the Presidio's overall population. And, beginning in the 1810s, companies of Indian Auxiliary troops visited the Presidio to train with the colonial soldiers.

These labor and military relationships between presidio colonists and Native Californians were strongly gendered. Nearly all captive laborers were men; additionally, the record of negotiations for paid laborers in 1797 implies that those hired were primarily men. Without question, native women also labored at the Presidio: recall, for example, that Moraga's 1782 directive explicitly discussed conduct concerning the employment of Native Californian women to "mill grain or do other chores" (Milliken 1995:76). However, it appears that the indigenous women who worked at the Presidio did so through arrangements that were not recorded in official military records—for example, laboring as domestic workers hired by individual families rather than as members of a large labor gang.

Understanding colonial ethnogenesis at El Presidio de San Francisco requires attention to the ever-present relationship between the colonial military settlers and the substantial number of paid, impressed, and captive Native Californians upon whose labor the colonists depended. Each body of archaeological evidence examined in this study must be considered in light of this relationship. While documentary sources describe groups of Native Californian laborers as discrete entities, separate from the colonial population, the daily reality was much different. Native Californians working at the Presidio did not labor in isolation. They worked under the supervision of military officers; alongside soldiers and civilians and imprisoned colonists; and in the settlers' homes, corrals, and fields. Clearly, labor relations shaped one of the most consistent and ongoing contexts for colonial-indigenous relations at the Presidio.

Colonial Homelands, Racialization, and Casta Mobility

In many popular and scholarly treatments of Alta California's history, the military settlers are referred to as "Spanish soldiers." In one sense, this is true—Alta California was a colony of Spain, and any military personnel living there were serving the Spanish crown and its interests. In many other ways, the reference to "Spanish soldiers" is grossly misleading, conjuring images of European conquistadors and Iberian Spanish culture.

Historical studies and colonial documents provide a more nuanced understanding of the homelands and racial classifications of the colonists who lived at the Presidio. The colonists were nearly all born in New Spain, most in the Interior Provinces. Under colonial law, the settlers' primary legal identity was their casta, or racial status. The Spanish-colonial sistema de castas was strikingly different from present-day Anglo-American constructions of race, in that the former provided explicit recognition of mixed heritage and opportunities for individual upward mobility. During the first fifteen years of San Francisco's colonization, most of the military settlers changed their casta, downplaying their Mesoamerican Indian and African heritage. Together, these individual actions undermined the sistema de castas and minimized the racial differences among the colonial population of the settlement.

Homelands

All the residents of El Presidio de San Francisco were subjects of the Spanish crown (and later, following Mexican independence in 1821, became Mexican nationals). Yet nearly all originated from what today is northwest Mexico. William Marvin Mason's (1998) analysis of Alta California's 1790 census provides the most comprehensive information about the geographic origins of the military settlers. Of the sixty-seven men and women listed as residents of the Presidio in 1790, twenty-five came from Sinaloa and nineteen were from Sonora, together constituting two-thirds of the Presidio's adult population. Eighteen had been born in other provinces in New Spain, including Baja California, Jalisco, Chihuahua, Zacatecas, Nayarit, Querétaro, Durango, and Mexico City. One resident, a retired soldier named Manuel Buitrón, had been born in Spain. Additionally, four colonists had been born in Alta California: mostly teenaged women married to older soldiers, they represented the beginning ascendancy of the first generation of California-born colonists (Mason 1998:65–72, 100–104).

Most members of the Catalonian Volunteers (1796–1803), the San Blas artillery company (1796–1801), and the San Blas infantry (1819–1823), whose short-term deployments to Alta California temporarily boosted the Presidio's population and troop strength, had also been born in North America, most in the Interior Provinces (Sánchez 1990). In sum, the settlement was founded and sustained by people born in the Americas. As historian Leon Campbell (1972:594) penned, "Although this fact has been recognized before, it is necessary to reassert it again in order to dispel the romantic myth of Spanish California as a land of titled caballeros."

Racialization and the Sistema de Castas

As American-born subjects of the Spanish crown, the residents of the Presidio were racialized through colonial legal estates that prescribed different laws, obligations, and privileges for people of Spanish, African, and Native American descent. Most were classified as castas, a group of designations that referred to people of mixed heritage.

The Spanish-colonial system of legal estates rested on the concept of *limpieza de sangre*, or purity of blood, which had developed on the Iberian Peninsula during the seven hundred years of coexistence between Muslims, Jews, and Christians. Limpieza de sangre was initially a religious rather than a racial concept, used to distinguish those Christian families who had not intermarried with non-Christians from those who had. While limpieza de sangre has been associated with whiteness or European identity, the concept also allowed people whose appearance did not match expectations of whiteness to establish a Spanish identity, by certifying their family's allegiance to the Christian faith and by adhering to European manners, customs, and styles (Mörner 1967:12–16; Stallaert 1998). This changeable aspect of social identity became a core principle of social life in Spanish-colonial Latin America: an individual's status was constrained by his or her birth, but under favorable circumstances, social identities could be transformed through social practices and by legal petition (Twinam 1999).

With the Spanish conquest of the Americas, the concept of limpieza de sangre shifted to emphasize geographic origin rather than religion. People from three geographic groupings—American, Iberian, and African—were considered to be "pure" races. Spain's American colonies were incorporated into two concurrent legal republics, the República de Españoles and the República de Indios. Enslaved Africans formed a third legal estate. Each estate was subject to different judicial proceedings, taxation requirements, and sumptuary laws, which mandated certain clothing styles for each estate. These legal estates racialized the power differences between colonizer and colonized and between slave owner and enslaved.

Within the first decade of colonization, sexual unions between men and women of different legal estates produced offspring of uncertain legal status. Initially, children of mixed unions were assigned to an estate based on the legitimacy of their parentage: if the father acknowledged the child as his own, the child usually belonged to the estate of the father; if the child was not acknowledged by the father, he or she usually belonged to the estate of the mother (Mörner 1967:29). Soon, however, American-born Spaniards (criollos) sought to distinguish themselves from those of mixed parentage. The sistema de castas developed in the early 1600s as a means to distinguish criollos from mixed-heritage peoples and to differentiate among various racial mixtures (Cope 1994:24).

Legal codifications of casta identities were quite elaborate, sometimes including up to forty different classifications (Cope 1994:24; Mörner 1967:58–59) (table 3). The complicated casta matrices not only differentiated those of mixed heritage from those belonging to a single estate but also fostered distinctions between higher- and lower-ranked castas. Although the sistema de castas was partially a "pigmentocracy" (Mörner 1967:55), in which lighter skin loosely corresponded with higher rank, casta identities were not solely determined by parentage or physical attributes of the body. Casta identities also referenced other indications of status such as legitimacy of birth or economic means, along with a diverse constellation of social practices that included dress, speech, mannerisms, diet, material culture, occupation, and leisure pursuits.[6] Transcripts of court cases and other legal and religious proceedings show that in most cases, a person's moral conduct, occupation, clothing, and other behaviors were the primary subjects of testimony related to determination of racial estate and casta (for example, Carrera 2003; Twinam 1999).

In its recognition of mixed heritage, the sistema de castas was substantively different from the Anglo-American racializing practice of hypodescent, in which people born to parents of different races are assigned to the race of the lower-status parent. Within the casta system, a person of mixed parentage could be classified as español if he or she presented cultural traits associated with Europeanness or was one or more generations removed from non-European ancestors. People with African and/or Indian ancestry could consolidate español status by purchasing a license, called a cédula de gracias al sacar, that entitled the bearer to the rights and privileges of the español racial class (Chance 1979:160; Mörner 1967:45; Twinam 1999). Further, the fine gradations in the sistema

TABLE 3. Examples of casta terms used
in eighteenth-century New Spain

Parents' Casta Rankings	Classification of Offspring
Spaniard and Indian	Mestizo
Mestizo and Spanish woman	Castizo
Castizo woman and Spaniard	Spaniard
Spanish woman and negro	Mulato
Spaniard and mulato	Morisco
Morisco woman and Spaniard	Albino
Spaniard and albino woman	Torna atrás
Indian and torna atrás	Lobo
Lobo and Indian woman	Zambaigo
Zambaigo and Indian woman	Cambujo
Cambujo and mulato woman	Albarazado
Albarazado and mulato woman	Barcino
Barcino and mulato woman	Coyote
Coyote woman and Indian	Chamiso
Chamiso woman and mestizo	Coyote mestizo
Coyote mestizo and mulato woman	Ahí te estás

SOURCE: Mörner 1967:58.

de castas also provided extralegal opportunities for racial mobility. Historians have documented hundreds of cases in which individuals shifted casta during their lifetimes, through court cases, marriages, patronage, migration, changes in personal appearance, and, in many cases, simply by declaration.[7] British, French, and Anglo-American visitors to Alta California were often perplexed and disturbed by this racial mobility. As one traveler complained, "The least drop of Spanish blood, if it only be a quadroon or octoroon, is sufficient to raise one from the position of a serf, and entitles him to wear a suit of clothes . . . and to call himself Español, and to hold property" (Miranda 1988:275).

Although it was possible to change casta or even estate status, not all colonial subjects were able to do so. Because of sumptuary laws, occupational restrictions, and anti-miscegenation policies, people of African heritage had the greatest incentive to shift to mestizo and other non-African casta designations. They were also subjected to the greatest scrutiny and surveillance in their identification practices (Althouse 2005; Carrera 2003; Haas 1995). Overall, for people of both Indian and African heritage, their ability to shift to a higher-status casta, and especially to español status, depended not only on their own conduct but also on their economic means, occupation, social alliances, legitimacy of birth, and the respectability of their family members (Jackson 1999; Schwartz 1995; Twinam 1999). Even people of mixed heritage who successfully claimed español status continued to be differentiated from "true" Spaniards, who were called *peninsulares* if born in Spain and criollos if born in the Americas.

Although the sistema de castas was primarily an instrument of colonial racialization, casta identities also referenced gender and sexuality, especially masculine honor.[8] Historians of colonial New Spain trace ideologies of masculine honor from practices in Europe that had been introduced to the Americas during the fifteenth and sixteenth centuries.[9] In part, masculine honor was accrued through sexual conquests outside the family and by preventing female relatives from engaging in dishonorable sexual relationships (Gutiérrez 1993b:705). The sistema de castas was used to delineate honorable and dishonorable sexual relationships: brothers and fathers of women who had sex with men of a lower casta were especially dishonored because their grandchildren, nieces, and nephews would lower the family pedigree. Under certain circumstances, secular law granted male relatives the right to prohibit a woman's marriage to a man of inferior casta status (Castañeda 1993a:729–730; Seed 1988:151–152).[10] The intersections between gendered and sexual ideologies and the sistema de castas meant that casta status affected men and women differently.

Frontier Practices of Race and Identity

In the frontier regions of northwest New Spain, the sistema de castas was not followed with the same rigidity as in the colonial metropoles (Jackson 1999; Jones 1979; Mason 1998:9; Weber 1992:326–329). Nearly the entire colonial population in the Interior Provinces was composed of castas, Christianized Mexican Indians, and free Africans, with only the highest-ranking military, religious, and government posts being filled by peninsulares and criollos. Rather than using the elaborate ranking system involving sixteen to forty categories, most colonial settlers were described as belonging to one of four major casta groupings. *Indio* referred to those who were mainly of indigenous Mesoamerican descent. *Mulatos* and mestizos were people of mixed ancestry who were viewed as primarily African or Indian, respectively.[11] The final category, español, granted a person of mixed ancestry most of the legal privileges held by peninsulares and criollos, affording opportunities for upward mobility for people with Indian and African heritage (Chance 1979:160; Mörner 1967:45).

The racial composition of New Spain's northern frontier became increasingly more "European" as Indians and Africans claimed mestizo status and mestizos claimed español identity (Jackson 1999; Weber 1992:327). By 1773, 49.3 percent of the soldiers garrisoned in New Spain's frontier presidios were listed as español (Moorhead 1969:40). An eighteenth-century Jesuit missionary living in Sonora stated that of the españoles, there was "scarcely one who could trace his origin to a Spanish family of pure blood. Practically all those who wish to be considered Spaniards are people of mixed blood" (Miranda 1988:269). Many historians have observed that frontier presidios contributed to this phenomenon, since soldiers were usually recruited "on the basis of justice and competence rather than of social standing, and without reference to color or circumstance of birth" (Moorhead 1975:104).[12]

The degree to which an español identity altered an individual's social status in the Interior Provinces is uncertain. David Weber argues that the increased racial "whitening" evident in demographic records may have affected only legal or sumptuary components of ethnic/racial identity: "the term español, however, never erased memories of a person's racial origins among his neighbors" (Weber 1992:328). In contrast, Mason suggests that the military settlers in Alta California "were virtually free from whatever stigma may have been attached in Mexico City to *mestizos* and *mulatos*" (Mason 1998:61). The *testimonios* (dictated memoirs) and autobiographies of prominent colonial settlers further highlight the ambiguous role of race in frontier society. These accounts often emphasize that all colonists had equal standing regardless of heritage, but the same documents also used casta terms to describe named individuals or as racial slurs (Mora-Torres 2005; Osio 1996; Sánchez 1995). This latter usage was particularly common for casta terms that referenced African heritage (that is, *lobo, cholo,* and *coyote*).

Casta Identities and Casta Mobility
at El Presidio de San Francisco

By the time the Presidio was established, casta identity alone could not be read as a literal indication of a person's African, Mesoamerican Indian, or Iberian heritage. This reality has methodological implications for archaeological research. There is a tendency in North American historical archaeology to investigate the archaeology "of" a circumscribed racial or ethnic group, such as the archaeology of African American or Chinese immigrant life.[13] The archaeology of colonial San Francisco must proceed with a different approach, one that acknowledges that colonial documents were contested discourses that both constituted and exposed the arbitrariness of racial classifications. What can be said with certainty is that the Presidio was a pluralistic community, composed of people descended primarily from Mexican Indians and Africans and to a lesser degree from Europeans, among whom racial and ethnic identities were under continual negotiation.

Census records from the Presidio's first fifteen years provide an opportunity to examine how the military settlers' racial status was represented in colonial documents.[14] In a roster of the members of the 1776 Anza expedition, 39 percent of those adults whose casta was recorded were listed as español, 31 percent as mestizo, 18 percent as mulato, and 12 percent as indio. There was little difference in the frequency of each casta designation among adult men and adult women (fig. 8). In comparison with the overall casta rankings of frontier troops in the Interior Provinces, the military settlers who founded the Presidio were from lower-status castas than their compatriots. This difference may have to do more with their limited economic resources than with their specific heritage. Anza deliberately recruited respectable but impoverished and landless civilians, people who were less likely to have the financial resources and social connections that fostered casta mobility.

Within the first fifteen years of their arrival in Alta California, many of the military settlers who founded El Presidio de San Francisco changed casta. Census records from 1782 and 1790 provide an opportunity to view this process. While only 39 percent of the military settlers were listed as español in 1776, this number increased to 44 percent in 1782 and to 57 percent in 1790. The percentage of colonists listed as mestizo also initially increased, from 31 percent in 1776 to 33 percent in 1782, but then dropped to 29 percent in 1790. The percentage of the colonial population listed as mulato and indio decreased sharply during this period. This overall pattern held for both adult males and adult females, although women's casta status increased more dramatically. In sum, a colonial community that began as majority indio, mulato, and mestizo emerged in fifteen years as a majority español population.

The increase in the number of colonists identified in the census records as español is borne out by the records of individuals whose casta status changed over time. Soldiers Ignacio Soto, Pedro Bojorques, and Ignacio Higuera, all listed as mestizos in 1776 and 1782, were classified as español in 1790. Others moved between different mixed-heritage designations: soldier Juan Arnesquita changed from mulato in 1782 to mestizo in 1790, and soldier Ignacio Linares changed from mulato to indio. The casta assigned to some colonists' children in their baptismal records further illustrates the variability with which casta labels were applied. For example, in two cases, the children of español parents were classified as mestizo, suggesting that the priest did not believe the parents' claimed identity. In another case, the offspring of two mestizos were variously classified as mulatos, españoles, and mestizos (Forbes 1983:178–183).

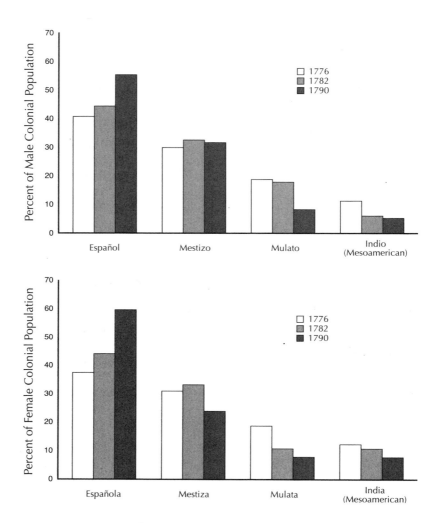

FIGURE 8. Casta composition of El Presidio de San Francisco's adult colonial population, by sex. Over time, individuals were increasingly described as español or mestizo, at the expense of mulato and indio identities (Langellier and Rosen 1996:191–193; Forbes 1983:178–183; Mason 1998:100–104).

The confusing and contradictory application of casta terms to different children of the same parents underscores the fact that, in colonial Alta California, the sistema de castas was not followed consistently and that colonial records cannot be used to reconstruct the cultural heritage or racial phenotype of any one individual. What is clear is that by the 1790s, members of the community increasingly presented themselves or were seen as español or mestizo, downplaying their Indian or African heritage.

The 1790 census is the last historical document I have been able to find that systematically recorded the casta rankings of Alta California's colonial population. To be sure, casta terminology was still used sporadically in military enlistment papers and church records. But, overall, government and church efforts to continue to track colonists' casta status were futile. One mission priest, charged with reporting on the casta composition of the colonial settler population, responded that it was impossible to do so because the settlers all considered themselves Spaniards (Miranda 1988:271). The designations español and española were common substitutions for lower-ranked casta terms, but during the 1790s, settlers, colonial officials, and missionaries also began to describe colonists with noncasta terms such as "gente de razón."

The changes in casta status among the Presidio's colonial population from 1776 to 1790 can be understood as participation in the broader trend of casta mobility and español identification in the Interior Provinces. Yet these shifts occurred during a period when Alta California was profoundly isolated from the rest of New Spain. Without disregarding the regional perspective, these changes also need to be understood as the cumulative result of social negotiations among the colonists living at the Presidio.

Both casta mobility and the growing use of noncasta identifications provided two important social resources for the later development of Californio identity. The first was that the military settlers who resided at the Presidio came to experience their racial identity as malleable and open to negotiation. The second is that the overall erosion of the sistema de castas as a viable method of classifying colonial subjects signaled a profound shift in the basic terms of social identification, one that rejected racialization as the means for creating distinctions among the military settlers. Chapter 4 continues to examine these precursors of ethnogenesis and trace the emergence of Californio ethnicity in the early decades of the nineteenth century. But first it is necessary to consider the other prominent components of colonial identities in New Spain: gender and sexuality.

Gender, Sexuality, Colonization, and Ethnogenesis

In colonial New Spain, gender and racial identities were produced through very different relationships to the body. Within the Spanish-colonial racial estates and the sistema de castas, possible racial identities were numerous and were determined not only through reference to the physical body but also in relationship to social practice. This aspect of racialization allowed a degree of play and metamorphosis that was not socially possible for gender identities. Spanish-colonial ideologies of gender and sexuality rested firmly on a binary gender system in which gender was assigned at birth based on the physical morphology of the infant's genitalia. Gender transgression was policed and, when discovered, was severely punished. In such cases, the "truth" of a person's gender identity was resolved by inspecting the unclothed physical body. Whereas those accused of racial deception might successfully defend themselves by reference to their mannerisms, clothing, occupation, and social relations, when it came to gender, such social practices were always trumped by the assignment of the body to one of two categories: man or woman.

This is not to suggest that transsexual, transgendered, and intersexed people were absent from the Spanish-colonial Americas. However, their existence was precarious and, if discovered, they were forced to assume the gender identity perceived to be congruent with their genitalia. Examples include Catalina de Erauso, who served as a lieutenant in the Spanish colonial army in sixteenth- and seventeenth-century Perú (de Erauso 1996); Gregoria Piedra, also known as La Macho, tried in 1796 for dressing as a man (Carrera 2003); and the colonial persecution of Native Californian "two-spirits," whose identities combined masculine and feminine traits (Roscoe 1998; Voss 2000a; Williams 1986).

Although gender identities were rigidly ascribed according to the sexed body, the colonists' concepts of male and female roles were not entirely static. Gender and sexuality were contested realms of social practice in Alta California. Gendered and sexual ideologies extended beyond sex assignment into realms of colonial policy and practice, from the most official regulations to the intimate details of social life. In other words, gender and sexuality in Alta California were as historically produced as race and casta. While they represented distinct realms of identification, gender identities were intrinsically connected to racial identities; consequently, colonial ethnogenesis was as much about changes in gender and sexuality as it was about ethnicity or race.

Racial Others and Sexual Others: Gender and Alta California's Colonization

"California" was first encountered by Spanish explorers in the 1530s, during Cortés's quest to locate the mythical island of the Amazons, a land of women and wealth rumored to exist in the Pacific Ocean. When ships made landfall on the southern Baja California peninsula, the land was named California after a fictional island in the chivalrous novel *Las Sergas del muy esforzado caballero Esplandián* (The exploits of the very brave knight Esplandián), by Garcí Ordóñez de Montalvo. The novel, first printed in Spain in 1510 and distributed in the Americas in the late 1520s, describes the Christian conquest of a heathen island inhabited by attractive black women. Their leader, Queen Calafia, was as wealthy in gold and pearls as she was beautiful. The mythical place was a reversal of the actual order of the colonial world: on the island of the Amazons, women of color were powerful, and the Spanish men who encountered them were either killed or forced to be their mates. Montalvo's fictitious knights converted the Amazons to Christianity and then married them; Queen Calafia, on her conversion and marriage, presented the island and all its wealth to the Christian knights. By conquering the island and marrying Calafia, Knight Esplandián set the world right again.[15]

Eighteenth-century territorial colonization of Alta California exposed the inversion of the California myth. Colonial sexual abuse of Native Californians was rampant; marriages between colonists and indigenous women were rare; and Native Californians fiercely resisted colonial appropriation of their lands and resources. The colonial sexualization of the Alta California landscape is considered in greater detail in chapter 6; first, however, we must examine the policies that structured the gendered composition and practices of the colonial population.

Spain's colonial military recruited only men to serve as soldiers and officers; this practice was so taken for granted that to my knowledge it was never explicitly stated in military regulations of the time. Likewise, the Catholic Church barred women from serving as priests, and the Alta California mission projects did not include nuns. However, women participated as agents of colonization through Spain's policy of domestic unity, which had been in effect since the first decades of its New World empire. This policy supplied royal funds to transport the wives and children of colonists to new settlements and also offered financial incentives for single colonial men to marry. The intent was to lend greater stability to colonial settlements, promote the social and biological reproduction of colonial society, curtail the troubles caused by single men on the frontier, and solve the problem of women and children left behind with no means of support. Further, colonial women's labor—farming, animal husbandry, food preparation, craft and textile production, healing, and teaching—was necessary to the survival of colonial settlements.[16]

Anza took this policy one step further, recruiting not individual soldiers but entire families with proven reproductive capabilities. In doing so, he undoubtedly discouraged and excluded transgendered people and nonheterosexuals from participating in the colonial venture unless they could successfully pass as normative men or women.[17] Once the Presidio had been established, military officers and mission priests continued to monitor colonists' gender identities, sexual behaviors, and reproductive capacity (Voss 2000a). Thus, while some scholars suggest that frontiers provide a less regulated space within which gender and sexual transgressives have greater latitude (Gutiérrez 1991; Hurtado 1999; Williams 1986), the institutional character of Alta California was such that colonists were under greater surveillance in sexual and gender matters than they had been in the civilian towns from which they were recruited.

The colonial women who lived and worked at El Presidio de San Francisco were integral to the imperial project of conquest. However, their role as military settlers has been largely ignored in historical and archaeological scholarship, in part because of gender stereotypes that link military conquest with masculinity and presume that women are more peaceful and nurturing than men. But these women were neither domestic angels amid the demons of war nor exceptional women who heroically rose above the limitations of conventional gender roles to enter a man's world. They were recruited, alongside their husbands, to serve as craftsworkers, farmers, ranchers, healers, parents, and educators in the military-colonial enterprise. With most soldiers assigned away from the Presidio on guard duty and military expeditions, many of the daily operations of the settlement were likely directed by the colonial women residing there. Their safety depended on successful pacification of local indigenous populations; their daily concerns almost certainly included questions of defense and military actions. They were no less implicated in the state-sanctioned violence of colonization than their male partners.

Fully accounting for women's involvement in military ventures can substantially alter the ways that we interpret the archaeological remains of colonial settlements like the Presidio. In the archival records of the settlement, women were rarely mentioned; it was even less common that they themselves guided pen to paper. If the archaeological record can be conceptualized as a different sort of text, the colonial women who lived at the Presidio were among its most prominent authors. Archaeological research thus provides an important opportunity to investigate the history of military women as well as the workings of gender and sexual ideologies on the colonial frontier.

Between Ideology and Practice: Gender and Sexuality in Colonial New Spain

Perhaps the biggest tension in historical scholarship about gender and sexuality in New Spain revolves around the investigation of patriarchy, on the one hand, and women's agency, on the other. The first emphasizes women's subordination and the very real ways that ideologies and practices of male supremacy acted as constraints on women's lives. The second traces women's political, economic, and cultural influence and highlights women's involvement as integral members of colonial society. These divergent perspectives are, of course, two sides of the same coin. There is an unfortunate tendency in either case to portray women and men as separate, with entirely different interests. In practice, men and women often shared much in common. Without discounting the divisions between people of different genders, we must also consider how their lived experiences were interwoven.

Both ecclesiastic and secular ideologies of patriarchal control were influential in structuring gender and sexuality in colonial New Spain. The positions of men and women in society were defined, in part, from the Genesis story, in which Eve, created to serve Adam and be his mate, succumbed to temptation and introduced original sin. Catholic doctrine thus opposed any actions that might elevate women over men; for example, any sexual postures other than the "missionary position" were classified by the church as unnatural perversions "because they made the woman superior to her husband, thus thwarting God's universal plan" (Hurtado 1992:374). The Catholic Church also retained ultimate authority over baptism and marriage, two sacraments that involved determination of gender identities and sexuality.

Under Catholic precepts, both men and women were viewed as equally lustful, inherently desiring sexual relations as part of the stain of original sin. Sexual activities were divided into two fundamental categories: conjugal (marital) intercourse was required by the sacrament of marriage, the bonds of which could be broken only by death; any other sexual activities were mortal sins. Rituals of confession included explicit questionnaires designed to aid parishioners in recalling sexual acts and lustful thoughts that required penance and absolution (Bouvier 1995:342, 359). Together, religious doctrines of female inferiority and the necessity and indissolubility of marriage placed women under the spiritual and material control of their husbands.

Ecclesiastic orthodoxy operated in tandem with, and at times in opposition to, secular ideologies of honor and shame.[18] The honor/shame complex was not only a sexual and gendered ideology but also an "ideology of personal subordination to familial concerns" in which society was divided "along both a vertical (honor-status) and a horizontal (honor-virtue) axis" (Castañeda 1993a:728). While honor was related to many social practices, including economic standing, hospitable behavior, and social conduct, sexuality was the most volatile aspect. Unlike religious ideologies that condemned all nonmarital and nonreproductive sexual acts, secular ideals of honor and shame evaluated sexual conduct from varying standpoints. Whereas, with few exceptions, men amassed honor through extramarital sexual conquests,[19] their female sex partners and assault victims lost honor and shamed themselves and their families. Even marriage could dishonor a woman and her family if the groom or his family were of lower casta or had a dishonorable reputation. In order to protect family honor, men and senior women were obligated to control the sexuality of their female relatives, even to the point of corporal punishment, physical confinement, and arranged marriages.[20] Women without such protection, especially lower-casta, indigenous, and poor women, were especially vulnerable to sexual predation and loss of social standing.

In addition to shaping relations between men and women, ideologies of honor and shame differentiated men of honor from less masculine and less honorable men. Similarly, virtuous women were elevated above those of *mala vida* (literally, bad living). Colonial gender identities were thus constructed not only into opposed binary categories but also relationally within each category. Like casta identities, a person's masculine or feminine honor could change during his or her lifetime and was more closely related to social behavior than physiology. Honor, which was always gendered, was a form of cultural capital that could be used to support claims to a higher casta ranking.

Neither religious doctrines of women's inferiority nor secular practices of sexual control relegated women to a position of complete powerlessness, however. Colonial women exerted considerable influence in society and participated in military, religious, and civilian institutions as well as ranching and commerce (Bouvier 2001; Castañeda 1992, 1998). That women participated so fully in public life despite ideologies of female subordination may be understood in part by reevaluating gender stereotypes that associate women and femininity with private domesticity, and men and masculinity with the public realm. In colonial Alta California, there was no clear boundary between public and private life. The smallest details of daily life were politicized through military regulations and religious scrutiny, while what might be considered public relationships were personalized and made intimate through bonds of kinship and mutual obligation that extended far beyond individual households. Consequently, "women inhabited a world where the 'public' domain of politics and government and the 'private' space of the domestic hearth . . . blurred and frequently merged. . . . women's activities in and outside the home, traditionally viewed as 'private' and 'public' realms, often overlapped and were interdependent" (Chávez-García 2004:xviii).

Colonial women were supported in their negotiations of family and public life by Spanish-colonial law, which (unlike contemporary British and U.S. legal systems) afforded women a degree of legal autonomy from their male relatives while still reaffirming the doctrine of *patria potestas* (paternal authority) (Chávez-García 2004:28). Colonial women maintained economic and legal status separate from that of their husbands, retaining their own property, wages, and maiden name after marriage. They could inherit, own, mortgage, convey, and pawn real estate and other personal property as they liked; and they could enter into independent contractual obligations without the knowledge or consent of their husbands (Chávez-García 2004; Haas 1995; Lothrop 1994). They could also bring legal complaints against men, including their own husbands, fathers, and brothers, for not fulfilling their obligations or for exceeding their power and authority (Chávez-García 2004:29; Langum 1987).

Historian Steve Stern (1995) proposes that this tension between patriarchal domination and women's agency can be understood by viewing gender relations in colonial New Spain as conflict-filled arenas of power in which men and women entered into "patriarchal pacts." Although neither men nor women contested patriarchal domination per se, they interpreted the principles of patriarchal privilege so differently that conflict over gender and sexuality was a routine aspect of daily life. Whereas men tended to view their patriarchal privileges as absolute, women understood patriarchal privilege as contingent on certain rights and obligations. For example, a wife might argue that a husband who was lazy and didn't work, was having affairs, or was a drunkard had forfeited his right to patriarchal authority; because of his bad actions, she was no longer bound to fulfill her conjugal duties or share her resources with him. Recent historical scholarship has unearthed numerous examples in which colonial women in Alta California diffused the power of abusive and controlling men by actively negotiating the terms of patriarchal privilege (Castañeda 1992, 1998; Chávez-García 2004; Haas 1995; Sánchez 1995; Voss 2002:336–346). (Chapter 6 discusses the strategies used by one such woman, Juana Briones.) Such tactics did not necessarily contest patriarchal privilege itself; in fact, women often invoked ideologies of female subordination and the honor/shame complex in order to convince other male relatives and men in positions of authority to intervene on their behalf.

Tracing these ideologies and practices is an important step toward understanding how gender and sexuality were transformed by colonial ethnogenesis in Alta California. At the Presidio, competing sexual ideologies meant that there was considerable room for dissension, strategy, and maneuvering. Gender relations and sexual codes were constructed and contested through institutional regulations and practices, within family relationships, and across broader social networks. As practices of racial identification changed through colonists' manipulation and eventual rejection of the sistema de castas, gender and sexual ideologies were also transformed.

.   .   .

This chapter began by discussing one artistic representation of life at El Presidio de San Francisco, a historical reconstruction produced by National Park Service artists, shown in figure 3. Let us now turn to another image, an 1873 painting called The Fandango, by the German-born American artist Charles Christian Nahl

FIGURE 9. *The Fandango*, by Charles Christian Nahl, 1873. Crocker Art Museum, E. B. Crocker Collection.

(fig. 9). The setting of the painting is unknown, but it most likely was intended to depict a pueblo or rancho in post-independence Alta California. Like the reconstruction in figure 3, Nahl's painting contains an adobe house, but it is only partially depicted in the shadows of the image. For Nahl, people take center stage. They have gathered for a *fandango*, a community party, and sexual energies are flowing—even the two horses in the bottom left of the image are nuzzling each other in anticipation. The revelers are vital, energetic, and active; their faces are visible and detailed. There are mulatos, mestizos, and Native Californians; men and women; children and adults; rich and poor. They are dancing, riding horses, playing music, fighting, talking, conspiring, and teasing the family dog.

A visitor to the Presidio would see nothing like Nahl's imaginative and sensationalized depiction of Spanish-colonial society. Nahl was notorious for his "fanciful history paintings" (Driesbach 2000) that included risqué depictions of muscle-bound men and scantily clad women. As Yolanda Venegas (2004) points out, Nahl's painting was part of the canon of literary and artistic works produced in the 1870s that romanticized Spanish-colonial California for an Anglo-American audience. *The Fandango* conveys a lifestyle of indolence, leisure, and sexual license in a world populated by "wild-eyed vaqueros, handsome bandidos, and scantily clad señoritas" (Venegas 2004:81).

What Nahl does successfully accomplish in this painting is to place social life, in all its complexity, at the center of his historical reconstruction of Spanish-colonial Alta California. In this chapter, I have tried to achieve a similar effect, albeit with less sensationalism and romanticism. The Presidio was a settlement composed of people from diverse geographic backgrounds: colonists recruited from throughout central and western Mexico, and Native Californians brought to labor in the settlement from local communities as well as from villages over a hundred miles away. Among the colonists, there were more children than adults, and nearly as many women as men. From the settlement's founding, racial and ethnic identities were in flux, as people classified with various degrees of Mexican Indian and African heritage increasingly were instead described as españoles and, eventually, with racially neutral terms. The next chapter continues to follow these transformations of social identification, including the emergence and consolidation of a shared colonial ethnicity, that of the Californios and Californianas.

4 FROM CASTA TO CALIFORNIO, II

Social Identities in Late Spanish and Mexican-Era Alta California

The ethnogenesis of Californio identity was both immediate and incremental. Within only two decades of their arrival in Alta California, the military settlers had cast away the racializing taxonomies of Spanish imperialism, drawing on historical antecedents from alternative practices of identification in seventeenth- and eighteenth-century New Spain. Into the early 1800s, the regional ethnonym "Californio" was used alongside other forms of shared colonial identification. Even after "Californio" became the primary identity for colonial settlers, the term's meaning continued to shift as the province's residents adjusted to the economic, political, and demographic changes resulting from Mexican independence and U.S. annexation. We can thus conceptualize ethnogenesis in Alta California as a multigenerational process, one balanced on the fulcrum of the middle decades of Spanish-colonial rule (1790s–1800s) and stretching backward and forward in time through the eighteenth and nineteenth centuries.

This chapter first traces the emergence of Californio identity among military settlers from the 1790s through the 1810s and its development during Alta California's Mexican era, 1822 to 1846. Since the 1850s, historians have produced countless studies of Mexican-era Californio identity, culture, economy, and political activity; in order to contextualize these studies, the chapter presents a brief synopsis of the historiography of Mexican-era Californio society. Although these historical studies are particularly valuable because they reveal the changefulness and multivalence of Californio identity during the years immediately before and after U.S. annexation, they are also limited by their overreliance on documentary evidence and by their neglect of earlier transformations of colonial identity that occurred within Spanish-colonial presidios. This chapter closes with a diachronic model of Californio ethnogenesis that integrates the shifting settler identification practices of the precolonial, colonial, Mexican-era, and American periods. Archaeology, in particular, provides essential lines of evidence; the extant physical remnants of colonial settlements reveal how shifts in spatial practices and material culture participated in changes in social identity.

"Self-Identity Fascination": Gente de Razón, Hijos del País, and Californios

From the 1790s onward, casta terms were increasingly absent from military and church records. This is not to say that the sistema de castas and its associated racialized identities disappeared altogether. One presidio commander, when pressed to report the castas of the soldiers under his command, reported vaguely that his company was about one-third españoles, one-third mestizos, and one-third *color quebrados* (literally, broken color). Most priests and military officers responded to similar requests by stating that such classifications were impossible because the population was too racially mixed to categorize or because the colonists would respond only that they were españoles (Mason 1998:62–63).

Simultaneously, other identities—gente de razón, hijos del país, and Californios—first supplemented, and eventually supplanted, the sistema de castas. These classifications marked a shift away from individual- and family-based identification strategies and toward community-based identities. It was one thing for a parent to argue with a priest that her newly baptized child should be recorded as español rather than mestizo; it was another thing altogether to refuse to state the infant's casta. Colonists' direct challenges to the legitimacy of the sistema de castas ushered in what one historian terms a period of "self-identity fascination [in] early California society" (Miranda 1988:265).

The colonial settlers' new identities emerged from earlier colonial practices and from shared historical conditions. Initially, the most common alternative to the sistema de castas was the distinction between gente de razón and *gente sin razón* (literally, people without reason, in contrast to people with reason). The issue of "reason" and its relationship to social identity originated in sixteenth-century theological debates about the divine status of Native Americans. In 1537, Pope Paul III resolved the issue by releasing a papal bull, *Sublimus Deus* (In the Image of God), which declared that Native Americans were "true men," capable of reason (Miranda 1988:267). In the seventeenth and eighteenth centuries, missionaries in the Interior Provinces of New Spain adapted concepts of *de razón* and *sin razón* to classify Native Americans according to the Indians' relationship with the Christian faith. Those who refused conversion were considered sin razón (also called *gentiles*), unwilling to hear the gospel. Neophytes were also categorized as sin razón; as recent converts who had not fully mastered Catholic doctrine, they had the same legal status as children (Mason 1998:178). To achieve de razón status, baptized Indians were expected to accept Christianity fully and to adopt colonial language, lifeways, and mannerisms (Miranda 1988:268). Gente de razón status held secular importance for Christianized Indians, low-ranking castas, and free Africans: only gente de razón were permitted to own land, participate in local governance, enter into contractual agreements, and enlist in the military.

From Alta California's founding, the military settlers—most of them descended from Christianized Indians and formerly enslaved Africans in the Interior Provinces—shared the common status of gente de razón for legal and religious purposes (Haas 1995:2). Significantly, however, in Alta California, the meaning of gente de razón shifted to indicate "not Native Californian."[1] For example, in 1814, the Franciscan priests at Mission San José stated that "the only two castes we know of here are the gente de razón and Indians" (Weber 1992:328). Although in theory Alta California's native populations should have been granted de razón status when they accepted Christianity, in practice the difference between gente de razón and gente sin razón became synonymous with the distinction between colonizer and colonized, "between civilization and savagery" (Haas 1995:31). Referring to all Native Californians, Christian or not, as gente sin razón served to deny the rights and rational capacity of Alta California's indigenous population and justified colonial appropriation of indigenous land and labor by missionaries and by military and civilian settlers.[2]

Other shared colonial identities connoted a regional pride: hijos and hijas del país (sons and daughters of the land), Californios and Californianas. These categories appear to have come into widespread use in the early 1800s, a time when the offspring of the original settlers were coming into maturity and assuming positions of responsibility in colonial settlements, and a time when Alta California was increasingly isolated from the rest of New Spain. Like gente de razón, the regional identities hijos del país and Californios pertained exclusively to colonial settlers, not to Native Californians.

In 1824, shortly after Mexican independence, the new republic abolished the sistema de castas. Alta California's military settlers had anticipated this change in identification practices by nearly three decades. At the dawn of the Mexican Republic, "Californio" had emerged as the most common term of identification used by military and civilian colonists in Alta California. "Gente de razón," "hijos del país," and "español" continued to be used, sometimes but not always interchangeably with "Californio." Thus the ethnogenesis of Californio identity was not a uniform process, but was rather the emergence of a tentative consensus that existed alongside other congruent practices of social identification.

"Land, Labor, and Cattle": The Historiography of Californio Identity in the Mexican Era

Historical accounts of Californio ethnogenesis have surprisingly neglected the metamorphoses in colonial identity that occurred during Alta California's years as a Spanish province. Instead, historians have overwhelmingly situated Californio identity within California's Mexican era (1822–1846), particularly after 1834, when the secularization of the missions and related expansion of ranching transformed the region's economy. Even though such histories of Mexican-era California fall outside the temporal span of this study, they are important here for two reasons. First, since the 1860s, these histories have dominated public and scholarly perceptions of what it meant to be Californio; and as a result, certain romantic tropes of pastoralism and feudalism have been interpolated into historical imaginings of Californio identity. Second, these histories of Mexican California have traced substantive changes, controversies, and internal tensions in Californio identity during the years immediately before and after the U.S. conquest. Such studies demonstrate that colonial ethnogenesis produced not a single fixed identity, but rather a complex and contested realm of identification practices. Having emerged during Alta California's Spanish-colonial era, Californio identity was in no way static. During the Mexican era, it was deployed in multivalent and contradictory ways, much as casta identities had been in earlier decades.

Testimonios, Imperialist Nostalgia, and Chicano/a Reclamation

The history of Mexican-era Californio society has been refracted through multiple lenses. In the 1850s, Anglo-Americans and European immigrants described Californios as lazy, indolent, backward, wasteful, uneducated, and immoral; such portrayals served to justify the U.S. annexation of California and Anglo-Americans' seizure of Californios' lands and livestock. From the 1850s through the 1870s, some Californios, most of them men formerly of high standing, penned memoirs and dictated oral testimonios that countered these negative portrayals by recounting historical events that illustrated the industry, sense of honor, responsibility, and fairness of the Californios. Their accounts were important discursive sites of political struggle for representation by the former leaders of a conquered people (Mora-Torres 2005; Sánchez 1995).

Beginning in the 1880s, a series of popular histories and novels initiated a durable rhetorical tradition that depicted the Californios as romantic historical figures, a graceful and aristocratic society of virile rancheros and beautiful women who were tragically but inevitably displaced by Anglo-American progress and enterprise. Hubert Howe Bancroft's seven-volume *History of California* (1886–1890) and, most notably, his *California Pastoral* (1888) are credited by many as the primary source of these romantic myths and stereotypes, along with the extraordinarily popular novels *Ramona*, published in 1884 (Jackson 1970), and *The Squatter and the Don*, published in 1885 (Ruiz de Burton 1997).[3]

Such texts paradoxically claimed a place for the displaced Californios in the history of the United States and simultaneously portrayed Mexican-era California as a cultural backwater that was "simple, often ignorant, unsophisticated, and, even if smart, quite helpless" (Mora 1949:175) in the face of Anglo-American progress. This scholarly rhetoric is perhaps best understood as a recitation of anti-Californio propaganda widely distributed in popular culture from the 1840s through the 1860s. For example, an 1866 business pamphlet published in San José read: "This result is inevitable; for it is but a repetition of the old story of the triumph of the stronger and more vigorous over the weaker; of the peaceful, but nonetheless sure, extermination of the indolent native Californian— half-Indian and half Spanish or Mexican—by the hardy, energetic Anglo-Saxon and his descendants" (Sanchez 1984:1). Such characterizations, which persist today in both scholarly and popular works, exemplify what Renato Rosaldo (1989) terms "imperialist nostalgia," in which conquerors mourn the passing of the traditional culture that they themselves have transformed.

In the latter half of the twentieth century, historical studies of Mexican-era California expanded to consider the tension between the Californios' contradictory position as the colonizers of California's native populations and their later victimization by U.S. territorial expansion. This led to an increased focus on the fate of Californios following the U.S. acquisition of California and on the historical connections between eighteenth-century colonial settlers and present-day Mexican American populations.[4] In the 1990s, the Columbian Quincentennial spurred a resurgence of historical scholarship on Spanish-colonial and Mexican-era Alta California. Diverse in its methodological and theoretical stance, this body of work is shaped by the growing influence of Native Californian and Chicano/a studies and draws on feminist, materialist, and postcolonial approaches. Many of these recent studies emphasize interethnic interaction as a central force in producing California's history. In this context, Californios in Mexican California are portrayed not as an autonomous bounded group, but as a population embedded in and constituted by the cultural negotiations and contests among Native Californians, colonial settlers, more recently arrived Mexican immigrants, and Anglo-American and European immigrants.

Many historical and archaeological studies explicitly foreground the experiences of Native Californians, who often appeared only as passive victims in earlier historical works. Additionally, for the first time, questions of gender figure prominently in some historical analyses.[5]

Californio Identity in Mexican-Era California

The recent focus on interethnic exchange in Mexican-era California has reopened inquiries into Californio ethnogenesis. While the earliest histories attributed the emergence of Californio identity to Alta California's isolation and the perceived cultural backwardness of its inhabitants, more recent studies, whose arguments are summarized here, have located this transformation of social identities in five interrelated phenomena: the emergence of ranchero culture; a seigniorial society; aristocratic pretensions; liberal politics and protonationalism; and immigration to Alta California in the 1830s and 1840s.

Most historians have associated Californio identity with the emergence of ranchero culture and its accompanying economic triumvirate of land, labor, and cattle. *Rancho* land grants allowed "sons of original soldiers to emerge as a powerful class" (Sánchez 1995:52) so that "political influence, economic power, and enormous landholdings quickly became synonymous in Mexican California" (Hackel 1998:132). Notably, the proliferation of landownership did not occur until after the 1834 secularization of the missions. No more than 25 ranchos were granted in Alta California during the entire Spanish-colonial period, and only 26 were awarded between 1822 and 1834. In contrast, 300 ranchos were granted between 1834 and 1842, and a staggering 453 were allotted during the years 1842 to 1846 (Greenwood 1989). By the time of U.S. annexation, private landholdings had become a distinctive feature of Alta California's social geography, though this explosion in landownership was a comparatively recent phenomenon.

For some historians, it was the ongoing interactions between men and livestock that imbued Californio culture with a unique character and rhythm, the seasonal hard work of calving, branding, and *matanzas* (large-scale slaughters) balanced by alternating periods of fiestas and community celebration (Sánchez 1993). Others focus on labor relations, arguing that the rancheros' exploitation of Native Californian labor was as central to the production of Californio culture as slave ownership was to plantation culture in the southern United States. The rancho economy depended on indigenous labor to convert the large herds of free-range cattle into marketable hides and tallow and to perform other tasks related to subsistence and craft production. While small ranchos might have had only two or three Native Californian workers, larger ones typically had a permanent labor force of fifty to two hundred, which could swell to as many as a thousand during peak agricultural seasons (Greenwood 1989; Hackel 1998; Sánchez 1993; Silliman 2004a). The argument is that these labor relations allowed the colonial settlers to see themselves as distinct from Native Californians and to develop a shared Californio identity based on that differentiation. "This," Douglas Monroy (1998:190) opines, "was a society based on the work of others. . . . [of] men who presumed entitlement to the service of women and especially people of color."

The ranchero culture was accompanied, according to many scholars, by a patriarchal family and social structure that closely bound members of Californio society to each other through ties of reciprocal obligation and uneven power. Following this argument, Californio identity emerged through what might be described as a feudal or seigniorial culture: a "personalist" society in which relationships were more important than individualism, notions of honor bound wives to husband and children to parents, and obligations of debt and labor attached the landless to the landed. This web of obligations and authority was not limited to the family but extended across the entire community (Chávez-García 2004:xvii, 26–28). The landowning ranchero was at the top of this hierarchy: "All lines of dependency radiated outward from his *casa* and embraced his children, his in-laws, other relatives, orphans, a bevy of Indian servants, sometimes also residents of the nearest village" (Pitt 1971:11). Californio identity was thus negotiated not through tropes of individuality or citizenship but through patron-peon and kinship relationships composed of "patterns of submission, hierarchy, and obligation" (Monroy 1990b:143).

Some historians contend that the convergence of rancho culture and seigniorial society was expressed through Californios' pretensions to aristocracy and an anticapitalist ethos that rejected the accumulation of profit for its own sake. Landownership had transformed humble settlers into *hidalgos*, people of importance. For these Californios, it is commonly written, social standing was everything, and wealth was important only insofar as it enabled its owner to maintain his social position. Openhandedness and hospitality were prized, as generosity strengthened the power-laden ties of obligation and reciprocity. The rancheros' resources were thus directed toward sponsoring social events: religious festivals, dances, fandangos, music, cockfights, bull-fighting, bear baiting, horse races, and feasts (Clark 1974:82; Monroy 1990b:100; Pitt 1971). Imported consumer goods obtained through the hide and tallow trade were another means through which Californios enacted their aristocratic aspirations. Lavish dress, furnishings, architectural embellishments, transfer-printed dinnerware, and metal serving dishes and utensils were all part of "a new awareness of self born of preoccupation with one's image" (Monroy 1990b:138; see also Haas 1995:52).

In their aristocratic self-presentations, some Californios also capitalized on their former allegiance to the Spanish crown to claim Iberian bloodlines: "There are [a] great many families in whose veins circulates much of the *sangre azul* [blue blood] of Spain" (Ignacio Sepúlveda quoted in Haas 1995:37).[6] The ability to present a white or European racial identity became increasingly salient in the 1840s and 1850s, as the Californios faced the stricter racial ideologies of Anglo-American, British, and other European immigrants. Studies of marriage patterns in Mexican-era Alta California document that during this period, many Californio families married their daughters to Anglo-American and British traders and immigrants, a practice interpreted as strategic *blanquemiento*, or "whitening" of the family lineage (Castañeda 1998; Cook and Borah 1979:305; Hurtado 1999:25). As Antonia Castañeda (1998:242) concludes, "The intermarriage of daughters of the Californios to Euro-Americans . . . became the basis for the 'old Spanish Californio family ancestry.'"

In contrast to historical accounts that emphasize ranchero culture and its expression in an aristocratic, seigniorial society, other studies argue that Californio identity emerged primarily through engagement with Enlightenment liberal politics and the development of protonationalist sentiments.[7] The growing influence of secular liberalism in the province is generally attributed to the political activities of a network of high-status young men, most connected by kinship, who eventually became members of the *diputación territorial* (provincial deputation) of Alta California. Through their debates with the Mexican government over topics such as secularization of the missions, economic liberalization, and immigration policies, these elite young men came to realize that their interests as Californios separated them from the rest of Mexico. A turning point in these debates was the 1834 compilation and widespread distribution of the *Manifiesto a la República Mejicana*, a collection of documents that historian Lisbeth Haas claims "expressed, for the first time, a collective Californio political identity" (1995:36).

By implementing its own plan for secularizing missions and distributing land, the Alta California diputación territorial ensured that descendants of the original military settlers would receive preferential access to land. The legislative body also established new laws that forced former neophytes from the disbanded missions to labor on the ranchos (Haas 1995:32–38). This contrast between the Californios' engagement with secular liberalism and their simultaneous subjugation of indigenous populations was a persistent tension in Mexican-era Californio cultural identity. It was, as Rosaura Sánchez notes, an ambiguous and aristocratic liberalism in which "long-held tenets of birthright and 'blood'" remained "the determining factors of an individual's standing" (1995:96).

Finally, some historians posit that Californio identity crystalized not through the province's isolation, the growth of the ranch-based economy, or political activities, but rather as a result of the influx of immigrants from other Mexican provinces, the United States, and Europe (primarily Britain) in the late 1830s and 1840s. For the first time since the 1770s, immigration in those years surpassed natural increase as the driving force of nonindigenous population growth. Encouraged by the Mexican government, these *extranjeros* (strangers or foreigners) could become naturalized citizens by converting to the Catholic faith and taking an oath of allegiance. Their presence was not negligible: in the 1840s, about one-third of new land grants went to settlers with non-Spanish surnames (Hackel 1998). This argument, in brief, is that the influx of these new immigrants made the Californios conscious of how distinct their culture had become from that of their homeland. In response, they dissociated themselves from other Mexicans by referring to themselves only as Californios and sought economic and marriage alliances with the Anglo-Americans and European immigrants.

Although these historical studies generally neglect transformations in settler identities prior to 1834, their findings indicate that the meanings of Californio identity substantially changed during the last fifteen years of Mexican rule. Increased self-governance combined with the closure of the missions and the diminished role of presidios ended the influence of the colonial institutions that had dominated Alta California since the 1770s. The concurrent exponential increase in the availability of land and indigenous labor for private agriculture, the growth of the hide and tallow trade, and greater contact with both Mexicans and Anglo-American and European extranjeros all signaled structural changes in the fabric of Californio society. Historians have assigned different levels of importance to these factors, but such developments were interwoven, and all contributed to the emergence of Californio identity.

Recent historical analyses raise two major points of contention related to these changes in Californio society in Mexican-era California. Both concern the degree to which Californio identity indicated an elite standing within the nonindigenous population. As feminist and Chicana scholars point out, most historical studies presume that becoming Californio was a masculine endeavor, that it fell within the realm of men who owned vast tracts of land, who controlled the labor of landless settlers and Native Californians, who were key players in political maneuvers, who were the patriarchal heads of vast extended families, and who used their female children as pawns in arranged marriages designed to improve their own racial and economic standing. Without denying the very tangible disadvantages that Californianas faced, recent research has questioned these tacit assumptions and demonstrates that women played a substantive role in the rancho society of the 1830s and 1840s.[8]

The wives, daughters, and sisters of male rancho owners were crucial participants in the economic workings of their families' agricultural enterprises.

But Californianas were not limited to serving as their male relatives' helpmates. Women were the direct recipients of fifty-five of Alta California's land grants, and an even larger number of ranchos were inherited by the widows and daughters of rancheros (Lothrop 1994). Other women owned smaller town plots (*solares*) and garden or orchard plots (*huertas*) (Chávez-García 2004). Californiana landowners directed agricultural laborers, negotiated with Anglo-American and European traders, and participated fully in the reciprocal relationships of mutual aid, generosity, and obligation that have been viewed as characteristic of seigniorial society. Nonetheless, there was a distinct gendered economic disparity in Mexican-era Alta California: women's landholdings, on average, were smaller than those of men; and women who owned no land had few economic options other than family support or domestic service, since they were barred from military or civil service employment. Landless women, both Native Californians and poorer Californians, were particularly vulnerable to sexual predation and to abuse by male family members (Chávez-García 2004).

The second controversy involves the degree to which Mexican-era Californio identity was used by those with economic and political power to differentiate themselves from poor and landless settlers, from people whose appearance indicated their African and Mexican Indian heritage, and especially from the growing numbers of recent immigrants from other Mexican provinces. Most historical scholarship on Californio identity focuses on landowning members of the political elite, who commanded the allegiance and labor of their social and economic inferiors and whose aristocratic pretensions may have been bolstered by claims to Spanish ancestry. At the same time, many other sources suggest that Californio identity was shared among non-Native Californians throughout the province, regardless of skin color or economic standing. Al Camarillo (1979), Antonio Ríos-Bustamante (1993), and Albert Hurtado (1999), in particular, argue that Californio identity was never separate from Mexican identity.[9] They stress that Californio culture differed only slightly from that in northern Mexico; that Californios had networks of relatives throughout Baja California and Sonora; and that Californio critiques of the Mexican Republic were not indications of protonationalism but rather signs of a commitment to participatory citizenship in the Mexican nation. As Antonio María Osio penned in 1851, "I am a *californio* who loves his country and a Mexican on all four sides and in my heart" (Osio 1996:23). For men like Osio, to be a Californio was to be Mexican, and the more recently arrived Mexicans were part of their *patria*, or homeland.

Archaeological investigations of rancho sites have also complicated the portrayal of elite ranchero life found in many historical studies. While some investigators have excavated the remains of the grand estates of Alta California's prosperous rancheros (Greenwood, Foster, and Duffield 1988; Silliman 1999,

2004a; Treganza 1958), still more have studied ranchos of average size. They have found that most rancho homes were of modest scale, typically two or three adobe rooms arranged in lineal order. In many cases, unusually thin walls and the absence of foundations suggest a scarcity of construction labor. Household debris and food remains recovered from rancho sites suggest that imported consumer goods were scarce and that European-produced ceramics were heavily supplemented by locally made pottery. Diversified, self-sufficient agricultural enterprises were more typical than the cattle-driven economy of the hide and tallow trade (Chace 1969; Felton and Schulz 1983; Frierman 1982, 1992; Greenwood 1989; Silliman 2004a:33–39). These investigations of the material conditions of rancho life serve "to balance the glorified image of the wealthy ranchero" (Greenwood 1989:458).

Two important points emerge from these debates about the gendered, racial, and economic exclusivity of Mexican-era Californio identity. The first is that the structural conditions that shaped social life in Alta California were rapidly changing in the 1840s. The gendered imbalance in rancho landholdings grew exponentially during this period with the increase in land grants to recent immigrants. Likewise, if Californio identity was ever used to distinguish prosperous landholding settlers from those who were poorer, darker-skinned, or more recently arrived, that use may have emerged or intensified during the rapid rise in extranjero landholdings, the increase in new arrivals from other parts of Mexico, and the U.S. conquest of Alta California. Consequently, scholars should use great caution in generalizing accounts of Californio identity from the 1840s and 1850s to the earlier Spanish-colonial occupation of Alta California.

The second, and perhaps more important, point is that available documentary sources and historical analyses reveal a great deal of variability in what constituted Californio identity. Individual historians emphasize different aspects of social life in their explanations of Californio ethnogenesis because being Californio was—like any other social identity—overdetermined, produced not through some unilineal chain of cause-and-effect but emerging from and reproduced through multiple social practices. The multivalent and ambiguous aspects of Californio identity were resources in negotiations of social power. Lower-status settlers and women could assert Californio identity to include themselves as members of the body politic. Upper-status settlers could also use the more inclusive definition when they wished to forge a sense of solidarity and unity across class, racial, and land-status lines (Sánchez 1995:179). In other contexts, the same elite might use the term "Californio" to differentiate themselves from other sectors of the province's population. It was this malleability that made Californio identity such a potent axis of social identification during Alta California's Mexican era.

Damaging Silences and Archaeological Possibilities

In sum, a review of the historiography of Californio identity reveals some surprising limitations, including an overreliance on documentary evidence; a temporal bias that emphasizes the late Mexican era and the early period of U.S. rule; an institutional focus on ranchos and, secondarily, missions and the neglect of presidios and pueblos; and an overemphasis on discourse at the expense of practice. Far from being trivial, these limitations have perpetuated damaging silences that allow romantic myths of Spanish conquistadors and aristocratic rancheros to continue to overshadow the contributions that women, Mesoamerican Indians, Africans, Native Californians, and those of humble economic means have made to California's history.

The near-exclusive reliance on documentary evidence is perhaps the biggest weakness of this historiography. As many historians acknowledge, the majority of Californios were illiterate; most of those who could read and write were elite men. Consequently, documents that survive from the Spanish and Mexican periods were produced by a small handful of military officers, priests, clerks, and educated rancheros. In addition to the differential effects of literacy on documents from the Spanish and Mexican periods, the later memoirs and testimonios that form the basis for so much historical research on the Californios were shaped by the effects of memory and by the author's or the interviewee's knowledge of the political context of their work. Not all Californios get "equal time" in these documents—the political exploits of the owners of large ranchos are prominent, but few women are represented, and the less prosperous laborers and owners of smaller rancheros are rarely mentioned (Sánchez 1995:10). The accounts written by Anglo-American and European travelers are equally biased; these too are penned predominantly by elite men, and their perceptions of Californio society were profoundly affected by racism, anti-Catholicism, and their designs on the future of Alta California.[10]

In other words, the vast majority of documentary records concerning Spanish-colonial and Mexican-era Alta California were produced by an extremely small percentage of the population, and the content and form of these texts were shaped by the high status, male gender, and political allegiances of their authors. There is much to be said for postcolonial and feminist methodologies that give voice to the silences and omissions in colonial texts by reading between and around the lines to produce a more inclusive history of Californio identity and society (Beebe and Senkewicz 2006; Chávez-García 2004; Pérez 1993, 1999). Still, such methodologies are constrained by the texts themselves. Archaeology provides a broader and more inclusive perspective on the emergence of Californio identity—as amply demonstrated by the findings of archaeological investigations of ranchos. If the written record illuminates the perspectives of elite men (the owners of large ranchos, the light-skinned, the economically prosperous, and the politically powerful), archaeological research can obtain direct evidence of the daily lives of women as well as men, children as well as adults, the landless and the landed, those of lower castas, and people of adequate or barely adequate means with little political leverage.

The second core limitation of extant scholarship relates to temporal focus. Theories of Californio identity that center on the emergence of ranchero culture focus on the short, final period of Mexican governance in Alta California. Those who emphasize political consciousness, rather than rancho economics and labor relations, mark the emergence of Californio identity scarcely earlier, in the early 1830s. Yet colonial records show that the formation of a regional, collective identity among the colonial settlers began no later than the 1790s and continued through the early 1800s. There is no doubt that political activity, landownership, and labor relations came to have a profound effect on Californio culture and identity, but the *emergence* of this shared identity occurred through the interactions among colonists and between colonists and Native Californians during the years from the 1770s through the 1810s. We must reach back beyond the proliferation of ranchos to include individual and collective manipulations of the sistema de castas and consider the ways that gente de razón status morphed into a regional identity.

The third limitation relates to institutional focus. Overwhelmingly, the story of Californio identity has been set on the ranchos of the 1840s, with some historical antecedents related to labor extending back to the missions in the days before secularization. Lisbeth Haas (1995) and Miroslava Chávez-García (2004) convincingly show that this approach has excluded the growing populations of *pobladores* who lived in the expanding pueblos and smaller semi-rural villas in the 1840s. But to my knowledge, no historian has substantively engaged with presidios as institutional sites for the cultural negotiation of colonial social identity. For nearly sixty years, these presidio communities were the residential, commercial, and political centers of Californio life. Any historical analysis of Californio identity must necessarily address the role of presidios as institutions of colonial ethnogenesis. Failure to do so hazards a denial of the military character of California's colonization.

The fourth shortcoming of these investigations is that they have focused considerably more on representation than on practice. With the notable exception of Haas's (1995) innovative use of spatial analyses and social geography, histories of Californio identity have relied on what people have written about themselves or others. As Sánchez (1995) aptly points out, such texts were potent sites of political struggle over representations of identity. Textual analyses need to be balanced by research on the material practices that also participated in colonial identity negotiations. Attention to material practice goes far beyond remediating the evidentiary limitations of documentary evidence. A focus on practice interrogates the ways in which social identities are *materialized*—made real and tangible social facts through the social production of space, the production and use of material objects, the preparation and consumption of food, and the adornment of the body (Bourdieu 1977, 1980; Butler 1993a).

A Diachronic Model of Californio Ethnogenesis

To remedy these shortcomings, scholars must recognize that understanding Californio ethnogenesis requires a longer-term diachronic perspective that encompasses historical events spanning several generations and political regimes. Such a model is presented here, based on the demographic research presented in chapter 3 and the historical scholarship reviewed in the preceding sections. It is important to note that identifying particular historical benchmarks does not imply that ethnogenesis in Alta California was linear or totalizing. Without question, these ongoing changes in colonial identities were uneven, incomplete, and contested. This model emphasizes that even changes in social identities that occur somewhat rapidly (in a matter of years or decades) are accomplished through incremental alterations of social practices in relationship to the structural conditions of particular historical moments.

Historical Antecedents
(1)   The decades prior to Alta California's colonization included a suite
       of changes to identification practices in eighteenth-century New
       Spain, especially in the Interior Provinces. These changes included
       social and legal practices that located racialized identities in social
       behavior and social standing as well as in the physical body; the
       simplification of the sistema de castas in the Interior Provinces; the
       expansion of the español casta classification to confer status and
       legal privileges on people of mixed heritage; and the modification
       of the classifications gente de razón and gente sin razón to differen-
       tiate Christianized and non-Christianized colonial subjects, regard-
       less of race.

Spanish Colonization of Alta California
(2)   During the first two decades of colonization (1776–1790s), indivi-
       duals and families manipulated casta status by declaring casta rankings
       with greater association to European ancestry than those assigned

to them at birth. This reclassification minimized their association with Mexican Indian and especially African heritage and later lent documentary credibility to some Californios' claims of Spanish heritage.

(3) Military and civilian colonists displayed a collective disinclination toward the use of casta terms in documents related to social identity, so much so that by the early 1800s, local colonial priests and military officials declared that it was impossible to enumerate settlers' castas.

(4) As early as the 1780s (and with increasing frequency in the 1790s and early 1800s), the colonists increasingly identified themselves as a social collectivity by distinguishing themselves from Native Californians. Gente de razón and gente sin razón, classifications formerly used to contrast Christian and non-Christian colonial subjects, shifted meaning and became discrete categories separating all colonial settlers from all Native Californians, baptized or not.

(5) Beginning in the early 1800s, second- and third-generation colonists claimed Alta California as their homeland, or patria, and began to refer to themselves as hijos and hijas del país and as Californios and Californianas. This practice was bolstered by isolation from the rest of New Spain during the years 1800 to 1821.

Mexican-Era Alta California

(6) Mexican independence resulted in a suite of structural changes, including economic liberalization and an increase in provincial self-rule. During the 1820s, the role of presidios as the centers of settler society diminished, corresponding to growth in pueblo populations and civilian governance as well as greater political engagement with secular liberalism on the part of some elite male Californios.

(7) Mission secularization in 1834 ended the dominance of religious institutions and expanded the availability of land, a necessary precondition for the emergence of ranchero culture among Californios. This was accompanied by the development of agrarian labor regimes that brought Native Californians under the control of the rancheros. According to some historians, Californio identity in the rancho era was also forged within patron-client relationships in a society increasingly dominated by elite seigniors with pretensions to Spanish heritage and aristocratic lifestyles.

(8)   In the 1840s, the rapid expansion of immigration meant that Califor-
      nio identity was more frequently experienced in opposition to Anglo-
      American, European, and perhaps Mexican identities. Some historical
      research suggests that during this period Californio identity was also
      becoming associated with elite status and (usually fictive) Spanish
      ancestry.

U.S. Annexation

(9)   After 1846, the Californios became colonized residents of an occupied
      territory, many losing their land, livestock, political power, and social
      standing. The harsh U.S. racial policies of hypodescent complicated the
      racial politics of Californio identity. Most Californio self-representations
      were penned or dictated during this era of displacement and loss and
      are best interpreted within this particular historical context.

Together, these changes in colonial racial and ethnic identities involved five
interrelated trends. The first was a shift from individual or family-based identities to a collective colonial identity. The second, closely related trend was a
transition from a heterogeneous society, diverse in heritage and places of origin, to one that represented itself as internally homogeneous. Third, the internal homogeneity of colonial society was contrasted against Native Californian
"others." Fourth, the growing distinction between the colonial settlers and the
Native Californians among whom they lived and worked was supported by the
colonists' repudiation of their own indigenous and African ancestry in exchange
for español and Californio identities. Fifth, distinctions among colonists were
increasingly expressed not as racial differences but as differences in honor, economic means, landownership, and political affiliation. One of the primary aims
of this study is to trace continuities and changes in material and spatial practices that occurred during this shift from a pluralistic, multiracial, colonial population to one defined by its common status as colonizers and by a regional and
ethnic Californio identity.

·   ·   ·

The research presented in this book offers scholars of California history an opportunity to consider the elements that have been absent from previous writing on Californio identity: a temporal focus on the early decades of colonization, an institutional focus on military presidios, and a methodological focus
on spatial practice and material culture. For anthropologists, archaeologists, eth-

nohistorians, and historians concerned more broadly with the issue of how colonization shapes practices of identification, it allows an examination of the ways in which colonizing populations are themselves transformed by their imperial actions and ambitions, and how such changes in identification practices are negotiated within and despite the structural conditions of powerful colonial institutions such as presidios.

Perhaps most important, this study strives to avoid the all too common archaeological tendency to "fix" social identity, to reduce complicated daily negotiations of social meaning to neat, bounded, transhistorical categories suitable for linear comparative analysis. The archaeological evidence and documentary record provide indications of the material and discursive practices that served as potent resources for changing individual and collective identities. Yet these social negotiations were ambiguous and multivalent, and their material traces—the fragmented remains of adobe buildings, broken sherds of cooking pots, charred remains of porridge spilled into a cooking fire, a lost button—must be considered within the specific contexts in which they were obtained, used, and lost or disposed of. The next chapter turns to these contexts of archaeological deposition, discovery, and interpretation.

A total of 86 underground storage tanks containing
bunker oil, fuel oil, gasoline and diesel fuels, waste
oils, and solvents, and associated pipelines, features such
as tank cradles, and contaminated soils were removed
at specific locations at the Presidio of San Francisco,
California. . . . Archaeological construction monitoring
and post-tank removal inspections were conducted at
fourteen tank removal [sic] located in archaeologically
sensitive areas. Pursuant to OSHA Regulation 29 CRF
1910.120, all field personnel working at the tank
removal locations during construction activity had
completed current hazardous waste operations and
emergency response training certification. During the
course of construction monitoring behind Building 12,
a stone feature and related clay tile and ceramic artifacts
were identified. Subsequent excavation revealed that
the stone feature was a typical Spanish Colonial-period
wall/foundation. The results of excavations to assess
this archaeological site are forthcoming.

Woodward-Clyde Consultants 1994:1.1−1.2

June 3, 1993, was unseasonably cold, even for San Francisco's infamous fog-
banked summer weather. All day, the coastal winds had whipped rain through
my "waterproof" jacket, and I was chilled to the bone. When I arrived at the
site of the last tank removal operation for the day, I was already anticipating a
return to dry clothes and a warm office. It was only 1:30 P.M., and if everything went quickly, I could still get some work done on an overdue report. So
when I inspected the pit in the backyard of Officers' Quarters 12, I was momen-
tarily inclined to dismiss the stones that appeared incongruously in the pit's
wall. But I had monitored sewer line replacements and tank removals in this
area for months, and until now I had never seen any stones of this type or size
in the natural soil. Furthermore, the stones were clustered tightly together; they

117

were mirrored on the opposite side of the pit by a similar cluster. Both group-ings of stone were flanked by fragments of soft, rust-red curved ceramic called *tejas*, or roof tile.

Archaeological monitoring is one of the most humble activities of the disci-pline, and one of the most emotionally exacting. You watch construction crews go about their business, doing your best to observe their excavations while avoiding close encounters with heavy equipment. On most days, the work is excruciatingly boring. Then, in the moment when something unusual appears, you are faced with split-second decisions. Is it "something"? Should you halt construction immediately or wait and see? The situation is compounded by the ever-present awareness that unwarranted delays in construction can result in enormous costs and loss of good faith.

Consequently, archaeological discoveries that occur in construction settings are more often moments of great anxiety than moments of exhilaration. June 3, 1993, was no exception. I pulled myself out of the pit and phoned Vance Benté, director of the cultural resources division in the environmental engi-neering firm where we both worked. I had found "something," I told him, maybe something Spanish-colonial because of the tile fragments, maybe a wall, certainly an alignment of rocks. It's raining, he reminded me; was I sure? No, I admitted, I wasn't sure. Vance instructed me to go back and "make sure," and then call him again.

I spent another half hour in the muddy pit, scraping down the sidewalls with my trowel and detailing the exposed stones. I uncovered several more pieces of roof tile and some fragments of tableware ceramic called majolica and also started to notice differences in soil color and composition that suggested some sort of historical trench cut. I called Vance again: I could not dismiss the un-usual clusters of stones and the artifacts associated with them, and I could only hope that I was not triggering a false alarm. While Vance alerted agency archae-ologists, I informed the tank removal contractor that they would not be able to return to the job site that day. Then I waited.

One by one, that afternoon they arrived: Vance, Army Corps archaeologist Sannie Osborn, and National Park Service archaeologist Leo Barker, all of them specialists in the archaeology of colonial-era California. My anxieties quickly vanished as they talked excitedly to one another. We had discovered the ar-chaeological site of El Presidio de San Francisco.

For decades, no one had been sure whether archaeological remains of the Presidio existed. The land once occupied by the Spanish-colonial settlement had been under continuous use by the U.S. Army since 1846. The daily operations of the army post involved constant earth-moving projects. No one knew the extent to which the roads, buildings, parking lots, utilities, and landscaping that are typical of urban military installations had affected any archaeological remains. The only above-ground physical remnants of the historical settlement were six bronze cannons that decorate various locations throughout the Presidio and fragments of adobe walls that had been encapsulated within the post's Officers' Club.

In 1972, while it was still an active military installation, the Presidio was included within the boundaries of the Golden Gate National Recreation Area (GGNRA). Consequently, when the army post was closed in 1994, the Presidio was transferred to the National Park Service. In 1996, the U.S. Congress created the Presidio Trust, a new federal agency, to jointly administer the park with the National Park Service. Both the incorporation into the GGNRA and the transfer of property between the army and these federal agencies created new opportunities for archaeological research on a historical site that had been little studied. The 1993 discovery of El Presidio de San Francisco initiated what today is perhaps the largest ongoing research program in historical archaeology in the western United States. Directed by the Presidio Archaeology Center, a joint facility of the Presidio Trust and the National Park Service, this program fosters collaboration among archaeologists from two federal agencies, eight universities and colleges, and numerous state and local government agencies, heritage groups, nonprofit organizations, and private-sector cultural resource management firms.

This book is based on the findings of thirteen years of research at the archaeological site of the Presidio. This chapter presents a synthesis of the methods used in field investigations of the site, including predictive studies, archaeological monitoring, geophysical prospecting, pedestrian surveys, and excavations. This discussion is especially important because the site itself poses specific methodological challenges. First, because it is located in an urban setting, not all regions of the site are equally accessible. Archaeologists often must seize windows of opportunity when study of a particular area is possible—for example, during a road repaving project or a building rehabilitation. Second, each field and laboratory project is initiated with different goals in mind. Some are compliance-oriented, aimed at identifying specific impacts to the archaeological site and mitigating these effects by recovering data that would otherwise be lost. Compliance-oriented projects may also be forward-looking, designed to gather information needed to develop plans for site use and preservation. Others are driven by research programs aimed at addressing specific questions about the history and culture of the people who once lived at the historical settlement. Still other investigations are initiated in order to generate opportunities for public interpretation of the Presidio's history. Third, over the years, different research teams have conducted field investigations, selecting somewhat different field and laboratory methods and procedures to accomplish their goals.

Because of these factors, it is especially critical that archaeologists studying the Presidio pay rigorous attention to depositional processes, preservation bias, archaeological sampling, and research technique. The sections that follow examine specific issues involved in these matters, but first it seems germane to mention a few broader principles that have guided my archival, field, and laboratory practices.

Archaeological interpretations, it is generally argued, are inherently underdetermined: that is, the available evidence is never sufficient to conclusively prove a given finding or conclusion. The practice of archaeological interpretation is fraught with ambiguity—an ambiguity, some suggest, that reflects the complexities of social life. Even researchers who study present-day communities must acknowledge that their findings are partial and fragmented, conditioned by their own vantage point, and constrained by material limits on observation. Scholars who study the past, such as archaeologists and historians, must grapple with even more uncertainty in our efforts to understand events and phenomena that occurred long ago.[1]

To acknowledge that there is ambiguity and uncertainty in any study of the past does not foreclose the possibility of meaningful interpretation. What it does suggest is that attention to evidentiary support should be at the forefront of any archaeological endeavor. During the past quarter century, the issue of the relationship between evidence and interpretation has been at the center of theoretical debates in archaeology. One of the most important developments has been a renewed emphasis on context—not only the physical archaeological context in which a given object is found but also the social contexts in which it was once used and the present-day contexts that generated its excavation and interpretation.[2] A concern for context, in all its aspects, is central to this study.

While there is ambiguity in archaeological interpretation, there are also very real evidential constraints that delimit the universe of possible interpretations. Alison Wylie (1986, 1992a), in particular, argues that the use of multiple lines of evidence is one means by which archaeologists can strengthen the empirical foundation of their interpretations. By itself, a single type of evidence, such as ceramic decoration, may provide rather wispy support for any particular interpretation, but when other kinds of information are brought to bear on the research topic, a more robust understanding of the past begins to take shape.

This study takes the call for multiple lines of evidence very seriously. In addition to placing the findings of archaeological investigations in dialogue with the information gained from archival research on historical documents and images, this book also considers the question of colonial ethnogenesis from the vantage point of a wide range of material practices: landscape, architecture, ceramics, foodways, and dress. Doing so allows us to attend not only to points of convergence among different bodies of data but also to dissonance and divergence. In historical archaeology, the most frequent cases of evidentiary divergence are those in which archaeological evidence provides a different understanding of the past than that afforded through documentary evidence (Voss 2007). The interpretive danger is to privilege resolution of these evidentiary conflicts at the cost of oversimplifying our understanding of the past. Attending to divergence as well as convergence enables us to identify arenas in which social life was more complicated, incomplete, or contested than one type of evidence alone might indicate.

As a discipline, archaeology has two strengths that, when combined, offer a unique perspective on culture. The first is its persistent focus on the material of social life; the second, its ability to provide a long-term perspective on social life. A diachronic, comparative approach thus joins context and multiple lines of evidence as a third methodological pillar of this study.[3] Ethnogenesis is a temporal phenomenon, the setting aside of older practices of identification and the emergence of new ones. This process can occur with great rapidity, or it can unfold slowly over centuries; regardless, investigating ethnogenesis requires attention to rhythms of change and continuity, of stasis and transformation. Chapter 4 outlined the sequences of incremental changes that facilitated the transition from casta to Californio and suggested that such transformations in social identity can be generally associated with specific episodes in the Presidio's history. Archaeological research thus affords an opportunity to chart, chronologically, the coincidence between different aspects of material practice and shifts in social identification.

Throughout, it must be remembered that these archaeological traces and fragments are the surviving remains of tangible objects that were taken up in the patterned routines and social dramas of daily life. In this process, they became part of material practices that structured and communicated social meaning and social identities. The ultimate goal of the field research described here is to foster a more nuanced understanding of the relationship between the material world and social life.

The Project Area

The Presidio of San Francisco, in its entirety, is a National Historic Landmark District (Alley et al. 1993). Overall, the park's archaeological research programs encompass a chronology that includes, on the one end, prehistoric Native Californian shellmounds and, at the other extreme, the physical remnants of 1950s and 1960s defense systems from the cold war era. The focus of this study, however, is the comparatively brief but profoundly transformative forty-five-year period of Spanish-colonial occupation. For this purpose, the project area is more precisely defined as those areas of the park that have yielded archaeological remains dating to 1776–1821 (map 6). To date, these finds have been limited to two adjacent regions: the Main Post and the upper valley floor of the Tennessee Hollow Watershed, where three deposits have been identified. The most well-defined feature of this archaeological landscape is the external wall of the Presidio's main quadrangle as it stood from approximately 1815 onward. In practice, we have come to refer to the project area by two different designations: the architecturally defined quadrangle site, and the more amorphous "extramural areas" surrounding the quadrangle. While useful for resource management purposes, this practice most likely overstates the lived historical division of space, for there are many indications that the boundary between the main quadrangle and the surrounding landscape was often quite permeable and flexible.

Casual visitors walking through the project area today have little indication that the remains of a 230-year-old Spanish-colonial settlement lie beneath their feet.[4] The main quadrangle site is one of the most developed regions of the Presidio of San Francisco, covered with officers' quarters from the Victorian era and the early twentieth century, World War II barracks, a massive cold war–era concrete command center, and other twentieth-century structures. With few exceptions, the alignment of these structures and that of their associated streets nearly exactly traces the outline of the historical main quadrangle (fig. 10)—an effect produced by the U.S. Army practice of reusing and incrementally replacing extant Spanish-colonial buildings and facilities when the Americans first occupied the settlement in 1846. These buildings surround an enormous asphalt parking lot that itself covers much of the quadrangle's former plaza. The only standing remains of the Spanish-colonial and Mexican-era quadrangle are adobe walls that are encapsulated within portions of the historical Officers' Club. As of this writing, the Presidio Archaeology Center is directing the Officers' Club Adobe Initiative, which includes above-ground "excavation" of this architectural fabric, carefully removing layers of more recent construction materials that have obscured and protected the surviving adobe bricks (fig. 11).

The constant use of the quadrangle site has transformed its archaeological remains. The best preserved are those architectural elements and accumulated deposits that were below or at the average ground surface at the time of U.S. occupation in 1846. These include the foundations of buildings, such as post molds, stone foundations, and, in some cases, the lower courses of adobe brick walls. Occasionally, but not always, floor surfaces are still preserved, having been protected by layers of adobe wall and roof tile collapse. Midden deposits

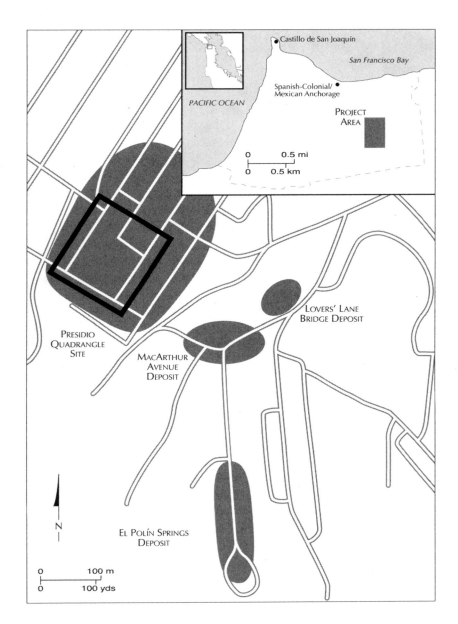

MAP 6.   Presidio of San Francisco, showing archaeological project area and major deposits.

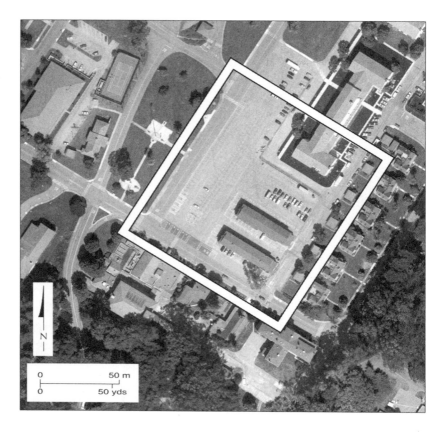

FIGURE 10. Relationship of the historical Presidio quadrangle to present-day streets and buildings in the Main Post.

are also generally well preserved because, for the most part, the colonial settlers disposed of their refuse in borrow pits, the broad depressions originally excavated to harvest the clay-rich subsoils for adobe brick and clay tile production. Consequently, many historical midden deposits lie beneath current grade and have been protected to various degrees from near-surface, ground-disturbing activities.

Most of the extramural area surrounding the main quadrangle was developed into suburban-style military housing, with the remaining lands designated as open space. Much of the region was drastically altered between the 1880s and the 1910s, when army landscapers planted a forest across much of the post to transform the formerly grassy coastal hills into a woodland landscape

FIGURE 11. Interior excavation of the Officers' Club to expose Spanish-colonial adobe walls and packed clay floors.

(Thompson and Woodbridge 1992:53). Consequently, the feel of the region surrounding the main quadrangle site is vastly different than it would have been during the Spanish-colonial, Mexican, and early American eras; the forest has reduced visibility by blocking sightlines and has increased the feeling of distance from one part of the project area to the other.

Archaeological field investigations in the project area have been ongoing since 1992 (table 4). Especially in the early years (1992–1996), most excavation projects were small undertakings aimed at answering specific questions about the presence or absence, location, and condition of architectural or depositional features within the main quadrangle site. Beginning in 1995, the scope of research expanded to include multiyear field investigations guided by comprehensive research designs. In 1997, research expanded further to include investigations of extramural areas outside the quadrangle itself. Until 1999, most field investigations were internally referenced: each proceeded according to field methods determined by the principal investigator in consultation with agency archaeologists, developing individual data points and project grids for each undertaking. Increasingly, site mapping, recordation, and field methods have been standardized under the leadership of the Presidio Archaeology Center, supporting current efforts to develop a comprehensive archaeological management plan for the site (Presidio Archaeology Center 2004).

Monitoring the Past

For the first five years of research (1992–1996), archaeological construction monitoring was the most commonly used method of investigating the Presidio site, with more than thirty monitoring projects undertaken during this period. Archaeological construction monitoring is not usually discussed in textbooks or taught in field schools, but in practice it is a widespread technique used to identify and assess archaeological resources under conditions that preclude preconstruction testing, such as the urban environment of the Presidio. The transformation of the army post into a National Park required innumerable ground-disturbing construction projects, including environmental clean-up efforts, utility work, and building rehabilitation. Planned, systematic archaeological monitoring has been an effective means of transforming these construction-related excavations into a broad-scale archaeological testing program.

At the Presidio, this systematic approach to archaeological monitoring is based on predictive models that identify sensitive locations for the discovery of prehistoric and historical archaeological resources. The first predictive models (Alley et al. 1993; Barker 1992) relied primarily on historical research commissioned by the National Park Service (Langellier and Rosen 1992; Thompson and

TABLE 4. Archaeological field investigations of El Presidio de San Francisco

Investigation	Type	Date	Lead Organizations	Technical Reports
Archaeological resources inventory	Pedestrian survey	1991	National Park Service (NPS)	Ivey 1991
Archaeological investigations related to Base Realignment and Closure (BRAC) and Defense Environmental Restoration Program (DERP)	Monitoring	November 1992–July 1996	Army Corps of Engineers (ACOE), Woodward-Clyde Consultants (WCC)	Voss and Benté 1996c, 1996d, 1996e
NPS-related archaeological monitoring	Monitoring	1995–1996	NPS, Dames and Moore	Dames and Moore 1995; Hale and Bevill 1997
Building 12 Field Investigation	Test excavation	June 8–9, 1993	ACOE, WCC	Voss and Benté 1996b
Officers' Quarters Excavation, Phase I	Test excavation	June 21–25, 1993	ACOE, WCC	Voss and Benté 1996b
Officers' Quarters Excavation, Phase II	Test excavation	October 4–8, 1993	ACOE, WCC	Voss and Benté 1996b
Pershing Square Field Investigation	Monitoring, test excavation	November 2–8, 1993	ACOE, WCC	Voss and Benté 1996b
Building 39 Excavation	Test excavation	March 28–April 1, 1994	ACOE, WCC	Voss and Benté 1996b
Building 15 Excavation	Test excavation	May 9–13, 1994	ACOE, WCC	Voss and Benté 1996b

(continued)

TABLE 4 (continued)

Investigation	Type	Date	Lead Organizations	Technical Reports
Sheridan Avenue Field Investigation	Monitoring, test excavation	May 26–31, 1994	ACOE, WCC	Voss and Benté 1996b
Wayside Exhibit Field Investigation	Monitoring, test excavation	September 16–22, 1994	NPS, WCC	Voss and Benté 1995
Geophysical investigation	Geophysical remote sensing	November 7–13, 1994	ACOE, WCC, and Golder and Associates	Cross and Burk 1995; Cross and Voss 1996
Building 49 seismic retrofit	Monitoring, test excavation	July–August 1995	NPS	L. Barker, personal communication, March 20, 2006
Fiber Optic Cable Installation Investigation	Monitoring, test excavation	February 7–12, 1996	ACOE, WCC	Voss and Benté 1996a
Archaeological groundtruthing	Test excavation	June 1–August 2, 1996	ACOE, URS Greiner Woodward Clyde	URS Greiner Woodward Clyde 1999
Chapel Investigations	Test excavation, excavation	Summer 1996, 1997, 1998, 1999, 2006	Cabrillo College, Golden Gate Parks Association, NPS, Presidio Trust (PT)	Simpson-Smith, Edwards, and Barker 1997; Simpson-Smith and Edwards 2000
Extramural survey	Shovel probe survey, test excavation	Summer 1997, fall 1997, and summer 1998	University of California, Berkeley (UCB), NPS	Voss 1999, 2001a, 2001b
San Francisco State University geophysical training	Geophysical remote sensing	Winter 1997 and summer 1998	San Francisco State University (SFSU), NPS	San Francisco State University 1997a, 1997b, 1997c, 1997d, 1998

Project	Activities	Dates	Institution	References
Officers' Club Mesa Room investigation	Subfloor excavation, architectural analysis	1998–2000	NPS, PT	L. Barker, personal communication, November 2, 2006
Building 39 Retrofit Investigation	Monitoring, test excavation, salvage data recovery	December 1998–January 1999	PT, NPS	E. Blind and L. N. Clevenger, personal communication, April 4, 2006; Hughes 2005; Origer 2005a, 2005b; Parr 2005
Funston Avenue Archaeological Research Project	Geophysical remote sensing, test excavation, excavation	Summer 1999 and 2000	UCB, PT	Ramsay and Voss 2002; Voss, Ramsay, and Naruta 2000
Tennessee Hollow Watershed Archaeology Project	Test excavation, excavation	Summer 2003, 2004, and 2005 (ongoing)	Stanford University, PT	Simmons 2006; Voss et al. 2004; Voss et al. 2005
Officers' Club Adobe Initiative	Structural stabilization, architectural analysis, test excavation, micromorphology, dendrochronology	2003–present (ongoing)	PT, NPS	Blind 2005; Blind and Bartoy 2006; Clevenger 2006; Crosby et al. 2004; Goldberg 2005; Rico 2006; Simmons 2006; Worthington 2006
Levantar	Site management and public interpretation	2004–present (ongoing)	PT, NPS	Presidio Archaeology Center 2004

Woodbridge 1992).[5] These initial models have been refined through continued analyses of historical maps, drawings, and photographs (Blind and Blakely 1999a, 1999b) and through landform modification studies that seek to identify naturally formed paleosols, soil erosion and deposition patterns, and historical episodes of grading and filling that have either promoted the formation and preservation of archaeological deposits or, alternatively, destroyed them (for example, Barnaal 2006; Meyer 2005). In the process, the predictive model has shifted from a two-dimensional printed map to a multidimensional interactive geographic information system (GIS) maintained by Presidio Archaeology Center staff. This approach has dramatically increased the precision and reliability of the predictive model, enabling Presidio Trust and NPS archaeologists to identify avoidance measures that protect both known and predicted archaeological resources.[6]

During monitoring, an archaeologist is present during ground-disturbing construction activities, observing soils as they are exposed and halting construction if an archaeological feature or deposit is discovered. The monitor also collects any artifacts found in the excavation back dirt, sometimes screening back dirt through a wire-mesh shaker screen to inspect excavated soils more closely for small artifacts. A daily report notes the location and dimensions of the construction excavation, describes any findings, and includes at least one diagram of the exposed soil stratigraphy. Most construction actions do not result in the discovery of archaeological deposits, but the cumulative compilation of stratigraphic data contributes to a general understanding of background soil conditions throughout the park. This system allows us to more easily recognize anomalous features, such as the concentration of stones described at the beginning of this chapter.

Overall, discovery-oriented monitoring at the Presidio has been most effective in identifying two kinds of Spanish-colonial archaeological resources. The first are durable architectural remains, such as the stone wall-foundations typical of later-phase constructions of the Presidio's main quadrangle. The second are depositional features with high artifact concentrations, especially midden deposits. Because of their strong visual signatures, architectural features and middens are easily recognized even during rapid excavation by a backhoe or grader. In such cases, construction excavation can be either routed around the archaeological feature or halted until the feature can be studied and recorded. In contrast, monitoring is less effective in identifying sheet scatters and subtle stratigraphic layers such as historical floor or yard surfaces.

Consequently, we have learned far more about the stone foundations that once supported the buildings of the main quadrangle than about any other type of archaeological remains. In comparison, we have collected very little information about more ephemeral forms of architecture or about patterns of spatial practices that were not defined by architectural features. Likewise, discovery of middens has spurred substantial investigations of these deposits, but, with notable exceptions (Voss 2002:526–584; Voss et al. 2005), there has been little research directed at recovering archaeological assemblages that could be attributed to a smaller-scale social units such as a neighborhood or household. Without doubt, this shapes the kinds of research questions that can be investigated as well as the ways such questions are answered.

Remote Sensing and Surveying

Although archaeological monitoring has been the primary means of detecting archaeological remains at the site, remote sensing and pedestrian surveys have also been used to detect archaeological deposits. Geophysical remote sensing refers to a suite of instrumental survey methods designed to detect anomalies in soil composition, density, moisture, and magnetism, which sometimes indicate the presence of archaeological features or deposits. Two major geophysical remote sensing studies were conducted within the main quadrangle site, the first in 1994 by Guy Cross (Cross and Voss 1996; Cross and Burk 1995) and the second in 1999 by Anna Naruta (2000).[7] Both studies relied on ground penetrating radar as their primary mode of detection, with additional information gathered through techniques that measure variations in the earth's magnetic field. In both studies, geophysical remote sensing was followed by excavation programs (described in the following section) used to evaluate the remote sensing findings (Ramsay and Voss 2002; URS Greiner Woodward Clyde 1999; Voss, Ramsay, and Naruta 2000).

Like archaeological monitoring, geophysical remote sensing has been most useful in predicting the locations of architectural remains in the main quadrangle. The stone foundations that once supported the settlement's adobe walls have a particularly strong and distinct reflective signature that can be positively identified with ground penetrating radar. Other anomalies identified through remote sensing have revealed depositional features such as middens and small pits, but the overall correspondence between anomalies and such archaeological deposits has been less reliable.

Outside the main quadrangle, I have used pedestrian surveys to identify Spanish-colonial and Mexican-era deposits and features in the surrounding landscape (Voss 1999). Because the lawns, meadows, and forests surrounding the Main Post have extremely low surface visibility, we have used shovel test survey techniques. Shovel test surveys combine conventional pedestrian survey with systematic subsurface testing. Crew members traverse the survey area on foot, mapping and collecting any surface findings and excavating small test pits, 12 inches in diameter, at 30-foot intervals. In addition to screening the excavated soil through ⅛-inch mesh and collecting any culturally modified materials, the survey crew records the stratigraphic profile revealed by each probe.

Like all field methods, shovel test surveys are more likely to detect certain kinds of archaeological resources.[8] This method is particularly well suited for discovering near-surface artifact scatters and features with a moderate and evenly dispersed artifact density—exactly the kinds of deposits that are less visible during archaeological monitoring and geophysical remote sensing. Linear features such as walls, roads, and aqueducts; deeply buried remains; and very small deposits are less likely to be detected, as are deposits from historical areas that have a very low artifact density, such as swept floors, yards, and plazas.

The shovel test survey collected 861 artifacts that clearly date to the Spanish-colonial and Mexican periods. Most of these are fragments of ceramic construction tiles (tejas and ladrillos); there are also thirty-two tableware ceramic sherds, two bottle glass shards, and a single glass bead that all conclusively date to the Spanish-colonial/Mexican era. Additionally, the survey recovered 457 artifacts that date to either the Spanish-colonial, Mexican, or early American periods (1776–ca. 1900). These include groundstone tools, flaked stone, wrought metal hardware, lead shot, animal bone, shell, charcoal, and additional bottle glass fragments and ceramic sherds whose manufacture spans the Spanish-colonial era through the early American occupation of the Presidio of San Francisco. The location of each find was plotted on the project area map; distinct clusters of artifacts were interpreted as likely indicators of archaeological sites and deposits.

In this manner, three distinct deposits were identified, all within the valley floor of the Tennessee Hollow Watershed. Each is located either at a springhead or at the confluence of two or more freshwater drainages. The artifacts recovered during the survey are congruent with what would be expected from residential deposits, an interpretation that has been substantiated through excavations at the southernmost site, El Polín Springs (Voss 2001a, Voss et al. 2004; Voss et al. 2005).

Excavation

Excavation is the next step after archaeological deposits and features have been identified through monitoring, geophysical remote sensing, or survey. The methods and techniques used in excavation at the Presidio have varied depending on the goal of each research project. However, since 1999, most excavation projects have been guided by best practices that include the following:

(a)   horizontal control of archaeological provenience in units of no greater than 4 feet squared or 1 meter squared

(b)   excavation following geological and cultural strata rather than arbitrary levels

(c)   use of the Harris Matrix system (Harris 1989; Harris, Brown, and Brown 1993) to record and analyze site stratigraphy and to control artifact provenience

(d)   wet-screening all recovered soils through 1/8-inch mesh to maximize artifact recovery

(e)   systematic soil sampling, including recovery of archive soil samples and flotation samples from each stratum in each unit

(f)   comprehensive recordation using standardized forms and photography

Map 7 shows the general areas where excavations have been conducted within or immediately adjacent to the main quadrangle of the Presidio.

Excavations of Quadrangle Architecture

Excavations of architectural remains in the main quadrangle site provide the empirical foundation for the analyses and interpretations presented in chapter 6. It is useful to briefly trace the sequence of research activities that generated this rich corpus of archaeological data about colonial architectural practices at El Presidio de San Francisco.

In response to the June 1993 discovery of the stone foundation in the Officers' Quarters 12 tank removal pit, the Army Corps of Engineers sponsored a series of small-scale test excavations with five goals in mind: to determine what historical building was represented by the stone foundation, to trace the extent of that building, to investigate its layout and construction, to compare the archaeological findings with extant historical plans, and to identify changes in the building over time. Test excavation units were located by projecting the alignment of the wall-foundation exposed in the tank removal pit. These excavations were conservative, consisting primarily of narrow, manually excavated units generally no greater than 30 inches deep, aiming only to expose the upper extent of the stone foundation. By October 1993, sufficient evidence had been obtained to determine that the archaeologically discovered foundations represented the eastern wing and northeast corner of the main quadrangle. Similar procedures were used in November 1993 and March 1994, when archaeological construction monitoring identified foundations in the west and

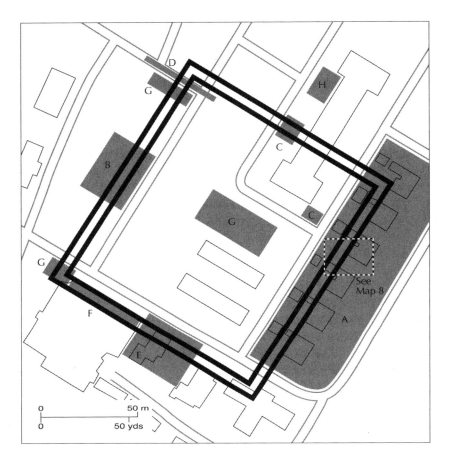

MAP 7. Presidio quadrangle site, showing project locations of major archaeological excavations. To conserve archaeological resources, only a small fraction of each shaded area has been sampled during excavations. A: Building 12 Field Investigation; Officers' Quarters Excavation, Phases I and II; Building 15 Excavation; Wayside Exhibit Field Investigation; Fiber Optic Cable Installation Investigation; Funston Avenue Archaeological Research Project. B: Pershing Square Field Investigation. C: Building 39 Excavation. D: Sheridan Avenue Field Investigation. E: Building 49 seismic retrofit; Chapel Investigations. F: Officers' Club Mesa Room investigation; Officers' Club Adobe Initiative. G: Archaeological groundtruthing. H: Building 39 Retrofit Investigation. See table 4 for project information.

north wings of the site. By the end of 1994, historical research and archaeological excavations had provided sufficient data to develop a working architectural plan of the main quadrangle of the Presidio (Voss 1996; Voss and Benté
1996a).

The second major phase of architectural research aimed to investigate the disparities between documentary and archaeological evidence regarding the size
and configuration of the main quadrangle. In brief, the archaeologically discovered quadrangle was 2.4 times larger in area than Spanish-colonial plan drawings and military records suggested. One working hypothesis, now substantially confirmed, postulated that the larger quadrangle was a later-phase
construction that replaced an earlier, smaller quadrangle. Geophysical remote
sensing (as described earlier) was used to identify soil anomalies that might
represent traces of these earlier buildings (Cross and Voss 1996; Cross and Burk
1995). Because most of the area under investigation lay beneath paved streets
and parking lots, mechanical backhoe and grader excavation served to groundtruth the findings of the remote sensing survey. Perhaps the most significant
findings of this research were the discovery of several post molds, perhaps from
a former palisade or wattle-and-daub wall, and an irregular linear alignment
of serpentine rocks that might represent a remnant of a foundation from an
earlier-phase construction (URS Greiner Woodward Clyde 1999).

Since 1996, archaeological investigation of the main quadrangle's architecture has shifted from broad-scale discovery to more focused investigations of
specific regions of the quadrangle. The first of these are the Chapel Investigations, a research program spurred by the discovery of Spanish-colonial architectural features during a seismic retrofit project. The Chapel Investigations
excavated portions of the southern wing of the main quadrangle, exposing architectural remains of the settlement's chapel and sacristy, the quadrangle's
southern exterior wall, and portions of adjacent structures. Through careful attention to site stratigraphy and correlation with historical documents, the researchers identified a detailed sequence of construction/demolition episodes
spanning the years 1784 to 1826 (Simpson-Smith and Edwards 2000:40–44).
These data highlight the dynamic architectural history of the main quadrangle.
(Clothing-related artifacts recovered during this project are included in an analysis of colonial dress in chapter 10.)

The Funston Avenue Archaeological Research Project was the second major
investigation to focus on a specific region of the quadrangle. In this case, field
research was initiated to aid the Presidio Trust in planning for the rehabilitation
of the thirteen Victorian-era Officers' Quarters (Buildings 4–16) on Funston Avenue, an area that encompasses the eastern wing of the main quadrangle. The

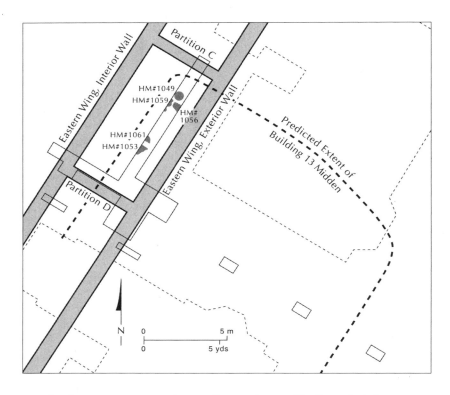

MAP 8. Summer 2000 excavations on Funston Avenue. The linear shaded areas indicate the stone foundations of the eastern wing of the expanded Presidio quadrangle. Smaller shaded areas indicate hearth features located within the one-room apartment. The heavy dashed line shows the estimated extent of the Building 13 midden. Lighter dashed lines show outlines of the present-day Officers' Quarters.

two-year field research program began in summer 1999 with a geophysical survey and test excavations throughout the entire Funston Avenue housing area (Voss, Ramsay, and Naruta 2000). In summer 2000, excavations were concentrated in an area that contained not only well-preserved architectural features but also depositional features such as floor deposits, trash middens, and borrow pits (Ramsay and Voss 2002) (map 8).

The Funston Avenue project contributed two major findings regarding the architectural history of the main quadrangle. First, the excavations further substantiated the hypothesis that the larger, archaeologically identified main quadrangle was constructed fairly late in the settlement's history. The archaeological excavations encountered a remarkably well-preserved stratigraphic sequence representing fifteen major depositional episodes, which together included fifty-nine stratigraphic units (Voss 2002:367–382) (fig. 12). The stone wall-foundations of the main quadrangle had been constructed in trenches that had been dug into an earlier Spanish-colonial era deposit, the Building 13 midden (fig. 12, IV). Artifact analyses indicate that the midden accumulated primarily ca. 1776–1800; the upper extent of the midden also includes a very small number of artifacts manufactured ca. 1800–1810. This indicates that the eastern wing of the expanded quadrangle was constructed post-1810, at least thirty-five years after the settlement was founded.

Second, research on Funston Avenue revealed detailed information about the architectural production of the expanded quadrangle's eastern wing. The archaeological evidence indicates that the eastern wing was built in a single construction episode. The massive, load-bearing foundations that form the interior and exterior facades of the eastern wing are continuous, without breaks or seams at the corners of rooms (fig. 12, V). Packed clay was emplaced to level interior floors prior to internal partitioning (fig. 12, VI). The space between the two foundations was then partitioned at regular intervals to create one-room apartments measuring 6 varas wide and 12 varas long (fig. 12, VII). (A *vara* is a Spanish measure of length, usually equivalent to about 33 inches and often translated into English as a yard.)

The most recent investigation of the main quadrangle's architecture is the Officers' Club Adobe Initiative, which combines the architectural research needed for structural stabilization of this unreinforced masonry building with archaeological study of both the standing historical fabric and the floor surfaces and substrata. Among the many findings of this study, two have particular relevance to the investigation of the quadrangle's architectural history. The first is that the Officers' Club adobe walls may be remnants of one of the earlier buildings constructed at the colonial settlement. The second is evidence of substantial remodeling episodes, including the construction of at least one new partition wall, later in the history of the building's use (Blind 2005; Blind and Bartoy 2006; Clevenger 2006; Goldberg 2005).

The archaeological investigation of the main quadrangle's dynamic architectural history is far from complete, and plans for continued research and public interpretation are already in development (Presidio Archaeology Center 2004). Archaeological monitoring, geophysical remote sensing, and excavation have, however, generated a solid working plan of a larger, expanded quadrangle constructed ca. 1815. Measuring 192 varas north-south and 172 varas east-west, this main quadrangle was constructed all of a piece, using uniform construction methods and materials. Archaeological traces of earlier architectural

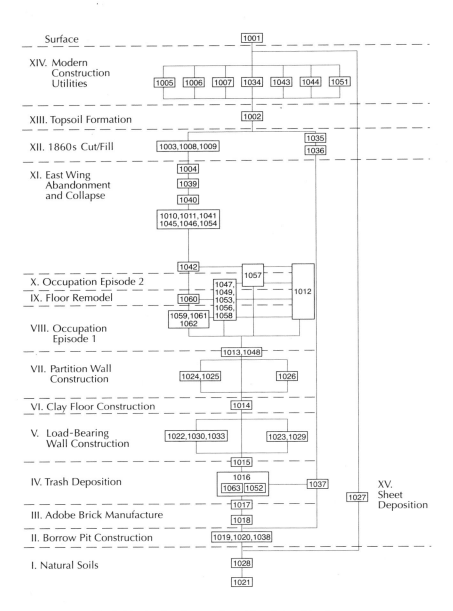

Surface   1001

XIV. Modern
     Construction
     Utilities   1005   1006   1007   1034   1043   1044   1051

XIII. Topsoil Formation   1002

XII. 1860s Cut/Fill   1003,1008,1009   1035   1036

XI. East Wing
    Abandonment
    and Collapse   1004   1039   1040   1010,1011,1041 1045,1046,1054

X. Occupation Episode 2   1042   1057   1012

IX. Floor Remodel   1060   1047, 1049, 1053, 1056, 1058   1059,1061 1062

VIII. Occupation
     Episode 1   1013,1048

VII. Partition Wall
     Construction   1024,1025   1026

VI. Clay Floor Construction   1014

V. Load-Bearing
   Wall Construction   1022,1030,1033   1023,1029

     1015

IV. Trash Deposition   1016   1063 1052   1037   1027   XV. Sheet Deposition

III. Adobe Brick Manufacture   1017   1018

II. Borrow Pit Construction   1019,1020,1038

I. Natural Soils   1028   1021

FIGURE 12.   Harris Matrix showing stratigraphic relationships between deposits excavated in summer 2000, Funston Avenue Archaeological Research Project.

structures have been more elusive, both because the area in which they are most likely to be found is largely covered with roads and parking lots and because the architectural materials and techniques themselves, such as wood palisade or wattle-and-daub, leave much subtler archaeological signatures than stone wall-foundations. In chapter 7, the archaeological data gathered through the investigations described here is revisited, in dialogue with evidence gathered from historical text and visual representations.

Excavations of Residential Space

Archaeological deposits formed during the occupation of residential units within the main quadrangle are rare at the site of the Presidio; in most areas, American-period grading either obliterated such deposits or severely compromised their integrity. However, the summer 2000 excavations on Funston Avenue encountered well-preserved floor deposits located within an apartment in the eastern wing of the expanded quadrangle (see fig. 12, VIII, IX, X). The excavation strategy used to sample these floor deposits was straightforward: first, the partition walls segmenting the eastern wing into individual rooms were located using test excavations; and second, two perpendicular trenches were excavated to obtain samples of floor deposits and to expose stratigraphic profiles. The excavation exposed about 25 percent of the room's total area. As would be expected from a floor deposit with a relatively short period of occupation (ca. 1815–1825), the accumulated deposits are very thin: the total volume of excavated soil attributed to the occupation of the room is only 0.63 cubic meters.

The excavation revealed four hearth features—discrete deposits of charcoal- and ash-rich, heat-affected soil—associated with the occupation of the apartment (see map 8). One was a well-defined circular deposit with evidence of multiple episodes of use. The others were more amorphous but nonetheless spatially discrete deposits that also evidenced in situ burning. All are either set into or rest immediately on top of the apartment's packed clay floor. All the soils excavated from these deposits were collected for flotation to recover charred plant remains, yielding a total of 8,379 botanical specimens. This rich assemblage of botanical specimens from the hearth contexts is unparalleled in archaeological studies of presidios and provides an important source of evidence for investigating human-plant interactions at El Presidio de San Francisco. These data figure in subsequent discussions of landscape (chapter 6) and foodways (chapter 9).

Excavation of Midden Deposits

The Spanish-colonial and Mexican-era residents of the Presidio disposed of their household refuse in community middens. Most middens were located in borrow pits, which had been excavated in order to harvest clay soil for adobe brick and ceramic tile production, a typical practice in Spanish-colonial settlements throughout western North America. These middens contain dense concentrations of material culture and dietary refuse, allowing researchers to obtain a large sample of artifacts and other materials through excavation of a relatively small area. The greatest interpretive asset of middens is their association with a community group rather than with individuals or households. Instead of reflecting fluctuations in the composition of individual households or activities, middens present the dominant trends in material and dietary practices within the community as a whole.

At the Presidio, seven midden deposits have been identified, all named after nearby buildings or landscape features (map 9). One of these—the Building 13 midden—is an archaeological gem, one of those rare sealed contexts that have excellent integrity and tight chronological definition. Materials found in this midden provide the primary empirical evidence for chapters 8, 9, and 10.

As noted earlier, the Building 13 midden was discovered in 1999 during test excavations aimed at identifying architectural remains of the east wing of the expanded main quadrangle. To our great surprise, we discovered the midden deposit *underneath* the wall-foundations and clay floors of the east wing. This meant that the midden must have been formed before the new expanded quadrangle was constructed. We returned to this location in summer 2000 and conducted systematic excavations of both the midden and the architectural remains above it. The resulting data allowed us to reconstruct the sequence of events that first created and then sealed this midden deposit. First, a shallow pit (2–3 feet deep) was excavated to harvest clay-rich soils for adobe brick and, possibly, for ceramic production (see fig. 12, II). At the time that the pit was excavated, it was located to the east of the main quadrangle. Its known extent measures approximately 80 feet east-west and 40 feet north-south, with an estimated minimum area of 2,500 square feet. For a short time, the pit was used for wetting the clay-rich soils and mixing them with sand, straw, and manure—tempering materials that increase the durability of adobe bricks (see fig. 12, III). A small layer of this mixture remains at the base of the pit. The colonial settlers began using the pit for refuse disposal before the layer of tempered clay had fully dried, allowing a few large and heavy objects to sink into the wet muck. Most of the refuse accumulated above this layer and in time formed a deposit of very dark grayish brown, loamy silt with dense concentrations of household refuse, butchery waste, and charcoal. As noted earlier, most of the deposit accumulated between 1776 and 1800, with a few materials added ca. 1800–1810 (see fig. 12, IV).[9] The midden was then sealed by a thick layer of clay packed on top of the

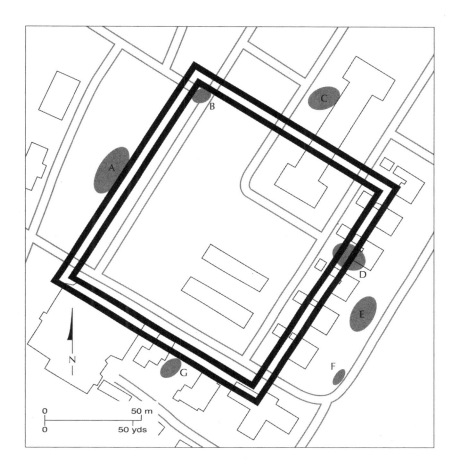

MAP 9.   Midden deposits in the vicinity of the Presidio quadrangle.
A: Pershing Square household waste deposit. B: Sheridan Avenue borrow pit/
disposal pit. C: Building 39 midden. D: Building 13 midden. E: Building 15
midden. F: Building 16 midden. G: Building 49 midden.

trash deposit, in order to create a floor surface for apartments in the new eastern wing of the expanded quadrangle (see fig. 12, VI).

The excavations intersected 200 square feet of the midden, an area equivalent to roughly 8 percent of the deposit's known horizontal extent. The volume of soil excavated from the midden totaled 140 cubic feet (4 cubic meters).
More than 37,400 archaeological specimens were recovered; collectively, these
materials weigh 49,586.2 g. Table 5 summarizes the frequency of specific ma-

TABLE 5. Materials recovered from the Building 13 midden,
by counts, weight, and relative frequencies

Material Type	Count	Weight (g)	Frequency by Count (%)	Frequency by Weight (%)
Construction ceramics	4,240	8,277.6	11.33	16.69
Household ceramics	7,467	12,302.6	19.96	24.81
Glass	157	102.3	0.42	0.21
Lithics	177	581.5	0.47	1.17
Metals	436	1,428.8	1.17	2.88
Bone	~22,000	26,601.9	58.80	53.65
Shell	126	16.0	0.34	0.03
Botanicals (including charcoal)	2,809	275.5	7.51	0.56
TOTAL	37,412	49,586.2	100.00	100.00

terial types, both by count and by weight.[10] By either measure, the most frequent type of material recovered from the Building 13 midden deposit is animal bone (nearly 59 percent by count, 54 percent by weight). The remaining materials include household ceramics, construction ceramics, glass, lithics, metal objects, shell, and botanical remains.

The Building 13 midden provides an important body of evidence for this study of colonial ethnogenesis. Not only does the midden have exceptional archaeological integrity, but it also dates to the exact period when colonial identities were undergoing rapid transformation through individual manipulation of the sistema de castas and the emergence of a shared Californio identity. The contents of the Building 13 midden thus afford a rare opportunity to examine the material routines of a community in transition.

. . .

As the foregoing demonstrates, investigating an urban archaeological site like the Presidio is methodologically and logistically challenging. Because of the urban landscape covering the quadrangle site, statistically driven sampling programs and large-scale exposures of room blocks or plaza areas are currently not feasible. Instead, we excavate in the grassy medians along well-traveled streets and jogging paths and in parking lots and the narrow yards surrounding former military housing, and we inspect the earth displaced by construction projects for indications of previously unknown deposits. The accumulated information gained from monitoring programs, geophysical remote sensing, surveys, and smaller-scale excavations can be brought together to provide a rich body of evidence about the colonial community that once lived on this wind-swept and fog-shrouded plateau and to afford a new perspective on social life in San Francisco's colonial era.

PART 2   SPATIAL AND MATERIAL
              PRACTICES

The importance of landscape in the study of colonial ethnogenesis in Alta California is far from coincidence. After all, the colonial settlers took their new collective ethnonym, Californios, from the toponym of the province. In doing so, they grafted themselves onto the land, and the reproduction and transformation of social identities became entangled with the reproduction and transformation of place. The strong bonds between colonial identity and place are a reminder that, at its most fundamental level, the colonization of Alta California was a transformation of spatial relations (Cook 1943): an appropriation of indigenous lands for colonial ends, and the ongoing movement of diverse human populations across both short and long distances as a means to accomplish these ends.

For the military settlers at El Presidio de San Francisco, making the landscape their own was an ongoing project, one that first and foremost involved military undertakings to secure indigenous lands as colonized space. The military presence was intertwined with building and infrastructure construction, agricultural endeavors, and projects that harvested raw materials (both organic and mineral) from the land. In addition to these deliberate actions, new habitual patterns of land use gradually began to form, related to daily movement, travel, trash disposal, and other activities. Through all these practices, the military settlers shaped a new land for themselves and shaped themselves to fit this new land.

The relationship between social identity and landscape is a recursive one.

Space, writes social geographer Allan Pred (1990:26), "is both the medium and the outcome of human agency and social relations." The intimate connection between space and identity stems from the body's material continuity—the uninterrupted path through space and time that is traced through each person's life. Collective and individual identities are formed in part through patterns of bodily movements that generate knowledge of one's place in the world and one's relationship to the social order. Feelings of being "lost," "out of place," or "in the right place" are practical expressions of this knowledge. Power is thus often materialized through control of space and bodily movement. Even the most mundane routines socialize people into prescribed roles and rules through the repetition of bodily practices (Bourdieu 1980; Butler 1990, 1993a). Michel Foucault (1975) particularly draws attention to physical manipulations of space (for example, buildings and structures) as power-laden technologies that control the movement of the body.

Simultaneously, it is through bodily movement that people are capable of transforming their world by taking social action, for the meaning of a place is produced through the interactions and activities that occur there. Anthony Giddens approached this social production of place by employing two closely related concepts: locale and regionalization. Locales are physical sites where social interactions occur; regionalization refers to the patterned differentiation among locales (Giddens 1984:110–131). Regionalization includes such phenomena as the construction of an unevenly developed built environment, the shaping of land-use patterns, the appropriation and transformation of natural resources and natural landscape features, the generation of patterns of movement, and the accrual of symbolic meaning to certain places (Pred 1990:10). Although it is not always deliberate, regionalization is never random or meaningless.

Through regionalization, power is materially expressed and materially contested. Space, like identity, is never homogeneous or fixed. Although there is often a persistent connection between place and community—as with the Californios and Alta California—there are always, in fact, multiple communities moving within and through contested and contingent places (Massey 1994). As chapter 3 describes more fully, the Presidio settlement housed a complex and diverse population: colonists and indigenous peoples; persons with varying mixtures of African, Mesoamerican Indian, Native Californian, and European heritage; officers, soldiers, auxiliaries, and civilians; prisoners and wage laborers; men and women; children and adults. As this heterogeneous population coalesced into certain larger social collectivities and at other times fractured into smaller affiliations and groupings, as people sought solidarity and mutual rapport with some and differentiated themselves from others, these constant negotiations of social boundaries occurred in and through spatial relationships. However, we must avoid simple conflations of social boundaries with spatial boundaries. At times, social difference is expressed and achieved through separation; but at other times, it is close proximity that allows the continued enactment of hierarchy and differentiation.

This chapter considers the interplay between landscape and colonial ethno-genesis on four interrelated scales. The first is the role of military regulations and policy, especially the Bourbon Reforms, in structuring the colonial landscape of Alta California. The second explores the spatial organization of colonial military aggression and defense in the San Francisco Bay area. Third, we turn to El Presidio de San Francisco, tracing the diachronic production of the settlement's immediate landscape and observing how space was socially produced at the scale of community life through a dialectic between military ideals and local practices. The fourth scale allows us to consider individual experience of identity and landscape through an archaeological exploration of the spatial life-history of one colonial woman, Juana Briones. This multiscalar approach to landscape analysis highlights the ongoing play between institution and community, and between structure and practice, in the transformation of social identities.

Geometry, Symmetry, Rationality: Colonization and Spatial Order

El Presidio de San Francisco was established during a period when the spatial practices of colonization were under increasing scrutiny. In 1764, King Carlos III had initiated a comprehensive reform of military institutions in the Spanish-colonial Americas. Like the larger body of Bourbon Reforms of which this was a part, the new military regulations applied principles of Enlightenment thought in the hope of reducing expenditures and improving Spain's hold on its diminishing New World territories. Codified in the 1772 Reglamento (Brinkerhoff and Faulk 1965), the reforms ordered the centralization of presidio administration and a systematic spatial reordering of frontier defenses throughout the Interior Provinces of New Spain. These directives were formulated and implemented, often over the objections of local commanders, by military engineers and tactical officers who had been born and trained in Europe. In focusing on the spatial order of frontier defenses, the 1772 Reglamento embraced Enlightenment philosophies of space that viewed architecture and landscape as mechanisms for social engineering (Etlin 1995; Foucault 1975; Markus 1993; Vidler 1987). By aiming to transform the presidios of the Interior Provinces into a precisely regulated defensive clockwork, the 1772 Reglamento articulated a vision of a frontier defense system that would be coherent, effective, mechanical, and rational (Voss 2007).

The 1772 Reglamento was a sharp departure from earlier military policies under which each presidio had developed largely in response to local conditions. The new policies replaced these diverse local tactics with two centralized strategies: the defensive cordon and the architectural master plan, both of which employed the concepts of enclosure and exclusion in frontier defense.

Defensive Cordons and the Geography of Threat

The defensive cordons were envisioned as military defense perimeters that would create an impenetrable boundary between colonized regions of New Spain and those areas still controlled by indigenous tribal groups. Between 1771 and 1776, the military command ordered the abandonment of the majority of existing presidios and established new ones along an east-west line that would come to approximate the present-day border between the United States and Mexico. This cordon of presidios, ideally spaced 40 leagues (about 100 miles) apart, formed a chain of positional defenses. The 1772 Reglamento specified that the area between each presidio on the cordon would be protected by patrols following a tightly regulated schedule. To complement this east-west cordon, a new north-south cordon was created by expanding the existing line of settlement on the Baja California peninsula northward into Alta California (map 10). In addition to containing indigenous resistance in the interior of the continent, the California cordon provided a coastal line of defense against maritime encroachment by other European nations. Thus, in Alta California, the cordon faced military threats on two fronts.[1]

The cordon strategy structured Alta California's colonial landscape along two roughly perpendicular axes. The first traversed the length of the colonized coastal zone. Although roughly trending north-south, this axis curved along the shores of strategically vulnerable inlets such as the Monterey and San Francisco bays; there, presidios were supplemented with castillos and baterías to further strengthen coastal defenses. This coastal axis was the main artery of the colonized world along which people, goods, raw materials, and information traveled from settlement to settlement.

The second axis, from west to east, ran from the waters of the Pacific Ocean through the colonized coastal zone and on to the interior mountain ranges and valleys. This axis traced gradients of risk and danger. To the west, the sea signaled the ever-present threat of foreign encroachment.[2] To the east, the interior lands were zones of active military contest between colonists and Native Californians. Moving east from the coastal zone beyond the edges of direct colonial occupation, this axis traversed three clines: areas left almost entirely vacant by both colonists and Native Californians; zones of direct colonial-indigenous contact and military conflict; and regions beyond direct colonial

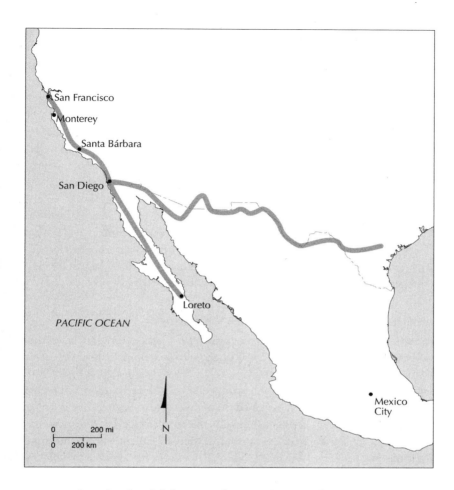

MAP 10. Spanish-colonial defensive cordons in western North America.
Adapted in part from Brinkerhoff and Faulk 1965.

incursion where Native Californians were faced with the indirect effects of colonization (disease vectors, environmental change, population movement inland from colonized areas, and introduction of new material culture through down-the-line trade). Although the boundaries of these areas were in constant negotiation, these regions corresponded roughly with the coastal mountain ranges, the Central Valley, and the Sierra foothills and mountains. Colonial movement into these areas was always tactical: explorations to gain knowledge of unfamiliar landscapes and the peoples who lived there, recruiting parties to enroll indigenous people as mission neophytes or presidio laborers, and military expeditions to harass, punish, and conquer those perceived as a threat to the colonial undertaking.[3]

The structured orientation of the colonial landscape was strongly gendered. Along the north-south coastal axis, both female and male settlers participated fully in colonial endeavors. Yet with rare exceptions, the only colonists to traverse the east-west axis were adult male soldiers and priests. A matter of practice rather than policy, this gendered pattern of movement created a region of colonial activity in which colonial women were largely absent. Not coincidentally, the east-west axis was also sexualized. During some expeditions to the interior, colonial soldiers deployed rape as an unofficial but widely accepted military tactic. The eastern inland thus became what Joane Nagel (2000, 2003) terms an "ethnosexual frontier"—in this case, a zone of interethnic sexual violence perpetrated by colonial men on Native Californians (Castillo 1994a; Hurtado 1999; Voss 2000a). The formation of the north-south coastal cordon was structured by military policy, but the accompanying gendered and sexualized regionalization emerged through local routines of movement and interethnic violence.

Architectural Master Plans: Defense and Surveillance

In addition to applying Enlightenment principles of spatial order in the formation of defensive cordons, the 1772 Reglamento also stipulated that the architecture of each presidio must conform to a master plan designed by military engineer Don Nicolás de Lafora.[4] Notably, this was the first and only time that the Spanish colonial military specified the architecture to be used in constructing frontier presidios.[5] In establishing this master plan, the 1772 Reglamento politicized architectural practices at colonial military settlements. Architectural decisions that had once been made locally, by presidio captains and the soldiers and families under their command, now had broader significance in terms of compliance with or deviation from the colonial master plan.

The 1772 Reglamento's plan for presidio construction turned to the aesthetics of the European Enlightenment, bringing geometric symmetry and principles of enclosure and surveillance into military architecture (fig. 13). It ordered that presidios should take the form of a rectilinear quadrangle and should be

> strengthened, constructing them according to the plan of the same engineer [Lafora]. . . . [and] that the buildings be done in accordance with the new plan, the exterior walls are to be built first of adobes, with two small bastions in the angles; afterward on the interior will be built the chapel, the guardhouse, residences for the captain, officers and chaplain, and quarters for the soldiers and Indians, sheltering everyone during the construction in campaign tents and temporary barracks. (Brinkerhoff and Faulk 1965:49, 63)[6]

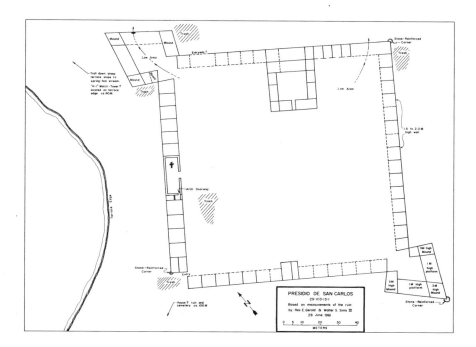

FIGURE 13. Archaeological plan of El Presidio de San Carlos. The plan of this presidio quadrangle is generally viewed as reflecting the architectural requirements of the 1772 Reglamento and the related master plan developed by Lafora, no copy of which has yet been found (Gerald 1968:36).

As anchor points of the defensive cordon, presidio quadrangles were designed to withstand siege and hold the line. Visual surveillance was central to this plan: lookouts stationed in each presidio's bastions and along the ramparts of its exterior wall would provide early warning of attack. At the first sign of danger, the community could enclose itself within the quadrangle's solid adobe exterior. The bastions also provided the tactical advantage of crossfire along all four exterior walls, improving defense of the compound's perimeter.

As chapter 7 discusses at greater length, it is clear that the military settlers at El Presidio de San Francisco chose to follow certain architectural stipulations and ignore others. Designs for the quadrangle, drawn in 1776, 1795, and 1796, all indicate that the settlement's commanders intended, at least on paper, to comply with the master plan. Indeed, archaeological and historical research shows that the settlement's central compound was always a constellation of buildings arrayed in a rectilinear quadrangle, facing inward toward a central plaza. However, the Presidio never met regulation standards for defensive capabilities. This finding seems especially surprising when we recall the settlement's primary purpose: to provide security and defense against both indigenous and foreign aggressors.

The 1772 master plan embedded three core defensive attributes in presidio design: complete enclosure, a defensive wall, and bastions. Complete enclosure of the settlement was perhaps the most fundamental building block of defense. The archaeological and historical evidence indicates that El Presidio de San Francisco's quadrangle was enclosed for only three brief periods: 1776–1779, 1792–ca. 1800, and 1816–1823. During the first two periods, the enclosure was more symbolic than tactical, achieved not with solid adobe but with wooden palisade, described in 1777 as "slight fences of sticks" (Governor Felipe de Neve quoted in Bancroft 1886a:331). Only in the 1815 construction of the third, enlarged quadrangle was the settlement enclosed with adobe walls; and even this was not completed until 1819, when sixteen Native Californian war captives "were put to work as forced labor . . . making adobes to replace the last of the wooden sections of the wall" (Langellier and Rosen 1996:140). Thus, for most of its history, the settlement was extremely permeable. It seems that the eastern (inland) side of the quadrangle was almost always the least protected, often standing entirely open without any buildings to create even the illusion of enclosure.

The second defensive attribute required by the 1772 Reglamento was a separate defense wall surrounding the perimeter of the quadrangle, intended to fortify the settlement's enclosure. Indeed, this exterior wall was to be constructed first, before any other buildings. Although no archaeological or historical evidence suggests that a *separate* defense wall was ever constructed at the Presidio, there are indications that builders paid special attention to the settlement's exterior facades.[7] Excavations have revealed that the exterior, or rear, walls of the quadrangle's buildings were often a few centimeters thicker than the interior walls that faced the central plaza (Ramsay and Voss 2002; Simpson-Smith and Edwards 2000; Voss 1996). Additionally, short wall segments were constructed to close gaps between some of the individual structures. However, given that the quadrangle was rarely completely enclosed, if at all, questions arise about whether these wall segments were constructed with defense in mind.

There is also no clear evidence of bastions—the third defensive attribute—at El Presidio de San Francisco. None of the colonial records of the Presidio's construction refer to bastions, nor do accounts by foreign visitors, which were extremely detailed and paid close attention to defensive capabilities. Likewise, none of the as-built diagrams and drawings or paintings of the quadrangle show bastions. There is, however, one tantalizing piece of archaeological evidence: a series of stone foundations that were exposed during test excavations immediately outside the quadrangle's northwest corner (URS Greiner Woodward Clyde 1999). The building represented by these foundations remains unknown, but the foundations are in an appropriate area to have been part of a bastion if one was ever constructed.

Bringing the Battle Home

Although colonial regulations dictated that presidio architecture be defensible, in practice the quadrangle at El Presidio de San Francisco rarely was, lacking complete enclosure, a separate defensive wall, and bastions. This absence of defensive capability certainly suggests a lack of fear by the military settlers that their homes, workshops, administrative offices, and storage buildings would be attacked. Had such a threat been perceived, the settlers would have no doubt made the defense of the quadrangle their first priority. We should not, however, misread this absence of defensive architecture as evidence that the colonial occupation of San Francisco was peaceful. Rather, colonial-indigenous violence was spatially segregated from daily life at El Presidio de San Francisco because of the dialectical relationship between colonial military tactics and Native Californian strategies of resistance and survival.

While the cordon was intended to function as a static barrier to indigenous and foreign incursion, the military command at El Presidio de San Francisco seems to have taken to heart the maxim that the best defense is a good offense. The colonial military attacked Native Californians in their own inland villages, regionalizing armed conflict farther and farther inland. Sexualization of military conflict through rape and sexual assault also terrorized Native Californian communities.

Native Californians were not passive in the face of colonial assaults. Although some historians assume that the colonists' technology (muskets, metal swords, and horses) was key in enabling such a small number of frontier soldiers to colonize Alta California, to the contrary, it was cultural differences in approach to warfare that gave the colonial military a distinct advantage. Armed conflict was not unknown among Alta California's precolonial indigenous societies, but among the coastal tribes most affected by colonization, intertribal warfare before contact with the colonizers consisted primarily of "highly ritualized forms of combat governed by rules designed to minimize fatalities" (Walker, Lambert, and DeNiro 1989:359). The willingness of colonial soldiers to kill large numbers of people was overwhelming to indigenous communities whose traditional combat strategies minimized casualties by using the tactics of assassination, flight, surrender, and negotiation. For some Native Californian communities, joining the missions was a tactical choice that at the time appeared to offer refuge from attacks by Presidio soldiers. Others formed fugitive communities in remote locations, defending themselves with elaborate systems of ditches, earthwork berms, and palisade fortifications (Castillo 1989:392; Milliken 1995:157; Phillips 1993; Voss 2000a). Both of these tactical responses solidified the formation of a no-man's-land between the colonized coastal cordon and the inland areas still occupied by indigenous communities.

El Presidio de San Francisco, although spatially removed from the front lines of conflict, was not insulated from the impact of colonial violence. Soldiers met violent deaths in mission uprisings and during inland battles; others returned home wounded and maimed. Nearly all colonial men carried physical scars of interethnic violence. Every monthly troop roster included a list of invalid soldiers on temporary or permanent leave from active duty.

Further, most inland military expeditions ended by marching war captives back to the colonized coastal zones. Soldiers deposited Native Californian women and children at the mission nearest the combat but usually brought captive men all the way back to the Presidio. There, captives were tried for their "crimes" and sentenced to corporal punishment (administered in public view in the quadrangle's central plaza) and forced labor. It was not unusual for captive Native Californian men to outnumber the colonial men resident in the settlement. At the Presidio, the colonists lived among their captured enemies and came to depend on their labor for the sustenance and maintenance of the settlement.

El Presidio de San Francisco was thus the cause—but rarely the location—of intercultural colonial warfare. The homes of the military settlers were largely removed from the routine skirmishes, punitive expeditions, and daily enforcement of discipline that characterized military interactions with Native Californians. The open, unfortified spatial organization of the military settlement must be understood in the context of the broader regionalization of the landscape, which segregated the coastal axis of colonial life from the inland locales of violence and struggle.

The Presidio Landscape

Regionalization, as noted earlier, is always meaningful, even when it is not deliberately achieved. In the institutional context of Spanish-colonial San Francisco, many spatial patterns were more intentional than not. At the very least, military regulations, church doctrine, and civilian laws set uniform standards for the spatial organization of colonial settlements, so that, at a fundamental level, spatial practices were measured by the extent to which they conformed with or deviated from such standards.

Nodes of Social Interaction, Layers of Practice and Meaning

Colonial San Francisco was dominated by two primary nodes of social interaction: El Presidio de San Francisco and Mission San Francisco de Asís (map 11). Linked by a well-traveled pathway capable of accommodating oxen carts, the settlements were less than four miles apart—a distance readily traversed on foot or horseback. These two institutions and the road between them constituted a local segment of the longer coastal axis of colonial Alta California. In the 1790s, two additional colonial nodes of activity—El Castillo de San Joaquín (1792) and La Batería de San José (1797)—were built along the coastal waterfront to provide additional defense against potential maritime encroachment. Other than these extensions of the presidio's military installations, San Francisco remained relatively undeveloped until the 1830s, when the Pueblo of Yerba Buena was chartered and former colonial soldiers began to receive rancho land grants.

The settlement of El Presidio de San Francisco can be conceptualized as a constellation of interrelated buildings, infrastructure facilities, and land use areas. The spatial anchor for the settlement was its main quadrangle. Located on a small plateau, the quadrangle was well situated for surveillance and afforded good views of the entrance to the San Francisco Bay and the bayshore. The establishment of the main quadrangle shifted the center of the cultural landscape inland and uphill from the bayshore. Flanked on the east and west by two riparian valleys, and on the south by sharply rising hills, the quadrangle also imposed a measured grid on the landscape; its rectilinear lines marked a decisive shift from the indigenous practice of aligning buildings with the contours of waterways and landforms.

In its idealized form, the quadrangle would have simultaneously facilitated landscape surveillance and channeled the focus of colonial life inward onto itself. If built to specifications, its bastions would have commanded views not only of the entrance to the bay but also of the surrounding hills and valleys, while its unbroken exterior walls would have directed the movements and gaze of its residents toward the plaza that functioned as the community's central gathering place. But in practice, this was not the case. The main quadrangle was rarely enclosed. Its facades were permeable, especially to the east, disrupting the internal focus of the community and facilitating connections between "inside" and "outside" spaces. This suggests a certain ambiguity: the quadrangle was a physical materialization of the colonial military presence in San Francisco, but its borders were more symbolic than effective, clearly demarcated yet easily traversed.

Beyond the quadrangle, the spatial development of the Presidio departed from the colonial grid and more closely followed the topographic and riparian features of the landscape. These extramural locales mediated the interface between

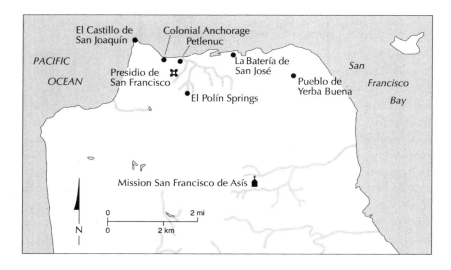

MAP 11.   Major settlements and facilities in colonial San Francisco.

the main quadrangle and the aboriginal landscape, creating a transitional zone that extended the spatial reach of the Presidio far beyond the quadrangle itself.

Archaeological monitoring and shovel test surveys have found that the areas immediately outside the main quadrangle contain a continuous scatter of artifacts as well as discrete features such as borrow pits, middens, and roasting pits. Here, the archaeological record retains traces of a wide range of productive activities: making adobe bricks, butchering animals, roasting food in prepared pits, burning shell and bone to produce lime for plaster, and disposing of trash. However, such activities were not confined to these extramural areas. To date, excavations in the main plaza area have been very limited, but one did uncover a scatter of angular sandstone fragments that might indicate a stoneworking area (URS Greiner Woodward Clyde 1999). Although the data are not conclusive, there is also limited evidence that other kinds of craft production (low-fired pottery, lead shot, and possibly blacksmithing) occurred within buildings in the quadrangle as well. In other words, the external wall of the quadrangle did not demarcate a boundary between a residential area and a work area. Rather, it seems that craft and food production went on throughout the quadrangle's buildings, plaza, and extramural areas, with a tendency for larger-scale and messier activities to be located immediately outside the quadrangle.

Beyond the quadrangle and the halo of activities immediately surrounding it, colonial use of the landscape focused on natural resources. A small wharf was built on the bayshore to provide a landing for supply ships and foreign vessels. El Polín Springs, at the head of the central tributary of the Tennessee Hollow Watershed, was developed as a major water source; our excavations there have uncovered traces of landform modifications that were likely undertaken to create a reservoir and ditch system. The hills immediately above El Polín Springs contain outcrops of serpentinite rock that had been quarried to provide foundation stones for adobe buildings. Firewood was scarce, and archaeobotanical evidence suggests that the colonists relied heavily on small trees, scrub brush, animal dung, and grasses as fuel. Collecting a day's fuel for cooking would have required increasingly long forays across the hillsides and valleys, as sources near the quadrangle itself were rapidly depleted.

One of the more interesting spatial changes at the Presidio was the formation of a small civilian neighborhood along the valley floor of the Tennessee Hollow Watershed (Voss 1999). As chapter 5 notes, archaeological surveys have identified three discrete residential deposits in this area, each located at the headwaters or confluence of spring-fed tributaries. Each residential area thus had access to a source of clean water, even if water in the main drainage was soiled by upstream activities. Historical sources provide the names of two of the extended colonial families who lived here—the Sánchez family and the Briones-Miramontes family—and also indicate that these households maintained small-scale farms and orchards. Archaeological investigations of this neighborhood are still in very early stages but do seem to show that Native Californians also lived and worked in Tennessee Hollow (Voss et al. 2005; Voss et al. 2004). Although the main quadrangle of the Presidio was largely deserted after 1837, both archaeological and historical evidence suggest that this extramural neighborhood continued to thrive well into the American period, its occupants departing only after the U.S. Army seized control of the area in 1849–1850.

Roads and more informal pathways linked these nodes of social interaction and activity, creating a web of patterned movement across the landscape. Perhaps not coincidentally, the agrarian neighborhood in Tennessee Hollow formed along two preexisting infrastructure facilities: a system of water collection and conveyance features, and the road between El Presidio de San Francisco and Mission San Francisco de Asís. As modern urban planners are well aware, infrastructure spurs development. In the example of Tennessee Hollow, we can see how earlier colonial patterns of movement and resource use structured the later development of new residential areas.

What Do Middens Have to Do with Ethnogenesis?

How did the diverse and multifaceted population of the Presidio co-occupy this cultural landscape? One clue may lie in patterns of waste disposal that have been uncovered through archaeological research. Anthropologists and archaeologists

TABLE 6. Native Californian artifacts found in the Presidio quadrangle area

Field Project	Total Number of Artifacts Collected	Artifacts Associated with Native Californian Material Culture
1993–1994 Woodward-Clyde Consultants excavations (Voss and Benté 1996a)	11,193	2 mending groundstone bowl fragments 1 *Olivella biplicata* shell, with spire missing
1996 Groundtruthing excavations (URS Greiner Woodward Clyde 1999)	180	1 hammer stone 1 obsidian projectile point fragment
1996–1999 Chapel Investigations (Simpson-Smith and Edwards 2000)	~13,600	1 worked chert flake
1999–2000 Funston Avenue Archaeological Research Project (Ramsay and Voss 2002; Voss, Ramsay, and Naruta 2000)	~ 440,000	2 obsidian projectile point fragments 2 chert projectile point fragments
TOTAL	~ 465,000	10

have long acknowledged that waste disposal practices provide a window into the symbolic: through the habitual, practical routines of sweeping floors, washing surfaces, gathering debris, and depositing these discarded materials in designated locations, people enact and reproduce shared social meanings (Rathje and Murphy 2001; Hodder 1987b).

Examining the archaeological evidence of waste disposal across the landscape of the Presidio suggests practices of material segregation and material commingling that may be related to the social negotiation of ethnic boundaries between colonists and Native Californians. One of the most surprising findings of our excavations in the Presidio's main quadrangle is that we have recovered very few artifacts associated with Native Californian material culture—only 10 artifacts out of an estimated 465,000 (table 6). Five of these are fragments of projectile points; the others include a worked chert flake, two fragments of a groundstone bowl, a hammer stone, and a whole *Olivella biplicata* shell, sometimes used in its natural condition as a bead. This paucity of Native Californian artifacts in the main quadrangle is especially puzzling because historical records document a sizeable number of Native Californians living and working there.

In contrast, artifacts from colonial-era Native Californian material culture are found in significant quantities in two other areas. The first is the Building 39 midden, a deposit located north of the main quadrangle that was discovered in the course of archaeological monitoring (see map 9, C). The majority of objects recovered from the deposit are glazed ceramic sherds, roof tile fragments, glass and metal artifacts, and butchered cattle bone—all typical of Spanish-colonial assemblages. Intermingled with these objects are distinctive artifacts associated with Native Californian material culture: rolled clay pipes, carved fish vertebrae beads, obsidian projectile points, fragments of steatite groundstone bowls, shell beads, carved bird bone tubes, and bone awl tips.[8] The midden also contains dense pockets of shell, primarily *Macoma nasuta* (bent-nosed clam) and *Mytilus* sp. (mussel), a dietary by-product that is not found in significant quantities elsewhere at the site but is common at late prehistoric and contact-era Native Californian archaeological sites (E. Blind and L. N. Clevenger, personal communication, 2006). The depositional context and artifacts from the Building 39 midden deposit are still under analysis, so it is not possible to make quantitative comparisons between its contents and that of other middens located closer to the quadrangle. Nonetheless, the qualitative evidence is clear: the Building 39 midden includes a frequency and a variety of Native Californian material culture that have not been encountered within the quadrangle itself.

The Tennessee Hollow neighborhood is the second area where we have found Native Californian material culture. At the Lover's Lane Bridge site, shovel test surveys recovered a modified chert flake and several marine shells typical of late prehistoric and protohistoric sites in the San Francisco Bay area: *Macoma nasuta*, *Clinocardium nuttalli* (cockle), and *Saxidomus nuttali* (Washington clam). *Clinocardium nuttalli* specimens from one shovel test evince a regularity of shape that suggests they may have been intentionally formed as bead blanks for the manufacture of clamshell disk beads. One specimen appears to have been ground to smooth the exterior face. The MacArthur Avenue site likewise contains *Macoma nasuta*, *Clinocardium nuttalli*, *Saxidomus nuttali*, and *Mytilus* sp., albeit in lower concentrations.

The northernmost site—El Polín Springs—has no noticeable shell in its deposits but has yielded a wide variety of flaked chert, obsidian, and glass artifacts as well as groundstone pestle and bowl fragments and a cut and shaped trapezoidal abalone (*Haliotis rufenscens*) shell ornament (fig. 14). Lithic analyst Kathleen Hull inspected a sample of debitage recovered during preliminary test excavations in 1998. Her analysis found that the flakes represent numerous stages of stone tool manufacture, including core reduction and rejuvenation, platform preparation, and biface thinning. Both percussion and pressure flaking with

cm
inches

FIGURE 14.   Artifacts associated with Native Californian material culture
recovered from archaeological deposits at El Polín Springs. *a*: groundstone
pestle fragment; *b*: groundstone pestle fragment, possibly modified for use
as a chopper; *c*: cut and polished abalone shell.

hard- and soft-hammer tools were used. The range of production stages and techniques represented in the assemblage suggests that lithic tools were being manufactured on site and that the producers were highly experienced in creating projectile points and other bifacially worked tools.

It is important to emphasize here that objects are not people: in tracing the deposition of artifacts associated with Native Californian traditional material culture, we are not tracing Native Californians. There is no question, for example, that Native Californians were present in the main quadrangle of the Presidio, and yet the archaeological evidence recovered to date indicates either that they did not use traditional material culture in that area (either through lack of access, lack of inclination, or prohibition) or that they disposed of such objects elsewhere. In a physical space in which colonial and indigenous lives were spatially interdigitated, the segregation of material culture through practices of refuse disposal may have been one way to spatially materialize the distinction between the military settlers and Native Californians.

In contrast, the deposits found in Tennessee Hollow evince a strikingly different pattern. Material culture associated with both colonial and indigenous lifeways are commingled in Tennessee Hollow refuse deposits, and there is no evidence of other forms of spatial segregation. Yet we should not be too quick to read this spatial integration as an indication of some form of benign ethnic pluralism. The serpentinite quarry and agricultural fields in Tennessee Hollow were likely to have been areas where Native Californians labored (at times willingly, at times under duress) and where the relationships between colonists and indigenous peoples were undoubtedly shaped by strong power differentials. Nonetheless, spatial disciplines related to waste disposal were not practiced, suggesting a qualitative difference in the symbolic relationship between indigenous and colonial ethnicities in this portion of the Presidio's landscape.

Landscape Biography: Juana Briones

Landscape biography—tracing the movement patterns of an individual—allows us to examine the social and personal aspects of these landscape transformations on the micro-scale. It also illustrates the broader spatial connections between locales and regions within the settlement of the Presidio as well as with other locales throughout the San Francisco Bay area.

Juana Briones was a colonial woman who was affiliated with the Presidio from 1812 until the late 1840s. She was a first-generation Californiana, born in 1802 as one of at least nine children in a soldiering family then stationed at the Villa de Branciforte (map 12). Illiterate and from a respectable but undistinguished family, Juana was typical of the rank-and-file military settlers who

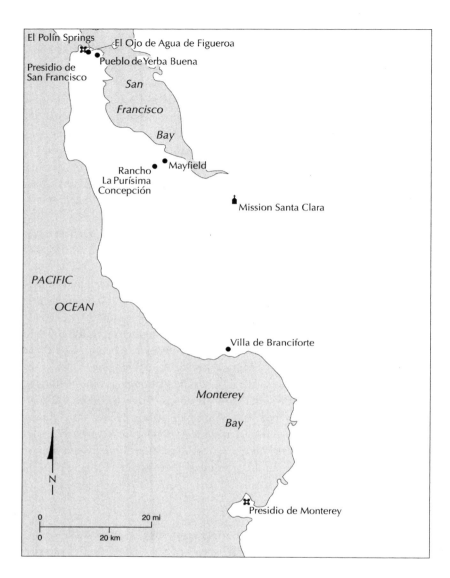

El Polín Springs

El Ojo de Agua de Figueroa

Pueblo de Yerba Buena

Presidio de
San Francisco

San

Francisco

Bay

Rancho
La Purísima
Concepción

Mayfield

Mission Santa Clara

PACIFIC

OCEAN

Villa de Branciforte

Monterey

Bay

N

0   20 mi

0   20 km

Presidio de Monterey

MAP 12.   Residences of Juana Briones.

constituted the majority of Alta California's colonial population.[9] Her parents were both mulatos who had immigrated to Alta California from towns in northwest Mexico. Juana's father, Marcos Briones, born in San Luis Potosí, enlisted as a young soldier in the expedition that founded El Presidio de Monterey. Her mother, María Ysiadora Tapia, was born in the Villa de Calisan; at the age of five, she traveled to Alta California with her family as a member of the Anza expedition and grew up at El Presidio de San Francisco. María Ysiadora moved to the Monterey district when she married Marcos Briones.

When Juana's mother died unexpectedly in 1812, Marcos moved his family to El Presidio de San Francisco. Juana was ten years old. Juana's older sister, Guadalupe, was married to Calendario Miramontes, a soldier garrisoned in San Francisco; Juana's mother's family, the Tapias, also still resided there. Perhaps Marcos wanted to be closer to the extended family during this time of grief and hoped that his married daughter and in-laws could assist him in raising Juana and her siblings. Presumably, they took up residence in the main quadrangle among the rest of the colonial settlers. At some point before 1824, Guadalupe and Calendario moved out of the quadrangle with Marcos to live at El Polín Springs.

In May 1820, Juana, at age eighteen, married Apolinario Miranda, the twenty-seven-year-old son of Alejo Miranda and María de los Santos Gutiérrez. Both of Apolinario's parents were listed in census records as indios from the Mexican towns of Pótam and Culiacán, respectively (Mason 1998:102). Apolinario's father had served as a soldier at the Presidio since at least 1790. In 1810, at age seventeen, Apolinario had enlisted at the Presidio, after working for some time as a herdsman. Like Juana Briones, he was illiterate and signed his filiación (enlistment papers) with the mark of the cross. His commander described him as olive-skinned with black hair and eyes and a broad thick nose (Argüello 1810). Between 1821 and 1841, Juana and Apolinario had eleven children, eight of whom survived infancy. They adopted a twelfth child, Cecelia Chocuilhuala, an orphan of deceased Native Californian parents (Bowman 1957:230).

It is likely that Juana and Apolinario initially lived in the main quadrangle of the Presidio, where Apolinario would have been allotted quarters. Sometime during the first few years of their marriage, they joined Marcos, Guadalupe, and Calendario at El Polín Springs (fig. 15). A third sister, María de la Luz, moved there as well. The Briones families maintained residences at El Polín Springs into the early 1850s. While the adult men participated in military service, the women cultivated food and raised farm animals, marketing produce, eggs, poultry, and dairy products. Archaeological evidence indicates that Native Californians lived alongside the Briones family throughout this period.

During this time, Juana began to develop a reputation as a *curandera* (traditional healer) and midwife. El Polín Springs, situated at the intersection of several en-

FIGURE 15. Excavated foundation of an adobe house that once stood at El Polín Springs, likely occupied by the Briones and Miramontes extended family.

vironmental zones, has the greatest biodiversity of any area in the Presidio of San Francisco; today, it provides the only remaining habitat for several threatened and endangered plant species. Several Briones family descendants have suggested that Juana may have chosen to live at El Polín Springs because of the opportunities it afforded for collecting herbs and roots for traditional remedies. Family history recounts that she worked closely with Native Californians to adapt Mexican remedies to the plants available in San Francisco. Indeed, archaeobotanical analysis of flotation samples from test excavations at El Polín Springs has identified a rich variety of nondomesticated plants (table 7), many of which are considered to have therapeutic uses.

In 1833, Juana and Apolinario requested a land grant for El Ojo de Agua de Figueroa, a small parcel adjacent to the Presidio, on the grounds that Apolinario was about to retire and that they had already built a house there. The land grant was half a mile from the extended family's El Polín residences and expanded the Briones sisters' agricultural enterprises. Juana developed the land into a farm with fruit tree orchards and a cattle corral.

Shortly afterward (possibly as early as 1835), Juana Briones obtained a lot

TABLE 7. Nondomesticated plant
seeds recovered at El Polín Springs

Plant	Common Name	Plant	Common Name
Asteraceae	Sunflower family	*Medicago* sp.	Burclover
Brassicacaea	Mustard family	*Myrica californica*	Wax myrtle, bayberry
Bromus sp. cf.	Brome grass	*Oxalis* sp.	Sorrel
Calandrinia sp.	Red maids	*Plantago* sp.	Plantain
Carex obnupta cf.	Sedge	*Poa* sp.	Bluegrass
Carex sp.	Sedge	Poaceae	Grass family
Caryophyllaceae	Pink family	*Ranunculus aquatilus* cf.	Buttercup
Claytonia sp.	Miner's lettuce	*Ranunculus* sp.	Buttercup
Cyperaceae	Sedge family	*Rubus* sp.	Blackberry, raspberry
Erodium sp.	Filaree	*Rumex* sp.	Dock
Galium sp.	Bedstraw	*Scirpus* sp.	Bulrush
Juncus sp. cf.	Rush	*Silene* sp.	Catchfly
Malva sp.	Mallow	*Solanum* sp.	Nightshade
Marah sp.	Wild cucumber	*Vulpia/Festuca* sp.	Fescue grass

SOURCES: Popper and Martin 2000; Popper 2002, 2005; Voss 2002:567–568.

in her own name in the newly established Pueblo of Yerba Buena (present-day North Beach in San Francisco) and built an adobe house there, located right on the trail leading between Yerba Buena and the Presidio. It appears that over the next five years Juana and members of her family alternated living at Yerba Buena, El Polín Springs, and El Ojo de Agua de Figueroa. They developed a prosperous business marketing fresh milk, meat, and vegetables from their farms to sailors and merchants on visiting ships. Ceramic tableware sherds recovered from El Polín Springs are almost all British-produced whitewares, primarily the more expensive transfer-printed wares (Voss 2001a; Voss et al. 2005; Voss et al. 2004) (fig. 16). Juana also used her vocation as a healer to forge close personal relationships with Anglo-American and British families living in the new pueblo. An early map of Yerba Buena, drawn in 1839 by Jacob P. Leese, refers to one stretch of bayshore as the *playa de Juana Briones*, an indication of her prominence in this new civilian community.

With the proceeds from her business, Juana Briones purchased yet another piece of land in 1844, the 4,400-acre Rancho La Purísima Concepción, located in present-day Palo Alto and Los Altos Hills. The land grant had been held by

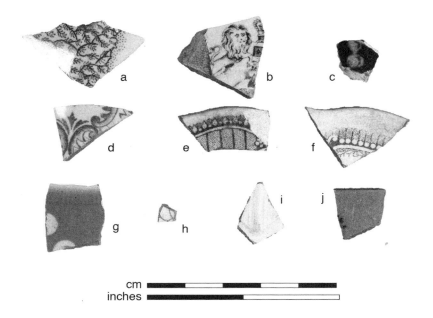

FIGURE 16. British whiteware sherds recovered from archaeological deposits at El Polín Springs. *a*: whiteware, black transfer print; *b*: white improved earthenware, black transfer print; *c*: whiteware, blue transfer print; *d*: blued ironstone, red transfer print; *e*: white improved earthenware, brown transfer print; *f*: white improved earthenware, brown transfer print; *g*: dipped whiteware; *h*: whiteware, green transfer print; *i*: creamware; *j*: whiteware, mocha.

two Native Californians from Mission Santa Clara, José Gorgonio and his son José Ramon. Juana paid them three hundred dollars for the deed and permitted them to continue living on the property. She began developing the ranch throughout the 1840s and eventually moved her children, her sisters, and other members of her extended family there during their land tenure disputes with the U.S. government.[10] Briones purchased additional land in Santa Clara in 1852 and later bought several residential lots in the town of Mayfield (now part of Palo Alto) in 1883, where she, two of her daughters, and her sister Guadalupe built homes. As Juana's health declined in the mid-1880s, she moved to Mayfield permanently, although her grandson recalled that she never resigned herself to town life (Mesa 1937). Juana died on December 3, 1889.

Residential Strategies

Juana Briones's landholdings are evidence of her prosperity and business acumen as a ranchera, businesswoman, and healer. There are also indications that her expanding claims on the Spanish-colonial and Mexican-era landscape were a means through which she negotiated personal difficulties.

Juana and Apolinario's marriage was a troubled union. Apolinario was a heavy drinker who physically abused Juana and their children. As the abuse worsened, Juana sought protection from military officers at the Presidio, but Apolinario ignored the reprimands he received. Finally, in 1844, Juana petitioned for ecclesiastical separation from her husband. As she was unable to read or write, her petition was transcribed by one of the priests at Mission Santa Clara. She stated:

> I do not fear to shoulder the conjugal cross that the Lord my Father and my Mother the Holy Church have asked me to bear, being in a state that I have freely chosen. What I truly fear is the loss of my own soul forever, and what is more, I fear the destruction of my unfortunate family due to the scandal and bad example of a man who has forgotten God and his own soul, whose only concern is drunkenness and all the vices that come with it, and who no longer cares about feeding his family, a burden that I alone carry with the labor of my own hands, a fact that I can prove with testimonials of exceptional strength if necessary. Moreover, my own labor and the labor of my poor family sustain my husband, not only providing him with clothes and food but also paying for his drunkenness. As to how much damage he brings home to me and my family, well, as soon as he is a little tipsy, he begins to utter his blasphemies, swear, and to put into practice his abominable behavior, not only publicly and imperiously demanding the conjugal debt from me, but also wanting to abuse it, as he has tried to do several times with my daughter María Presentación, who fortunately is already married.
>
> Your Lordship, none of the blows, beatings with clubs, and grave dangers that I have seen in my life, nor the brutality and cruelty with which I have been treated, merit consideration because, if my sufferings were mine alone, I would not bear them with pleasure, but at least I would accept them as divine will. . . . Your Lordship, my husband is the greatest obstacle placed before my children, because from him they learn nothing but swearing, blasphemy, and ugly, lewd, and dissolute behavior. How will I excuse myself before God if I do not seek, as much as I can, all possible means of ridding my family of such a bad example? (Briones 1844)[11]

Although no record has been found of whether the church approved or rejected Juana's petition for a separation, from that point forward she ceased using her husband's name and was referred to by others as a widow. She continued to conduct her business affairs independently and in association with her siblings and her children.

Through her negotiation of the Presidio landscape and the growing civilian communities beyond the military reservation, Juana Briones pursued residential strategies that provided her with safe havens from a dangerous marriage. For nearly all her adult life, Juana maintained at least two and at times as many as four places of residence, many of them only a short walk or horse ride away from each other. From the Presidio quadrangle to El Polín Springs, to El Ojo de Agua de Figueroa, to Yerba Buena, to the Rancho La Purísima Concepción and her houses in Santa Clara and Mayfield, she used her landholdings to maintain close ties with her kin and daughters and to create financial and spatial independence from her husband.

A Pluralistic Landscape

Tracing the landscape biography of Juana Briones illustrates how experiences of the Presidio landscape and the social meanings of structured space are standpoint-dependent. Her experience of the colonial landscape was shaped by her family history, her troubled marriage, her vocation as a traditional healer, and her agricultural business. It was also structured by military and colonial policy. Like most colonial women living in Alta California, Juana Briones never traveled beyond the narrow coastal strip of securely colonized territory, though she observed her father, brothers, and husband participating in more far-ranging military expeditions. Until later adulthood, her place of residence was tethered to the military posts of her male relatives. Unlike many male rancheros, she did not become involved in the lucrative hide and tallow trade but instead developed an agricultural niche in vegetable farming, fruit orchards, poultry-raising, and dairy farming.

Historians have emphasized that the ethnogenesis of Californio identity was driven by adult men who built personal empires based on the material rewards of their military service, their ability to "pass" as Spanish, and the political capital gained through social affiliations with other high-status men. By this formula, a woman like Juana Briones should have fallen to the bottom of the social hierarchy in Californio society. She was barred from military service by virtue of her gender, phenotypically marked by her African ancestry (throughout her adult life, others pointedly remarked on her dark face and "Moorish" features), and linked by marriage to a common soldier whose poor conduct was repeatedly censured by military officials; in addition, she incorporated Native Californians as members of her household. The case of Juana Briones's troubled marriage exposes the vulnerabilities of the adult women and lower-casta settlers who lived at colonial settlements like the Presidio. It also demonstrates that at least some nonelite subjects were able to create physical spaces in which to advance their own and their families' interests and to protect themselves, in some measure, from the abusive excesses of their social superiors.

Undoubtedly, the colonial landscape of El Presidio de San Francisco would appear markedly different from the perspective of other occupants. Even within Juana's own sphere of social interaction, we might consider how the landscape she inhabited was experienced differently by, for example, her sister's husband, Calendario Miramontes; the Native Californians who worked in her family's agricultural undertakings; the commanding officers considering her petition for land at El Ojo de Agua de Figueroa; or the Anglo traders and merchants who did business with her at Yerba Buena. For precisely this reason, landscape biography engenders more complicated, nuanced interpretations of the archaeological record. Further, it highlights the ways in which archaeological deposits are interconnected: far from being discrete "sites," they represent nodes of social interaction and material practices within a larger social landscape.

.   .   .

This chapter began by describing the Bourbon crown's effort to radically reconfigure the spatial organization of Spanish-colonial military defenses in North America. It closed with the biography of a San Francisco colonial woman who, from a fairly disadvantaged position in the lower stratum of colonial society, navigated the economic and emotional dangers of an abusive marriage through strategic movements and positionings across the landscape. What connects these two divergent perspectives on landscape and ethnogenesis are middle-range scales of place-making, within which reside the interplay between governmentality and community.

At the Presidio, the uneasy interface between colonial policy and local practice was a potent site for the emergence of colonial identity. As this chapter demonstrates, this locus of cultural production was not a conceptual realm but instead was concretely enacted in spatial practices. The 1772 Reglamento dictated the cordon system of defenses, but it was the decisions of the local military captains and the actions of the soldiers under their command that produced Alta California's unique colonial geography. Here, natural topography fused with the contours of colonial-indigenous warfare in creating a securely colonized coastal region, one marked as much by gender and sexuality as by ethnic difference. The nonconformist architectural plan of El Presidio de San Francisco's main quadrangle was intimately connected with this, as its weak defenses were possible only because of the spatialization of interethnic violence. Finally, the apparent spatial segregation of refuse generated by colonial and indigenous populations is perhaps one of the most provocative findings of our ongoing field research programs. It is highly likely that Native Californians were always present in the quadrangle, as servants, construction laborers, craftsworkers, field hands, prisoners, war captives, and members of military auxiliaries. Yet through practices of refuse disposal, the material objects most closely associated with indigeneity were deposited separately. This finding suggests that despite constant physical proximity, the military settlers used material and spatial practices to create a firm boundary between themselves and Native Californians.

Throughout the Spanish-colonial and Mexican periods, the San Francisco Bay area was a contested landscape, but it was increasingly dominated by colonial practices of spatial control. Nearly all historians writing of this era have identified landownership—the proliferation of ranchos in the 1820s and 1830s—as one of the most important factors contributing to the development of Californio identity. But it was actually the much earlier colonial transformation, reconfiguration, and, in time, dominance of the landscape, rather than individual landownership, that provided a spatial foundation for the emergence and consolidation of Californio ethnicity. The military settlers, working in concert with mission priests, established a fully colonized coastal axis in which Native Californians became trespassers, neophytes, prisoners, laborers, and servants in their own homelands. This was accomplished not by individual rancheros but rather through a coordinated, institutional program—one in which the entire colonial community participated—using an entwined strategy of religious conversion, labor regimes, and military domination.

There were, of course, limits to colonial domination of the Alta California landscape, especially as a result of Native Californian resistance to further encroachment on indigenous lands. Even within the securely colonized axis, Native Californians and those who occupied the fringes and lower rungs of colonial society deployed a broad range of spatial strategies to foster their physical and cultural survival. Nonetheless, they now did so within, against, or outside the colonial spatial order. Increasingly, the contested landscape of colonial Alta California was a place that the military settlers came to understand as their rightful patria. And in claiming this place for themselves, they simultaneously fashioned themselves as Californios and Californianas, people whose identity was entwined with the lands they occupied.

This chapter continues the investigation of space, place, and ethnogenesis by examining the architecture of El Presidio de San Francisco's main quadrangle. As the colonial transformation of the San Francisco landscape illustrates, places are socially produced and actively constituted by the people who inhabit them. Power is inherent in, rather than prior to or a result of, the social production of place. It is one of the means by which power relations are materialized through practice and strategy. This is especially apparent in the production of architecture.

Architecture is a technology that gives physical presence to the regionalization of social life. By building, people transform the physical world, altering paths of movement and sightlines; bending the flow of light, air, and sound; delineating inside from outside, here from there. The built environment gives material shape to social life, encouraging some patterns of movement and social interaction while discouraging or even prohibiting others. A focus on architectural practices affords an important perspective on ethnogenesis because it sheds light on the choices and strategies used by members of a community to establish their physical presence on the landscape.

The nucleus of colonial life in Spanish-colonial San Francisco, the Presidio's main quadrangle was the administrative and economic center for the entire presidio district and the place that most colonial families called home. Although its architectural form was dictated by military regulations, the settlers complied with some stipulations and ignored others. The architecture of the quadrangle can be understood as a hybrid expression of conflicting ideals: the regulatory visions of military planners, the architectural habits and aspirations of the settlers themselves, the labor of the settlers and Native Californians, and the resources and constraints of the local environment.

Whereas chapter 6 discusses the layout of the main quadrangle in relation to the broader landscape, this chapter examines the quadrangle itself as a physical artifact. It presents a synopsis of the quadrangle's architectural history as reconstructed through archaeological and historical research, focusing not only on conventional aspects such as form, style, design, and materials but also on the social relationships involved in architectural production and maintenance. Three major trends in architectural practices marked the quadrangle's development—homogenization, centralization, and expansion—and all three participated in the emergence and consolidation of Californio identity. By the mid-1810s, drastic architectural transformations were occurring at the settlement. This metamorphosis of the Presidio's built environment may have been motivated in part by increased contact with other European colonial powers. However, rather than establishing defenses, the architectural changes were aesthetic and signified a heightened concern with ethnic respectability. Such transformations also had gendered implications, reflected in the production of architectural forms related to sexual honor and shame.

Architecture as Product and Context

The methodological approach used here draws attention to architecture as a product of social relations as well as a material context for social life. The goal is not to produce a static or composite plan of the settlement's layout. Instead, I approach the main quadrangle as a constellation of constantly changing architectural elements (walls, floors, roofs, plazas, walkways, apertures, and infrastructure). This perspective highlights continuities as well as changes in the architectural history of the settlement. Multiple lines of evidence are used to trace the shifting influences of military regulations and local practices on the Presidio's architecture. The findings of archaeological investigations are thus in dialogue with evidence from historical plans, maps, drawings, and texts. Foreign scientific and trading expeditions often had the covert objective of assessing Spain's defensive capabilities; and the diaries, reports, and images of El Presidio de San Francisco produced by European maritime visitors provide a particularly important source of documentary information about the quadrangle's architecture.

The architecture of the Presidio's quadrangle has been the primary focus of archaeological research at the site. The studies completed during the past thirteen years constitute a robust body of evidence, though there are still areas of

considerable ambiguity. The southeast corner and portions of the northern fa-
cade of the quadrangle cannot be investigated because twentieth-century U.S.
Army construction destroyed any archaeological deposits or features that may
have once been present. Other areas have yet to be extensively excavated, especially the central area of the site, which is now a paved parking lot. Additionally, certain kinds of architectural features, such as stone wall-foundations,
have greater archaeological visibility than the residues left by organic building
materials such as wattle-and-daub or palisade construction. Consequently, our
investigations have generated considerably more archaeological information
about post-1810 architecture at the Presidio than about earlier periods. This
bias is balanced to some extent by the composition of the documentary record.
Most accounts of the Presidio's architecture are found in correspondence between local officers and their superiors in central Mexico. After the 1810 Hidalgo Revolt and the beginning of the struggle for Mexican independence, such
correspondence dropped precipitously. Hence, there is fairly strong documentary evidence, but weak archaeological evidence, of the main quadrangle's architecture before 1810, while the reverse is true for post-1810 construction.

One theme that consistently emerges from documentary accounts is the ongoing struggle to maintain the quadrangle against the destructive forces of the
elements. Rainstorms and the accompanying winds caused substantial damage
nearly every winter; persistent fog brought dampness that undermined the structural integrity of mud brick, mortar, and plaster; and earthquakes, sometimes
causing catastrophic damage, were not infrequent, with an especially concentrated period of seismic activity in the early 1800s. Fire was also a constant danger. Examining this interplay between architecture and the environment draws
attention to the cycles of repair and reconstruction needed to sustain even the
most rudimental shelter. Once constructed, buildings were not simply static
containers of social life. Walls, roofs, and floors were being continually transformed, on the one hand by elemental forces that promoted decay and collapse,
and on the other by human actions that maintained, repaired, modified, demolished, and recycled architectural fabric. These episodes of construction and
collapse, repair and remodeling, were moments of architectural decision-making
that give us insight into the habits, preferences, and aesthetic values held by
members of the Presidio community.

Architectural History of the Main Quadrangle

The first fact that became apparent through archaeological research was that
there had been not one quadrangle but many (at least three), each supplanting
the previous one. The first, constructed when the settlement was founded in

1776, was never completed; by 1780, it had been largely destroyed by storms and fire. The second quadrangle was apparently built incrementally between 1780 and 1800 and then deteriorated during the early 1800s. In 1815, most of the second quadrangle was razed, and a third was constructed in its place. With each iteration, the quadrangle was markedly altered, but there were also continuities. Notably, the general configuration—a single row of structures lining the edges of a rectangular central plaza—appears to have been consistent throughout the Presidio's history. In other aspects, the quadrangle changed significantly over time, especially regarding the building materials used, the organization of architectural production, the size of the quadrangle's footprint, and the degree to which the quadrangle was enclosed.

The First Quadrangle: 1776–1780

After moving to the site of El Presidio de San Francisco on July 26, 1776, the military settlers initially lived in temporary shelters while they waited for a delayed supply ship, the San Carlos. They had brought few tools and little hardware with them on their overland journey from Tubac, and no serious construction could begin until the needed materials were available. When the San Carlos finally arrived on August 17, 1776, Commander José Joaquín Moraga wasted no time in laying out the outlines of the quadrangle, drawing on the expertise of ship's captain, Don Francisco Quirós, and first pilot José de Cañizares: "A square ninety-two varas each way was marked out for it, with divisions for church, royal offices, warehouses, guardhouse, and houses for soldier settlers" (Palóu 1926:124). With the aid of sailors from the San Carlos, the Presidio soldiers constructed a warehouse, chapel, and comandancia. The soldiers and their families were responsible for building their own dwellings, which were largely constructed of palisade and wattle-and-daub with thatched roofs (Bancroft 1886a:289, 331, 472; Federal Writers' Project 1976:55; Langellier and Rosen 1996:31, 60).

No archaeological evidence of this earliest quadrangle has yet been discovered. However, a plan drawing of the proposed quadrangle survives; it matches the military regulations described in chapter 6 to the letter (fig. 17). The drawing's most unusual feature is that it depicts the settlement's buildings as separate, rather than connected, structures, each protruding into the central plaza from the quadrangle's massive defensive wall.

From written accounts, it appears that few of the structures depicted in the 1776 drawing were constructed. The plan is best interpreted as a record of colonial intentions rather than as a representation of the quadrangle as it actually stood. When Governor Felipe de Neve inspected the Presidio the following year, he noted that the quadrangle had not been enclosed; further, the adobe

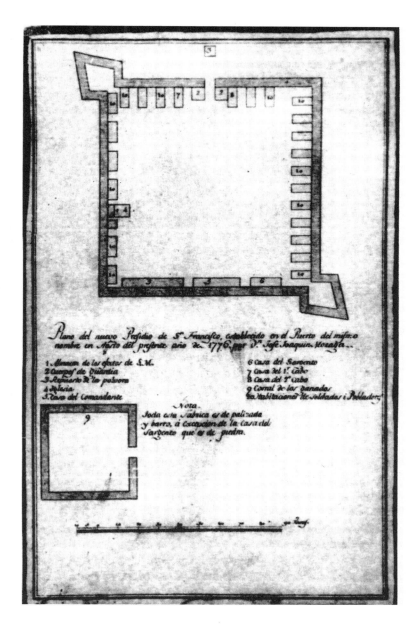

FIGURE 17.   1776 plan drawing of El Presidio de San Francisco. The
drawing is commonly attributed to José Joaquín Moraga, but Francisco
Palóu (1926:124) wrote that the plan had been formed and drawn by
José de Cañizares. See Langellier and Rosen 1996:34 for a translation of
the plan's text. Servicio Geográfico del Ejército, Madrid.

comandancia and warehouse were unsubstantial, and all other structures were "mere huts" (Langellier and Rosen 1996:38). Perhaps the most thorough description of the main quadrangle in its first years was written by Hermenegildo Sal, a soldier who later was promoted to *habilitado* (a military rank combining the duties of a quartermaster, paymaster, accountant, and storekeeper) and then to acting commander of the Presidio. In a 1792 report, he wrote:

> I am eyewitness that this Presidio was begun to be built on July 27th, 1776 and at the end of 78 the house of the Commandant was in adobe; one wall of 4 yards, height; a second 3 yards, the third, 2½; and the fourth also 2½. The [illegible] house in stone, stores, church, and habitations for the troops in palisade and earth. During a rain fall in the month of January of 1779, the stores, the slaughter house, the church, the house of the commandant and of the troops and the greatest part of the four pieces of wall fell, in such a way that at the end of the year 80, none of the houses built in the year 78 were standing. The lack of intelligent workers for the construction and direction of the works contributed much to this; and at present they are still lacking. (Sal 1976:47–49)

In October 1779, fire destroyed the community's hospital tent and gutted at least one house (Bancroft 1886a:331). By all accounts, the quadrangle had essentially collapsed by 1780, its residents presumably taking shelter in tents and other improvised structures.

The Second Quadrangle: 1780–1815

From 1780 to 1792, the colonists gained little ground in their attempts to build durable structures. Historical accounts indicate that soldiers and their families built their own shelters, usually of palisade; that gale force winds and winter storms repeatedly blew down large areas of the quadrangle; and that a lack of materials, labor, and skilled craftsworkers hampered the colonists' attempts to construct adequate shelter (Bancroft 1886a:472; Langellier and Rosen 1996:47–60).

Two historical documents provide comprehensive descriptions of the Presidio's quadrangle as it stood in 1792, a little over a decade after the first quadrangle had been destroyed. The first document is a plan map drawn by Sal to accompany his report to Governor José Antonio Romeu (fig. 18). Sal's plan depicts the main quadrangle as composed of three wings of rooms on the north, west, and south, with the eastern side of the quadrangle open. The plan's notes include measurements for most structures; Sal wrote that the quadrangle measured 116 varas (98 m) north-south, and 120 varas (102 m) east-west. In the

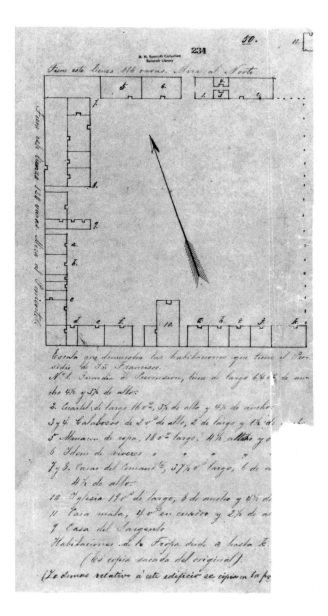

FIGURE 18.   1792 Sal plan map of El Presidio de San Francisco.
See Langellier and Rosen 1996:55 for a translation of the plan's
text. Courtesy of the Bancroft Library, University of California,
Berkeley.

accompanying report, Sal documented the poor condition of the quadrangle's structures:

> The storehouses are built in stone and mud without any support [plaster] and therefore exposed to rain.
>
> The guardia, the prison-cells, and the soldiers' houses are in stone and adobe; its walls are crumbling and for this reason they have put in the side of the square [plaza] counterfort [buttresses] of stone to support [the walls].
>
> The sergeant's house is made of stone without support and is falling down. The one of the commandant and others are of adobe. The soldiers' dwellings are not equal to it.
>
> All the walls of the church are crumbling and deteriorating and [the cracks] are wider in the upper-part than in the lower. All the roofs in what is built in the Presidio are of straw [zacate] and tule and are very much exposed to a fire, as far as the authorities can realize it.
>
> The winds blow in such a way, in the summer from the northwest, and in the winter from the south and the northeast, that they are like hurricanes which make notable harm in said roofs and every year one must attend to them with endless work. . . .
>
> The adobe is bad in itself because of the dampness it crumbles; and thus, it is indispensable that the roofs in the South and in the Southwest side cover [protect] the greatest part of the walls.
>
> The lumber is found at a distance of more than ten leagues and if everything is favorable a trip may be made every week and this is not in all the seasons of the year. . . .
>
> All this that I manifest and expose is notorious and therefore I sign it. (Sal 1976:47–49)

In November 1792, the British ship HMS *Discovery* landed at El Presidio de San Francisco. The ship's captain, George Vancouver, was one of the first foreigners to visit the Presidio. His account largely corroborates that provided by Sal:

> The only object of human industry which presented itself, was a square area, whose sides were about two hundred yards in length,[1] enclosed by a mud wall, and resembling a pound for cattle. Above this wall the thatched roofs of their low small houses just made their appearance. On entering the Presidio, we found one of its sides still unenclosed by the wall, and very indifferently fenced in by a few bushes here and there, fastened to stakes in the ground. The unfinished state of this part, afforded us an opportunity of seeing the strength of the wall, and the manner in which it was constructed. It is about fourteen

feet high, and five feet in breadth, and was first formed by uprights and horizontal rafters or large timbers, between which dried sods and moistened earth
were pressed as close and as hard as possible; after which the whole was cased
with earth made into a sort of mud plaster, which gave it the appearance of
durability, and of being sufficiently strong to protect them, with the assistance
of their fire-arms, against all the force which the natives of the country might
be able to collect. . . . [The colonists'] houses were along the wall, within the
square, and their fronts uniformly extended the same distance into the area,
which is a clear open space, without buildings or other interruptions. The only
entrance into it, is by a large gateway; facing which, and against the centre
of the opposite wall or side, is the church; which, though small, was neat in
comparison to the rest of the buildings. . . . in the winter, or rainy seasons,
[the houses] must at the best be very uncomfortable dwellings. (Vancouver
1984:708–709)

To date, archaeological evidence of the second quadrangle corroborates the
Sal plan (fig. 19). Field research first focused on the predicted location of the
north wing of the second quadrangle. Geophysical remote sensing identified
several reflective anomalies suggestive of wall alignments (Cross and Burk 1995;
Cross and Voss 1996). In 1996, we conducted mechanical excavation using
backhoes and graders to groundtruth these survey findings. The excavations exposed several post molds, perhaps from a former palisade; a rammed earth or
wattle-and-daub wall; and an irregular linear alignment of serpentinite rocks
that appear to represent a robbed foundation trench (URS Greiner Woodward
Clyde 1999). The 1996 to 1999 Chapel Investigations, in the middle of the
southern wing of the main quadrangle, identified architectural remains of the
chapel and sacristy, the quadrangle's southern exterior wall, and portions of
adjacent buildings. Significantly, the configuration and size of these buildings
conform to the Sal plan. Additionally, the distance between the archaeologically identified chapel and sacristy and the robbed foundation trench and post
molds approximates the distance indicated by the Sal plan (Simpson-Smith and
Edwards 2000). More recent archaeological investigations of the Officers' Club
indicate that the dimensions and locations of these extant adobe walls are congruent with those shown on the 1792 Sal plan (Blind 2005; Blind and Bartoy
2006; Clevenger 2006; Goldberg 2005).

With few personnel or funds available, Acting Commander Sal was unable
to maintain—let alone improve—the condition of the quadrangle. At the end
of 1792, he wrote another report in which he stated that "the labor spent on
the presidio is incredible and yet there are now but slightly more or less [build-
ings] than at first." He repeated that the quadrangle had been enclosed on the

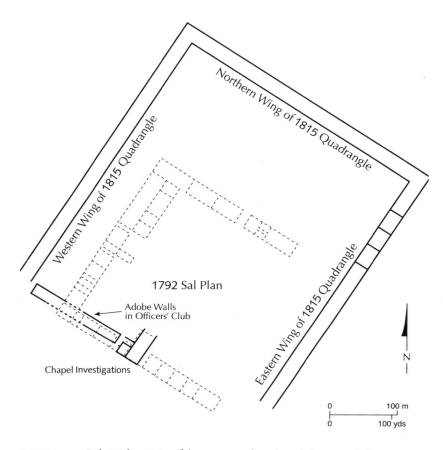

FIGURE 19. Relative locations of the 1792 quadrangle and the expanded 1815 quadrangle. The location of the Sal plan (see fig. 18), shown here in dashed lines, is projected by "keying" the plan to the chapel, sacristy, and exterior wall-foundations revealed in the 1996–1999 Chapel Investigations.

east side by a new palisade wall, but added that the three wings of structures desperately needed repairs and the chapel and soldiers' residences needed to be razed and reconstructed. Sal concluded the report with a request for funds to hire Indian laborers (Langellier and Rosen 1996:61).

The eight years following Sal's 1792 report saw renewed colonial attention paid to the Presidio. While most personnel and funding were directed to the construction and staffing of new defensive facilities such as the Castillo de San Joaquín and the Batería de San José, some resources were devoted to the quadrangle itself. Beginning in 1795, Governor Diego de Borica began to explore

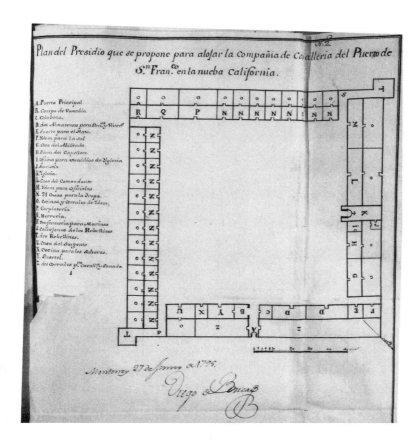

FIGURE 20. *Plan of the Presidio That Is Proposed to House the Cavalry Company of the Port of San Francisco in New California.* This plan was submitted on June 26, 1795, by Acting Commander Hermenegildo Sal to Governor Diego de Borica, along with an itemized list of previous construction and repair expenses (Langellier and Rosen 1996:104; Whitehead 1983:75). See Whitehead 1983:74 for a translation of the plan's text. Courtesy of the Bancroft Library, University of California, Berkeley.

the possibility of moving the quadrangle to a more sheltered location within the settlement, even commissioning two plans for the proposed construction (figs. 20 and 21). Except for the relationship between the chapel and the main entrance to the quadrangle, the two plans are remarkably similar and meet the military regulations of the time to the letter. The proposed quadrangle would have had a separate defensive wall, creating protected corrals and yards behind residences. Both plans depict a somewhat larger quadrangle than the one de-

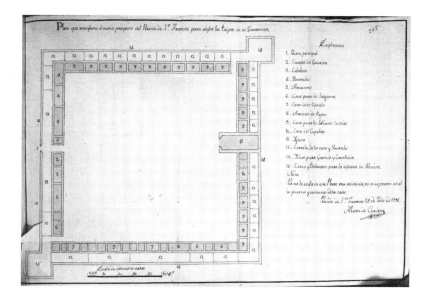

FIGURE 21.   *Plan That Shows the New Design of the Presidio of San Francisco for Housing the Troops of the Garrison.* Prepared by engineer Alberto de Córdoba, July 24, 1796. See Whitehead 1983:76 for a translation of the plan's text. Courtesy of the Bancroft Library, University of California, Berkeley.

picted on the 1792 Sal plan, each measuring approximately 130–140 varas to a side. In the end, plans to relocate and rebuild the quadrangle never passed the proposal stage; in 1799, Governor Borica conceded that he lacked the funding to underwrite the ambitious scheme (Langellier and Rosen 1996:102).

Throughout the rest of the 1790s, the Presidio settlers focused their available resources on the effort to gain ground against the elements. They established a forge and a tile kiln at the Presidio to provide a ready supply of hardware and to replace the thatched roofs with fire- and rain-resistant tile (Langellier and Rosen 1996:73, 90). During this time, the responsibility for building and maintaining residences and barracks began to shift from individual households to the Presidio company as a whole. Construction projects included a new wing of nine individual quarters and a barracks to house those soldiers whose duty alternated between the castillo and the quadrangle. These and other centralized construction projects, such as work on the perimeter wall, a new warehouse, and a guardroom, were accomplished largely by native laborers and colonial civilians working under military direction (Langellier and Rosen 1996:73, 89, 95, 107–108). Acting Commander Sal, in particular, worked to build alliances with the leaders of Native Californian villages to ensure a stable supply of labor (Bancroft 1886a:614).

After 1800, the Spanish crown reduced its expenditures on its North American colonies, further limiting financial support for Presidio building projects. El Presidio de San Francisco was once again largely isolated from its parent polities of New Spain and Spain, a condition further exacerbated by the 1810 Hidalgo Revolt and the beginning of the Mexican War for Independence. During this period, the quadrangle's architecture suffered both from the effects of winter storms and from a series of strong earthquakes. By all accounts, the architecture of the main quadrangle was falling into a state of considerable disrepair.

The Third Quadrangle: 1815–1821

In 1815, the Presidio community undertook a massive construction campaign that replaced the deteriorating second quadrangle with a greatly expanded third quadrangle. This construction represented a turning point in architectural practices at the Presidio. Examining how the colonists were transforming their built environment during this period affords an important opportunity to investigate the relationship between the emergence and consolidation of Californio identity and the material practices of the community.

As no plan or direct account of its construction has yet been found in colonial records, our knowledge of the third quadrangle comes primarily from archaeological evidence.[2] Excavation has been most extensive in the east wing and northeast corner of the expanded quadrangle. Investigations of the north wing, northwest corner, west wing, and southwest corner have consisted primarily of archaeological monitoring discoveries and geophysical remote sensing studies, followed by mechanically excavated trenches. Excavations in the south wing have provided detailed information about the architectural history of the settlement's chapel, and current work in the present-day Officers' Club is yielding information about the standing adobe remnants encased within its walls (see fig. 11).

Taken together, the findings of these investigations make up a robust body of evidence from which to construct a working model of the third quadrangle. This quadrangle was a substantial expansion of the settlement's architectural footprint. Measuring 192 varas (163 m) north-south and 172 varas (145 m) east-west, it occupied an area more than 2.4 times greater than the second quadrangle (see fig. 19). Its west, north, and east wings were constructed all of a piece, using uniform materials and methods. Each wing consisted of two parallel adobe brick walls set at a uniform distance of 6 varas from each other. These load-bearing walls rested on stone foundations that had been set into a U- or V-shaped trench extending about 60 cm below the historical grade. The stones were generally angular rocks ranging from 10 cm to 50 cm in diameter and had been set in three or four rough courses, with the interstices between the stones filled with a simple mud mortar. The stone foundation generally projected 10–20 cm above the historical grade. The upper surface of the foundation was smoothed with a leveling course of small cobbles and pebbles set into mud mortar. The adobe walls rested atop this stone foundation. Generally, the interior (plaza-facing) wall measured about 1 1/3 varas (1.12 m) thick, with the exterior wall slightly thicker, about 1 1/2 varas (1.27 m). The entire compound was roofed with clay tiles.

In the eastern wing, the space formed by the two parallel adobe walls was subdivided by partition walls. The partitions were less substantial than the interior and exterior walls: only 1 vara (0.84 m) thick, they rested on a single course of small serpentinite cobbles that had been laid directly on the historical ground surface. The partition walls created rooms of identical size measuring 6 varas deep and 12 varas wide; each room was likely an apartment allotted to a soldier and his family. We do not yet have sufficient archaeological evidence to determine whether these regularly spaced partitions continued along the north and west wings.

The architectural development of the south wing during this period is less understood. It appears that some older buildings were incorporated into the new quadrangle, such as the chapel complex and the building represented by the adobe walls in the Officers' Club. There is some archaeological evidence of remodeling and repair during this time, especially of the chapel, which had been badly damaged by an earthquake in 1812. Nonetheless, the buildings on the south wing seem to have been rebuilt in place rather than completely redesigned.

That this new quadrangle was constructed primarily in 1815 is supported by both archaeological evidence and documentary sources. Portions of the expanded quadrangle's east wing rest directly above the Building 13 midden deposit. Most of the ceramic sherds recovered from this midden date to the late 1700s, but a few—about 1 percent of the assemblage by minimum vessel count—are Aranama majolicas and British whitewares that were not manufactured before the early 1800s. These ceramic dates suggest that the east wing was constructed after 1810.

Another indication of the third quadrangle's construction date comes from a foreign source: the records of a Russian naval expedition whose ship, the Rurik, visited El Presidio de San Francisco in 1816. Russia had established its mercantile settlement of Colony Ross in 1812 and concomitantly increased its surveillance of Alta California's coast. The Rurik's naturalist, Adelbert von Chamisso,

FIGURE 22.   Detail of *View of the Presidio of San Francisco*, by Louis Choris, 1816.
Watercolor. Courtesy of the Bancroft Library, University of California, Berkeley.

reported that the quadrangle was newly built and covered with tiles, although the chapel was still unfinished (Rezanov 1926). Louis Choris, the official artist of the expedition, painted a detailed watercolor of the main quadrangle and the surrounding landscape (fig. 22). The watercolor depicts a quadrangle that is closed on all four sides with continuous exterior and interior facades.

While direct documentary evidence of the Presidio's architectural transformation is limited, one second-hand account provides an interesting perspective. In 1996, Rose Marie Beebe and Robert Senkewicz published a translation of a handwritten memoir penned in 1851 by Antonio María Osio. Originally from Baja California, Osio and his family moved to Alta California in 1825 and settled in Monterey. Although most of Osio's memoir is based on personal experience, some of it derives from oral tradition (Beebe and Senkewicz 1996:15–16). His account of the construction of the third quadrangle, which had occurred ten years before he moved to the province, falls into this latter category.

Osio tells a story about the 1815 quadrangle reconstruction to illustrate how the settlement's commander, Luis Antonio Argüello, became friends with the newly appointed governor of Alta California, Pablo Vicente de Solá. Osio wrote:

> When the pace of their military service permitted it, Captain Argüello liked
> to keep his soldiers either well entertained with honest diversions or involved
> in hard work, which he would direct. Once, when he and his men were
> returning to the presidio at sunset after a day on horseback, he stopped on
> the crest of the low ridges that overlook the military square. From that vantage

point, he pointed out to them that all of the homes were in poor condition. He suggested that, if they agreed and were willing, the homes could be quickly and completely destroyed and then tastefully rebuilt around a larger square, which would provide each house a larger lot and a better appearance.

One of the sergeants, with whom he would discuss nonmilitary matters or converse informally as if he were his own nephew, answered that his sergeants, corporals, and soldiers had never demonstrated any other desire than to do the captain's bidding. Therefore, he would soon see them all working on the project he wished to complete. Since everyone was in such a good mood, the new presidio square was sketched out by dawn the next morning. Sergeants, corporals, and soldiers were appointed to begin to break ground and lay the foundation as soon as they could obtain the assistance of the Indians. Other men were appointed to go to the spot named Corte de Madera de San Rafael to prepare the different types of timber. (Osio 1996:32)

Osio next discusses the difficulty of transporting timber for the new structure. As the local surroundings were completely deforested, the nearest source of timber was located across the bay, to the north. Argüello built a barge and learned to navigate the bay waters from a Native Californian named Marín. The quadrangle project was well underway when Argüello received a communication from the new governor ordering him to turn over the barge, which had been constructed without permission and which, the governor charged, could be used to trade with smugglers. To defend his honor against this accusation, Argüello relinquished the barge and traveled to Monterey, personally telling the governor "that he had not asked for permission because he, his officers, and his men were all living in ramshackle homes, which were threatening to fall down. Before that calamity could occur, everyone agreed to work like *peones* [laborers] for their own benefit, so as not to place any burden whatsoever on the royal treasury" (Osio 1996:37).

Argüello's audacity in the exchange won Solá's respect, and the two men became friends. However, the loss of the barge kept Argüello from finishing the project. When Solá visited the Presidio later that year, the new quadrangle was unfinished (Osio 1996:38).

Construction continued for several years. José María Amador, a soldier stationed at the Presidio from 1809 to 1827, wrote in his memoirs that the quadrangle was in the process of reconstruction in 1818 and that the old structures were made of wooden stakes and the new structures were adobe (Mora-Torres 2005:43–45). Also in 1818, Governor Solá wrote to the viceroy of New Spain that the southern wing of the quadrangle, where the chapel was located, was yet to be finished (Bancroft 1886b:372). In 1819, sixteen captive Native Californian men were put to work making adobes to complete the last sections of the quadrangle (Langellier and Rosen 1996:140).

In its centralized construction and use of uniform building methods and materials, the Presidio's third quadrangle marks a significant shift in the colonial community's production of its built environment. It also presents an interpretive paradox: ironically, the third quadrangle most closely matched the stipulations of military regulations, yet it was built during a time when the Presidio had the greatest autonomy and the least oversight by colonial officials. We are well advised to take Osio's account with the proverbial grain of salt, but nonetheless it is clear that this architectural undertaking was a local endeavor, not one that was ordered by colonial officials in Monterey or Mexico City.

Architectural Decay during the Mexican Era: 1822–1848

After the end of Spanish-colonial rule in 1821, the ambitiously conceived third quadrangle began to physically deteriorate and slowly lost its primacy in colonial life at the Presidio. New fenestrations in its exterior walls permitted easy passage between internal and external spaces; and within a few short years, most of the newly constructed eastern wing had collapsed.[3] The archaeological deposits associated with the third quadrangle provide further evidence of this; rooms on the east wing contain only thin occupational deposits capped by layers of roof and wall collapse. These layers of structural debris are mixed with butchering refuse that was apparently disposed of in the decaying buildings (Voss 2002:379–380).

The architectural dissolution of the main quadrangle in the 1820s anticipated the events of the 1830s that would end El Presidio de San Francisco's role as the nucleus of Californio daily life. In the early 1830s, many of the military settlers received land grants and began to shift their primary residences to their agricultural holdings; even more departed in 1834 and 1835, as the Pueblo of Yerba Buena was granted its charter and Commander Mariano G. Vallejo moved most military personnel to the newly formed Sonoma Barracks. Vallejo authorized the salvaging of usable construction materials from the Presidio to erect buildings at both new settlements. By 1840, only the Presidio's comandancia, chapel, prison, and some workshops still stood (Langellier and Rosen 1996:170).

The post-1821 decay of the quadrangle indicates a decline in the symbolic importance of architecture among the colonial community as well as an actual decline in architectural productivity. The rapid dissolution of the Presidio's main quadrangle in the 1820s highlights its importance as a colonial institution. The main quadrangle was a spatial form that rapidly lost its salience within the new political and economic conditions that accompanied Mexican independence.

Architectural Trends: Homogeneity, Centralization, and Expansion

Certain continuities in the architectural form of the main quadrangle were evident throughout its history. The general configuration of the quadrangle—a single row of structures lining the edges of a rectangular central plaza—was particularly consistent. And, as chapter 6 notes, the main quadrangle never incorporated the defensive capabilities dictated by military regulations. In other aspects, however, the quadrangle changed significantly over time. Three trends are apparent between 1776 and 1821: greater homogeneity in architectural materials, technique, and form; increased centralization of architectural production; and expansion of the quadrangle's footprint. Though they began earlier in the Presidio's history, these trends all culminated in the 1815 construction of the third quadrangle. Together, they suggest the growing symbolic and functional importance of the main quadrangle to the Presidio community during the Spanish-colonial era.

Homogeneity

The increasing homogeneity of architectural practices at El Presidio de San Francisco is evident in both building materials and building form. Given that military regulations specified that presidio quadrangles should be constructed entirely of adobe (Brinkerhoff and Faulk 1965), it is perhaps the initial *heterogeneity* of El Presidio de San Francisco's architecture that needs to be explained.

The first quadrangle was constructed of a variety of materials and techniques, all of them endemic to the northwest Mexican provinces from which the Presidio settlers had been recruited. The Presidio's incomplete enclosing wall was a palisade fence; the comandancia was adobe; at least one building was made of stone; and the rest of the buildings, including the church, storehouses, and settlers' residences, were constructed of palisade, rammed earth, *jacal* (wattle-and-daub), and *zacate* (thatch).

The persistence of these mixed architectural materials and techniques into the 1810s, relatively late into the settlement's history, is striking. Palisade, jacal, zacate, and rammed earth construction continued at El Presidio de San Francisco long after the surrounding missions and their outbuildings were being built entirely of stone and adobe with tiled roofs (Barker, Whatford, and Benté 1997). Economic and environmental factors underscore the challenges faced by the settlers in constructing shelter in this new environment, but they do not explain the failure to follow military regulations and the use of mixed materials and architectural techniques. We can perhaps understand this heterogeneity as an improvisational response to the new natural and cultural environment that the colonial settlers were striving to inhabit, one in which an array of familiar techniques were deployed in an unfamiliar setting. The diversity of architectural practices also may have been a venue in which the pluralistic ethnic composition of the settlement was being negotiated. For example, Diana DiPaolo Loren's investigations of El Presidio de Los Adaes in the frontier Tejás province found that most colonists lived in houses that mixed colonial and indigenous architectural styles, allowing them to "put on" different ethnic and class identities that might be advantageous in specific situations (Loren 1999:204–205).

Even as architectural heterogeneity persisted, the 1790s marked the beginning of increasing homogenization at El Presidio de San Francisco. Adobe began to be used more often than other materials in new construction, especially for nonresidential buildings that served the community as a whole. The transition to adobe was complete by the 1815 construction of the third quadrangle: the mixed groupings of adobe, stone, palisade, and jacal were demolished and replaced with continuous wings of adobe rooms, constructed to uniform standards. This resulted not only in the homogenization of the quadrangle's appearance and the production of uninterrupted exterior facades but also in the standardization of building width and room size. By 1815, each household, regardless of origin or ethnicity or heritage, lived in identical apartments, indistinct from each other in appearance.

The shift toward adobe construction cannot be interpreted as an adaptive response to San Francisco's natural environment. Importing mud-brick architecture to the foggy California coast can only be viewed as colonial folly: as Hermenegildo Sal observed, "The adobe is bad in itself because of the dampness it crumbles" (Sal 1976:47–49). Nor can military regulations explain this late choice, for compliance with the architectural stipulations of the 1772 Reglamento came only when El Presidio de San Francisco was relatively autonomous and most isolated from colonial military command.

Instead, adobe architecture may have been one of the ways that the military settlers asserted their status as colonizers during this critical period in the emergence of Californio identity. Most of the building materials and methods used throughout the Presidio's first four decades had close correlates among local Native Californian architectural practices. Adobe alone was distinctly colonial, associated with colonial institutions such as the mission complexes and earlier buildings at the Presidio that had a community-wide function (the chapel, warehouses, guardhouse, and comandancia). The wholesale adoption of adobe as the preferred building material at the Presidio was an important means through which the polyracial colonial population materialized a clear distinction between themselves and local indigenous populations.

Centralized Labor, Centralized Production

Labor relations and the scale of architectural production at the Presidio also changed over time. Overall, the responsibility for architectural production shifted from the household to the military command, and work was increasingly performed by Native Californian laborers rather than by the colonists themselves.

Administrative buildings and the chapel had always been overseen by the military command, but for the first two decades, the settlers themselves were responsible for building their own residences (Langellier and Rosen 1996:33). Not until the 1790s did the military command began to concern itself with the construction and maintenance of the settlers' housing. Beginning in 1795, the governor and Presidio commanders began to plan to replace the quadrangle. The surviving plans indicate that residential structures were included in the proposed construction (see figs. 20 and 21), although this never came to fruition.

In 1798, the Presidio's officers directed the construction of a new wing of nine individual quarters and a barracks to house those soldiers whose duties alternated between the main quadrangle and the newly constructed Castillo de San Joaquín. This was the first instance in which the Presidio's military command assumed responsibility for providing residential housing for its troops. It was also during this period that the settlement developed infrastructure for producing its own architectural materials, with the construction of a tile kiln and a forge (Langellier and Rosen 1996:89, 73, 90). Not coincidentally, the increased involvement of the military command in household architectural production during the 1790s coincided with the growing use of Native Californian labor at the settlement. Large Native Californian work parties were recruited from indigenous villages and also hired under contract from the missions.

The scale of architectural production at El Presidio de San Francisco shifted most dramatically with the 1815 construction of the third quadrangle. Constructed all of a piece, the west, north, and east wings of the new quadrangle could have been produced only with a centralized effort. Osio's narrative provides one account of how this might have occurred: the settlement's commander "suggested" the project and, through his second-in-command, obtained his troops' pledge to implement the plan. During this period, however, the primary source of construction labor was Native Californian prisoners of war. Argüello wrote in February 1816 that construction work had halted because eighteen of the captive workers had escaped; in September of the same year, fourteen of the prisoners escaped again and were not recaptured (Bancroft 1886b:372; Langellier and Rosen 1996:131). The third quadrangle was completed in 1819 after sixteen new captives were put to work as forced laborers making adobe bricks (Langellier and Rosen 1996:140).

The archaeologically recovered dimensions of the expanded third quadrangle help us understand exactly how labor-intensive this massive undertaking was. Laying foundations for the west, north, and east wings involved quarrying, transporting, and laying a minimum of 590 cubic meters of serpentinite stone. The walls and roofs required quarrying, mixing, and forming clay to produce no less than 2,800 cubic meters of adobe brick and enough fired-clay roof tile to cover an area of over 4,800 square meters.[4] All of this was accomplished entirely with manual labor. These estimates do not include the work involved in erecting internal partition walls, preparing and applying substantial quantities of mud mortar and plaster, acquiring and emplacing timber beams and the lattice-work roof substructure, applying floor surfaces, or building in the south wing of the expanded Presidio.

Two historical documents, both written in 1796, provide still another perspective on the labor required for the third quadrangle (Schuetz-Miller 1994:45). In that year, Governor Diego de Borica asked master stonecutter and stone layer Manuel Esteban Ruiz to estimate the materials, tools, professional artisans, and assistants that would be required to construct an entirely new quadrangle for El Presidio de San Francisco, according to the plans that the governor had commissioned (see figs. 20 and 21). Ruiz's list was then given to Sal, to calculate the amount and cost of labor necessary to enact the plan. From their estimates, it appears that they planned to construct the new quadrangle over a one- or two-year period. During that time, the work force would have included three master artisans, ten peones (civilian laborers), five soldiers, and no fewer than ninety-four Native Californian laborers.[5] Altogether, Borica's proposed construction project would have required at least 28,600 person-days to complete.

The 1815 quadrangle, which was 180 percent larger than the one proposed by Borica, undoubtedly required an even greater labor force—by conservative calculations, no fewer than 50,000 person-days, and most likely a great many more. By any measure, the 1815 quadrangle was a massive undertaking that created a demand for a constant supply of Native Californians to perform grueling, back-breaking labor. Argüello's boast that the construction could be accomplished "all by the labor of Indian captives without cost to the King" (Bancroft 1886b:127) gave added incentive to the Presidio soldiers' ongoing battles with inland native villages in the Central Valley.

These estimates of material and labor also point to a possible relationship between the organization of architectural labor and the choice of materials. Throughout the world, mud brick construction has been and continues to be undertaken on the household scale; this was historically true in Alta California, especially at smaller ranchos. Nonetheless, the labor involved in quarrying stones for building foundations and the difficulty of transporting wooden beams for ceiling rafters might have been prohibitive for individual households. Some materials—such as tile for roofs—were simply unavailable unless their production was coordinated in some way by the community, either through centrally organized production or specialist craft workshops. Accounts of Native Californian workers at the Presidio especially indicate that they were assigned the most repetitive, heavy tasks of quarrying and hauling stone and excavating, mixing, and molding clays. This observation is not meant to posit a causal relationship between architectural materials and the organization of architectural labor, but rather to note that changes in one would have encouraged changes in the other.

The increasing centralization of architectural production also had gendered implications. For most of the Presidio's history, architectural production was organized primarily at the household level. Women, men, and children all likely participated in the architectural design, production, and maintenance of their homes. How each household organized architectural decision-making and labor seems to have been a private matter, so we can surmise that there might have been considerable variability from residence to residence.

By 1815, with the construction of the third quadrangle, production of residential architecture had shifted from the household to the military command, and all architecture was subject to centralized directives. These centrally organized construction projects were segregated by gender: only men participated in the new undertakings. The masculinist character of Osio's narrative concerning the 1815 quadrangle illustrates this dynamic, recounting a process in which architectural decisions were made by colonial officers and implemented by male soldiers who supervised the labor of Native Californian men. How the colonial women at El Presidio de San Francisco may have reacted to these changes is a matter of informed speculation: some may have welcomed relief from the work involved, feeling that the military command was finally fulfilling obligations it had long neglected; others may have resented being excluded from the process or the imposition of uniform architectural forms.

What is certain is that architectural production increasingly became a venue in which the differences among men were materially enacted through chain-of-command decision-making and labor regimes. By creating situations in which higher-ranking military colonists supervised and controlled the labor of lower-ranking colonial soldiers and Native Californian male laborers, these centralized construction projects participated in the growing importance of differential masculinities in Californio social life. Whereas male colonists had once been distinguished by racial casta, some men now used their military rank to exert

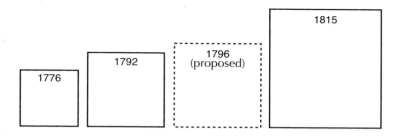

FIGURE 23.   Size-based comparison of El Presidio de San Francisco's main quadrangles.

greater power over the details of daily life. Most significantly, through these labor projects, colonial men of all ranks came to experience authority over Native Californians not only in military conflict, where outcomes were uncertain and danger was ever present, but also in the context of structured daily routines of labor supervision and discipline. While materially transforming the place they called home, colonial men simultaneously consolidated their status in the social order and put Native Californian men "in their place" as subordinate manual laborers.

Expansion

With each reconstruction of the quadrangle, its footprint increased, ultimately covering an area nearly four times the area of the first quadrangle (fig. 23). The first quadrangle measured 92 by 92 varas; the second, 116 by 120 varas; a proposed (but never constructed) quadrangle, 130–140 varas to a side; and the third, 172 by 192 varas.

Archaeologists usually interpret increases in site size as evidence of a growing population, but in the 1810s, the Presidio's population was at best stable and possibly declining. It is also worth noting that the 1815 quadrangle did not expand through incremental replacement and augmentation of individual structures (as would generally be the case if expansion were driven by population growth) but rather by deliberately tearing down older structures, establishing a new grid, and constructing continuous blocks of apartments. We might even think of the third quadrangle as San Francisco's first urban redevelopment project—a wholesale demolition followed by master-planned new construction.

I initially assumed that the 1815 expansion was undertaken to create more buildings, especially to create more and bigger apartments. However, the expansion increased interior room space by only approximately 25 percent, a gain that could have been realized by constructing new homes on the eastern, undeveloped side of the second quadrangle. Alternatively, at the presidios of San Diego, Santa Bárbara, and Monterey, the residential capacity of the settlement was increased not by enlarging the quadrangle but by adding rows of rooms along the exterior of an existing wing or by building into the plaza itself. Certainly by 1815, many of the residential areas of El Presidio de San Francisco's quadrangle had been damaged by storms and earthquakes and needed repair, but these structures could have been rebuilt in the same location, as was done on the south side of the quadrangle.

If the quadrangle was not expanded to create more or larger residential buildings, why was such a massive project undertaken? Notably, the 1815 expansion increased the size of the plaza by more than 220 percent. Perhaps this growth was motivated not by a desire for more rooms, but rather by a desire for a larger central public space. The plaza increase could have served many functions. For example, with greater participation of Indian Auxiliaries in military campaigns, the existing plaza might have been inadequate for training exercises and drills. More space in the main quadrangle might have been needed for craft production or other activities. Or the central plaza might have served as a safe space where children could play or work with minimum direct supervision, since their activities would be visible to anyone in the community.

Another factor that merits consideration is how plazas facilitate social performances—both ritual and routine—in community life. In prehistoric archaeology, increases in plaza space (both in number of plazas and in their size) are often interpreted as shifts in the social organization of community ritual or an increase in the importance of social visibility (Kidder 2004; Perry and Joyce 2001). It is interesting to note that the expansion of the quadrangle's plaza occurred during the early years in which the military settlers were asserting a collective Californio identity in place of the ethnic/racial markers of the sistema de castas. Might the increased visibility of social practices have been an important way in which this shared identity was enacted and consolidated during the routines of daily life? What interests might have been served by creating a more prominent venue for social performance and ritual?

Honor, Shame, and Ethnic Respectability

There are powerful parallels between the transformation of social identity produced through Californio ethnogenesis and the architectural transformation of El Presidio de San Francisco's built environment. The sistema de castas was replaced by a community-based identity shared among people who had been previously differentiated by racial and ethnic heritage. Likewise, a heterogeneous built environment formed by the actions of individual households was transformed into a unified quadrangle, homogeneous in appearance and produced through the coordinated efforts of the community. The organization of labor involved in the production of this new place was also a social structure through which other hierarchies were enacted and consolidated, especially those among men: between high- and low-ranking military personnel, and between colonists and Native Californians.

The changes in the Presidio's architecture may have also participated in changes in gendered practices. The sistema de castas referenced not only race but also gender and sexuality. Casta designations were used to delineate honorable sexual relationships from dishonorable ones; and sexual relationships, in turn, produced the contested spectrum of racialized subjects who constituted the next generation of castas. Castas simultaneously carried the honor of their European ancestors' sexual conquests and the shame of illegitimacy and descent from lower-status Indian and African forebears. The military settlers' rejection of casta rankings and the concomitant ethnogenesis of Californio identity must have had concurrent effects on gendered and sexual ideologies and practices.

The honor/shame complex provides a particularly useful lens through which to examine the intertwined transformation of ethnic, racial, and gendered identities. As chapter 3 describes, the honor/shame complex was one of several secular ideologies that influenced social negotiations of gender and sexuality in Spanish-colonial California. Within honor/shame ideologies, men's masculine honor was affirmed by sexual conquests and by protecting the sexual virtue of female relatives. Men who failed to accrue honor, or whose female relatives were not sexually virtuous, were "less than men." Honor and shame also differentiated between virtuous and fallen women, the latter deemed undeserving of protection from sexual assault and the degradations of poverty. The honor/shame complex thus informed not only relations between men and women but also relationships among men and among women.

Architecture, Privacy, and Sexual Surveillance

In societies in which ideologies of sexual honor and shame are prominent, architecture often participates in enacting daily routines related to the preservation of feminine honor. Most commonly, residential architecture and public areas are partitioned or otherwise subdivided to create visual privacy and discrete enclosures, allowing women to conduct their daily activities away from the public gaze. Architectural partitioning also aids male and elder female relatives in their efforts to prevent unchaperoned contact between the women in their charge and unrelated men. Architectural partitioning does not necessarily create gender-segregated spaces, but it often delineates public areas from more private ones (for example, visitors may be received in the front room of a house, but only family members would customarily enter more private interior rooms).

Historical and archaeological evidence of partitioned space—or the lack of it—suggests the extent to which honor/shame ideologies influenced architectural decision-making at the Presidio. Formal spatial analysis is a methodology that can provide a quantitative measure of the degree of partitioning and spatial segregation in an architectural space (see, for example, Gilchrist 1994: 161–167; Markus 1993). One can quantify degrees of access within a structure by counting the number of thresholds that must be crossed to move from an entrance of a building to its most secluded room(s).

Analysis of the three quadrangle plan drawings produced in the 1790s shows that partitioned residential space was not evenly distributed across the community; such private space was apparently a privilege associated with military rank (table 8). In the 1792 Sal plan (see fig. 18), the only "as-built" representation of the quadrangle's architecture, most residential buildings have only one level of access; these are all labeled *Habitaciones de la Tropa* (soldier's quarters) (Sal 1792). Two other soldiers' quarters (labeled c and d on the plan) are two-room complexes with two levels of access. The sergeant's quarters is a three-room compound with two buildings that open directly onto the plaza and a third that is accessed only through an interior passage. Finally, the comandancia is a sizeable four-room complex with an additional private, walled courtyard. This structure afforded the greatest degree of privacy for its residents: they could perform outdoor tasks out of public view, and two of the rooms could be accessed only by first passing through the private courtyard.

The 1795 and 1796 drawings (see figs. 20 and 21) were plans for future construction; they are not evidence of actual spatial practices but instead represent the intentions of military officers and engineers, who had been asked to envision an improved replacement of their built environment. One striking difference between the Sal plan and these two drawings is that the latter, if constructed to plan, would have provided a private, walled yard for almost all residential buildings, even those allocated to rank-and-file soldiers and their families. The only exceptions would have been the male-only barracks for unmarried soldiers shown on the 1796 plan. Like the quadrangle depicted in the Sal plan, these proposals would have allocated moderately larger apartments to sergeants and significantly larger ones to officers in the higher ranks. The officers' apartments in the 1795 plan were to be unpartitioned, while those in the 1796 plan were depicted as a line of two or three adjoining rooms with an enclosed rear yard.

Analyzing these three plans indicates that, in the 1790s, partitioned residential space that provided privacy and enclosure was a privilege associated with mil-

TABLE 8. Formal spatial analysis of
residential buildings in plans for the Presidio quadrangle

	Residential Buildings			
	In 1792 Plan	In 1795 Plan	In 1796 Plan	In 1815 Quadrangle
Number of rooms/enclosed spaces per residential building				
1	9	0	2	Most appear to have
2	2	28	21	only one room
3	1	0	3	
4	1	0	3	
5	1	0	0	
TOTAL NUMBER OF RESIDENTIAL BUILDINGS	14	28	29	Unknown
Levels of access per building				
1	9	0	2[a]	Most appear to have
2	4	28	24	only one level
3	1	0	3	of access
4	0	0	0	

[a] Unfortunately, doorways are not depicted in the 1796 plan, so calculations of levels of access require certain assumptions. The analysis here presumes that each residential building could be entered from the plaza by only one door and that adjacent rooms were connected with doorways.

itary rank. This is shown most dramatically in the Sal plan, where only the commander's family had access to private outdoor space, with the remainder of the community presumably performing their outdoor work in public view in the plaza. The 1795 and 1796 construction plans illustrate an intent to allocate walled yards to all households. At least to the engineers and officers developing plans for the Presidio's architectural rehabilitation, such spaces were considered important locales of domestic life.

When these plans are compared to the archaeologically known third quadrangle, it is clear that a shift in spatial practices and preferences occurred between the 1790s and the 1810s. Archaeological research on the configuration of the third quadrangle is far from complete, but current information indicates that all residential quarters had only one level of access. The east, north, and west wings were all composed of a contiguous line of single-room apartments; the buildings on the south wing, while not contiguous, were also only one room deep. There is no evidence of enclosed rear yards or the kind of multiroom structures depicted on earlier plans. It is certainly possible that the apartments occupied by elite families were composed of two or more contiguous rooms, although preservation conditions are such that this may not be apparent from the archaeological remains. Nonetheless, the plans developed in 1795 and 1796 to provide each apartment with a private yard do not appear to have materialized.

I interpret this change in architectural practices and imaginings as an indication that the Presidio's third quadrangle marked a transformation of spatial practices associated with the honor/shame complex. In the 1810s, practices related to honor and shame may have been increasingly implemented at the community level rather than within individual households. The primary outcome of expanding the enclosed main quadrangle was an increase in the size of its central plaza. This must be seen as a deliberate choice: a quadrangle of the same total footprint could have provided ample private yards for each dwelling without expanding the plaza. In addition, the years from 1815 to 1822 were the only time that the quadrangle was completely enclosed by adobe walls. With entrance to and egress from the quadrangle now controlled—perhaps for the first time—through the narrow guarded gate on its north end, the plaza became a secure, visually protected interior space within which the residents of the quadrangle could conduct their daily routines. In sum, the architectural evidence suggests that the honor/shame complex shifted from being a household-based elite practice to a paternalistic obligation of the military command toward the community at large. As with the social relations of architectural production, there was a parallel transfer of household responsibilities to the military leadership.

The Face of the Community

The 1815 transformation of the Presidio community's built environment signals several turning points in social relations during the emergence of Californio identity: the transfer of household-based rights and responsibilities to the military command; the homogenization of community architecture and differentiation from Native Californian architectural practices; the increasing importance of the plaza as a venue for social routines and ritual; and the consolidation of hierarchical relations among men through labor regimes. These internal changes in social relations coincided with external shifts in the broader sphere of social, economic, and political interactions surrounding El Presidio de San Francisco.

After 1800, the Presidio's increasing isolation from its parent polity of New Spain was accompanied by intensified interactions with maritime expeditions from European countries. The settlement had particularly frequent contact with Russian visitors, first with maritime voyages from the Russian-American Company's Alaskan settlements and then, after 1812, with Colony Ross, a mere sixty miles north. Hostility and territorial tensions between El Presidio de San Francisco and its northern Russian neighbors were interwoven with social and economic networks that linked the two communities. The Presidio, no longer receiving regular supplies from San Blas, became especially dependent on Colony Ross for access to manufactured goods, while the Russians desperately needed agricultural products. Social events between the two settlements (such as dinner parties, fandangos, bear-and-bull fights, and dances) fostered friendships, alliances, and romance among the two colonial communities. In addition to this close relationship with the Russian-American Company, the Presidio increasingly hosted the crews from visiting French, Dutch, English, and Yankee ships that anchored in the bay while traversing the Pacific coast.

The transformation of the settlement's built environment during this period may have had as much to do with settlers' relationships with outsiders as it did with social relationships within the colonial community. As increasing numbers of European visitors sailed through the mouth of the San Francisco Bay, the Presidio community could no longer define itself solely in relationship to colonized Native Californians. The settlement's original diversity—its strong African-Latino and Mexican Indian heritage—was a liability in its interactions with other colonial powers. To their European visitors, the Presidio's quadrangle presented the face of the community. The military command's concern with the appearance of the quadrangle, the homogenization of architectural materials and form, the complete enclosure of the plaza, and the gendered implications of these practices—all of these may have been motivated in part by a desire to present an image of ethnic respectability to European visitors.

. . .

Architecture functions not simply as a spatial container of social life, but rather as a form of material culture that is produced through and simultaneously structures social relationships. By treating architectural remains as artifacts with complex histories of production, use, maintenance, discard, and reuse, we can see that the social relations involved in constructing and maintaining a building can be just as important as the social activities that occur within that building. The diachronic, comparative approach taken here draws attention to continuities and changes in architectural practices during the dynamic transformations of social identity involved in Californio ethnogenesis.

During the Spanish-colonial era, the Presidio's main quadrangle was the most prominent physical materialization of colonial life in San Francisco. Just as social identities at the Presidio were overdetermined—constructed in reference to race, ethnicity, religion, gender, sexuality, rank, and economic status—so too was the architecture of the community. Environmental influences, architectural traditions, colonial regulations, economic constraints, labor regimes, the military chain of command, racially inflected notions of taste and aesthetics, sexual and gendered ideologies—all of these factors influenced the production of architectural forms, sometimes conflicting with each other and at other times converging. Throughout, the Presidio's architectural metamorphoses unfolded in a manner that differentiated the military settlers from Native Californians and that emphasized colonial commonalities over ethnic and racial variation. In this regard, architectural practices were one strategy used by the Presidio's polyracial community to negotiate anxieties about ethnic and gendered respectability within an increasingly transnational social universe.

El Presidio de San Francisco's military settlers inhabited a world of clay. The vertical walls that defined their built environment, whether of wattle-and-daub, rammed earth, palisade, or adobe, were surfaced in clay; the settlers walked across floors and plazas made of packed clay and fired-clay ladrillos; and, after the 1790s, they slept under roofs of curved clay tejas. The settlement was ringed with wide pits excavated to harvest clay for these constructions. Portable ceramic vessels were ubiquitous and resonated with the fabric of the settlement itself, linking fixed architecture to the activities of everyday life. Our excavations have recovered thousands of ceramic sherds—broken pieces of storage jars, pots and griddles, cooking bowls, serving vessels, and tablewares that were essential to the daily routines of every colonial resident at the settlement.

Household ceramics are central to this archaeological study of colonial ethnogenesis for several reasons. Preservation is a significant factor: the durable, largely inert sherds remain relatively unchanged long after other household objects made of organic materials or metals have decayed or corroded. Further, ceramics are brittle and break regularly, creating a steady stream of debris that contributes to archaeological deposits. More than this, however, pottery is an expressive as well as a functional medium. Ceramic manufacture is an additive technology, one that fosters infinite variety in form, surface, and decorative elements. The regularity and variation of the choices made, whether deliberate or habitual, reveal patterns of practice and aesthetic preferences that are often related to social identity. Tradition (the way things are done) and taste (the way things are done right) are in constant play with function and innovation.

This chapter examines two categories of ceramic artifacts from the Presidio. The first group consists of sherds from imported tableware vessels that were used to serve and consume food. The second group is made up of sherds from locally produced, low-fired earthenware vessels, all of which were used in food preparation and cooking. The two sets of ceramic sherds could not be more different—one was highly varied and beautifully decorated, and the other, uniformly plain and poorly made—and it is unusual for them to be considered together. This analysis connects them through attention to the aesthetics of procurement, production, and use.

Ceramics in Context: The Colonial Marketplace, Depositional Processes, and Archaeological Analysis

It is important to first discuss the artifacts' contexts: the procurement networks that limited the options available to colonial consumers; the depositional processes that resulted in the formation of the Building 13 midden; and the archaeological analysis procedures that generated the observations on which this chapter is based.

Ceramics and the Economy of Empire

Until the 1810s, Alta California's presidios were economically dependent on the Naval Department at San Blas, which dispatched an annual shipment of manufactured goods to the province. These imported materials were supplemented by foodstuffs and craft goods made from local sources. The ceramic assemblage from the Building 13 midden reflects this economic structure. The collection is dominated by three waretypes: Mexican galeras (lead-glazed, red-bodied earthenwares), Mexican majolicas (tin-glazed earthenware), and locally produced unglazed earthenwares. Together, these waretypes account for 87 to 96 percent of the assemblage, depending on which quantitative measure is used (table 9).[1] Some of the Mexican ceramics can be traced to the towns of Puebla and Tonalá, but the majority were likely products of the many ceramic manufactories established in western Mexico during the 1750s (Barnes 1980). Chinese porcelains, which had been obtained by the Spanish through trade in the Philippines, were also distributed through the San Blas supply ships (Dado 2006). The Building 13 midden provides little evidence of trade with British and American vessels, indicating that Spanish prohibitions against commerce with foreign merchants were largely effective during the 1770s–1810s (fig. 24).

Colonial memorias and facturas (requisitions and invoices) document what was

Waretype	Sherd Count		Weight		MNV	
	Number	Frequency (%)	g	Frequency (%)	Number	Frequency (%)
Galera	4,383	58.70	8,140.3	66.20	134	53.39
Majolica	1,725	23.10	1,381.8	11.24	40	15.94
Unglazed earthen-ware	883	11.83	2,333.9	18.98	45	17.93
Bruñida de Tonalá	351	4.70	275.1	2.24	10	3.98
Chinese porcelain	62	0.83	81.5	0.66	8	3.19
Unidentified glazed earthenware	29	0.39	4.6	0.04	0	0.00
British whiteware	21	0.28	20.7	0.17	7	2.79
Black-glazed earthenware	7	0.09	7.2	0.06	2	0.80
Olla de aceite	3	0.04	33.8	0.27	2	0.80
Stoneware	2	0.03	15.2	0.12	2	0.80
Faience	1	0.01	2.5	0.02	1	0.40
TOTAL	7,467	100.00	12,296.6	100.00	251	100.00

requested and what was actually delivered to Alta California's presidios via the San Blas supply ships. Each year, the San Francisco Presidio's habilitado compiled a list of the settlement's needs for the following year and dispatched it to San Blas. The goods received from supply ships were documented in invoices that included the fixed government prices charged against the settlement's account.

In 1987, National Park Service archaeologist Leo Barker traveled to the Archivo General de la Nación in Mexico to retrieve microfilm copies of colonial documents related to El Presidio de San Francisco, including the invoices and requisitions. These sources were later amended with a contribution of additional microfilmed documents from Francis Weber and Catherine Rudolph of the Santa Barbara Presidio History Center (Barker 2007). Through a partnership between the Presidio Archaeology Center and the International Council on Monuments and Sites (ICOMOS), archivist Veronica Dado (2003, 2004, 2006) transcribed and translated twenty-six requisitions and seven invoices, which represent seventeen shipments to El Presidio de San Francisco.[2] These

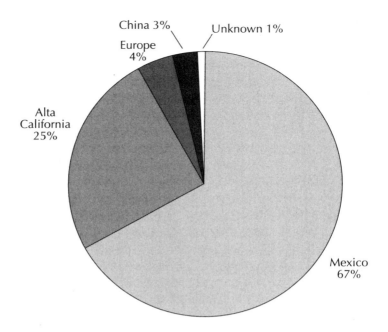

FIGURE 24. Places of manufacture for the ceramic vessels recovered from the Building 13 midden. Frequencies are calculated using minimum number of vessels.

documents are contemporary (1781–1810) with the Building 13 midden and provide a valuable source of information about how ceramics were supplied to Alta California presidios.

Just over half of the requisitions and invoices listed ceramics, which were referenced in three contexts: orders of *losa*,[3] or household ceramics; orders of empty *botes* (large jars), for storing water and liquid foods; and jars used as shipping containers for wet foodstuffs such as olive oil, cured olives, and honey. Losa produced in Mexico was shipped by the crate, with each crate usually holding twenty or twenty-five dozen (240 or 300) pieces.

Descriptions of household ceramics were remarkably vague. Most entries simply referred to them as *losa surtida* (assorted pottery) or sometimes as *losa blanca* (white pottery). The latter could be a specific reference to majolica, a low-fired earthenware with an opaque tin glaze that creates a white background color on the vessels' surfaces. Rarely, the documents mentioned place of manufacture (such as Puebla or China) or quality (fine, ordinary, or regular). The invoices and requisitions mentioned vessel forms only occasionally, typically listing plates, cups, bowls, serving plates, water jars, jugs, pans, pots, skillets, and chamber pots.[4] A dozen pieces of losa generally cost two to four *reales* (one peso was equal to eight reales), although in one order, Chinese porcelain plates were valued at ten reales per dozen. Some larger vessels, such as chamber pots and serving dishes, were priced individually, from a half real to six and a half reales each. In comparison, a pair of adult-size leather shoes cost five to six reales, and a pair of scissors cost one real (Dado 2004).

Military settlers at the Presidio had little specific control over the waretypes, vessel forms, decorative styles, or other attributes of available ceramics. The major purchasing decisions were made by military agents in the San Blas Naval Department (who determined what goods were shipped) and by each presidio's habilitado, who requisitioned, accepted, and distributed the goods. In this context, the imported ceramics recovered from the Building 13 midden provide evidence of the interplay between local practices of the Presidio community and the structural constraints imposed by the military supply system.

Depositional Processes

The ceramic sherds analyzed in this chapter were excavated from the Building 13 midden during 1999 and 2000. Accounting for nearly a quarter (24.8 percent) of the midden's contents by weight, this assemblage is composed of 7,467 sherds (12.3 kg), representing a minimum of 251 vessels. As chapter 5 explains, the Building 13 midden accumulated in an open pit that had once been excavated to harvest clay-rich soils for adobe, tile, and ceramic production. Manufacture dates for ceramics and other chronologically sensitive artifacts found in the midden indicate that the majority of the deposit accumulated between 1776 and 1800 (Voss 2002:694–695). This was a particularly important period in colonial ethnogenesis, when settlers were actively rejecting casta designations and beginning to self-identify as gente de razón and Californios.

The fragmentation and spatial distribution of ceramics found in the deposit indicate that the Building 13 midden was an open-air dumping area where refuse from household activities was deposited in an incremental, repetitive fashion. The deposit contains the full functional range of ceramics that would be present in most households, representing all aspects of food storage, preparation, and consumption (fig. 25). The ceramic sherds are highly fragmented: the mean average sherd weight is only 1.65 g, with more than 70 percent of the sherds weighing 1 g or less. Sherds from a single vessel were rarely found in close association, and some cross-mends occurred among sherds recovered as far as 10 m apart. Additionally, some of the softer-bodied ceramic wares had abraded and rounded edges. The high degree of fragmentation and dispersion and the presence of post-depositional abrasion indicate that the midden's con-

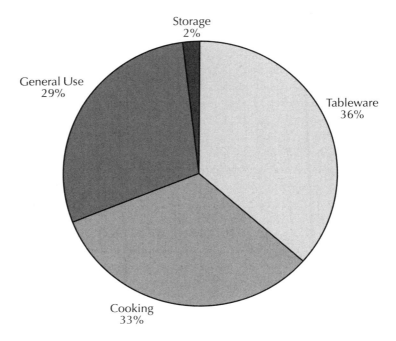

Storage
2%

General Use
29%

Tableware
36%

Cooking
33%

FIGURE 25. Functions of the ceramic vessels recovered from the Building 13 midden. Frequencies are calculated using minimum number of vessels.

tents were mixed as a result of animal or human scavenging and foot traffic. Consequently, it is impossible to trace objects in the midden to specific households or other social groups within the colonial population. The midden is thus best interpreted as a record of community practices during the time when most of the deposit formed.

Analyzing the Ceramic Assemblage

This specific context of acquiring, distributing, utilizing, and discarding ceramics informed the methods we used to analyze the ceramics from the Building 13 midden. Archaeologists generally analyze ceramics by following classification systems that emphasize differences or similarities in paste, glaze, technology, and decorative motifs. The ceramic transactions listed in the colonial memorias and facturas, however, suggest that place of manufacture, vessel form and function, and, to a lesser degree, quality were all salient attributes, while the fine distinctions that archaeologists often make between different waretypes and decorative styles were not. This does not mean that archaeological classifications have no analytical value; rather, it argues for using the information provided in the memorias and facturas to analyze vernacular attributes (location of manufacture, form, function, appearance) independently from archaeologically defined waretypes.

In this effort, I integrated sherd-level and vessel-level analyses using both quantitative and qualitative methods. First, each sherd was individually cataloged and analyzed, with a record of attributes related to waretype, decoration, vessel part, thickness, burning, surface treatments, and manufacture technique. Next, the sherds within each waretype were assigned to minimum vessel groupings using a qualitative method that accounted for paste composition and inclusions as well as vessel form, vessel size, and decoration. Each minimum vessel grouping was analyzed to determine vessel form, including rim form and vessel dimensions (rim diameter, base diameter, vessel height, and wall thickness); manufacture technique; surface treatment (presence or absence of glaze, slip, or decoration); surface and interior color; paste composition, inclusions, and temper; presence or absence of soot residues; and the percentage of the original vessel represented by the original sherds as well as the degree of crossmending among sherds (Voss 2002:657–701).

The high degree of fragmentation posed challenges in determining vessel form and function. Over half the vessels could not be attributed to specific forms, but most could be identified as either flatware (such as plates, soup plates, *comales* [flat ceramic griddles], platters, and saucers) or hollowware (including bowls, cups, jars, and pots). Vessels were then assigned to one of four functional groupings (see fig. 25): tableware vessels used to serve and consume food; cooking wares, used for heating foods and identifiable archaeologically by the presence of soot residues on the exterior of the vessels; general use wares, bowls of medium and large size, without soot, that could have been used for food storage, preparation, and service; and storage wares, in this assemblage represented by only two *ollas de aceite* (oil jars).

On the Colonial Table

Archaeological analyses of ceramic tablewares provide a window into the "finegrained relationship between people and the material culture of the home" (Miller 2001:15). Chapter 3 argues that social life at the Presidio was not organized into distinct "private" and "public" spheres. Instead, what we might term "domestic" life was inextricably intertwined with the colonial military endeavor and its institutionalization. The home was thus an important locale where institutional policies and practices interfaced with small-scale interpersonal relationships. Archaeological evidence indicates that colonial residents of the Presidio prepared and consumed food in small groups, which were

TABLE 10. Tableware vessel form counts
(MNVs) found in the Building 13 midden, by waretype

Waretype	Cup or Bowl	Jarro or Chocotero	Plate or Soup Plate	Platter(?)	Unidentified Form	Total
Majolica	7	—	28	1	4	40
Galera	6	8	3	—	8	25
Bruñida de Tonalá	4	—	—	—	4	8
Chinese porcelain	6	—	—	—	2	8
British whiteware	1	—	—	—	6	7
Black-glazed earthenware	—	—	—	—	2	2
Faience	1	—	—	—	—	1
TOTAL	25	8	31	1	26	91

sometimes—though not always—organized along familial lines (see chapter 9). Meal sharing afforded an intimate sphere of social interaction among small groups of community members.

As durable, material objects repeatedly taken up in these social settings—meal after meal, gathering after gathering—ceramic tablewares provide one indication of the aesthetics and physical form of meal sharing. Tablewares account for 36 percent of the Building 13 midden ceramic assemblage, totaling ninety-three minimum vessels (see fig. 25). In comparison with the other functional ceramic groupings, tablewares show the greatest diversity in both waretype and form (table 10). Most of the tableware ceramics are decorated, ranging from simple handpainted rim bands to more elaborate polychrome decorative styles. They were all imported, primarily from central New Spain (present-day Mexico) but also from China, France, and Britain. The only other tableware objects represented in the Building 13 midden are two glass drinking vessels, one a molded, gadrooned stemware glass, and the other a copper-wheel engraved crystal tumbler (Voss 2002:450). Without question, ceramics were the dominant material on the colonial table.

Status, Gender, and Race in the Archaeology of Spanish-Colonial Ceramics

Archaeologists studying Spanish-colonial settlements throughout North America have long considered tableware ceramics to be an indicator of economic and ethnic status in colonial society. Most such studies are based on certain assumptions related to status and gender. The most common approach, for example, assumes that ceramics imported from Spain, China, or England are the highest-status wares; that those produced using European methods in New World potteries are next in status; and that locally produced ceramics are lowest in status. Majolica, a tin-glazed earthenware produced primarily in Puebla, Mexico, is commonly presented as the highest-status American-produced ware because of its similarity to Spanish majolica and Italian talavera ceramics. This latter claim is perhaps best expressed, in all its contradictions, by Charles Fairbanks (1973:165): "The archaeological evidence supports the conclusion that majolica originating in both Spain and the New World was largely a luxury item. Often used in hospitals and by apothecaries, it was also found as a widespread tableware. . . . Culturally, majolica is a luxury item, although it is found in even the more impoverished sites."

In declaring such waretypes to be status items, archaeologists have simultaneously associated majolicas, porcelains, and European-produced waretypes with masculinity and the public sphere. Perhaps the most well-known study of this kind is Kathleen Deagan's investigation of ethnicity and gender in Spanish-colonial St. Augustine. Deagan compared the archaeological remains of criollo and mestizo households to identify the archaeological signatures of different ethnic groups. In her analysis, she postulates that food preparation was a domestic, private, female realm, while dining was a more public activity associated with male status. She argues that majolicas were high-status items, likely used for social display in the male realm, and locally produced indigenous wares were low-status items used in the female realm (Deagan 1983b).

The status, ethnic, and gender associations of majolica and other ceramics in colonial New Spain have recently been reexamined by Diana DiPaolo Loren (1999) in her study of how material culture was depicted in casta paintings (see chapter 10). As Loren documents, majolica and Chinese porcelains are visible in the background of Spanish and high-status casta portraits, whereas lower-status casta paintings often show Native American or African women cooking stews in undecorated ceramic vessels. Majolica and other high-status ceramics are not absent from the lower-status casta paintings, however; instead, such tableware ceramics are shown in a chipped or broken state as part of a suite of elements meant to signify the unclean living situations of the lower castas (Loren 1999:150–155). Loren's study suggests that it was not waretype per se, but rather the context of use, that imbued ceramics with ethnic or status connotations in colonial New Spain.

Colonial memorias and facturas provide a different perspective on the purported association between ceramics and ethnic or economic status. Majolica—losa de Puebla and losa blanca—was no more expensive than most other types of

TABLE II. Majolica traditions and types found in the Building 13 midden

Tradition/Type[a]	Dates of Production	MNV
Puebla Tradition	1700–present	30
San Agustín Blue-on-White	1700–1780	2
Puebla Blue-on-White	1700–present	6
Huejotzingo Blue-on-White	1700–present	4
Wavy Rim Blue-on-White	1700–1800	5
San Elizario Polychrome	1750–1800	11
Green and Yellow Huejotzingo variants	1780–1800	2
Aranama Polychrome	1750–1850	6
Monterey Polychrome	1800–1830	—[b]
Tumacacori Polychrome	1780–1860	1
Other polychrome varieties[c]	—	3

[a] Puebla and Aranama Tradition classifications follow the typology developed by May (1972, 1975). Tumacacori Polychrome, a decorative type identified by the blue tint given to the background glaze color, has been extensively described by Barnes (1972:11) and Goggin (1968:198–199).
[b] All of the Aranama Tradition minimum vessels were defined through rim sherd analysis. The presence of numerous Monterey Polychrome body sherds in the assemblage suggests that some of these minimum vessels are associated with that type.
[c] See Voss 2002:667 for descriptions of these three unidentifiable varieties.

ceramics; in fact, Chinese porcelains appear to have been the most costly (Dado 2004; Perissinotto 1998). The requisitions and invoices also indicate that in colonial descriptions of ceramic vessels, the form and function of pottery were more important than waretype.

Thus, while organized broadly by waretype, the following analysis of table-ware ceramics does not assume a priori that, for example, majolicas and porcelains in the Building 13 midden assemblage were used by officers, Spaniards, and men; or that lead-glazed wares were used by enlisted soldiers, mixed-race castas, and women. Instead, it focuses on the form, function, and aesthetic appearance of these vessels by asking what place each vessel occupied on the colonial table.

Waretypes and Vessel Forms

Mexican Majolica   The majolica sherds recovered from the Building 13 midden represent a minimum of forty distinct vessels. Mexican majolica is part of a larger family of tin-glazed, soft-bodied earthenwares; metal oxides painted onto the glazed surface before firing create vivid in-glaze decorations. Although

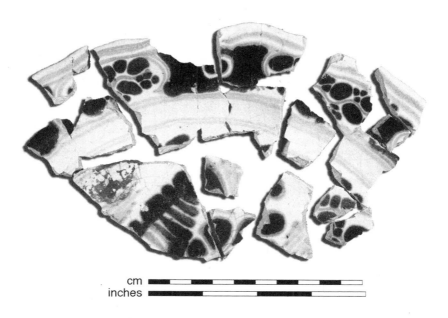

cm
inches

FIGURE 26.   Sherds of a majolica soup plate, San Agustín Blue-on-White; recovered from the Building 13 midden.

Mexican majolica was produced in several locations, the city of Puebla has dominated the industry since the 1600s (Goggin 1968). The losa de Puebla mentioned in colonial requisitions and invoices almost certainly refers to majolica.

Most majolica found in the Building 13 midden falls into one of two major stylistic traditions (table 11).[5] The Puebla Tradition is characterized by monotonal and bitonal blue decorative elements on a white field and by polychrome decorations containing blue and black-brown elements. The Aranama Tradition was also primarily produced in Puebla and fuses the design elements of the Puebla Tradition with the green/orange/brown color scheme of Italianate and Spanish talavera ceramics (May 1972). However, there is little indication of what, if any, meaning these archaeologically identified stylistic traditions and types had for the military settlers who owned and used the vessels.

Majolica ceramics played a very specific role on the tables of the Presidio's residents. Most of the majolica vessels (70 percent) are plates or soup plates, wide, shallow vessels used for individual servings of main dishes such as stewed and dry-cooked meats, grains, and vegetables (fig. 26). In fact, the twenty-eight majolica vessels account for 90 percent of the plates or soup plates recovered from the midden. An additional seven minimum vessels were cups or bowls (see table 10).

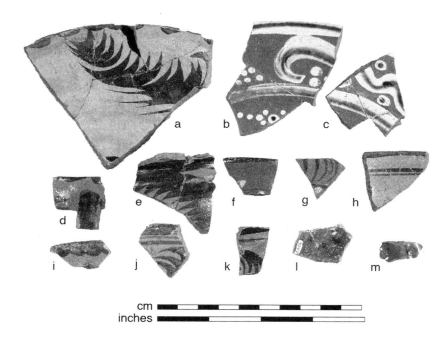

cm
inches

FIGURE 27.   Decorated galera tableware sherds recovered from the Building
13 midden. *a*: monochrome dotted rim motif soup plate; *b* and *c*: polychrome
white and green slipware soup plate; *d*: monochrome dotted rim motif
cup/bowl; *e*: monochrome jarro/chocotero; *f* and *g*: polychrome brown
and white jarro/chocotero; *h*: monochrome banded rim motif, cup/jarro/
chocotero; *i*: monochrome wavy rim motif; *j*: monochrome banded rim
motif; *k*: monochrome banded rim motif; *l*: plain green-glazed; *m*: monochrome green-glazed.

Mexican Galera   Twenty-five of the tableware vessels are galeras. "Galera" is
a ceramic term used primarily in California and the southwest United States to
describe a subset of Mexican lead-glazed earthenwares that are red-bodied and
are coated with a translucent or transparent lead glaze. Galera vessels found in
the Building 13 midden were produced in both Alta California and the area that
is now northwest Mexico. However, all of the *tableware* vessels are from Mexican, not Alta Californian, potteries.

Most of the tableware galera vessels are decorated (fig. 27), most commonly
with handpainted underglaze designs executed in brown, reddish-brown, or
black pigment. They are sometimes embellished with dots and lines of pale yellow slip; sometimes areas of the slip are tinted by adding small amounts of green

cm
inches

FIGURE 28. Rim sherds of a Bruñida de Tonalá cup recovered from the Building 13 midden.

colorant.[6] The decorations consist primarily of curvilinear geometric design elements. At a minimum, most vessels have horizontal bands (straight, wavy, or dotted) at the rim, joints, and inflection points. These bands define decorative zones that are filled in with clusters of dots, wavy lines, crescents, and spirals. The glaze surface treatment on galera tablewares provides another set of aesthetic options: some vessels are entirely glazed; others are glazed only on the interior or exterior; and at times the glaze itself is tinted red or green by adding iron or copper oxide powders to the glaze mixture. The galera tablewares present a range of aesthetic variety connected through shared design elements and techniques.

The galera vessels are all hollowwares. While there are a few soup plates, cups, and bowls, the most striking forms in the galera assemblage are eight distinctive *jarros* (jars) called *chocoteros* (Barnes 1980: 104–105). As their name implies, these vessels were typically used to serve hot chocolate and other warm beverages.

Bruñida de Tonalá   The Building 13 midden assemblage includes sherds representing ten minimum vessels of Bruñida de Tonalá, eight of which were tablewares (the other two were storage vessels, likely used to keep water) (fig. 28). Also known as *losa de olor* (fragrant pottery), Bruñida de Tonalá has been manufactured since the early 1600s in Tonalá, Jalisco, and is found in relatively small frequencies in Spanish-colonial archaeological sites throughout the Interior

Provinces.[7] The ware is known for its distinctive taste and smell, qualities obtained from coatings of a thin translucent slip made from special clay found about 50 km south of the town. Bruñida de Tonalá ceramics were especially prized because the ware's porous, low-fired body facilitates evaporation and aids in keeping liquids cold (Charlton and Katz 1979:47). Further, the clay and slips emit a pleasant aroma when wet (hence, losa de olor) and give a good taste to liquids. Water stored in Bruñida de Tonalá vessels was thought to be a health tonic, and broken pieces of the soft pottery were sometimes eaten to promote good health (Diaz 1966).

The ten minimum vessels represented in the Building 13 midden are all hollowwares; some are identifiable as cups and bowls, and some larger and thicker sherds likely came from pitchers or jars. These vessels are decorated with red and black metal oxide pigments applied between layers of the translucent slip, which produces a four-color decorative palette (red, pink, black, and blue-gray). Bands, curvilinear motifs, and spirals are the most common design elements on sherds excavated from the Building 13 midden, as well as a fine-brushed hatching identified as the *petatillo* style, said to resemble the lines of woven mats (Katz 1977). After the decorations and layers of slip are applied, the vessels are burnished (*bruñida*) with a lead ore stone, giving the ware a subtle sheen (Katz 1977:54–61).

Chinese Export Porcelains   Eight minimum vessels are porcelain, a white, vitrified, high-fired ceramic that is usually translucent. Although porcelains were being produced in both Asia and Europe at this time, all of the porcelains from the Building 13 midden were manufactured in China. Spanish traders procured Chinese porcelain in the Philippines and transported it to New Spain via the Manila Galleon trade route; these goods were referenced in requisitions and invoices as *losa de China* and *losa enchinada* (Dado 2006).

Six of the minimum vessels are bowls and cups; the other two could not be identified to form. Two have blue-on-white underglaze decorations, one with what is often described as "standard river and lakescapes with pavilions, bridges, and boats" (Staniforth and Nash 1998:4) (fig. 29). The other six vessels are *famille rose* overglaze polychromes executed in reddish, gold, and brown enamels (Staniforth and Nash 1998:3–7); these include banded and floral motifs.

British Whitewares   Seven minimum vessels are British whitewares, a category that encompasses the wide variety of white-bodied, clear-glazed earthenwares that have been produced since the 1700s in the Staffordshire ceramics industry in England (Majewski and O'Brien 1987). Their production began during the industrialization of the British ceramics industry, when improvements to ves-

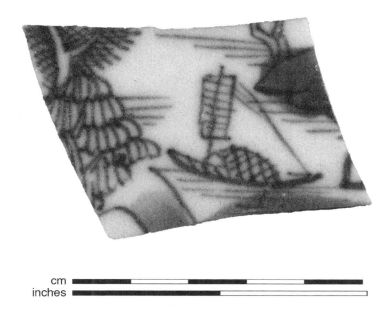

| cm | |
| inches | |

sel body, glaze, and decoration were being rapidly developed. Consequently, the beginning production dates for most British earthenware types, decorative techniques, and colors are well known (table 12).

British whitewares from the Building 13 midden are of interest for several reasons. Although the assemblage represents seven minimum vessels, these are derived from only twenty-one small sherds. Hence, while whiteware accounts for 2.79 percent of the entire ceramic assemblage by minimum vessel count, it is only 0.28 percent by sherd count and 0.17 percent by weight (see table 9). Only one minimum vessel can be identified to form (a cup/bowl), which, combined with the late manufacture date for at least three of the vessels, cautions us that these wares were not prominently used in table settings during the primary period of the midden's formation. In Alta California, British whitewares were generally acquired through gift exchange and trade with American, British, and Russian vessels. Variety in waretype and decorative features indicates that these vessels were likely acquired piecemeal rather than as matched sets.

Other Wares   One minimum vessel is a faience bowl. Like majolica, French faience is a tin-glazed earthenware, which is commonly found at Spanish-colo-

TABLE 12. British whitewares found in the Building 13 midden

Waretype/Decoration	Beginning Production Date[a]	MNV
Creamware	1764	2
Pale blue underglaze	1764	1
Undecorated	1764	1
Pearlware	1779	2
Tortoiseshell mocha	1790s	1
Overglaze painted rim bands	Early 1800s	1
Whiteware	1810	2
Blue transfer print, floral motif	1810	1
Undecorated	1810	1
White improved earthenware	1805	1
Undecorated	1805	1

[a] Beginning production dates from Majewski and O'Brien 1987.

nial sites in the former colonial provinces of Texas and Florida (Loren 1999; Tunnell and Ambler 1967). Two other minimum vessels, unidentifiable to form, are composed of gray-bodied earthenwares coated with an opaque black glaze.[8] Both faience and black-glazed ceramics are rarely found in Alta California and, like British whitewares, were probably acquired through trade or gift exchange with British and French explorers who visited Alta California in the 1790s and early 1800s.

Ethnic Ambiguity and the Pluralistic Table

By attending to form and function as well as waretype and style, the analysis of tableware ceramics from the Building 13 midden refutes the association between specific waretypes and economic, ethnic, or gender status. Instead, the vessels indicate a pattern of ceramic usage in which different waretypes were functionally integrated to complete the colonial table. On a typical table setting, one would likely see majolica soup plates for serving stews, beans, and other main dishes; galera chocoteros for hot beverages; Bruñida de Tonalá cups and pitchers for cool beverages; and a selection of galera, majolica, porcelain, faience, and British whiteware bowls and cups—and the occasional glass vessel—for soups, gruels, and spirits. Nearly all of these tablewares were decorated, their aesthetic appearance unified by the prevalence of handpainted linear and curvilinear geometric and vegetal motifs. But no single color scheme dominated: the base color of vessels ranged from white and blue to tan and or-

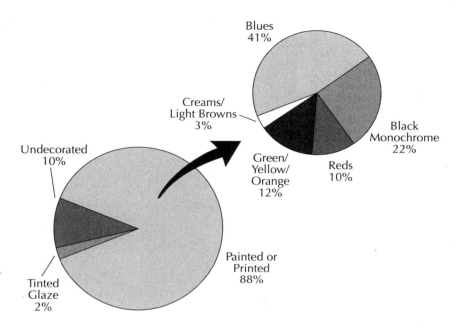

FIGURE 30. Decorative attributes of tableware ceramics recovered from
the Building 13 midden. Frequencies are calculated using minimum vessel
groupings.

ange. Black monochromes and blue monochromes, bichromes, and polychromes are the more prevalent decorative colors; but the assemblage also includes red, green, yellow, orange, and brown decorative elements in both
monochrome and polychrome configurations (fig. 30).

"Taste," Pierre Bourdieu (1984:6) writes, "classifies, and it classifies the
classifier." It is the logic behind the cultural economy of material goods. Inculcated through upbringing and experience, taste is one means through which
social subjects, themselves categorized economically, racially, and ethnically,
distinguish themselves. Whether conscious or unconscious, the aesthetics of
daily life are thus never neutral.

What, then, can be made of the heterogeneous table settings used at daily
meals by households and other small social groups at El Presidio de San Francisco during the 1790s and early 1800s? As discussed earlier, the military settlers might not have had much choice in the ceramics they used. Upon joining
the colonial military and traveling to Alta California, the soldiers and their families exited the local market economies of their home villages and became largely

dependent on the colonial administrative bureaucracy for their material needs and wants. Although 25 percent of the ceramics found in the Building 13 midden were produced locally, none of these functioned as tablewares. Although the military settlers clearly had the capacity to produce their own tablewares, they chose not to, relying on ceramics imported from San Blas and occasional gifts or trades with foreign visitors.

At a time when ethnic and racial identifications were in considerable flux, and when the colonists were beginning to form a shared sense of regional identity, the residents of the Presidio used table settings that mirrored their own situation as colonial agents. Gathered through the transportation and economic infrastructure of the colonial military, the ceramic tablewares reflected the aesthetic and functional diversity of pottery produced throughout New Spain. Like the settlers themselves, the individual tableware pieces were no longer embedded in the specific regional and social context of their production. Instead, the variety of waretypes and specialization of forms present at the Presidio resonated with the community's connection to the larger Spanish-colonial empire. Whether through policy or preference, the ceramic assemblages on Presidio tables reflected the dislocated, heterogeneous community that used them.

The findings of this analysis draw attention to meal sharing as a cultural practice that may have been particularly important in the transformation of social identities at El Presidio de San Francisco. Meals were occasions when institutional practices of procurement interfaced with household practices of consumption. The aesthetics of meal sharing may be understood as a product of the military settlers' negotiations of these two scales of material practice.

Making Pots

Although the Presidio settlers relied on imported goods for their table settings, a substantial portion of the ceramics they used for cooking and food preparation were locally produced wares. Sixty-three, or 25 percent, of the vessels represented by the assemblage were made in Alta California, almost certainly at El Presidio de San Francisco or at nearby Mission San Francisco de Asís (see fig. 24). I have analyzed these locally produced earthenwares[9] with the goal of reconstructing, to the extent possible, the social relations of their production and use as well as the stylistic and technological choices made by the potters who created them. The locally produced ceramic vessels found at the Presidio differ markedly from those found at some other Spanish-colonial settlements in Alta California. The vessels represented in the Building 13 midden were generated through at least three different modes of production. Making pots in colonial

San Francisco thus involved a range of social and economic relations, and the vessels themselves suggest that potters' proficiencies varied from rank beginner to accomplished craftsworker. Nonetheless, as a group, the locally produced pots evince strikingly narrow functional, morphological, and stylistic ranges. This suggests that conservatism, rather than innovation or synergy, governed the making of pots for the Presidio's households.

Ceramics and Colonization in Alta California

While archaeologists have often interpreted imported and commercially available tablewares as markers of colonial status, locally produced earthenwares have usually been interpreted as evidence of colonial influence on indigenous culture. Sherds of these vessels are recovered at every excavated Spanish-colonial site; at many presidios, these earthenwares make up the vast majority of ceramic artifacts. It is generally thought that these vessels were the result of the presidios' trade relations with local indigenous communities. In most areas, this was indeed the case, and the local earthenwares usually demonstrate a continuation of prehistoric indigenous ceramic traditions, with modifications to appeal to colonial tastes.[10]

The situation was quite different in the Monterey and San Francisco presidio districts. Native Californians indigenous to these central California coastal regions used baskets instead of pottery to store, prepare, and cook food and, consequently, did not provide a ready supply of pottery to the colonial settlements in the region. The presence of locally produced earthenwares in the ceramic assemblage at El Presidio de San Francisco must therefore be understood from a different vantage point.

Many researchers have assumed that Native Californians residing at missions were the primary producers of locally made pottery and that this work indicated indigenous acculturation and assimilation into colonial lifeways. This emphasis has drawn attention away from a second potential source of pottery production in Alta California: the military and civilian colonists themselves. Guadalupe Vallejo, niece of Mariano Guadalupe Vallejo, who served as commander of El Presidio de San Francisco from 1831 to 1834, wrote of the Alta California colonists:

> The settlers themselves were obliged to learn trades and teach them to their servants, so that an educated young gentleman was well skilled in many arts and handicrafts. . . . He could also make soap, pottery, and bricks, burn lime, tan hides, cut out and put together a pair of shoes, make candles, roll cigars and do a great number of things that belong to different trades. (Vallejo 1890:185)

In his study of presidios along the present-day Mexico-U.S. border, Rex Gerald similarly describes unglazed earthenwares as "the common utility wares which were made by local specialists or by each presidial wife" (Gerald 1968:54).

Sarah Ginn (2005:2) draws attention to locally produced earthenwares as a product of "the fluid process of cultural interface" among European priests, Native Californians, and colonial settlers of Mexican Indian and African heritage. Ginn posits that by producing pottery, people of diverse backgrounds and cultural traditions formed communities of practice based on shared technological and stylistic strategies. The locally made pottery from the Building 13 midden is a valuable source of information about the negotiation of social identities through the practices of production.

Making Pots for El Presidio de San Francisco

During the 1790s, Alta California's military settlers and mission priests were increasingly focused on improving the province's material self-sufficiency. As part of this initiative, the Naval Department of San Blas recruited craftsworkers and sent them on contract to Alta California. Two were potters, one of whom was briefly stationed at Mission San Francisco de Asís in 1798 and later moved to El Presidio de San Francisco, where he was joined by some neophytes from the mission (Schuetz-Miller 1994:14–20; Webb 1952:69). Two soldiers enrolled at the Presidio also participated in this effort, teaching pottery-making to neophytes at the San Francisco, Santa Clara, and Santa Cruz missions (Langellier and Rosen 1996:125). In this same period, ceramic production for construction projects began in earnest at El Presidio de San Francisco, and kilns were built for firing roof tiles and paving tiles.

Consequently, the locally produced earthenware sherds found in the Building 13 midden must be considered not only within the context of indigenous-colonial interactions but also in light of the colonists' efforts to lessen the Presidio's dependence on the military supply chain. It is surprising that no tableware vessels are represented among the sherds of locally made earthenware excavated from the Building 13 midden; all sixty-three minimum vessels are utilitarian forms designed for cooking and general kitchen use. The vessels are functionally congruent with the ninety Mexican galera vessels, with the Mexican galeras providing most of the cooking vessels and the local wares accounting for more of the general use vessels (fig. 31).

These limited historical accounts of ceramics production in 1790s San Francisco indicate that pottery-making at the missions was intertwined with similar production at the Presidio. Instrumental neuron activation analysis (INAA) has also found that pottery from the San Francisco mission and the Presidio have identical chemical signatures (Skowronek et al. 2001, 2003, 2005; Skowronek,

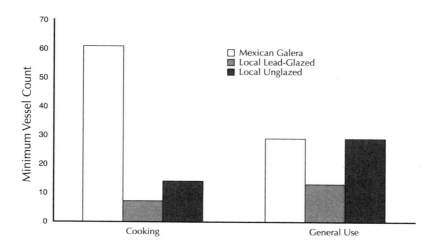

FIGURE 31. Waretypes of utilitarian vessels recovered from the Building 13 midden.

Blackman, and Bishop 2007), further evidence that craftsworkers, laborers, raw materials, and finished products were circulated between the mission and the Presidio.

Analysis of Locally Produced Earthenwares

Household ceramics found in the Building 13 midden were identified as "locally produced" only if paste attributes, temper, and inclusions matched those observed in locally made construction tiles (tejas and ladrillos). Locally produced clay tile fragments and their household ceramic cognates have a very narrow range of paste colors, which are significantly redder than those observed in Mexican-produced earthenwares.[11] Additionally, locally produced household earthenwares and construction tiles share a high volume (20–30 percent) of subangular quartz sand particles that are absent from Mexican-produced earthenwares (Hirata 2001:23). The association between these local construction tiles and earthenwares is further substantiated by trace element analysis (Skowronek et al. 2001).

Analysis of the locally produced ceramic assemblage was undertaken with assistance from Rita Hirata (2001), whose own experience as a trained ceramic artist was invaluable in reconstructing the sequence of movements and tools involved in creating each vessel. Analysis included macroscopic and microscopic observations oriented toward determining paste composition, vessel manufacture, surface treatment, firing conditions, vessel form, and vessel use. Based on

TABLE 13. Comparison of vessel attributes of locally produced earthenwares

	Quantity (MNV)	Manufacture	Surface Treatments	Firing	Form	Function	Quality
Group 1	9	Hand-built (mostly pinching and drawing)	Smoothing, brushing, burnishing (all vessels)	Low-temperature, open-air, oxidizing, short	Hollowwares, flat bases	2 cooking; remainder general use	3 good, 6 poor
Group 2	29	Wheel-thrown	Smoothing to reduce or eliminate rilling marks (only 7 vessels)	Low-temperature, open-air, oxidizing, short	Hollowwares, including bowls; flat bases	13 cooking; remainder general use	22 good, 7 poor
Group 3	20	Wheel-thrown	Lead oxide glaze, 5 tinted green	Kiln-fired	Hollowwares, including bowls and constricted-mouth vessels; flat and round bases, one footing	6 cooking; remainder general use	17 good, 3 poor

cm
inches

FIGURE 32. Locally produced, hand-built, unglazed earthenware recovered from the Building 13 midden. These sherds exemplify the wide variety of skill, form, and technique found in the assemblage. *a*: burnished exterior; *b*: unfinished interior; *c*: rough exterior; *d*: burnished interior; *e*: smoothed interior and fire clouding; f: burnished interior.

these observations, the locally produced vessels were classified into three primary categories based on method of manufacture and presence or absence of glaze: hand-built, unglazed earthenwares; wheel-thrown, unglazed earthenwares; and wheel-thrown, lead-glazed earthenwares (table 13).[12]

Hand-Built, Unglazed Earthenwares   Nine minimum vessels were formed by hand (fig. 32). Hand-building encompasses a variety of free-form ceramic manufacture techniques; most vessels in this category appeared to have been formed primarily through pinching and drawing. None were glazed, but all showed indications of other surface treatments. Three of the vessels had visible traces of smoothing and scraping to remove or redistribute excess clay. Four were burnished, and five were brushed. Burnishing and brushing are surface treatments used to create a more uniform vessel surface; burnishing also reduces the porosity of the vessel's surfaces.

The quality of these hand-built, unglazed vessels varied widely. Three had even sidewalls and good vessel surfaces. The remaining six were poorly built.

Many were manufactured from clay with large inclusions, including gravels as large as 7 mm in diameter that protruded from some vessel walls, causing star-shaped surface fractures. These inclusions generally indicate little preparation of the clay body before the vessel was formed. Several vessels had uneven and undulating walls (a given vessel might change more than 10 mm in thickness across a 2–3 cm distance) with rough, uneven surfaces. Overall, the wide range in vessel quality suggests that they were shaped by potters who were relatively unskilled or inexperienced. The presence of brushed and burnished vessels suggests that although the potters were not very proficient, they were knowledgeable about techniques that could improve the durability and usability of their wares.

The vessels were soft and porous, with little iron oxidation; one vessel had fire-clouded surfaces, which can result when vessels are fired in low-temperature, open-air fires for short periods. Additionally, many of the vessels had a dark, dull brown core (different from the black or gray core caused by firing in a reducing environment), with brighter colors showing only within the 1 or 2 mm closest to the vessel's surfaces. All of these attributes indicate that oxygen was freely available but that only vessel surfaces received sufficient heat to oxidize ferrous compounds in the parent clay. While short, open firings tend to produce more friable and porous wares, they are economical in fuel use and require less labor and capital expenditure than pit and kiln firings. Open-air firings are typically used for sporadic, low-quantity ceramic production at the household level (Rice 1987:154–156).

The hand-built, unglazed vessels were all hollowwares; none could be identified to specific form. All the base fragments in the assemblage were flat, with no evidence of vessel feet or footrings. Two had soot residues, indicating that the vessels were used in cooking.

Wheel-Thrown, Unglazed Earthenwares   The second group consists of twenty-nine minimum vessels that were wheel-thrown and were unglazed (fig. 33). Wheel-thrown vessels are produced with a different suite of technical skills than hand-formed vessels, as the potter harnesses the momentum of the rotating wheel by pulling, pressing, and squeezing the clay into the desired form. Wheel-thrown vessels are easily identified by the presence of horizontal rilling marks that form as the vessel rotates against the pressure of the potter's hands or shaping tools. Most of the vessels represented in the assemblage had no surface treatments, but seven had been smoothed on their exterior surfaces to reduce or eliminate rilling marks. Like the hand-built, unglazed earthenwares, the wheel-thrown, unglazed earthenwares seem to have been fired in low-temperature, open-air conditions.

cm

inches

FIGURE 33. Locally produced, wheel-thrown, unglazed earthenware recovered from the Building 13 midden. These sherds demonstrate the range of skill and technique represented in the assemblage. *a*: Uneven grooves and ridges indicating wobbling while the pot was thrown. *b*: High, evenly spaced, raised ridges. *c*: Raised ridges, attempts at smoothing. *d*: raised ridges; *e*, *f*, and *h*: well-thrown, with fireclouding on sherd *f*; *g*: uneven thickness and roughness from scraping out interior base.

The vessels in this category exhibit qualities indicating that they were produced both by experienced, skilled potters and by potters less capable of manipulating the clay on the wheel. Twenty-two of these vessels were of good quality, with no apparent flaws, and had thin, uniform walls with even surfaces. The quality of the other seven vessels varied widely. In five cases, the defects were minor: unevenly spaced, low, horizontal raised ridges on the vessel surface; and uneven wall thickness. In the other two vessels, the defects were more severe. One was lopsided, with high, raised horizontal bands on the interior. Another was unusually thick, with high, raised horizontal bands on the interior and a rough, uneven surface. These potters were apparently of varied ability and were likely novices or relatively inexperienced nonspecialists.

All of the wheel-thrown, unglazed vessels were hollowwares, two of which were identifiable as bowl-shaped vessels. Twelve minimum vessel groupings had sufficient rim sherds to allow measurement of the rim diameter. Four of these vessels measured 10–20 cm in diameter; seven others were 20–30 cm; and one vessel measured 32 cm. All had flat bases with no evidence of vessel feet or footrings. Thirteen of the wheel-thrown, unglazed vessels had soot residues on the exterior surface and thus were identified as cooking vessels.

Wheel-Thrown, Lead-Glazed Earthenwares   The third group of locally produced wares consists of twenty wheel-thrown, lead-glazed vessels (fig. 34). The presence of these vessels in the Building 13 midden is a significant discovery, as these sherds were among the first locally produced glazed wares identified in Alta California (Voss, Ramsay, and Naruta 2000). Other researchers have since confirmed the presence of locally produced glazed earthenwares at other Spanish-colonial sites in the province (Ginn 2005; Skowronek et al. 2001).

Like the Mexican galeras, these vessels generally had a translucent lead glaze. The body characteristics of the vessels (even, red color, and hardness) and the presence of the glaze itself indicate that the vessels were kiln-fired. Most vessels were glazed on both interior and exterior surfaces, but six were glazed only on the interior. Those with interior glaze all contained soot residues on their exterior, suggesting that they were used for cooking. The glaze on five of the vessels was tinted green, an effect achieved by adding copper to the glaze recipe. On some of the vessels, portions of the glaze had oxidized to a matte pale yellow color; this lead oxide residue is a by-product of glaze decomposition and is especially common on vessels that were dusted with a lead oxide powder rather than being coated with a lead oxide liquid suspension. It can also occur if the firing conditions are not sufficiently hot or of sufficient duration to allow the lead glaze to fully fuse (Barnes 1980:92–93).

The wheel-thrown, glazed earthenwares showed a wide range of quality,

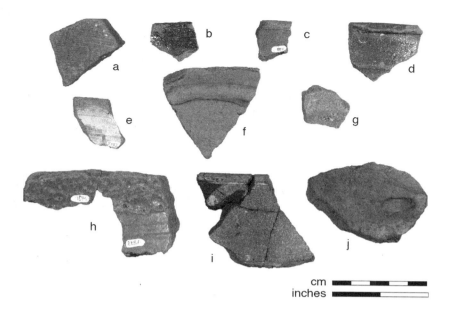

FIGURE 34. Locally produced, wheel-thrown, lead-glazed earthenware recovered from the Building 13 midden. These sherds exhibit distinctive characteristics in form and manufacture. a: rilling marks; b: green-tinted glaze; c: typical rim form; d: unusual comma-shaped rim form; e: decomposing glaze; f: raised footring; g: flat base; h: glaze firing defects; i: burnt exterior; j: burnt exterior, note pit mark from stone or plant material.

similar to that seen in the first two categories. They were generally robust, utilitarian vessels. Most were well-formed and evenly glazed. Three showed deficiencies in form, including deep ridges typical of vessels produced by potters inexperienced with wheel-throwing. One of these vessels also had undulating walls of variable thickness. Another of the three showed several glaze defects, including pinholes, bubbles, discoloration, and spalling, which suggest that the vessel was either poorly fired or that the glaze was not mixed or applied properly.

All of these glazed vessels were hollowwares, with a greater variation in form than the unglazed locally produced wares. Two vessels were clearly bowl-shaped, with an additional three also likely formed as bowls. One of these was unusually delicate, with walls measuring only 3–4 mm thick. At least two vessels had gently constricted mouths, one measuring 20 cm in diameter at the vessel orifice and at least 24 cm at its maximum diameter. While most vessel bases were rounded or flat, one had a footring. The vessels were of moderate size: one measured 8–10 cm in diameter; five measured 10–20 cm; and four others were greater than 20 cm.

Social Organization of Ceramic Production

This analysis affords insight into the organization of craft production at the Presidio. The three broad groupings of locally produced earthenwares were each crafted through different modes of production. The first group of hand-built, unglazed wares suggests the least formally organized mode. These vessels required no specialized equipment or materials and were highly variable in form and quality. The poor quality of the vessels, combined with the prominence of burnishing, suggests that the potters who made these vessels had little experience or formal training but were aware of techniques to reduce vessel porosity. Most likely, these potters were individual colonists at the Presidio who drew on their knowledge of vernacular pottery production in northwest Mexico to fashion makeshift pots from local clays. It is probable that these vessels were produced to replace broken cooking vessels and kitchen bowls that could not have otherwise been replaced—either because of reduced inventory in the Presidio's stores or because of the limited economic resources of the household.

The wheel-thrown vessels, both glazed and unglazed, indicate the presence of a more organized workshop, at either the Presidio or the mission, where pottery was being produced with more regularity and using specialized technology. They show greater consistency and quality in both clay preparation and vessel formation, although a few vessels were still produced by inexperienced potters. It is most likely that the wheel-thrown wares were produced by Native Californians working under the supervision of the artisan potter who visited the San Francisco area during the late 1790s. Consequently, these vessels were more likely to have been distributed through the Presidio's storehouse rather than being made by particular households for their own use. Finally, the third group of glazed, wheel-thrown vessels evinces the greatest technical specialization, requiring imported glaze materials and kiln-firing. Both El Presidio de San Francisco and Mission San Francisco de Asís had this capacity, so the vessels may have been produced at either or both locations.

This analysis suggests that between 1790 and 1810, craft production at El Presidio de San Francisco was changing in a manner that paralleled the concurrent transformation of architectural production (discussed in chapter 7). Military settlers and their families still fulfilled some of their own needs through household-level production, but more ceramics were being produced in centralized workshops by Native Californian workers under the supervision of colonial craft specialists. The colonists were becoming more reliant on indigenous labor for the material necessities of daily life. This development is important because it implies that the growing centralization and homogenization of colonial material culture at the settlement was not limited to manipulations of space and landscape, but extended to those objects used in the home and in smaller-scale social occasions.

.   .   .

Tradition is a common metaphor used to describe the relationship between the aesthetics of production and ethnicity: this, tradition says, is how *we* do things, such that tradition and the social group recursively define each other. Taste and style—the choices that encapsulate what is preferred from the universe of possible choices—are means by which individuals and groups forge connections between aesthetics and identity. Taste and tradition "work" because people are shaped by the material culture that surrounds them, just as they make their own physical imprint on their surroundings. The military settlers at the Presidio were constrained in their aesthetic choices by the supplies made available to them by the military command. Yet they were no less affected by their material world because of this.

The locally produced ceramic vessels found in the Building 13 midden afford an opportunity to examine aesthetic choices that the colonists may have been able to influence more directly. When viewed in the broader context of locally made earthenwares found at colonial sites throughout Alta California, it becomes apparent that those used by the Presidio's residents represent an exceedingly narrow range of technical and stylistic possibilities. Recently, Ginn surveyed locally produced earthenwares in archaeological collections from a broad sampling of Alta California colonial sites. She documented that colonial-era Alta California potters were making vessels using a wide variety of techniques, including paddle-and-anvil, coiling, slab building, and molding (including molding on basket forms) as well as the pinching, drawing, and wheel-throwing seen at El Presidio de San Francisco. The collections also show a diverse range of vessel forms throughout Alta California. They include not only the utilitarian bowls and cooking pots found in the Building 13 midden but also ollas, jars, and tablewares such as soup plates, small bowls, and cups (Ginn 2005). Why did El Presidio de San Francisco—host to a guest artisan potter as well as home to two soldiers proficient in ceramics—have only the most rudimentary forms, produced with a narrow range of ceramic production methods?

Striking in their plainness, the locally produced wares from the Presidio display none of the synergistic play, innovation, or improvisation often seen in the material culture of other colonial settlements. Instead, it is clear that the colonists were making and selecting vessels that imitated, in form and appearance, the utilitarian vessels supplied to the settlement by the San Blas supply ships. The military settlers apparently pursued aesthetically and technologically conservative material strategies that minimized the appearance of cultural differences within the colonial population.

In this regard, the absence of locally produced tablewares is particularly of interest. Such vessels would have evoked the increasing importance of labor-based interactions between the settlers and Native Californians. The exclusion of locally made vessels from the table indicates that the colonists' growing dependence on indigenous labor was ambiguously received, perhaps a source of discomfort rather than pride for the military settlers. Instead, with each table set with the goods procured through military supply channels, shared meals were social gatherings that reinforced the community's colonial status and participation in the broader project of empire building. Like the heterogeneous tablewares joined into a unified place setting, so too the diverse colonial population of the Presidio was transforming itself into a unified community.

"Tell me what you eat, and I shall tell you what you are." Since 1825, Jean Anthelme Brillat-Savarin's aphorism (1999:3) has succinctly pointed to the tense and persistent relationship between food and social identity. The act of consuming food—taking foreign substances into the body for sustenance—is both intimate and intensely social (Dietler 2006). Food and ethnicity are closely intertwined and often mutually categorized: modern restaurant guides and supermarket aisles are commonly organized with ethnonyms. Food is not only a medium through which ethnic authenticity is enacted and debated but also a venue in which social boundaries are installed in bodily responses. The foods one craves, the foods that give comfort, and the foods that repulse are all refracted through lenses of ethnic, racial, and economic identities. Hunger, satiation, malnutrition, and corpulence all inscribe economic relations of power onto the bodies of social subjects.

As chapter 8's analysis of ceramic artifacts showed, meal sharing and food consumption were highly symbolic practices for the colonial residents of the Presidio. Decorated, imported ceramic wares adorned the Presidio's tables, contributing what today's epicures might term "presentation value" to the dishes being served. This chapter considers the food itself. "Foodways," a term that refers to a broad range of practices associated with food, may be conceptualized in two interrelated components: diet (the actual goods consumed) and cuisine (cultural beliefs and practices concerning food) (Crown 2000). Both are supported by a food-related infrastructure that includes all aspects of production, procurement, trade, processing, and storage.

This chapter draws on archaeological analyses of faunal, botanical, and ceramic data, along with other food-related artifacts and historical sources that document colonial food practices. It establishes the economic and social context for interpretation of archaeological remains and then addresses the issue of diet. Evidence from supply ship requisitions and invoices, food container artifacts, and archaeologically recovered animal and plant parts all contribute to an understanding of the foods eaten by the military settlers. We will also return to the ceramic assemblage discussed in chapter 8 to investigate how settlers prepared and consumed foodstuffs. This chapter is complemented by the book's appendix, which presents the methods and findings of zooarchaeological and archaeobotanical analyses of animal bone, shell, and plant remains.

Feeding the Colony

From the beginning, the Spanish crown intended to develop Alta California as a self-sufficient colony that would support itself through farming and animal husbandry. The Anza expedition, which established the Presidio, was also a cattle drive, bringing nearly a thousand head to Alta California. Additionally, the colonists and missionaries brought seeds and cuttings to establish cereal, bean, and vegetable crops. At the same time the military settlers were struggling to construct the Presidio quadrangle, they were also working to establish agricultural enterprises at the Presidio and, beginning in 1777, at the Pueblo of San José and the San Francisco and Santa Clara missions. During the first few years, the settlement relied on shipments of food staples from San Blas. But David Hornbeck and David Fuller (1983:52–57) estimate that Alta California became agriculturally self-sufficient by the late 1770s, as did the more recently established San Francisco presidio district a few years later. As more Native Californians came into the missions in the late 1780s, the missions became the primary agricultural producers in the province.

By the 1790s, the military settlers living at the Presidio were obtaining their sustenance from three sources: the Presidio's own cattle range, gardens, and agricultural fields; the missions and, to a lesser extent, the San José pueblo, which provided agricultural staples, especially cereals and beans; and the annual supply ships from San Blas, which brought low-bulk, high-flavor foods such as oils, sweeteners, and seasonings. All these foods were distributed by the Presidio's habilitado, with the price of goods charged to each soldier's account. What is less clear in historical documents—but is an issue that can be investigated through archaeological evidence—is the extent to which soldiers and their families supplemented their rations by hunting, trapping, fishing, gathering wild plants and shellfish, raising their own livestock, and tending personal gardens.

Historical studies of colonial-era foodways allow an intimate view of how food was distributed and prepared at Alta California presidios. Approximately half of a soldier's weekly ration was usually maize; the other half consisted of *menestra* (a mixture of beans, garbanzos, and lentils), chiles, and beef. Small amounts of imported rice, *panocha* (brown sugar loaves), lard, and chocolate supplemented the "humdrum fare largely of corn and beans" (Mason 1978:408).

José María Amador, who grew up at the Presidio and served there as a soldier from 1809 to 1827, later described the meals he had eaten as a young boy (Mora-Torres 2005:141–143). His family, like other well-off households, would start the day at six or seven in the morning with a light breakfast consisting of a chocolate beverage or maize atole (a thin gruel) made with milk. About an hour later, the family would eat their main breakfast of cooked beef and beans with bread or corn tortillas. For the noon meal, Amador recalled, "Each of my sisters would get a small glass of wine from my mother. The main dish was rice or noodle soup, a pot of boiled beef with vegetables, and beans. Sometimes we got dessert cheese or sweetbreads for dessert. After our meal, the males would get a small glass of aguardiente from Spain" (141). The evening meal was taken at eight or nine o'clock at night and consisted of beans and beef cooked in a chile sauce and a little wine.

While Amador's family ate well, "the poor would eat whatever they could" (Mora-Torres 2005:143). According to Amador, families with fewer resources would have a simple breakfast of maize atole or roasted fresh corn or pumpkin stewed in milk. For their noon meal, the poor "would boil corn or wheat until it burst and with hot water, a little lard, salt, and chiles, they would cook it. For dessert, the most they would have was cheese and, on some occasions, *asaderas* [a particularly rich cheese] with panocha." Evening meals included "cooked meat or roasted meat, beans, corn atole, or migas, which was a type of atole cooked in lard with the corn partly cracked" (143). The poor, Amador recounted, could not afford either wine or aguardiente to accompany their meals.

Married soldiers were allotted only slightly more rations than those without families. To cope with this situation, "married women at the presidios managed to obtain some extra rations by making tortillas for bachelor soldiers and preparing other food for them. In exchange for such work it was customary to give some corn, beans, or whatever other food the soldier could spare" (Mason 1978:408; see also Langellier and Rosen 1996:51–52; Mora-Torres 2005:217).

These and other historical accounts suggest that food preparation was a strongly gendered set of tasks primarily associated with colonial women, although adult men and children were also enlisted in this necessary work. In this preindustrial colonial province, transforming raw agricultural materials into edible food required considerable skill and time-consuming labor. Food preparation may have been a central node of a micro-economy involving labor exchange and barter. While the military command, especially the habilitado, dominated the official economy of the settlement, the unofficial household-to-household economy was likely conducted among rank-and-file soldiers and female heads of households. Consequently, attention to food preparation and dietary composition affords opportunities to examine female-gendered practices that contributed to colonial ethnogenesis.

The Colonial Diet

Both historical and archaeological sources offer rich indications of the composition of the colonial diet. Evidence is provided by four data sets: colonial documents, food containers, animal bone and shell, and preserved seeds and plant parts.

Food Supplies from San Blas

As chapter 8 notes, the records of colonial requisitions to the Naval Department of San Blas and the invoices of the goods actually shipped contain a wealth of information about materials imported into the settlement (Barker 2007; Dado 2004; Osborn 2006). Early shipments typically included many staple items such as maize, flour, and legumes. After the 1780s, food shipments were dominated by agricultural goods not available in the province, especially rice, oils, olives, nuts, sweeteners, chocolate, coffee, seasonings, and liquors.

The invoices and requisitions contain some surprising items. Dried shrimp and crab powder are recorded in several shipments, although colonial settlers could have easily harvested shellfish and crustaceans from the nearby ocean and bay. In addition, the shipments included no meat products other than lard and preserved ham, indicating that Alta Californians became self-sufficient in supplying meat relatively quickly. One requisition (Dado 2004:doc. 102) specifies ammunition for hunting rabbits, hares, and waterfowl; curiously, this is the only mention of hunting activities I have found in the historical documents.

With rare exceptions, the foodstuffs shipped to Alta California were processed goods that were fully consumed, leaving behind little archaeological evidence. The volume of imported foodstuffs was small and contributed no more than a small fraction of the settlers' dietary needs. Nonetheless, these imported foods were of great cultural significance and were used to enhance and flavor the agricultural products that made up most of the colonists' diet. The resulting dishes combined local foodstuffs with flavors from northern Mexico (Osborn 2006).

Food Containers

Containers are an important indirect source of information about processed and stored foods such as oils, beverages, and seasonings, which often leave little direct archaeological residue. The Building 13 midden deposit yielded evidence of only five food containers, a surprisingly low number. Two are ollas de aceite, amphora-shaped jars with constricted openings that were used to transport liquid goods, usually cooking oils, during sea voyages. The sherds representing these containers match descriptions of Mexican-produced ollas de aceite (Caywood 1950:78–84; Di Peso 1953:223); these vessels undoubtedly arrived at the Presidio as containers for liquids shipped from San Blas and may have been reused, until they broke, for other liquid storage.

Additional containers include two minimum glass bottles, represented by 107 shards of glass (89.1 g): a dark green ("black glass") British wine bottle and a French blue-green bubbled bottle, both typically used to transport wine, brandy, and other liquors (Harris 1979; Jones and Sullivan 1989). As the supply ship invoices list wine and liquors transported by the barrel, these bottles may have been acquired through gift exchange or small-scale trade with visiting foreign ships. The fifth container is a ferrous metal food canister with a pinched and rolled edge, which indicates the presence, in low frequencies, of canned goods at the settlement.

The general paucity of food containers is striking, suggesting that most imported foods were transported in bulk in wooden boxes, barrels, casks, or sacking. It is possible that six ferrous metal strapping fragments recovered from the Building 13 midden are remnants of these shipping containers, although metal strapping was also used in wooden chests and other furniture.

Bone and Shell: Meat Foods

For several decades, archaeologists have concluded that the colonial diet in Alta California followed a general pattern of meat consumption. Beef was by far the primary meat source, followed by sheep and goats, then pigs and domesticated fowl.[1] This pattern is so persistent that one researcher stated that in Alta California, the "faunal evidence indicates a remarkably consistent diet in the face of major economic changes. . . . This evidence seems to support the cross-cultural observation that foodways are among the most tenacious of our material cultural habits" (Costello 1989a:93).

The archaeology of the Presidio allows us to investigate meat consumption in the colonial diet during the earlier years of colonization, when a shared Californio identity was emerging among the settlers (see appendix). Was the colonial diet always so standardized and regimented? Does the general pattern posited by archaeologists thus far match the diet followed by military settlers at the Presidio?

Zooarchaeological analyses of animal bone and shell from the Building 13 midden confirm the centrality of beef in the colonial diet. Forty-three bone specimens were identified as *Bos taurus*, and many of the Artiodactyla and the unclassified large mammal specimens were also likely derived from cattle. Both element distribution and the locations of cut marks indicate that settlers slaughtered and butchered cattle on site and disposed of excess parts of carcasses along with other household waste. This evidence suggests that households, either singly or in groups, were herding and managing their own meat supply rather than relying on the central stores maintained by the habilitado.

Domestic chickens were also relatively numerous, with twenty-eight specimens identifiable to this species. Chickens, like cattle, were probably raised and tended by individual households, as there are no historical records of more centrally organized poultry-raising. The chickens represented in the excavated sample were sexually mature at time of death, which may indicate that they were raised primarily for eggs and were slaughtered for meat only after their egg production declined.

Besides cattle and chickens, other domestic mammals are curiously absent from the assemblage: sheep and goats are represented by only nine specimens, and no pig remains have been identified. The diversification of domestically raised meat products evidenced in later-period mission and rancho deposits seemingly had not yet occurred at the Presidio during the years 1776 to ca. 1800. Instead, there is substantial evidence that the colonists were supplementing their beef-based diet with wild game such as deer, hares and rabbits, waterfowl, turtles, and fish. Predatory mammals (coyote/dog/wolf, gray fox, grizzly bear) are also present in low frequencies; these animals may have been eaten, but it is more likely that they were shot or trapped for sport, to protect domesticated animals, or for their fur.

One of the most striking findings of the zooarchaeology analysis is the presence of 117 fish specimens. Many fish bones are cartilaginous and are not preserved archaeologically; additionally, their small size decreases the chance of recovery and recognition even when fine-mesh screens are used. The recovered specimens likely indicate an even greater prevalence of fish in the colonial diet than simple bone counts would suggest. The fish specimens are primarily surf perch with some pile perch, herring, lingcod, and plainfin midshipmen. These taxa share several similarities: they are all saltwater taxa that are small to medium in size, and all are in-shore species found on the sandy or muddy bottoms of bays. They are species that would have been readily available on the sandy and rocky littoral shores immediately north of the settlement's main quadrangle.[2]

In contrast to the abundance of fish bones, the remains of shellfish were few and highly fragmented. The shell assemblage consists primarily of mussels that are found in rocky areas near the low tide line along both the ocean and the bayshore near the Presidio. A few very small shell fragments were identified as red abalone. What is most significant, however, is the low frequency of shell in the deposit, which indicates that the colonial inhabitants of the Presidio were not utilizing the abundant shellfish resources only a short walk from the main quadrangle.

In summary, the faunal analysis of the Building 13 midden assemblage suggests a greater reliance on wild species than is commonly found in zooarchaeological studies of deposits at other Spanish-colonial sites. While cattle were undisputedly the dominant source of meat, other domesticated mammals frequently identified at other sites (sheep, goats, and pigs) are present only in extremely low frequencies or not at all. The beef diet was significantly supplemented by wild mammals, wild and domesticated birds, and fish. But the remains of another readily available wild food resource, shellfish, are nearly absent from the assemblage and are not found in significant frequencies anywhere at the site. In contrast, shellfish constituted such a prominent component of the diets of local Native Californian populations that most prehistoric sites in the area are classified as shell middens. Could the scarcity of shellfish in the Building 13 midden, and in other archaeological deposits associated with the Presidio, be an indication that the colonists were avoiding a food source closely associated with indigenous foodways?

Seeds: Plant Foods

The role played by plant foods in the colonial diet was equally important. Historical accounts of colonial foodways emphasize that cereal and bean dishes were central to every meal. Historical descriptions often emphasize maize as a primary dietary constituent, but colonial records reveal that wheat was also grown and consumed in significant quantities in Alta California, especially in the northern districts (Costello 1989b; Hornbeck 1989; Hornbeck and Fuller 1983). To date, archaeologists have paid far less attention to the plant components of the colonial diet in Alta California than to the meat components, because plant remains do not preserve as well as bone and are difficult to retrieve without targeted sampling procedures. This is the first study to undertake substantive archaeobotanical analysis from deposits at an Alta California presidio site (see appendix).

Physical evidence of plant use at El Presidio de San Francisco comes from two archaeological contexts, which together provide a diachronic perspective. The first is the Building 13 midden; the second is the clay floor located within an apartment in the eastern wing of the third, expanded quadrangle (see map 8). Four hearth features (discrete lenses of charcoal and ash-rich, heat-affected soil) were identified in the floor deposits; they yielded dense concentrations of botanical specimens. The Building 13 midden deposit formed primarily during the years 1776 to 1800. The apartment was occupied no earlier than 1815 and likely was abandoned and had collapsed, or at least had fallen into disrepair, by 1824.

One challenge in archaeobotanical analysis is distinguishing plant remains that were burned as fuel from those that were produced or collected for food. As figure 35 shows, bluegrass (*Poa* sp.) makes up the majority of the plant assemblage (54 percent from the midden, 60 percent from the apartment floor). This taxon includes a variety of indigenous and introduced species, including several species of short grasses that grow on the coastal bluffs, sand dunes, grassy slopes, and grasslands typical of the ecological zones surrounding the Presidio. It is most likely that these short grass specimens entered the archaeological record as fuel. The grass stems with seeds may have been used for kindling, or the seeds may have been contained in animal dung that was collected for fuel. Some of the other wild plants in both assemblages, such as *Erodium* sp. (filaree) and *Malva* sp. (mallow) are also common animal forage and may have entered the archaeological record as dung burned for fuel (Popper 2002).

Edible Cultivated Plants   In both the midden and apartment floor deposits, cultivated plants are limited to a narrow range of cereals and legumes. The midden yielded 58 cereal specimens, of which 34 could be identified to taxa. Of these, 20 (59 percent) were maize, and the remaining 14 (41 percent) were wheat. The apartment floor and hearths yielded 2,742 cereal specimens, of which 1,520 could be identified to taxa. These were overwhelmingly wheat (98.6 percent), with the remaining specimens consisting of very small amounts of domesticated barley and maize.

Because of the vast difference in the size of these two assemblages, these quantitative differences are difficult to interpret. Nonetheless, the prominence of wheat in the apartment deposits is of considerable interest. At the time the apartment was occupied, the Presidio was producing roughly equal quantities of maize and wheat (Hornbeck and Fuller 1983:52–53). But this does not account for foodstuffs obtained through trade with the missions and pueblos, which could have brought a greater amount of wheat into the community. As a result, the interpretations are ambiguous: either maize was not a prominent component of the diet of the apartment's inhabitants, or foods containing maize were prepared outside the apartment, or maize had already been ground into

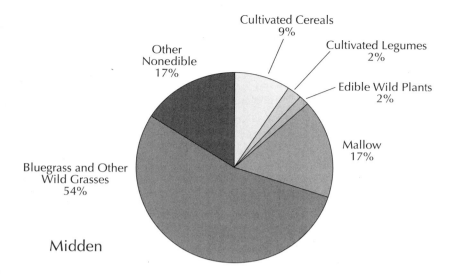

Cultivated Cereals
9%

Cultivated Legumes
2%

Other
Nonedible
17%

Edible Wild Plants
2%

Mallow
17%

Bluegrass and Other
Wild Grasses
54%

Midden

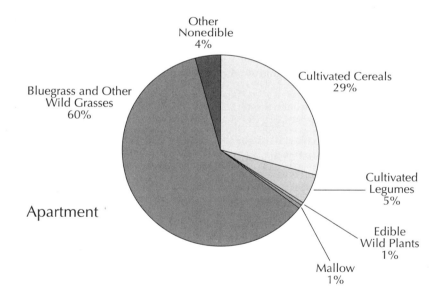

Other
Nonedible
4%

Cultivated Cereals
29%

Bluegrass and Other
Wild Grasses
60%

Cultivated
Legumes
5%

Apartment

Edible
Wild Plants
1%

Mallow
1%

FIGURE 35.   Frequency of plant types recovered from the Building 13
midden and the quadrangle apartment.

meal before it entered the apartment. Wheat, however, was clearly obtained in whole-grain form. Before being ground by hand, wheat grains are usually parched over a low fire to remove moisture. Grains may have fallen into the hearth fires during this process, which would have carbonized and preserved them.

Another striking absence in the cultivated plant assemblages is "the virtual lack of plant parts other than grains and kernels of wheat and corn," which suggests "that these foods were received cleaned of extraneous plant parts" (Popper 2002:6). This is true of both the broader stream of household waste entering the Building 13 midden and the floor deposits formed by the inhabitants of the apartment. In other words, the colonists received their maize shucked from the cob and their wheat and other cereals threshed and winnowed. If this labor was performed at the Presidio, it was performed away from residential areas, and the resulting debris was deposited separately from household refuse.

In comparison to cereals, both deposits contain smaller frequencies of cultivated peas and beans. The apartment deposit includes specimens identifiable to *Pisum* sp. (pea) and *Vicia faba* (fava bean). The botanical assemblage from the apartment deposit also includes fifty-eight pod fragments, which likely represent legume consumption and indicate that, unlike wheat and maize, some legumes were not shelled before being distributed to households.

Edible Wild Plants   The cultivated plants found in the deposits were likely grown, harvested, and processed for food. The situation is much more complicated when we consider the remains of nondomesticates, because historically many wild plants were used for more than one function. For example, the seeds of *Atriplex* sp. (saltbush) can be toasted and eaten (either ground or whole); its leaves have folk medicinal uses; its roots were commonly used as a soap; and it may also have been consumed as forage by grazing animals (Balls 1962:74–75). Further, many of the wild plants present in the assemblage could be identified only to genus or family, so that most archaeologically identified taxa represent both edible and nonedible species.

Wild plants that can be confidently interpreted as food-related appear only in very low frequencies in both the midden and apartment deposits. In the Building 13 midden, the remains of edible wild plants fall into three categories. First, there are plants known to have been used by Native Californians to make *pinole*, a flour made of toasted and ground seeds that was either eaten dry or cooked into gruels or small cakes (Heizer and Elsasser 1980:242, 246). These include *Atriplex* sp. (saltbush), *Carex* sp. (sedge), and *Juncus* sp. (rush). The second category is made up of nuts and berries such as *Corylus* sp. (hazelnut), *Rubus* sp.

(blackberry/raspberry), and *Sambucus* sp. (elderberry). The third category, represented by only one specimen, is wild legumes (Fabacae). Each of these taxa is represented by only one to three specimens; together, they account for only 2 percent of the seeds recovered from the Building 13 assemblage.

In addition to these three categories, the Building 13 midden had a relatively high frequency of *Malva* sp. (mallow) seeds (105 specimens, 17 percent). Mallow is a weedy annual that was introduced to Alta California during the early Spanish-colonial period and spread widely throughout the landscape. Mallow seeds have been found in archaeological deposits in at least two rancho sites (Petaluma and Ontiveros) and one mission site (Santa Cruz) (Silliman 2000:294–295). The plant is associated with both Native Californian and colonial uses. The leaves, root, and seeds of the plant are all edible (Roos-Collins 1990:118); one account describes how Native Californians used seeds from some mallows to make pinole (Silliman 2000:295). Both native and colonial healers used the leaves and stems medicinally (Cohen-Williams and Williams 2001:9; Heizer and Elsasser 1980:247). However, mallow also serves as forage for grazing animals and could have entered the archaeological record through the burning of animal dung for fuel. The function of mallow remains ambiguous, its presence possibly signaling use as food, medicine, or fuel.

There is minimal overlap between the wild edible foods represented in the midden and those represented in the apartment floor deposits. In the latter deposits, wild barley, peas, and legumes (*Hordeum* and *H. brachyantherum*, *Lathyrus* sp., and Fabacae) are the most prominent. Hazelnut and sedge are minimally present, represented by only one and three specimens, respectively. Mallow seeds were also found, in lower numbers (49 specimens) and in drastically lower frequencies (1 percent) than in the Building 13 midden deposit. These differences could indicate minor changes in the wild plants gathered for consumption by colonists living at the Presidio. The most significant result of these analyses, however, is the overall and consistently low frequency of wild edible plants.

Plants in the Colonial Diet   The archaeological evidence confirms that wheat, maize, and legumes were major staples in the colonial diet, with the botanical assemblage from the apartment indicating that wheat may have become increasingly prominent. The botanical evidence related to cultigens has implications for the organization of subsistence labor. Unlike animals (domestic and wild), which appear to have been procured on the hoof and butchered by individual households, cultivated cereals were obtained having already been cleaned of extraneous parts. Substantial amounts of wheat were provisioned in whole-grain form; if used as flour, the wheat would have been parched and hand-ground by members of the household. Alternatively, the wheat may have been cooked whole or cracked in boiled and simmered stews and gruels.

In contrast, by the mid-1810s, maize had either virtually disappeared from the colonial diet or was being provisioned in ground form. The former alternative would indicate that the settlers were avoiding a food that by all accounts had been central to the earlier colonial diet. Writing generally of colonial New Spain, Alfred Crosby (1972:107) suggests that maize, a New World cultigen, was culturally associated with Indians and scorned by elites. Perhaps the Californios, in shifting away from identification with their Mexican Indian heritage, similarly shunned maize as a food no longer appropriate for them.

Alternatively, if maize was being provided in ground form, who was performing the work of transforming the whole kernels into flour? In previous chapters, we saw that colonists increasingly relied on the labor of Native Californian men as construction and agricultural laborers. The workers most likely to have been assigned the task of grinding corn for the colonists were Native Californian women. Colonial records (for example, Milliken 1995:77) mention that indigenous women were being employed as early as 1777 to mill grain for households in the civilian Pueblo of San José. Travelers visiting the San Francisco area in the 1780s and 1790s likewise recounted that Native Californian women at the missions were assigned the "tedious and laborious" task of grinding corn "with a roller upon a stone" (La Pérouse 1989:86; see also Vancouver 1984). There are no documentary records of such labor practices at the Presidio, but this archaeological evidence may indicate that military families were also benefiting from the labor of indigenous women.

While the archaeological evidence related to maize and the colonial diet is, in the end, ambiguous, the botanical data regarding wild plants is definitive. The military settlers living at the Presidio made scant use of wild plants. The few wild seeds, nuts, legumes, and berries found in the midden and apartment botanical assemblages are present in such low frequencies that their consumption was occasional at best. Even more striking are the wild subsistence plants that are completely absent from the assemblage. Native Californian foodways in the San Francisco Bay area centered on two plant-based foods: acorns, usually ground and boiled into a thick soup; and pinole flour. In the archaeological deposits at the Presidio, seeds traditionally used to make pinole are incredibly scant (both in absolute count and in frequency), and acorns are not present at all. Botanical remains of such nondomesticated foods have been found in significant numbers at other Spanish-colonial and Mexican era sites (Silliman 2000:293–295); hence their absence is unlikely to be the result of preservation biases. That the colonial diet had not incorporated wild plant resources to any meaningful degree by the 1810s and 1820s suggests avoidance rather than lack of knowledge about the local environment.

Diet and Ethnogenesis

This historical and archaeological evidence sheds light on the complicated and ambiguous relationship between diet and ethnogenesis. Scholars of Alta California history will not be surprised that the military settlers at the Presidio were consuming a diet centered on the triumvirate of beef, cereal, and beans. The requisitions and invoices related to the San Blas supply ships give us information about imported seasonings, sweeteners, and oils that have little or no archaeological visibility. A small number of glass bottles and food canisters point to possible small-scale trade or gift exchanges with visiting foreign ships.

What the archaeological data do uniquely provide are indications of small variances and changes in the colonial diet that differ from the conventional model assumed by most historical studies. Wild game—deer, waterfowl, rabbits, turtles, fish, and perhaps also bears and foxes—appears to have been a more important source of meat than sheep, goats, or pigs. Yet shellfish and wild plant foods were not incorporated into the colonial diet in any meaningful amounts, perhaps because they were strongly associated with Native Californians. The near-absence of corn in the later-period apartment deposits could indicate a colonial avoidance of foods that were culturally associated with indigeneity or, alternatively, a growing reliance on Native Californian labor to grind grain. In sum, diet appears to be an aspect of social practice that both reinscribed and troubled the boundaries of colonial identity; such ambiguity is reflected not only in the content of the archaeological record but also in the plurality of interpretive possibilities.

Cuisine and Food Preparation

Dietary composition alone offers only one perspective on food practices and preferences. Food preparation transforms raw materials into products that are culturally recognizable as food. Such transformations have potentially infinite variety: consider, for example, the contrasts among common foods made of only wheat and water: a slice of bread, a steamed or boiled dumpling, a plate of noodles, a cracker, and a bowl of farina porridge. The person preparing food from raw materials faces an array of choices, and the patterned regularity in these choices points to conventions, traditions, and practices that are negotiated throughout the rhythms of daily life.

This section returns to the ceramic assemblage from the Building 13 midden (introduced in chapter 8) to reconstruct, to the extent possible, practices related to food preparation. Ceramic vessels are not the only artifacts representing food preparation, but they are by far the most numerous.[3] The ceramic assemblage includes sherds representing a minimum of eighty-two cooking vessels and seventy-three general use vessels. Both vessel size and vessel form afford insight into the patterns of food preparation at the Presidio.

Vessel Size

Institutions are notable in their tendency to centralize and regulate the daily practices of their inhabitants. El Presidio de San Francisco was no exception, and the archaeological and historical evidence generally indicates that in some areas, such as architecture, the military command increasingly assumed responsibility and control over practices that had previously been the purview of households and other smaller-scale social groups. One important question related to food preparation at the Presidio concerns the scale of this work. This is an issue of particular interest because it is well documented that food preparation at nearby missions was directed by priests and their assistants; there, cereals and legumes were stewed into porridges that were distributed three times a day (La Pérouse 1989; Langsdorff 1927; Milliken 1995; Webb 1952).

One useful measure of the scale of food preparation is the volume of cooking vessels. Because only a few of the vessels were sufficiently complete to allow volume calculations, rim diameter was used as a proxy.[4] The cooking vessels were surprisingly small; all the rim diameters fell within a range of 12 to 32 cm. General use vessels were similarly sized, with rim diameters ranging from 6 to 40 cm, and all but four vessels falling within a narrower 12 to 28 cm diameter range (fig. 36). The few general use and cooking vessels for which volume could be approximated had capacities from 1 to 4 L; the actual quantity of food prepared in such vessels was undoubtedly slightly less, since pots and bowls are rarely filled to the rim during use.

Since most tableware vessels could hold approximately 0.3–0.5 L of food or drink, most cooking pots and kitchen bowls seem to have been designed to prepare between two to ten servings of food. Food preparation at the Presidio, then, was likely carried out by fairly small social groups, such as households, although food may have been shared across households as well.

Vessel Forms

The vessel forms of both food preparation and tableware vessels reveal further information about how raw ingredients were prepared and served (table 14). Throughout the ceramic assemblage, hollowware vessel forms dominate, indicating that military settlers living at the Presidio consumed a diet almost entirely composed of liquid-based foods such as stews, bean dishes, gruels, and porridges.

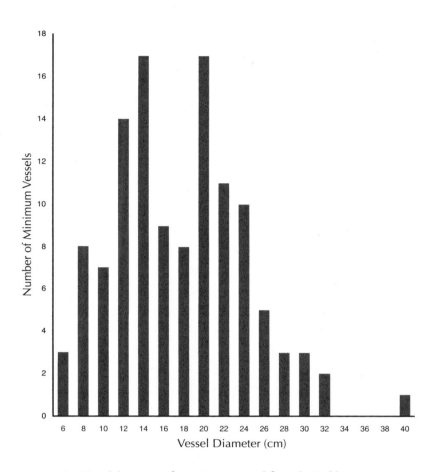

FIGURE 36. Vessel diameters of ceramics recovered from the Building 13 midden. In cases where diameter measurements fell within a range (for example, 12 to 16 cm), the least diameter was used.

Eighty-two minimum vessel groupings were identified as cooking vessels by the presence of soot residues on the exterior of the sherds. The most striking aspect of the cooking vessels is the relative scarcity of comales, the flat ceramic griddles used for cooking tortillas as well as for heating other types of dry food. Only one minimum vessel could be confidently identified as a comal; three others are also likely comales but could not be positively identified. Together, these four vessels represent fewer than 5 percent of the cooking vessels. Comales are especially susceptible to fracture because of their flat, thin shape and the extreme thermal stress involved in their use (Rice 1987:298); their low frequency

TABLE 14. Vessel form count and frequencies
found in the Building 13 midden

Vessel Form	MNV Count	MNV Frequency (%)
Flatwares		
Soup plate	3	1.2
Plate or soup plate	28	11.2
Comal	1	0.4
Comal (?)	3	1.2
Platter(?)	1	0.4
Other flatware	3	1.2
FLATWARE SUBTOTAL	39	15.5
Hollowwares		
Bowl	33	13.1
Bowl or cup	11	4.4
Cup, jarro, or chocotero	8	3.2
Bowl-shaped pot with flared collar	5	2.0
Shallow bowl-shaped pot with horizontal handles	5	2.0
Cup	2	0.8
Olla de aceite	2	0.8
Jar	1	0.4
Other hollowware	115	45.8
HOLLOWWARE SUBTOTAL	182	72.5
Other/unknown	30	12.0
TOTAL	251	100.0

NOTE: Slight discrepancies in subtotals are the result of rounding.

cannot be explained as a result of differential breakage rates. Their scarcity in the Building 13 midden is particularly surprising because many historical accounts indicate that military personnel of all ranks and their families consumed tortillas as a daily staple.

In contrast, seventy-three of the cooking vessels and sixty-five of the general use vessels are hollowwares (five cooking vessels and eight general use vessels could not be identified to form). All of the general use hollowware vessels and most of the cooking vessels are bowl-shaped and were likely used for storage, soaking, mixing, and other aspects of food preparation prior to cooking. In addition, two distinctive forms of cooking vessels were identified in the ceramic assemblage. Five minimum vessels are bowl-shaped pots with slightly constricted orifices and a low, flared collar; these were probably used to boil and simmer cereals, beans, and meats.[5] Five others are low, shallow, open bowl-shaped vessels with horizontally applied handles at the rim. Today, vessels similar in form are used in Mexican cuisine to thicken bean and rice dishes, as the shallow open form facilitates the evaporation of excess liquid.

The tableware vessel forms further substantiate the colonial emphasis on liquid-based foods. Forty-two of the tableware vessels are hollowwares. The remaining thirty-one tableware vessels are soup plates or vessels that could be either soup plates or plates. Soup plates are flatware vessels with a depressed central well, suitable for serving stews and other wet foods without spilling. Well over half, and most likely the vast majority, of the tableware vessels were designed for the consumption of liquid-based foods.

An Eighteenth-Century "Fusion Cuisine"

At the Presidio, food was being cooked and consumed in households or other small social groups, but each food-sharing group apparently prepared and served meals in very similar ways, using similar ingredients. The dominant pattern of household production of liquid-based foods may reveal information about the organization of labor related to food. In a review of ethnohistorical studies of women's participation in food preparation in Mexico, Elizabeth Brumfiel (1991:237–238) notes that griddle foods such as tortillas are particularly labor-intensive. Husking, boiling, soaking, hulling, grinding, forming, and cooking maize or wheat dough into enough tortillas to feed a family was a process that required at least eight to twelve hours a day. In contrast, pot foods such as stews, bean dishes, and gruels like atole were relatively labor-saving. The size and form of cooking vessels from the Building 13 midden suggest that households were making choices that minimized labor demands on the household cook. Since historical accounts hint that soldiers' wives were primarily responsible for preparing food, the prominence of liquid-based foods might indicate that their time and labor were highly valued.

Although liquid-based foods were undoubtedly labor-saving, the settlers may have also preferred them to dry-cooked foods. Brumfiel writes that a high pot-to-griddle ratio "reflects people's ability to indulge the Mexican preference for foods cooked in pots, foods that traditionally carried positive symbolic connotations" (Brumfiel 1991:240). She adds that gruels such as atole were thought to have health-promoting properties, and cooking pots were perceived as symbolic wombs. Archaeological studies of African diaspora communities in eighteenth-

and nineteenth-century North America have also noted that stewed and simmered foods were positively associated with African identities (Ferguson 1992; Franklin 2001). The high value placed on such foods in both indigenous Mexican and African diaspora food traditions might have provided a culinary common ground—a sort of "fusion cuisine," if you will—that supported the development of shared colonial foodways in the multiethnic settlement.

.   .   .

Food and shelter are material necessities. Cultural practices interweave biological needs with social structure, so that physical life and social identity merge and become inseparable in practical experience. It is no coincidence that, so far, this study of colonial ethnogenesis has interrogated archaeological evidence of colonial placeways and foodways: architecture, food-related ceramic vessels, food containers, animal bone, shells, and seeds and other plant parts. This chapter's explicit focus on diet and cuisine points us toward the fragile interface between body and society.

The colonial diet, based on the domesticated triumvirate of beef, cereals, and legumes, distinguished the military settlers from Native Californians who tended, but did not cultivate, wild plants and animals (Anderson 2005; Blackburn and Anderson 1993). The plant and animal remains excavated at the Presidio indicate that colonists had an ambiguous relationship to food resources available in the local environment. They supplemented their beef-based diet with wild game and particularly with fish. They gathered and consumed some wild plant foods but avoided acorns and shellfish. In later years, the colonists may have reduced their consumption of corn, a food generally associated with indigeneity in colonial New Spain, but the data are not conclusive. Dietary composition was a means by which the military settlers consolidated their status as colonizers and distanced themselves from their own indigenous heritage; yet this was not an impermeable boundary, since some wild foods were acceptable to the colonial palate.

With this in mind, the social organization of food preparation takes on added significance. Food was prepared for households or other small social groups; and the military settlers shared a common practice of preparing liquid-based foods such as stews, soups, gruels, and atoles. These shared culinary practices would have minimized, rather than highlighted, ethnic or racial differences among colonists.

Through their role as food producers, women living at the settlement certainly played a key part in the formation and emergence of a shared Californio identity among the racially and ethnically diverse colonial population. Decades before El Presidio de San Francisco's architectural modifications in 1815, which created an *externally* homogeneous appearance, members of the colonial population within were engaging in shared practices related to diet and cuisine. By eating similar foods, prepared in a similar manner, inhabitants of the Presidio began experiencing themselves as similar rather than different from each other—as a community of Californios. Adult women, responsible for procuring and preparing food for their dependents and boarders, were instrumental in effecting this transformation.

10   FASHIONING THE COLONIAL SUBJECT

Clothing

Five uniform buttons, two dozen dark glass embroidery beads, and a cheap glass costume jewel—the dense deposits of the Building 13 midden have yielded only a small handful of artifacts derived from the clothing of El Presidio de San Francisco's colonial settlers (fig. 37). This scarcity is echoed throughout the archaeological site. Buttons, beads, buckles, religious charms, and other traces of bodily adornment are so rare that they account for barely 0.01 percent of the artifacts recovered from the settlement. The low frequency of clothing-related objects is perplexing when compared to other archaeological investigations. Study after study has found that personal items "are among the most frequently encountered artifacts on colonial sites" (Deagan 2002:5). Why, then, does the reverse seem to be the case at the Presidio?

One might be tempted to disregard this small assemblage of artifacts, to conclude that the objects pictured in figure 37 can contribute little to our understanding of colonial ethnogenesis. But these buttons and beads provide a material entry point into the complex and contested realm of dress and social identity in colonial San Francisco.

Social Skins

Clothing and, more broadly, dress[1] are important media through which people negotiate, stabilize, and transform social identities. The low frequency of clothing-related items in the archaeological record of the Presidio should not lead us to

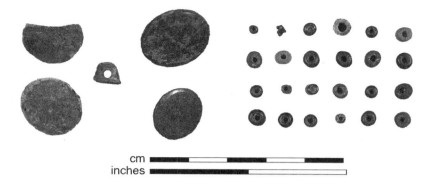

cm
inches

FIGURE 37   Copper-alloy uniform buttons and glass beads recovered from
the Building 13 midden. (A glass costume jewel, also found in the midden,
is not shown here.)

think that clothing was incidental to daily life at the settlement. Materials worn
and carried on the body are tangible means by which people create social surfaces that mediate the unstable interface between the body and the rest of the
world.[2] Through prosthesis and proprioception (one's knowledge of bodily position through internal sensations), people experience a physical extension of
their bodies into and through the materials that are put on the body.[3] Simultaneously, the body is experienced as separate, shielded, protected, hidden, covered, and restricted by these materials. This sensory dialectic fosters a subjectivity in which the physical boundaries of personhood are continually under
negotiation: "Paradoxically, dress simultaneously blurs and bounds the body's
borders" (Fisher and Loren 2003:228; see also Joyce 2005). Further, clothing
transforms movement and conditions the use of the body in daily life. Items of
clothing cannot be viewed as static objects draped on an already-defined and
stable body; nor do clothes project or communicate a preformed identity, for
clothing is a means through which social identities are inculcated and naturalized in the body (Bourdieu 1984; Butler 1990, 1993a; Cohn 1996). Clothing
participates in the ongoing production of embodied subjects.

Clothing, like other bodily manipulations and ornamentation, is particularly
potent in visual negotiations of identity, for in ongoing social interactions, dress
and the body are perceived simultaneously. The "social skins" (Turner 1980)
effected by dress, posture, ornamentation, and gesture facilitate identification
with a larger group (Comaroff 1996; Fisher and Loren 2003). In this sense,
dress is always a citational practice using reproduction, mimicry, parody, exaggeration, and transformation to refer to social precedents and to webs of sim-

ilarities and differences in appearance (Bhabha 2004; Butler 1990, 1993a; Joyce 2005; Turner 1995). Through dress, individuals can reveal or conceal different selves and move the body through multiple identities (Fisher and Loren 2003).

Constraints on dress also act to "fix" the range of possible identifications. Archaeological studies of clothing and dress in the Spanish-colonial Americas have tended to emphasize clothing as a means through which individuals could exercise agency and choice in the construction of their own identities (for example, Deagan 2002; Loren 2001b). Clothing-related objects allow an intimate scale of archaeological investigation, but this intimacy should not be misread as separate or removed from the workings of social power and governmentality. In eighteenth- and nineteenth-century New Spain, clothing was a highly politicized realm of social practice, part of what Hall (2000:70) terms the "microphysics" of colonial power. Sumptuary laws, trade relationships, military regulations, and religious doctrine, together with social customs and fashion, meant that the personal act of getting dressed was fully entangled with the politics of empire.

Castas and Clothing in New Spain

From the moment of their recruitment, the families who founded the Presidio were fashioned into colonial subjects. Juan Bautista de Anza insisted that the members of the expedition he led, most of whom had been recruited from impoverished towns in Sinaloa and Sonora, receive their initial compensation in clothes rather than cash, for "if paid in money, they would waste it or lose it in gambling" (Chapman 1916:293). Together, Anza and the expedition's purchasing agent, Juan José de Echeveste, anticipated the goods necessary to outfit the planned 30 male recruits, their wives, and an estimated 180 children (table 15). For the adults, Anza ordered ready-made clothes: military uniforms for the men, and a fairly plain wardrobe of shirts, petticoats, and shawls for the women. The clothes were tailored from serviceable fabrics: locally produced *manta*, a coarse cotton or woolen cloth, from Puebla; Silesian linen imported from Germany; flannel; and silk serge. Children's clothing was supplied to parents in the form of dry goods that were to be sewn into garments similar in form and fabric to those worn by adults. Additionally, men, women, and children all received ready-made stockings, shoes, hats, and hair ribbons.

Anza's decision to provide a full wardrobe to each member of the expedition was, in one sense, a practical approach to the challenge of outfitting a military company staffed by impoverished recruits. Within the broader political context of clothing in eighteenth-century New Spain, it is also apparent that

TABLE 15. Wardrobe items ordered
to clothe members of the Anza expedition

Wardrobe for a Man	*Wardrobe for a Woman*
3 shirts of good Silesian linen	3 shirts
3 pairs of underdrawers of Puebla cloth of 4 varas, each one	3 pairs of white Puebla petticoats
2 cloth coats, with which their lining and trimmings	2 pairs of petticoats, some silk serge, others of thick flannel, and an underskirt
2 pairs of trousers, ditto	2 varas of linen stuff for two linings
2 pairs of stockings	2 pairs of Brussels stockings
2 pairs of chamois-skin boots	2 pairs of hose
3 pairs of gaiter shoes	2 pairs of shoes
1 cloth cape lined with thick flannel	2 women's shawls
1 hat	1 hat
2 Puebla powder-cloths	6 varas of ribbon
1 ribbon for the hat and hair	
2 leather jackets	
30 shoulder belts	
Clothing for Ninety Boys	*Clothing for an Equal Number of Girls*
5 pieces of cloth containing 180 varas	270 varas of linen stuff for shirts
12 pieces of Puebla cloth for linings and white trousers	4 pieces of Puebla cloth for petticoats and linings
270 varas of linen stuff for shirts of about 3 varas	90 cloths for women's shawls of all sizes
50 hats	2 pieces of thick flannel for little petticoats
8 dozen shoes for children of various sizes	4 pieces of cloth of about 34 varas for underskirts
	12 pieces of ribbon for bands
	16 ditto of fine rope
	8 dozen shoes for girls of various sizes

SOURCE: Reproduced from Chapman 1916.

Anza was undertaking a social engineering project, one aimed at transforming the recruits' social identities and stabilizing their place in the colonial order.

Colonial Ideals: Bourbon Fashions and Racial Passing

In seventeenth- and eighteenth-century Spain, as well as in the Spanish-colonial Americas, rights and obligations were bestowed on legal estates, such as the castas, not on individuals. It was a person's membership in an estate that secured his or her position in society. Although lineage and physical traits were not disregarded, scholars are in accord that the primary attributes used to evaluate whether a person belonged to a particular estate or casta were dress and, to a lesser degree, speech, mannerisms, and occupation.[4] Clothing practices thus presented a social paradox. While those in power used clothing to regulate bodies and enforce arbitrary social hierarchies, nonelites could use clothing strategically to transform their social identities and blur social divisions. Attempts to separate the racial estates and different castas incited counter-practices such as racial cross-dressing, mixed clothing, and passing. Consequently, the politics of clothing in colonial New Spain were produced through "ordinary people in everyday life pushing, expanding, and testing the categories by grading themselves up and others down. In this they reordered their world as much as conformed to it" (Boyer 1997:66–67).

In the 1700s, the advent of the Bourbon monarchy brought visual inspection to the forefront of governmentality, and the Spanish government increased surveillance of bodily practices such as clothing. There was rising concern that it was becoming impossible to distinguish the different social groups that composed the legal estates. A climate of suspicion grew among colonial elites, centered on the fear that some people of Moorish and African heritage were successfully passing as Spaniards. Concern about racial passing was further intensified by heightened attempts to enforce estate-based tax codes and tribute requirements. Clothing, which lent itself to concealing and transforming identities, was a focal point of these anxieties.

The new French-influenced Bourbon fashions of the eighteenth century were shaped by this intensified scrutiny of appearance. Looser, billowing clothes fastened by laces and ties were supplanted by form-fitting, buttoned garments that revealed rather than concealed the contours of the physiological body. Bourbon dress for men included knee-length breeches that fastened with buttons at the waist and side seams and buckles at the knee; stockings covered the lower legs. White pullover shirts were drawn to the body by sleeveless waistcoats fastened with closely spaced buttons down the front. The waistcoats were framed by cutaway jackets with decorative buttons on the front and at the cuffs. Women's attire was composed of floor-length skirts topped by tight-fitting

FIGURE 38.   *De español e india, mestizo*, attributed to José de Ibarra, ca. 1725. This panel of a casta painting illustrates the contrast between Bourbon fashion and Mexican Indian dress. The español man displays the classic Bourbon silhouette, with form-fitting clothes and a cutaway jacket that reveals the figure. The india woman, in contrast, wears the flowing huipil, wraparound skirt, and multipurpose rebozo typically associated with indigenous dress. The older boy carrying the infant also wears indigenous dress of poorer-quality cloth; his head and feet are bare, indicating that he is probably a servant. Museo de América, Madrid.

bodices, which, like men's waistcoats, were usually fastened with closely spaced buttons on the front. These standard outfits were worn by most elites and nonelites alike. Social status was signaled through subtle differences in the texture, patterning, and quality of fabric; in the methods used to fasten garments; in the degree of elaboration of garment fasteners such as buttons and buckles; and in ornamentation (or its absence) with embroidery, ribbons, garlands, braided thread, broaches, and other jewelry (Deagan 2002; Fisher 1992:54–61).

Important exceptions to Bourbon patterns of dress were found in what might be considered national or ethnic costumes. In colonial New Spain, Bourbon dress contrasted with garments that had been historically associated with Mexican Indians, especially the *huipil* (fig. 38). The huipil was a flowing garment sewn from several lengths of handwoven cloth, with a neck opening to accommodate the head. It was worn loosely draped over the body. Other garments associated with indigenous dress were also made of uncut, rectangular pieces of handwoven cloth, such as folded and wrapped skirts and aprons, *rebozos* (narrow shawls used as headscarves), ponchos, and folded cloth headpieces (Carrera 2003:24; Fisher 1992:18, 50, 65–66; Katzew 2004:77). Bourbon fashion was hegemonically associated with Europe, the Enlightenment, and the metropole, whereas the huipil and other Mexican indigenous styles were associated with rural backwardness and racial impurity. However, non-Bourbon modes of dress were also sometimes worn to signify heterodox identifications and political stances. For example, in New Spain, it was not uncommon for prosperous indios and castas to continue to wear huipiles and other indigenous clothing forms, crafting them from the textured brocade cloth and multicolored printed fabrics prized in Bourbon fashion (Fisher 1992:65–66). Such outfits transformed the material substance of colonial elite appearance into performances of indigenous identity.

Sumptuary Laws

Sumptuary laws were one of the discourses through which Bourbon elites expressed their anxieties about social disorder and fashion. In their broadest form, sumptuary laws are legal measures taken by elites to maintain exclusivity of access to certain objects and substances and to enforce "a tight connection between status and its material signifiers" (Hall 2000:72). Sumptuary laws in colonial New Spain were initiated during the earliest years of conquest, but their promulgation and enforcement accelerated in the late 1600s and throughout the 1700s.[5] The foremost objective was to maintain the integrity of each legal estate. To this end, Spain's colonial sumptuary laws sought to prevent both upward and downward mobility among colonial subjects. However, sumptuary laws often had the reverse effect, awakening widespread desire for restricted commodities (Appadurai 1986:22–26, 32; Fisher 1992:62).

People with African heritage were especially targeted by sumptuary laws. *Negros* (people of full African ancestry), mulatos, and other castas with African ancestry were expected to dress in Bourbon fashion, but they were prohibited from wearing luxury textiles, especially silk and lace, and from adorning themselves with gold, silver, pearls, and precious stones. Women with African heritage were not allowed to wear the embroidered, full-length *mantillas* (headscarves) that were the hallmarks of elite Spanish women. Penalties for violation of these laws included confiscation of the offending articles of clothing for a first offense and one hundred lashes with a whip for a second offense. Exceptions were occasionally granted to mulatas who had married a Spaniard.[6]

The edicts simultaneously prohibited any person of mixed heritage from dressing as an indio. In New Spain, indios were exempt from some taxes and had exclusive access to certain lands and natural resources. Many castas also preferred to identify more with their Indian ancestry than with an ambiguous status as people of mixed heritage. But as the Bourbon monarchy intensified its enforcement of colonial tax codes, sumptuary laws increasingly aimed to visually separate indios from castas. With few exceptions, sumptuary legislation barred negros, mulatos, and mestizos from wearing Indian clothing. Punishment for men included one hundred lashes and jail sentences; women were to be stripped naked and publicly humiliated for their offenses.[7]

Overall, sumptuary legislation "attempted to define the castas' status as both non-Indian and inferior" (Cope 1994:16). People of mixed heritage, like the settlers who had been recruited to establish the Presidio, were quite literally caught in the middle of colonial racial hierarchies. Those with African heritage were in a particularly disadvantaged position, as they were the special target of sumptuary laws aimed at restricting their social mobility through the regulation of personal appearance.

Cuadros de Casta: Colonial Taxonomies of Race and Dress

While sumptuary laws attempted to provide a legal solution to colonial anxieties about racial cross-dressing, elite colonists also expressed their vision of colonial society through a new artistic genre: the *cuadros de casta*, or casta paintings, which emerged in the early 1700s.[8] Casta paintings were visual representations of the racial taxonomies that defined the colonial legal estates and the sistema de castas. More than one hundred series of these paintings were produced in the eighteenth century, nearly all of them in Mexico City (Katzew 2004:3). By the 1760s, casta paintings had become a common element of elite colonial visual culture.

Typically, a casta painting series consists of one or more rectangular canvases divided into eight to eighteen panels (fig. 39). Each panel depicts a triad of man, woman, and child, usually beginning in the upper left-hand corner with an español and an india and their mestizo child. Successive panels show the idealized outcome of subsequent cross-racial couplings and their casta offspring. Panels are clearly labeled to indicate the racial identity of each parent and child; because of this, casta paintings have been compared with contemporary scientific illustrations that provide identification of animal and plant species (Deans-Smith 2005). Yet more than depicting physiological bodies, the casta paintings are saturated with material culture. Clothing, work tools, household objects, foods, and buildings—alongside skin and hair color—are primary signifiers of racial difference. Commissioned by colonial elites at a time when the boundaries between estates were increasingly disrupted in real life, casta paintings visually represented the colonial fantasy of a racially stratified society, one in which each person's dress, occupation, diet, housing, and consumer practices were congruent with that person's lineage.

While sumptuary laws indicate what clothing items were prohibited for

FIGURE 39.   Casta painting, by Ignacio María Barreda, 1777.
Oil on canvas, 79 × 49 cm. Real Academia Española de la Lengua,
Madrid.

members of racial groups, the casta paintings provide a sense of what was expected from members of racial groups. Costume historian Abby Sue Fisher
(1992:91–97, 120–123) and archaeologist Diana DiPaolo Loren (1999:128,
133–172) have each analyzed casta paintings as sources of information about
colonial ideals regarding the dress of different castas. Their research indicates
that depictions of clothing in casta paintings cluster into four groups: Spaniards;
members of higher-ranking castas, primarily mixtures of Spanish and Indian
heritage; members of lower-ranking castas, primarily mixtures that include
African heritage; and Indians.

In the paintings, Spaniards are marked by their complete adherence to Bourbon standards of dress and the conspicuous display of expensive and rare materials. Tightly fitted outfits are clearly depicted as fashioned from richly colored silks, velvets, brocades, and patterned fabrics. The garments' openings and
edges are elaborated with fine lace, multilayered ruffles, and closely spaced lines
of filigreed and jeweled gold and silver buttons. Powdered wigs for men, heavily embroidered mantillas for women, and heeled shoes and jewelry for both
genders complete the image of elite Spanish appearance.

Members of high-ranking castas are also portrayed in Bourbon dress, but with
looser-fitting garments that are more functional than decorative and that are
made from less expensive materials, a mixture of imported and handwoven fabrics. Ornaments are simpler: ribbons, simple ruffles, and modest jewelry. Clothing fasteners such as buckles and buttons are fewer in number; are made of
copper, brass, or tin; and are plain rather than decorated. Instead of wigs, men
wear neckscarves and hats; women wear rebozos instead of mantillas.

In contrast, members of lower-ranking castas are depicted in dress that is at
odds with Bourbon fashion. Bourbon-style clothing, when worn, is portrayed
as dirty or tattered. Most commonly, men are shown wearing loosely fitted clothing associated with specific trades. Both men and women frequently wear a mixture of Indian and colonial garments, such as huipiles tucked into the waist-
bands of skirts or pants. Clothing is generally unadorned and is fastened with
laces or ties rather than buttons or buckles. Shoes and hats, when worn, are ill-
kempt; more often, members of the lower castas appear barefooted and bare-
headed.

Finally, indios in the casta paintings are portrayed entirely in indigenous dress
that, although free-flowing, is clean and in good repair. A few Indian women
partnered with Spaniards are pictured wearing elaborate huipiles, ornamented
headdresses, and costly jewels, suggesting marriages between upper-class Spanish men and women from elite indigenous families.

The analyses of the cuadros de casta by Fisher and Loren, along with the sumptuary laws, provide an index of the hegemonic meanings of the cuts, fabrics,

FIGURE 40. *MP Uniformes, 81 (Soldado de cuera, 1804, en la chupa)*. This diagram shows regulation military uniform and gear. The coat was shorter than the knee-length coats worn from the 1770s through the 1790s; additionally, the horse carried fewer protective leather coverings than in earlier years. España. Ministerio de Cultura. Archivo General de Indias, Sevilla.

fasteners, ornamentation, and condition of clothes worn by colonial subjects of the Spanish crown. Notably, archaeological investigations at the Presidio have not recovered any clothing-related objects that were associated with proper Spanish dress. The buttons, beads, and costume jewel recovered from the Building 13 midden are objects that would have been viewed by colonial elites as markers of the military settlers' mixed-race heritage. Additionally, the low frequency of clothing fasteners and objects of adornment in the archaeological deposits is a significant indicator of the military settlers' low status in the colonial racial hierarchy.

Uniforms and Military Regulations

The colonial settlers' dress was also subject to military regulations. The 1772 Reglamento specified a particular uniform for frontier troops (figs. 40 and 41). Called *soldados de cuera*, or leather jacket soldiers, for the thick leather armor they wore, presidio soldiers were outfitted far differently than their European counterparts (fig. 42).[9] Their uniform consisted of "a short jacket of blue woolen

FIGURE 41. A soldier at Monterey and his wife. The image is attributed to José Cardero, one of two artists working for the Malaspina expedition, which visited Monterey in September 1791. The soldier is depicted lifting his cuera to show the layers of protective material underneath. Note the buttons on the sleeve cuffs of his jacket and along the external side seams of his trousers. In contrast, the bodice of his wife's dress is fastened with laces drawn up the center front of the garment and with ribbon ties at the elbows. Museo de América, Madrid.

cloth, with small cuffs and a red collar, breeches of blue wool, a cloth cap of the same color, a cartridge pouch, a leather jacket, and a bandoleer of antelope hide, as is presently in use (the bandoleer to be embroidered with the name of the presidio in order to distinguish one from another), a black neckerchief, hat, shoes, and leggings" (Brinkerhoff and Faulk 1965:19–21).

In addition to this outfit, each soldier was to be equipped with a shield made from bull hide, a protective leather apron, a broadsword, a lance, a cartridge box, a musket, and pistols. This kit was a deliberate hybrid of indigenous Mexican and European military gear. The distinctive cuera—a heavy, knee-length, and sleeveless coat made of seven layers of buckskin—derived from both European styles of armor and the Aztec *ichcipilli* (a quilted sleeveless tunic) and

FIGURE 42. Uniforms of the Catalonian Volunteers (left) and artillerymen (right), some of whom were garrisoned at El Presidio de San Francisco
during the 1790s. In contrast to the specially outfitted soldados de cuera,
these military men wore uniforms resembling those of European troops.
Photograph provided and authorized by the Museo del Ejército, Madrid.

was intended to protect its wearer from arrows. The uniform, armor, arms, ammunition, and tack weighed about 123 pounds altogether, producing "a veri-
table human fortress on horseback" (Moorhead 1975:189). Frontier officers
dressed in similar garb, donning the cuera in battle and while leading expeditions, although they might wear Bourbon-style cloth waistcoats and jackets while
conducting regular business at presidios. Rank was signaled through subtle
differences in cloth, buttons, and decorative trim, such as gold braid, epaulets,
and stripes (Mackey and Sooy 1932; Perissinotto 1998:27).

In light of the sumptuary laws and the visual discourses on clothing related
in the cuadros de casta, the hybrid frontier uniform assigned to presidio troops
takes on greater significance. Colonial officials were careful to maintain the separation between the frontier presidio troops and the regular army, even going
so far as to caution frontier military commanders against providing presidio
troops with the lighter clothes and other comforts issued to soldiers in Europe.
Such "luxuries," they feared, would feminize the soldados de cuera and make
them less fit for the rigors of frontier warfare (Moorhead 1969:40). While the

cuera was valued for its utility in battle, it marked the soldiers themselves as coarse, unrefined, and distinctly non-Spanish, associating them through dress with the more stigmatized castas.

Anza's Shopping List: Clothing the New Recruits

Returning to the list of wardrobe items ordered by Anza (see table 15), we can now consider the implications of Anza's insistence on directly supplying the recruits with clothing. These recruits were primarily poor people of Mexican Indian and African heritage. By ordering clothing for soldiers *and* their families, Anza controlled the dress of the entire expedition, effectively eliminating differences in appearance that might have been related to cultural affiliation, casta, or economic means. Military-issue dress, for women and men, served as a social leveler, a veneer or camouflage cloaking their previous racial and economic status.

With the exception of the cuera worn by the troops while on duty, Anza's wardrobe plan dressed recruits in the Bourbon mode. By supplying men and women with fitted, ready-made clothing, as well as shoes, hats, and stockings, Anza foreclosed any possibility that recruits would dress themselves in the looser garments associated with indigenous identities. At the same time, the fabrics used to fashion these wardrobes sent an unambiguous message about the collective status of the members of the expedition. The cloth was functional and plain, most of it locally produced, the type of textiles associated with members of the lower-status castas in the casta paintings. The notable exception was the provision of a silk serge petticoat to each adult woman, which violated sumptuary laws prohibiting women of African heritage from wearing silk fabric.

Anza's use of clothing as a social equalizer contributed to the process through which the colonists at El Presidio de San Francisco increasingly viewed their co-settlers as their social equals and came to regard differences in casta status as irrelevant to social life. Distributing silk to the expedition's women may have communicated the message that restrictions on those of African heritage no longer applied. Perhaps not coincidentally, the most dramatic change in casta affiliation during the first decades of the Presidio's history was the movement away from casta ranks associated with African heritage in favor of mestizo and español identities. But while Anza's wardrobe plan would have dissolved some barriers to social mobility, it also established clear limits on the possibilities afforded to the recruits. The cut of their clothing was Bourbon in fashion, but the fabric they wore on their bodies was plain and utilitarian, continuing to mark them as members of the lower castas.

The End of the Journey: Native Californians
and a New Politics of Clothing

By the time Anza's recruits arrived in San Francisco, clothing had gained additional significance through the contrast between colonial and Native Californian dress. In the San Francisco Bay area, most Native Californians wore few garments. Women usually wore knee-length grass or deerskin skirts, and men had little or no covering over the genitals. In cold weather, both men and women draped cloaks of animal skins and hides over their bodies for warmth. In addition, women frequently wore layers of necklaces on their chest; men also wore jewelry, including necklaces, hair ornaments, and ear and nose piercings. Most adults wore basketry hats, the women's often decorated with elaborately woven patterns. The body's skin was a locus of deliberate adornment, both through permanent tattoos and more ephemeral body painting using clay pastes and vegetable pigments.[10] Although Native Californians intensively adorned and modified their bodies, the colonial priests and military settlers misread indigenous dress as nakedness, which was taken as a sign of sexual license, incivility, and cultural inferiority as well as sloth and lack of industry (Bouvier 2001:71–72; Hurtado 1999:10–12).

Colonial policy demanded that Native Californians be convinced to clothe themselves in a Christian manner (Bouvier 2001:71–72, 165–167). This project was undertaken primarily by mission priests, but military officers also distributed clothing to Native Californians who labored at the presidios or who participated in Indian Auxiliary military units. The colonial leaders expended considerable resources in this effort. One researcher estimates that, initially, up to 25 percent of the annual mission budget for the Californias was spent on clothing (Jackson 1999). Mission neophytes were issued clothes made of coarsely woven wool or cotton, usually white with blue striping; the loose-fitting, wrapped, and draped garments bore some resemblance to clothing associated with Mexican Indians (fig. 43).[11] "Spanish" clothing—garments resembling those issued to the military settlers—was sometimes given to neophytes as a reward for hard work and to those who had been designated as *alcaldes* (literally, mayors), creating visual hierarchies among the Indians at the missions (Bouvier 2001:165–167).

Undoubtedly, the members of the Anza party experienced a transformation in their understandings of their own appearances through their interactions with Native Californians, both in and outside the mission context. The homogeneous dress they had been issued at the beginning of their journey was now contrasted, on the one hand, with indigenous dress and its connotations of nakedness and, on the other hand, with the clothing issued to most neophytes and to Native

FIGURE 43. *Games of the Inhabitants of California*, by Louis Choris, 1816. Forty years after Mission San Francisco de Asís was established, its Native Californian inhabitants continued to wear traditional hairstyles and headdresses, along with the striped cloth issued by missionaries. Those pictured display a range of styles: some are clad only in breechcloths or wrapped loosely in a length of cloth, while others are wearing sewn shirts. Courtesy of the Bancroft Library, University of California, Berkeley.

Californians laboring at the Presidio. How did the military settlers participate in this new, local articulation of the politics of colonial dress? The sections that follow investigate this question through research on cloth and clothing fasteners at the Presidio.

Clothed in Empire

Beyond the clothing initially provided by Anza, the military settlers depended on their habilitado to order and maintain a stock of clothing, fabric, notions, and other sewing supplies. Because shipments from San Blas were irregular, clothing shortages were not uncommon (Langellier and Rosen 1996; Mora-Torres 2005). When shipments did arrive, they brought cargos of ready-made garments, textiles, ribbons, and embroidery floss as well as other objects of personal adornment from around the world.

The requisitions and invoices associated with these shipments reveal that a truly remarkable amount of attention was given to clothing (Barker 2007; Dado 2004). Garments, fabrics, and sundries were described at a level of detail far greater than that accorded to other types of goods. For example, a typical requisition might ask for "six crates of ordinary earthen dinnerware" (Dado 2004:doc. 208). In contrast, the authors of the requisitions and invoices went to great lengths to specify the manufacture, origin, quality, color, and style of clothing, textiles, and notions.

For example, stockings are variously described by material (silk, cotton, wool); by gender (for men or women); by color and decoration (black, white, red, scarlet, quince, embroidered, striped); by quality (ordinary, superior, fine); by weaving technique (worsted, double-stranded, footed stockings); and by place of manufacture (Barcelona, China, Toluca, Istlahuaca, England, Galicia). Similar attention to detail can be found in entries for other dry goods. In addition to entries for "common" cloth, specified according to quality and color, requests for textiles include baize, batiste, bombazine, calico, chambray, cotton, cotton velvet, creole cloth, crepe, crinoline, dimity, flannel, frieze, lanquin, linen, muslin, percale, rouen, serge, silk, and wool of various colors and grades. Within each kind of textile, further distinctions are made according to quality and place of manufacture. Linens, for example, include domestic linen, Brittany linen (further described as being wide or narrow, and of superfine, fine, ordinary, and medium quality), imitation Brittany linen (described as wide or narrow), Brabrant linen (fine, ordinary, and untreated), and glazed linen lining.

Without doubt, the invoices and requisitions confirm that the colonial settlers living at El Presidio de San Francisco were greatly concerned with personal appearance—an impression bolstered by the frequent orders of mirrors (small mirrors, ordinary mirrors, dressing table mirrors, and fine crystal mirrors) in the documents. Could Anza have anticipated that his plainly clothed expedition members would soon be spending their minimal salaries on imported European linens, Chinese silks, French lace, and other finery? And who were the intended audiences for these social performances of appearance? The Presidio lay at the farthest reaches of the empire, perhaps the most isolated outpost in Spanish North America. Therefore, it appears that this attention to garments, textiles, and notions was undertaken primarily as part of the ongoing negotiation of social relationships within the settlement and between the military settlers and mission priests, civilian farmers, and Native Californians with whom they interacted regularly.

Consuming Knowledge

Arjun Appadurai (1986:38) emphasizes that analyses of commodity exchange should not place luxury goods in opposition to necessities. Rather, luxury goods can be understood as goods whose critical use is rhetorical and social and, by extension, politically necessary. Specialized knowledge is a prerequisite for consumption of such goods, especially those procured through long-distance, intercultural flows of materials and capital. Traders and merchants provide critical bridges of knowledge that facilitate the movement of commodities across cultural gaps.

Alta California's colonial settlers are historically portrayed as geographically, politically, and economically isolated from the rest of the Spanish-colonial empire. While this was substantially true, the attention paid to clothing-related materials in the requisitions and invoices betrays a will to knowledge (after Foucault 1978) of global capitalism that is not evidenced in other aspects of the settlement's material practices. Architecture, household material culture, foodways—all of these primarily reference local cultural practices and the marketplaces of New Spain. Yet orders and invoices for clothing-related goods reveal that the colonial settlers were sophisticated consumers, familiar with the details of cloth production throughout the global marketplace.

Table 16 lists the places of manufacture that appear in the requisitions and invoices from the Presidio and the goods that were procured from those locales. The variety of locales and the specificity of requests—even listing the particular factory from which the goods should be procured—suggest that geographic origin was an important citational quality of clothing. The military settlers of the Presidio were quite literally clothed in empire, the goods on their bodies a physical testament to Spain's growing industrialization of its colonies and its economic relationships with other European countries, the Philippines, and China (Dado 2006). Table 16 also reveals the unevenness of settlers' geographic knowledge. In New Spain, places of manufacture are generally listed by reference to a specific town, whereas references to Spain and France include only major cities and provinces. China, England, Germany, and Holland are generally named only by country, with a few exceptions (Peking silk, rouen fabric from Silesia). The geographic discourse of dress was spatially stratified. Global consumption was imagined differently for goods produced within the empire than for those from outside it.

The requisitions and invoices point to the key role military bureaucrats played as the settlement's mediators of knowledge about commodities. Requisitions were formulated by the habilitado, then circulated for revision and approval among his commanding officers, and eventually submitted to the governor of the province. From there, the requisitions were sent to the warehouse manager at San Blas for fulfillment, who undoubtedly had to consult with his own superiors about any controversial or difficult requests. This written discourse about clothing and fabric was circulated among men whose literacy

New Spain (Mexico)

Blue domestic cloth, cabo cloth, blue baize, shawls

Benado: Chamois leather boots

Chimistlanes: Superior Mexican shawls

Cholula: Common cloth, fine lanquin cloth, fine closely woven cloth

Istlahuaca: Wool stockings

Las Carretas: Fine dark blue, yarn-dyed common cloth

Puebla: Black and white hats, common cloth, white cloth, small white cotton cloths, fine bombazines, wide striped cloth, shawls

Puruagua: Yarn-dyed cloth, blue cloth

Querétaro: Blue cloth

San Pedro: Cloth, strawberry-colored cloth

Sayula: Sturdy leather shoes

Tescuco: Hats

Toluca: Fine large double-stranded wool stockings, cotton stockings for men

Spain

Wide-toothed combs

Alcoy: Fine dark blue, yarn-dyed cloth

Barcelona: Calico, printed cloth, 2nd grade blue common cloth from the Marcola factory, colored kerchiefs, white silk stockings, shaving razors

Catalonia: Catalan baize

Córdoba: Shoes for women and men, dark stained shoes sewn like the English, ordinary spindle thread for stockings

Cuenca: 2nd grade scarlet cloth

Galicia: Superior footed stockings for men, understockings of thread

Grenada: Neckscarves, superior clean chatoyant ribbon, assorted ribbon

La Mancha: Wide lace

San Fernando: Blue, dark blue, deep red cloth

Sevilla: Wide chatoyant ribbon

TABLE 16   (continued)

France

Ordinary blue wool flannel

Brabant: Medium quality cloth

Brittany: Superfine cloth, wide cloth, linen

Lorraine: Wide lace

Pontivy: Superfine cloth from the Superior factory, fine cloth, ordinary cloth, shirts

Rouen: Genuine fine quality rouen fabric

China

Silks of various colors

Blue Peking silk

Nankeen cloth

Fine coco cloth for shirts

Ordinary percale

Bleached common cloth

Mamudies

Ninfa [coarse silk] cloth, red and scarlet, handwoven

Silk kerchiefs

Silk stockings (white, scarlet, red)

1st grade ivory combs

England

Fine dark blue imperial serge

Blue wool flannel

English striped cotton cloth

English boots

Germany

Imitation Brittany linen, narrow and wide

Rouen fabric from Silesia

Holland

Dutch cloth

SOURCE: Dado 2004

FIGURE 44.   *View of the Presidio of San Francisco*, by Louis Choris, 1816.
Engraving. Courtesy of the Bancroft Library, University of California, Berkeley.

and military position distinguished them from rank-and-file troops and their
families.

Worn on the Body

The colonial community of the Presidio was saturated with textures, colors,
and patterns of textiles, with ribbons, spangles, embroidery, and military in-
signia further enunciating the appearance of the social body. Writing of colonial South Africa, Jean Comaroff (1996:19) concludes that clothes "were to
prove a privileged means for constructing new forms of value, personhood,
and history on the colonial frontier." With clothing and identity so intertwined
in discourses of personhood and race in New Spain, it is perhaps no wonder
that apparel was a particularly charged arena of cultural practice among
colonists in Alta California.

The question of how these carefully described dry goods were used within
the settlement is difficult to address. Visual representations (drawings, paintings, and so forth) of people in Spanish-colonial Alta California are rare and
were generated almost entirely by visiting colonial officials and foreign travelers rather than by the province's residents themselves. Most are stylized representations of social "types" (as in fig. 41) rather than portraits of named persons. Only one, by Louis Choris, is of El Presidio de San Francisco (fig. 44).
The image includes three mounted soldiers, each clad in identical light blue

jackets and knee-length breeches, wearing tan hats with broad brims and low crowns. They are escorting Native Californian workers who are clothed only in breechcloths and who wear their hair in the topknot traditional to local indigenous groups. Other than this singular representation, we must turn to the invoices and requisitions, to other written accounts, and to the archaeological record for clues regarding the use of the goods ordered and received.

Although Anza had originally ordered ready-made clothing for both men and women, from the 1780s onward, the finished garments arriving at the Presidio were primarily for men. Stockings, footwear, and head coverings were supplied in finished form to both men and women. Additionally, the woven cotton shawls (rebozos) characteristic of casta women's dress were ordered directly from New Spain, with specific directions regarding place of manufacture, color, and embroidery. Beyond that, fitted clothing was limited to men: capes, jackets, waistcoats, shirts, and breeches were regularly ordered in plentiful quantities. Most adult men, it appears, were clothed in the Bourbon style in outfits conforming to the frontier military uniform dictated by the 1772 Reglamento.

The invoices and requisitions betray a meticulous attention to signaling rank among men through the details of these ready-made garments. For example, in 1796 one invoice specified two separate orders of short jackets: one order described "short jackets of fine dark cloth from Las Carretas [Mexico] with cuffs and collar of 2nd grade scarlet cloth and plain button and the other half of gold-colored button with loop, of 1st and 2nd sizes"; while the other asked for "short jackets of fine dark blue, yarn-dyed cloth from Alcoy [Spain] with cuffs and collar of 2nd grade scarlet cloth, plain metal gold colored button, lined in common cloth of 1st and 2nd sizes for sergeants, corporals, or distinguished ones" (Dado 2004:doc. 102). The same document distinguished between blue wool flannel breeches of "creole" cloth (made in New Spain) and breeches made with wool flannel from France, the latter specified for sergeants. While enlisted soldiers, sergeants, and high-ranking officers all wore similar garments, their rank was marked by subtle differences in the origin, color, and texture of fabric and in the color of their buttons.

Clearly, the ability to recognize and decode subtle differences in men's dress was necessary to negotiate the social world of the Presidio. But men's clothing may have functioned on a dual register. Overall, military uniforms were social levelers, greatly minimizing the larger distinctions in clothing that were common in civilian life in New Spain. While an outsider, especially from a distance, might have perceived adult men at the Presidio to be of identical social status, the soldiers and settlers themselves were keenly aware of the differences signaled by slight variations in fabric texture and color and in fasteners and trim. For example, as José María Amador recounted, "The officer wore the same uniform as the soldier with the difference that his materials were of finer quality. Obviously, they displayed their distinctive insignias and wore the three-corner hat for full dress but, for ordinary use, they wore the same [hat] as the soldier" (Mora-Torres 2005:227).

Significantly, differences in dress among men corresponded to military rank, not casta standing. In her research on colonial South Africa, Comaroff notes that, there, the "standard proletarian uniform for black males made little ethnic distinction. By contrast, the visual archive confirms that non-élite Tswana women became the prime bearers of emergent 'tribal' markings of a particularly modern sort" (Comaroff 1996:35–36). Perhaps clothing practices among colonial women in San Francisco might have become similarly significant. Given that men were supplied with ready-made uniforms, the majority of textiles and notions may have been intended for the local production of women's and children's clothing.

As the colonial women of the Presidio gradually replaced the drab clothing that had been issued by Anza and Echeveste, how did they fashion their new appearances in this isolated community? To what extent might they have returned to non-Bourbon styles of dress, such as the huipil, or developed new hybrid or synergistic fashions? How did women's dress relate to the ongoing negotiation of casta status and the emergence of Californio identity? The documentary evidence is ambiguous but provocative. Silks—silk cloth in a rainbow of colors, silk stockings, silk headscarves, silk stockings, silk embroidery floss, even silk rebozos—are listed in nearly every record of dry goods delivered to the settlement. Imported fabrics, flowery prints, lace trim, ribbons, embroidery—all of these are the trappings of women of high status, who were, if not Spaniards, at least women of the higher-ranking castas. These items would have particularly facilitated casta mobility among women of African descent, who had earlier been prohibited from wearing such materials by sumptuary laws. Yet the absence of mantillas and brocade fabrics, the lack of elaborated fasteners (discussed in the following section), and the prominence of rebozos and costume jewels (glass beads, fake pearls) conversely suggest material limits to colonial women's social performances of upward mobility.

It is also unclear whether these status-linked materials were available to all women in the community. The requisitions and invoices indicate no significant difference in the goods ordered specifically by officers and sergeants and those ordered for distribution to the general troops. Conversely, Amador's memoir suggests that women's dress was determined by economic means:

When I was fifteen or sixteen years old, this was around 1796 or 1797, the
women would dress in the following manner: a white underskirt with embroidery four fingers wide; over the underskirt, another skirt of blue, green, or
black coarse cloth. The stockings were black or red made of silk; the shoes
were low and had regular size heels and either metal or silver buckles. The
rebozos were either cotton or silk; the necklaces were made of pearls, or to
be more precise, imitation pearls.

This description was the common dress that women of some means wore
to receive guests or make visits, or to go out to entertain themselves. When she
was doing her house chores, she would wear a white underskirt of linen or
pontivil, and a skirt made of cheap serge of some color over it.

Poor women would dress in the same style as those with means but the
quality of their items was inferior, that is, instead of serge, they would wear
a coarse wool fabric or very coarse flannel. (Mora-Torres 2005:223–225)

Periods in which clothing supplies were scarce, Amador continued, heightened
the difference in dress between poor women and women of "some means."
Wealthier women might buy raw wool and hire native workers to produce
stockings and cloth and to make homemade cloth shoes, while others were
forced to wear "natural" stockings and shoes (that is, to go barelegged and barefooted) (Mora-Torres 2005:225).

Amador also recounted his experience on an expedition that visited the Ross
Colony in 1820 and traded for cloth during one of these periods of scarcity:

We left with supplies of all types: mantas, pieces of Indiana or Calico [fabric],
and also shoes. Those who were married got supplies for the married; those who
were single, received supplies for the single. We came ashore with shirts of saya
saya (a type of silk in a light/dark pink color), which made us into a spectacle—
poor people in silk shirts. We came back to San Francisco on the second day,
transformed into gallant men and causing much envy amongst our poor fellow
soldiers who had stayed behind at the presidio. (Mora-Torres 2005:51)

This "spectacle" of "poor people in silk shirts," "transformed into gallant
men," indicates that at the twilight of Spain's empire in North America, dress
continued to be a dangerous yet alluring medium of social mobility. Amador's
recollections, along with the requisitions and invoices, suggest that the politics
of clothing had substantially shifted from a practice based primarily on racialization to one engaged with military rank and economic means. To this extent,
Anza's social engineering project was effective, for there is no indication that
the colonists' dress ever reverted to signaling differences in casta status.

Dressing Up: Buttons, Buckles, Beads, and Baubles

Most garments, fashioned from plant fibers and animal furs and skins, decompose readily and are rarely preserved intact at archaeological sites except under the most fortuitous conditions. But as the fabrics decay, they leave behind the "hard parts" of clothing—bone, shell, metal, ceramic, and glass objects that served as fasteners or were worn as decoration. As noted earlier, the scarcity of such objects in deposits at the Presidio is itself striking, especially in comparison with other Spanish-colonial archaeological sites. Nonetheless, these archaeological traces provide insights into colonial dress that are not available through documentary evidence alone.

The small number of clothing-related artifacts in the Building 13 midden (see fig. 37) is typical of archaeological deposits at the Presidio. Most excavations at the site have recovered a few of these unremarkable buttons and beads. The notable exception to this general rule is the Chapel Investigations, an excavation of the central region of the south side of the quadrangle, where the chapel once stood (Simpson-Smith and Edwards 2000). The clothing-related artifacts from the chapel area display significantly greater variety than those found elsewhere in the settlement.

This section presents a comparative analysis of the buttons, buckles, beads, and baubles recovered from Building 13 midden and the chapel area.[12] These artifacts suggest a spatialization and temporal rhythm in the practices of dress and appearance at the Presidio. The chapel area was a charged arena in which social displays through clothing and adornment apparently were routinized aspects of community worship. Attending mass and other social and ritual events at the chapel were occasions for "dressing up" and putting one's "best" appearance forward for others to view.

Dressing up can be understood in part as a recognition that one is entering a tournament of social value, an occasion in which participants are simultaneously evaluating others and being judged themselves. Whether they are secular or sacred, such events are distinguished from everyday interactions by setting and ritual. At the Presidio, the confluence of religious worship and elaborated dress was not likely a simple coincidence. The celebration of mass was a rite of restoring spiritual order to the disorder of corporeal life, one in which communicants sanctified their own bodies by ingesting the transubstantiated flesh and blood of Christ. Further, Catholic worship in colonial Alta California incorporated lavish adornment: of bodies through vestments and statuaries, and of the material world through furnishings, ritual objects, altarpieces, and wall paintings (fig. 45). In such a context, the social presentation of personhood through dress surely resonated on multiple registers, both worldly and spiritual.

FIGURE 45.   Presbytery and side altars of the chapel at Mission San Francisco de Asís. In addition to the elaborately carved and painted wood *reredos* (altar backgrounds) and saints, shipped to the mission from Mexico City, the walls and ceilings of the mission chapel were completely filled with painted designs, some in Native Californian motifs and others in European style. There are no records of the interior appearance of the chapel at El Presidio de San Francisco, but it was likely the most decorated building in the settlement. Collection of Mission Dolores.

Fasteners: Buttons and Buckles

Clothing fasteners were particularly charged elements of apparel in late eighteenth- and early nineteenth-century New Spain. Buttons were hallmarks of form-fitting Bourbon fashions, supplanting the laces, ties, and belts of earlier periods. In the New World, buttoned garments contrasted with the draped clothes associated with indigenous dress. As Fisher (1992) and Loren (1999) both document, it was not only the presence or absence of buttons but their quality and abundance that marked status in colonial society. Rows of closely spaced buttons, filigreed and jeweled buttons, and buttons made of gold and silver were all used as markers of high status. In casta paintings, clothing with fewer, plain buttons was associated with the respectable castas, while missing buttons or mismatched buttons signaled the degeneracy of the lower castas. Buckles, especially shoe buckles, were similarly potent sites for claiming social status; here again, decoration and use of jewels and precious metals were markers not only of wealth but of Spanish pedigree.

The requisitions and invoices suggest that buttons at the Presidio fell within a very narrow range, primarily loop-back, gold-colored metal buttons of various sizes, ordered by the gross or double gross (Dado 2004). The five buttons and button fragments recovered from the Building 13 midden are typical of this kind of clothing fastener (see fig. 37). All are cast copper-alloy (likely brass), single-piece uniform buttons, four with drilled wedge shanks and one with a wire eye loop (table 17).[13] They range from 14.4 mm to 17.4 mm in diameter, which suggests that they were used for sleeve and trouser fasteners (buttons used on jacket and waistcoat fronts tended to be about 20 mm in diameter) (Deagan 2002:168). Two of the buttons are tin-plated, an inexpensive modification that would have given them a silvery appearance. All five buttons are typical of those used on military uniforms for frontier soldiers.

In contrast, the six fasteners (five buttons and one buckle) recovered from the chapel area show a greater degree of variety (fig. 46). The small, rectangular, plain copper-alloy buckle was likely used for a shoe fastening. Three buttons are copper-alloy uniform buttons, all with attached wire eye loops. Like those from the Building 13 midden, these three are likely to have been sleeve or trouser fasteners, as their diameters range in size from 11.3 to 16.0 mm. One is plain; the smallest appears to be copper-plated, which would have given it a gold-colored appearance; and the third is a phoenix button, decorated with the characteristic bird rising from a burning nest.[14] The other two buttons recovered from the chapel area are small parts that were usually used as decorative buttons on elite men's clothing. One is a copper-alloy floral filigree button cover, which would have been fastened over a gem or paste jewel that was mounted on a metal button backing. The second is a button backing typical of those used to mount bone, gem, or paste jewel button facings; its brass wire loop fastening is unusual in that it is not soldered to the reverse of the button back but rather threaded through a small aperture in the center (Deagan 2002:166–174). These decorated buttons were associated with social displays of higher status and would likely have appeared in the center front closing of a waistcoat or possibly on jacket cuffs. Attending chapel was a social occasion where at least some men were displaying their finery: civilian garments or dress uniforms enhanced with copper-plated and decorated buttons.

The buttons recovered from both the midden and the chapel deposits are associated with men's clothing, whether of rank-and-file military uniforms or civilian finery. Unless the buttons were used in an unorthodox manner, the archaeological evidence suggests that colonial women living at the Presidio did not adopt the Bourbon fashion of buttoned garments and were either

TABLE 17. Buttons and fasteners from
the Building 13 midden and the chapel area

Catalog Number	Object	Condition	Fastener	Decoration	Maximum Diameter (mm)
Building 13 Midden					
6014	Uniform button	Portion of disk and complete shank	Drilled wedge shank	Tin-plated	15.4
6031	Uniform button	Shank only	Drilled wedge shank	n.a.	n.a.
6039	Uniform button	Complete	Drilled wedge shank	Plain	17.4
6052	Uniform button	Complete, shank broken	Drilled wedge shank	Plain	16.1
6064	Uniform button	Complete	Soldered brass wire eye, no foot	Tin-plated	14.4
Chapel Area					
—	Uniform button	Complete	Soldered brass wire eye, no foot	Molded phoenix pattern, no. 9	15.8
02220	Button facing	Whole but bent	n.a.	Filigree flower motif	12.0
02250	Buckle	Incomplete	n.a.	None	14.3 x 13.0
03629	Button backing	Backing only	Soldered brass wire eye, with foot	Unknown	9.4
06541	Uniform button	Complete	Soldered brass wire eye, no foot	Copper-plated	11.3
07001	Uniform button	Complete	Soldered brass wire eye, with foot	None	16.0

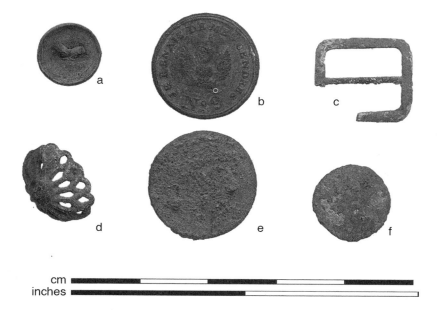

FIGURE 46. Clothing fasteners recovered from the chapel area of the Presidio. a: button backing; b: phoenix button; c: buckle; d: filigree button cover; e: plain uniform button; f: copper-plated uniform button.

wearing more flowing, draped clothes or fastening their clothes with laces and ties.

Ornaments and Charms: Beads and Baubles

Beads, charms, and other baubles also differ significantly between the Building 13 midden and the chapel area. In the chapel especially, two unique artifacts were found that attest to devotional practices (fig. 47). The first, a molded crucifix, was found emplaced next to a vertical line of lime mortar and red ocher in the southwest corner of the chapel's presbytery. It presumably served as an offering during the construction of the chapel to sanctify this most holy section of the building. The second is a *milagro*—an amulet, usually shaped like a body part, often offered to a statue of a saint along with prayers for healing. In eighteenth- and early nineteenth-century New Spain, the boundary between religious practice and personal ornamentation was a permeable one, as jewelry and other objects of adornment frequently had religious meaning or amuletic properties. Thus, in addition to these two explicitly religious objects, it is possible that other ornaments discussed here might have had dual meanings.

cm
inches

FIGURE 47.   Religious charms recovered from the chapel area of the
Presidio. The front of the crucifix (*top left*) shows the figure of Christ
on the cross; above his head is the inscription "INRI" (an acronym for
a Latin phrase translated as "Jesus the Nazarene, the King of the Jews").
The reverse side of the crucifix (*top right*) depicts the figure of the Virgin
Mary with the inscription "IMMACULATA / VITAM PRAESTA / PVADI"
("The Immaculate gives life to the purified one"). The milagro (*bottom*)
is identical on both sides.

With the exception of the costume jewel recovered from the Building 13 midden, the remainder of the ornaments are small glass trade beads, typical of those
found at colonial-era sites throughout North America. In contrast with missions,
ranchos, and other period contact sites, which often yield thousands of glass
beads, the archaeological deposits at El Presidio de San Francisco contain relatively few. Only twenty-four were recovered from the Building 13 midden, and
fifty-eight beads were found in the chapel excavations. In many respects, the
bead assemblages are more similar than different: they are dominated by cylin-

TABLE 18. Reflected colors of glass beads
from the Building 13 midden and the chapel area

Color	Building 13 Midden		Chapel Area	
	Count	%	Count	%
Polychrome				
Cornaline d'Aleppo	1	4	3	5
Costume pearl	—	—	4	7
Monochrome				
Black and dark gray	23	96	14	24
Blue and blue-green	—	—	13	22
Green	—	—	7	12
White	—	—	5	9
Clear	—	—	3	5
Red	—	—	2	3
Red-brown	—	—	2	3
Brown	—	—	1	2
Purple	—	—	1	2
Pink	—	—	1	2
Yellow	—	—	1	2
Unknown	—	—	1	2
TOTAL	24	100	58	100

drical, tumbled, monochrome, drawn beads, nearly all of which are short "embroidery" beads measuring less than 6 mm at least diameter.[15] However, the subtle differences between the two assemblages further support the interpretation of a spatialization of dress practices at the Presidio.

The most apparent difference between the two assemblages lies in the reflected color of the beads (table 18). All but one of the beads from the Building 13 midden are black or dark gray; the remaining one is a red-on-white, translucent Cornaline d'Aleppo bead (Sprague 1985:94). Black and dark gray beads are also prominent in the chapel area (24 percent of the assemblage), and Cornaline d'Aleppo beads are likewise present (5 percent). However, the largest grouping in that assemblage (34 percent) consists of monochrome beads falling within a color continuum from blue to blue-green to green. White and clear beads and costume pearls (clear glass beads overlain with silver paint) are also included, along with a variety of red, brown, pink, and purple beads. Together, the chapel area bead assemblage presents a significantly broader palette, one that suggests greater variety in bead use for personal adornment and for religious objects such as rosaries.

In addition, the chapel area has yielded one wire-wound bead, the only one in either assemblage that was not cane-drawn. Beads from the chapel area have a greater size range (1.5 mm–7.9 mm least diameter) than those from the midden (1.2 mm–4.3 mm least diameter); and, while embroidery beads still predominate, the chapel assemblage includes nine of the larger necklace-size beads. The beads from the chapel area also correspond more closely to the entries for beads and jewels found in the requisitions and invoices; there is no mention of the kind of black or dark beads found in the Building 13 midden, but the documents do list imitation pearls, white beads, and beads of "topaz, emerald, and amethyst" (Dado 2004:doc. 141).

Keeping Up Appearances

The archaeological data thus provide some indication of the rhythm of dress at the Presidio, one patterned on a spatial and temporal division between the sacred and the mundane. Garments worn in the home and during the routines of daily life were plain, with only minimal adornment, as suggested by the utilitarian buttons and black and dark gray glass beads. Understated dress has its own aesthetic. In Alta California, only provincial governors seated in Monterey— the highest-ranking colonial elites in the region—are recorded to have dressed in a gaudy and sumptuous manner. Among themselves, the military settlers, both officers and soldiers alike, seem to have negotiated the relationship between status and appearance through subtle indicators, such as the quality of cloth used in similarly colored and styled garments, rather than through overt displays of wealth and status.

This everyday aesthetic seems to have been punctuated by religious services and by other, perhaps secular, events in which "dressing up" was integral to the occasion. The Presidio was a small community. Its routines of movement and work centered on a shared, open plaza, so its members encountered one another on a daily basis. While religious services were a time of intensified copresence, it was more likely the ritual character of the event rather than the act of gathering itself that spurred heightened attention to self-presentation. Such events, themselves routinized according to the religious cycle of the week and the annual calendar of saintly festivals and other observances, were occasions when the colonists shrugged off their everyday wear and stepped into other social skins, ones in which displays of wealth and status were more overt. Many of the finer fabrics and notions listed in the requisitions and invoices were probably intended for such occasions rather than for daily wear.

This duality in clothing practices—understated dress for the mundane, overt displays of status for the sacred—is perhaps connected to tensions in emerging Californio identity. Becoming Californio meant the unification of a community, formerly partitioned by casta, under a shared ethnicity. Understated dress practices minimized the appearance of difference between neighbors and may have been encouraged by, and in turn supported by, nascent Californio identifications. Yet it is clear that Californio identity was also partitive, marked by divisions in gender, rank, and economic means, and that these internal hierarchies were an ever-present threat to the cohesiveness of this emergent ethnicity. Religious services celebrated the spiritual hierarchies of the heavens and, in doing so, naturalized the worldly hierarchies of the flesh—between men and women, the saved and the sinner, and the blessed and the cursed. As such, rituals at the Presidio chapel may have provided a mediated context for the display of status differences among the new Californios, one in which such distinctions were made apparent yet also discursively separated from routine, secular social interactions.

Above all, variation in colonial dress at El Presidio de San Francisco occurred within a very narrow range. This is especially apparent when the assemblages of clothing-related items recovered from the settlement are compared to those excavated from other Spanish-colonial sites. The men's copper-alloy buttons, both plain and decorated; the absence of metal fasteners for women's clothing; the glass costume jewel and glass trade beads—all of these signal appearances associated with life in the middle. Racially, the military settlers' appearance placed them on the cusp between lower and upper casta identities; financially, it signaled their status as people of modest resources. There were firm upper limits to the metamorphosis of social bodies at the Presidio, limits established not within the community itself but by the military and economic systems that structured the conditions of daily life at the settlement.

. . .

Archaeologists and historians studying the Spanish-colonial Americas have consistently suggested that clothing was a means through which people could transform their identity. The materials discussed here point to the other side of that equation—that dress was a means through which colonial military subjects were fashioned, not, as the cliché goes, from whole cloth but from a heterogeneous mixture of initial economic and casta positions within the imperial hierarchy. It is clear that the residents of the Presidio, at the very least the habilitado and the settlement's other officers, were fully interpolated into discourses of status and dress that required detailed knowledge of the intricacies of textile production and commodity exchange. Their connoisseurship of textiles and notions is evidence that the origins and material attributes of these goods mattered quite a bit in their social world.

Both archaeological and documentary evidence shows how colonial men negotiated their relative status with one another through practices and discourses of dress. The degree to which other colonial residents of the community—rank-and-file soldiers, women, and younger persons—participated in this rhetoric is less understood. Colonial women, as fashioned subjects, are most visible in relationship to sumptuary laws and racially charged standards of Bourbon fashion. Many were initially listed as mulatas or other castas related to various degrees of African heritage, but silks, laces, and other restricted goods apparently circulated among the colonial community with little if any regard to race. It also seems that the colonial women living in the Presidio had not fully adopted the trappings of Bourbon fashion. Whether by choice or out of necessity, they likely fastened their garments with cloth belts, laces, and ties rather than buttons and buckles and adorned themselves with only cheap glass baubles and beads.

Clearly, the colonial population of the Presidio was reinventing itself, first through changes in casta designation and eventually through the creation of a Californio identity. The modest and consistent modes of dress evidenced here probably supported these transitions, especially for those of African heritage, who perhaps faced the greatest challenges in shedding their casta status. Yet this process of reinvention, at least within the realm of dress, occurred within a very narrow scope.

The small range of variation in colonial dress at the Presidio becomes even more apparent when we consider the complete absence of objects of apparel that are associated with Native Californians. In much of New Spain, the social boundaries between castas and indios were somewhat permeable, so much so that sumptuary laws had to explicitly prohibit castas from wearing indigenous dress. This was true not only in the geographic heart of the colony but on the frontiers as well. For example, military settlers at the frontier presidio of Los Adaes commonly violated this prohibition, incorporating local indigenous garments and ornamentation into their apparel, much to the chagrin of visiting military inspectors (Loren 1999, 2001a, 2001b). Yet the archives and archaeological record of El Presidio de San Francisco suggest the opposite. None of the ornamentation typical of Native Californian dress—beads, earrings, pendants, and hair ornaments carved from shell, bone, and antler—is present in either the Building 13 midden or the chapel area. Nor do written or visual representations provide any suggestion that the military settlers incorporated deerskin and fiber skirts, fur capes, or woven hats into their dress. Although the colonists were structurally limited in their ability to acquire the trappings of truly elite appearance, the greatest evidence of their "agency" in matters of dress may be found in their disinclination to incorporate Native Californian dress into their routines of bodily presentation.

This study uses archaeological and historical evidence to approach an understanding of the sensory and embodied lives of the colonial subjects who once lived at the Presidio. Their patterns of movement across the landscape; the buildings in which they took shelter and the labor it took to construct such buildings; the portable household objects used in daily routines of food preparation and consumption; the pots fashioned by hands on wet clay; the foods taken into the body for sustenance; the objects worn on and extending the body— all these were media through which the military settlers recursively transformed their world and were themselves transformed. Not indigenous, not African, not casta, and not European: the emergent Californios were new kinds of social subjects, occupying an ambiguous middle space in the colonial order of people and things. As was the case for the spatial, material, and dietary practices discussed earlier, analyses of clothing and dress indicate that this precarious position was achieved as much through emphatic distinction from Native Californians as it was through challenges to the arbitrary racial hierarchies that permeated the Spanish-colonial Americas.

CONCLUSION

The Limits of Ethnogenesis

> My concern has been to show how real people . . .
> were caught up in larger social and cultural processes
> and how they articulated their sense of who they were
> in this context.
>
> Lucas 2006:177

This study has traced the history of a group of colonized subjects who were re-cruited and relocated to serve as colonizing agents of the Spanish crown. It is of-ten the most disadvantaged members of society—those with the fewest options, those who are viewed as expendable—who are pressed into service on the front lines of others' imperial projects. The military settlers who founded and main-tained El Presidio de San Francisco were no exception. Despite the known danger and deprivations, joining the Anza expedition offered tantalizing opportunities for economic betterment and a fresh start in a new land. Drawn into a web of nation building and empire, the settlers were subjected to military and religious disciplines and transformed by their new roles and responsibilities.

But the settlers were not simply passive cogs in a clockwork machinery of imper-ialism; they altered the very institutions that had enlisted them. Colonial ethno-genesis—the emergence and articulation of a shared identity as Californios—was one way that the military settlers transformed colonial systems of power. Their repudiation of the sistema de castas can be understood as a collective refusal to define themselves and their fellow settlers by their ancestry or the color of their skin. And yet their new, shared Californio ethnicity was a means through which the military settlers consolidated their new status as colonizers and naturalized their dominance over Native Californians.

This study has investigated the transformation of colonial identities on the micro-scale by closely examining the archaeological and documentary traces left behind by the military settlers garrisoned in San Francisco during Spain's domination of California's central coast (1776–1821). This approach is significantly different from that taken by the majority of historical studies on the subject, which generally attribute Californio ethnogenesis to macro-scale economic, political, and demographic events in California's later years as a Mexican province (1822–1847) (see chapter 4). As the foregoing chapters demonstrate, colonial ethnogenesis began during the earliest decades of colonization; colonial identities were never fixed and changed continuously throughout the Spanish-colonial and Mexican era. Moreover, these changes in colonial practices of identification occurred, in part, from the "bottom up"—through the routines, strategies, and tactics that settlers used in their everyday lives as residents of Spain's northernmost military outpost.

It is essential to focus on the ways that material practices participated in these negotiations of social identity. Material practices are potent sites where governmentality and institutional disciplines interface with social agency. They are a middle-range scale of meaning-making through which relations of power are negotiated and contested. In colonial San Francisco, every aspect of personal life—the house one lived in, the food one ate, and the clothes one wore—was structured by military and religious institutions. Yet the institutionalization of daily life was never complete. The residents of El Presidio de San Francisco always retained some capacity to act in ways that mattered and, in doing so, participated in shaping the social and material order.

This concluding section draws together the archaeological and historical analyses detailed earlier, highlighting those material practices that were particularly salient in the emergence and consolidation of Californio identity. It then returns to the theme of overdetermination (first elaborated in the introduction). Rather than attributing colonial ethnogenesis to any one "root cause," this book argues that colonists forged their new collective identity through a matrix of material practices and discursive strategies that contributed to within-group identification, distinction from Native Californians, the establishment of labor regimes, heightened attention to differential masculinities, changes in colonial women's roles in the community, and greater emphasis on the sexual politics of ethnic respectability, honor, and shame.

This conclusion next examines the broader implications of this study in the disciplines of archaeology and anthropology and in the history of colonialism, situating the case of El Presidio de San Francisco in comparative perspective by contrasting it with other colonial ventures. Structural conditions of colonization inform, but do not necessarily determine, how colonial identities are materialized and negotiated. Rather, the interface of global imperial systems with local contexts is always historically contingent because of the unpredictable actions taken by individuals and social collectivities affected by colonial projects.

In addition to demonstrating the importance of material practices in the on-going negotiation of social identities, this study provides an important caution against viewing hybridity, fluidity, and contingency as inherently liberatory strategies. In the case of Californio ethnogenesis, the transformation and ambiguity of social identities served to stabilize colonial structures of power and intensified gendered and sexual hierarchies. Thus, this chapter concludes with a consideration of the limitations of ethnogenesis, both as a theory of identity transformation and as a practical strategy of subaltern resistance.

Materializing Identity

Chapters 6 through 10 analyzed the archaeological and documentary record of El Presidio de San Francisco according to five genres of material practice. The first of these, landscape, is perhaps the most fundamental to studies of territorial colonization. It is no coincidence that Alta California's military settlers took their ethnonym from the toponym of the lands they had appropriated. This entanglement between place and personhood established the colonists' sense of legitimate entitlement to the land and the indigenous people and resources it contained. Could there be any doubt that California belonged to Californios? Although, as mentioned earlier, many historians emphasize the significance of rancho ownership in the 1830s and 1840s, the emergence of Californio identity and culture should actually be located in the much earlier appropriation and reorganization of the California landscape by colonial institutions from the 1770s through the 1780s.

California's early Spanish-colonial landscape was created through the rapid establishment of a cordon of institutions along its coast and the concomitant regionalization of the landscape along a north-south axis that served as the midline of the Californios' world and an east-west axis that traced gradients of risk, danger, and military conflict. Military engagements between the colonial soldiers and indigenous peoples were spatially segregated from the colonial settlements. This separation allowed the Presidio's quadrangle, required by military regulations to be a fortified enclosure, to take an ambiguous and less secure form. The quadrangle was the physical materialization of the colonial military presence in San Francisco, but its borders were more symbolic than effective, and it had little or no defensive capability. The colonial landscape was also gendered and sexualized. Colonial women rarely traveled outside the securely colonized coastal axis. In their absence, the eastern inland areas were masculinized through colonial men's military expeditions and sexualized through interethnic sexual violence perpetrated by some colonial men on Native Californians.

The centrality of space and place to colonial practices of identification is further exemplified by the architectural history of the Presidio's quadrangle, first built in 1776. Over time, the quadrangle expanded dramatically, culminating in the 1815 construction of an entirely new, master-planned adobe quadrangle that covered an area nearly three times greater than the first quadrangle. This expansion significantly enlarged the community's plaza, suggesting that this public gathering place was an increasingly important venue for routine and ritual performances of social identity. It may also have shifted spatial practices related to surveillance of colonial women's sexuality. Simultaneously, the building materials, building techniques, and architectural form of the quadrangle became more homogeneous; by the completion of the 1815 quadrangle, all households occupied adobe apartments that were nearly identical in size and shape.

Concurrently, there was a profound change in the social relations of architectural production and maintenance. Initially, each household was expected to build and maintain its own dwelling, but over time the military command assumed responsibility for the construction and upkeep of residential housing. Architectural production shifted from a small-scale endeavor shared by colonial men, women, and children to a centrally organized undertaking carried out by work gangs of Native Californian men under the direction of colonial soldiers. In the 1810s, the settlement's growing reliance on captive laborers contributed fuel to the already incendiary military campaigns against inland Native Californian communities.

Analysis of locally produced ceramics provides similar indications of material homogeneity and changes in labor practices. Such ceramics display little technical and stylistic variation, both in relation to locally produced ceramics found at other Alta California colonial sites and especially in comparison to the wide range of distinctive, regional ceramic styles from the rest of the Interior Provinces. This limited range may indicate that colonists were pursuing an aesthetically conservative strategy that minimized the appearance of differences among colonial households. As with architectural production, in the 1790s craft production of local goods such as ceramics became more centralized in workshops run by master craftsworkers and colonial soldiers who supervised the labor of Native Californian apprentices.

Recovered ceramic vessels and plant and animal remains indicate that meal sharing was an important small-scale social occasion that reinforced the settlers' colonial status and their shared role in empire building. Meals, prepared for and consumed by small groups, were events in which institutional practices of procurement and supply interfaced with household practices of consumption. Food preparation was a highly valued and gendered arena, one directed by adult colonial women, so much so that unmarried men did not prepare their own food but would instead barter their rations in order to board with a married couple. Consequently, archaeological investigation of foodways provides information about how colonial women negotiated a realm of material practice that was intimately tied to Californio ethnogenesis.

Analysis of ceramic sherds from vessels used for table service reveals that each waretype served a particular dining function, producing a heterogeneous table setting that had been assembled through the transportation and economic infrastructure of the colonial military. These table settings resonated with the military settlers' own situation as colonial agents, who had been similarly "procured" from diverse communities and assembled at a remote setting. Meals prepared and served in colonial households were apparently very similar, consisting primarily of liquid-based foods such as stews, gruels, and porridges. Drawing on the high value placed on stewed and simmered foods in both indigenous Mexican and African diaspora populations, these meals formed a "fusion cuisine" that emphasized aspects of culinary traditions that were shared by the diverse colonial population.

The content of the colonial diet consisted overwhelmingly of cultivated cereals and legumes and domesticated stock, especially beef and chicken, supplemented by a small but not insubstantial quantity of wild game, especially deer, rabbits, waterfowl, and fish. However, those foods most closely associated with Native Californians—shellfish and acorns—are conspicuously absent from colonial deposits, even though they were abundant in the environment surrounding the Presidio. The frequency of corn, relative to wheat, in colonial deposits decreased over time. These findings suggest that the military settlers deliberately sought to distinguish their diet from that of Native Californians and that they increasingly avoided corn, a food hegemonically associated with indigeneity throughout New Spain. Alternatively, it is possible that colonial households were being supplied with ground corn, perhaps because the repetitive and back-breaking labor of grinding grain was becoming more centralized.

Clothing was a particularly charged site for the negotiation of social identities in New Spain. The Spanish military used clothing as a tool of social engineering among the families recruited to establish San Francisco: ready-made clothing issued to both men and women functioned as an immediate social leveler, camouflaging previous racial and economic status differences. Colonial men were issued hybrid frontier uniforms that marked them as distinctly non-European. Women received Bourbon-style clothing made from functional and plain fabrics, including silk serge; their military-issue dress minimized their Mexican Indian and African heritage yet still marked them as nonelites.

Throughout the Presidio's years as a Spanish-colonial military post, the fabrics, fasteners, and other dry goods furnished to the settlement continued to place firm upper limits on the settlers' social mobility, marking them as mixed-race people of moderate means. In turn, the settlers themselves appear to have shunned any clothing-related objects associated with traditional Native Californian dress. Among the colonists, clothing ceased to function as a marker of racial distinction. Instead, subtle variations in fabric, fasteners, and ornamentation signaled differences in military rank and economic resources. Archaeological evidence suggests that while everyday clothing tended to minimize the appearance of differences in rank and class, religious services at the settlement's chapel were occasions for more overt social displays of status. This illuminates a persistent tension in the ongoing negotiation of Californio identity: Californio ethnogenesis united a racially heterogeneous community through a shared ethnic identity, yet the unity of colonial society was continually threatened from within by differentiation by gender, rank, and economic means.

Diachronic Perspectives

Chapter 4 demonstrates that Californio ethnogenesis was both incremental and immediate. Identity transformations occurred rapidly, with the middle decades of Spanish-colonial rule (1790–1810) being a pivotal period during which colonists rejected the racial terms of the sistema de castas and began to describe themselves using other collective identities. But ethnogenesis was also a multigenerational process. New practices of identification at El Presidio de San Francisco built on earlier changes in social identities that had occurred in the Interior Provinces during the early and mid-eighteenth century. Later, structural changes following Mexican independence, such as growing provincial self-rule, the secularization of the missions, and the expansion of the rancho-based economy, spurred further transformation in the meanings and uses of "Californio" as a term of social identification.

The material practices described in the preceding chapters correspond to this diachronic model of colonial ethnogenesis and can be ordered into three major temporal categories. The first dates to the beginning of the colonial project in the 1770s. These material practices were largely determined by military regulations and other governmental and bureaucratic procedures. Foremost was the rapid transformation of the Alta California landscape through the defensive cordon system. In addition to this colonial appropriation of place, the newly recruited settlers were interpolated into the military's system of procurement and supply distribution. Throughout the Spanish-colonial era, Presidio settlers had little control over the material culture and foodstuffs used at this remote outpost, relying largely on supplies shipped from San Blas. These imported goods were complemented by locally produced goods, which grew in importance over time.

The second temporal category involves material practices that developed from the 1780s through the 1790s. These correspond to settlers' individual manipulations of the sistema de castas and to the earliest assertions of collective, non-racial colonial identities. The artifacts and plant and animal remains recovered from the Building 13 midden provide the largest body of evidence of material practices during this period. These data point to the important social role of food preparation and meal sharing in the military settlers' negotiation of colonial identity. Material culture from this period, such as locally produced ceramics and clothing, evinces a narrow range of aesthetic choices. Foodways, material culture, and dress all emphasized the commonalities among colonists and downplayed differences related to race and ethnic heritage.

The 1790s were a pivotal time in the transformation of spatial and architectural practices, perhaps in part because of the Presidio's heightened role in international contests of empire. This decade witnessed the spatial expansion of colonial military defenses, as the Castillo de San Joaquín and the Batería de San José were established along the San Francisco bayshore. Appropriation of the inland landscape accelerated with the intensified development of colonial infrastructure (roads and water catchment and irrigation systems) and resource extraction sites (quarries, grazing lands, and timber harvests). Also during the 1790s, architectural practices at the settlement began to change: the military command took charge of the production of some residential architecture; adobe became the preferred building material; kilns were constructed to produce fired tejas and ladrillos for roofs and floors; and craft production became more centrally organized. These changes were possible only because of the increased reliance on Native Californian laborers. During this period, most indigenous workers were mission neophytes and wage laborers recruited from tribal villages. Some, however, were war captives serving terms of hard labor as punishment for raiding settlers' cattle or escaping from the missions.

The third temporal category includes material practices that emerged during the 1810s, after the widespread adoption of Californio identity. This decade was marked by isolation from the rest of New Spain and intensified interaction with non-Spanish Europeans, especially the newly established Russian outpost, Colony Ross, and British, French, and Yankee traders. The 1810s also saw the culmination of transformations in architectural practices that had begun in the 1790s. The homogeneous exterior of the 1815 quadrangle was perhaps intended to convey an appearance of ethnic respectability to outsiders. The enclosed and enlarged plaza may have also enabled a heightened surveillance of colonial women's sexuality. The expanded quadrangle was constructed almost entirely by the unpaid labor of Native Californian captives, further solidifying these labor regimes as a way for the Californios to differentiate themselves from local indigenous populations. Yet, simultaneously, civilian neighborhoods also began to develop in the valley immediately east of the main quadrangle. Archaeological investigations of these residential areas indicate a commingling of indigenous and colonial material culture, suggesting that the hierarchical segregation of Californios from Native Californians was never fully complete.

This diachronic perspective suggests that in Alta California, colonial ethnogenesis was an uneven process, with material practices and practices of social identification recursively transforming each other in each period. From the 1770s to the 1790s, changes in social identity were supported by practices of material homogenization, imposed both by military institutions and by the household-based practices of craft production and food preparation and consumption. From the 1790s onward, the adoption of shared forms of colonial identification (gente de razón, hijos del país, Californios) was accompanied by the centralization and greater homogenization of architectural and craft production at the Presidio. Also during this time, labor regimes involving significant numbers of Native Californian men became increasingly central to daily life at the settlement. In the 1810s, shared Californio identity was materially consolidated through a massive reconstruction of the Presidio's built environment, perhaps motivated in part by a desire to present an ethnically respectable face to the growing numbers of Russian, British, French, and Yankee visitors. The construction of the new expanded quadrangle marked an intensification of colonial labor regimes at the Presidio.

The beginnings of Californio ethnogenesis can be traced both to the homogenizing influence of governmental policies and military regulations and to the daily efforts by household cooks, seamstresses, tailors, and potters to help their families "fit in" with the larger community. In these efforts, some families and individuals came to assert a more "European" racial status than the one ascribed to them at the beginning of their colonial endeavor. Archaeological evidence suggests that the military settlers also began to differentiate themselves from local Native Californians by avoiding certain wild foods, by failing to adopt other aspects of local indigenous material culture, and by spatially segregating the refuse generated by colonial and indigenous populations living at the settlement. Only later, from the 1790s, did the local military command become instrumental in transforming social identification, through the growing centralization of architectural and craft production and the importance of hierarchical labor regimes involving first paid and then coerced work gangs of Native Californian men.

Overdetermination and Californio Ethnogenesis

Californio identity, while under constant negotiation, was overdetermined by the structural and institutional conditions of the imperial project and by the material practices and discursive strategies deployed by the military settlers themselves. Chapter 1 suggests that overdetermination might be understood through the metaphor of an iceberg, since what is enunciated is only a small fraction of the many factors that contribute to any particular practice of identification. A vastly larger configuration of social practices and identifications lurks beneath the surface of stated identities, and these hidden or unspoken referents lend considerable force and momentum to claims of social distinction.

Californio ethnogenesis was a historical process in which the parameters of social identification radically shifted from being anchored in racial hierarchies to being constructed through reference to a shared regional ethnicity. This transformation occurred within a matrix of material practices and discursive strategies that included within-group identification, distinction from Native Californians, differential masculinities, and changes in gender roles and sexual codes.

Within-Group Identification

Theories of ethnic identity formation that emphasize shared culture have been characterized as "primordialist," in that they generally presume that people form ethnic bonds to fulfill a universal need for a feeling of belonging. The findings of this study suggest that within-group identification can be promoted not because of inherent psychological needs but instead through structural conditions that generate shared histories and expectations of common destiny. Members of the heterogeneous population recruited to colonize the San Francisco Bay area were thrust together into circumstances beyond their individual control. Separated from extended kin, friends, and other associates, they endured the long overland trek from Tubac to San Francisco and the deprivations and dangers of the early years of colonial life. They were subjected to military discipline and bureaucratic procedures that further increased the material similarities of their daily lives. The military settlers actively participated in this homogenization of daily life through their own routines of craft production and meal preparation and consumption. In between the macro-scale conditions of military regulations and the micro-scale activities of particular households, local officers began to play a central role in coordinating and directing the homogenization of the built environment of the settlement. In sum, the military settlers' lives became more similar and less like those of the kin and townsfolk in the diverse communities they had left behind in the Interior Provinces.

Distinction from Native Californians

Collective identification among the military settlers was paired with extreme differentiation from Native Californians. In all aspects of material practice—landscape, architecture, foodways, craft production, and dress—the military settlers not only avoided adopting those material practices associated with Native Californian lifeways but also abandoned some colonial cultural practices, especially architectural ones, that had close parallels in traditional Native Californian material culture. This finding was one of the most surprising results of the archaeological investigations at El Presidio de San Francisco. Spain's empire in the Americas is historically noted for the prevalence of cultural and biological *mestizaje* (mixing) between colonizing and indigenous populations and for the syncretism that resulted from the ongoing entanglements of these two groups. I had anticipated an even greater degree of cultural mestizaje and creolization among the heterogeneous population that colonized San Francisco, especially because many colonists were themselves of indigenous heritage. Yet the military settlers maintained firm distinctions between themselves and local Native Californian populations. Californio identity thus emerged not only through a shared colonial culture but also in opposition to local Native Californians.

Differential Masculinities, Military Campaigns, and Labor Regimes

Differential masculinities—the hierarchical relations between men in their culturally prescribed roles *as* men—were central to Californio ethnogenesis, particularly in enacting social differences among military settlers and between military settlers and Native Californians. Recruited as soldiers, adult male settlers were differentiated from each other by military rank. As racial terms ceased to be used in the settlement, military rank became an increasingly prominent form of social distinction. Rank had material as well as symbolic consequences: higher rank entitled some men and their families to larger quarters and to substantially greater salaries, which gave them better access to foodstuffs and material goods and also improved their economic prospects. Colonial men engaged in subtle contests of social value among themselves, through heightened attention to status displays in men's dress. This is evidenced both in slight differences of fabric and fasteners in their everyday uniforms and in the elaboration of men's dress during religious services at the Presidio chapel.

During the Spanish-colonial period, all able-bodied colonial adult men (except priests) were enrolled in military institutions; even retired soldiers and civilians living in pueblos and villas were expected to serve in militias that supplemented the colonial army's meager troop rosters. This undoubtedly conditioned their daily relationships with Native Californians, for even the most casual interactions occurred within a general climate of violence and conflict. In their duties as mission guards, the soldiers enforced discipline among neophytes and attempted to stop fugitivism. On exploring parties and military campaigns, they engaged in direct combat with indigenous villagers. The connection between male colonists' roles as soldiers and their identities as men was heightened by the sexualization of military conflict. Rape functioned as an unofficial but widely deployed tactic in colonial military excursions into Native Californian villages. Within secular colonial ideologies of honor and shame, such sexual encounters brought honor to and marked the virility of the colonial men who perpetrated these assaults and, from this perspective, emasculated the Native Californian men who were unable to protect their communities from sexual predation.

The gendered pattern of labor relations at the Presidio reinforced hierarchies of military rank among colonial men and further enacted their control of Native Californian men. The Native Californians who labored at the Presidio— whether paid laborers recruited from outlying villages, contract workers from the missions, or captives of war—were primarily men. Construction projects in particular were social occasions that put social subjects in their place in the colonial order. Such projects were conceptualized and ordered by higher-ranking local officers and implemented by rank-and-file soldiers, who supervised Native Californian laborers. Throughout the Spanish-colonial era, these construction projects intensified, along with the degree of coercion involved. Perhaps the most significant product of these architectural endeavors was not the buildings themselves, but the social interactions that allowed the continued reenactment and consolidation of social hierarchies among colonial and indigenous men. While these social hierarchies were most dramatically and persistently materialized in the social production of architecture, they were echoed in other transformations of labor relations, especially the centralization of craft production at the Presidio from the 1790s onward.

Gender Relations and Sexuality

Changes in colonial men's roles, as well as changes in their relationships to one another and to Native Californians, were accompanied by transformations in gender relations between colonial men and women and a shift in the ways that colonial women participated in the community. During the earliest decades of colonization, realms of social practice hegemonically associated with women, especially food procurement, production, and preparation, were central arenas in which the military settlers materialized in-group cohesion and distinguished themselves from Native Californians. The micro-economy formed through household-based, food-related barter and exchange also strengthened social ties among the settlers. It was no simple task for colonial women to obtain and prepare food in their new environment, and we should be careful not to trivialize the importance of their expertise to the survival of the military settlement.

From the 1770s to the 1790s, colonial women participated fully in strategies of casta mobility that minimized their and their families' African and Mexican Indian heritage. In this context, women's dress was a serious matter: clothing fashioned from Chinese silks, imported European linens, and other fine fabrics allowed colonial women to break the stranglehold of sumptuary laws, which had particularly targeted the appearance and comportment of women of African descent.

From the 1790s onward, as the military settlers articulated a shared colonial identity, colonial women were often removed from direct involvement in certain aspects of social practice, especially craft production and architecture. Additionally, colonial women were excluded from the expanding colonized regions to the east and the north of the settlement. Changes in women's roles were further accentuated in the 1810s, with the construction of the 1815 quadrangle and the concomitant intensification of labor regimes. Additionally, the growing frequency of interactions with Europeans and Yankees during this decade spurred a growing concern with ethnic propriety and respectability, reflected in the architectural enclosure of the quadrangle, which may have been related to tightening social oversight of colonial women's sexuality.

We know so little about how women settlers living at the Presidio during 1800–1820 participated in and responded to these changes in the community's gendered and sexual dynamics. Having surmounted the racialized stigmas of the sistema de castas, were they now caught in a web of greater paternalistic control in their new identity as Californianas? Or did they welcome the material and social transformations in their community, perhaps feeling that, for the first time, the military command was finally living up to its obligations to provide shelter and protection to them and their families? Were colonial women, like colonial men, engaging in gendered hierarchies of differential womanhood and femininity? Did they direct and supervise a cadre of Native Californian women working as household servants, seamstresses, and agricultural laborers at the Presidio, whose presence has escaped mention in official colonial documents? Was the status of Californio women in the community dependent on their husbands' rank in the military hierarchy, or did they participate in other tournaments of social value among themselves?

The evidence, both documentary and archaeological, is inconclusive and ambiguous. There are, of course, the tantalizing indications that foodways were changing during this period, with maize either playing a significantly lesser role in the colonial diet or alternatively being provisioned in ground form through an as-yet-unidentified labor system. It was also during this time that some families, one of them headed by the Briones sisters (see chapter 6), moved out of the quadrangle and embarked on independent agricultural ventures. Although it is not yet possible to fully chart colonial women's participation in the consolidation of Californio identity, it is evident that Californio ethnogenesis depended on transforming the gendered lives of colonial men and women and the sexual ideologies and practices that informed their relationships with each other.

El Presidio de San Francisco in Comparative Perspective

In their recent monographs, Nan Rothschild (2003) and Kent Lightfoot (2005) demonstrate that comparative analyses of colonial contexts can produce new insights: "Such a comparison," Rothschild notes, "is enlightening as it brings out aspects of each situation that may be otherwise overlooked and shows the tremendous variation that may exist in what appear as similar situations" (2003:1–2). The research presented here on colonial identities and material practices at El Presidio de San Francisco takes on additional significance when compared to the findings of archaeological research at other colonial settlements.

As mentioned earlier, most of Spain's colonial ventures in the Americas resulted in biological and cultural mestizaje, the creolization, blending, and synergistic interplay between indigenous and colonial populations and cultures. Archaeologists have unearthed material evidence of cultural mestizaje at sites throughout the Spanish-colonial Americas. The most prominent study of this kind is Kathleen Deagan's investigation of St. Augustine (Deagan 1973, 1975, 1983a, 1983b), which found that colonial households combined Spanish and indigenous material practices in ways that were structured by gender and race. Spanish material culture persisted in what Deagan identifies as socially visible men's activities, such as architecture, tableware ceramics, and clothing; whereas areas that she classifies as domestic women's activities, such as food preparation, showed considerable indigenous cultural influence. This cultural pattern of male-public-European and female-domestic-indigenous material practices at colonial settlements has been broadly generalized as the "Augustine Pattern," and many argue that it was a pervasive colonial strategy throughout the circum-Caribbean region.[1]

Archaeological investigations in other regions of the Spanish-colonial Americas have similarly found that nearly all colonial households incorporated indigenous material culture, foodstuffs, food preparation methods, and other attributes into their daily routines, although not always according to the gendered pattern described by Deagan and others. For example, Diana DiPaolo Loren's research at El Presidio de Los Adaes (in the former Spanish province of Texas, now in Louisiana) found that colonial households there actively incorporated distinctive Spanish, French, and Native American material culture, architecture, and foodways. The deliberate mixing of culturally distinctive practices, Loren argues, gave individuals great flexibility in their social identities, allowing them to easily navigate social interactions with French, Spanish, African, Native American, and mixed-race peoples (Loren 1999:286–288). Rothschild traces the emergence of an intermediate colonial society in Spanish-colonial New Mexico that combined material elements from both Spanish and Pueblo Indian "cultural ancestors," largely as a result of the labor and cultural innovations of Native American women (2003:223). Mark Barnes's investigation of El Presidio de Tucson (in the former Spanish province of Sonora, now in Arizona) uses ceramic analysis to trace colonial incorporation of Piman material culture and foodways (Barnes 1983, 1984). Mary Van Buren (1999) documents Spanish reliance on indigenous technologies in the Andean Spanish colonies, and Ross Jamieson investigates how members of various castas in colonial Ecuador used colonial and indigenous material culture in their negotiations of mixed-race status (Jamieson 2000, 2004, 2005).

In contrast, by deploying material practices that created internal homogeneity within the colonial population and established rigid distinctions between themselves and local Native Californians, the military settlers at El Presidio de San Francisco made a series of historical choices that departed from the generalized pattern of Spanish-colonial mestizaje, creolization, and syncretism.[2] Surprisingly, their material practices more closely resemble those of Protestant mercantile colonies in northeast North America during the sixteenth and seventeenth centuries. Rothschild's research (2003) on Dutch settlements in the Hudson River Valley, in present-day New York (then known as New Amsterdam), provides a prime example. The Dutch, whose primary objective was to obtain beaver skins through trade with the Iroquois Nations, "clearly desired a distant relationship" with local indigenous peoples. They lived in separate towns, did not proselytize to the natives, did not enter into sexual or labor relationships with indigenous women, and generally "compartmentalized [their interactions] so that their only contact was in trade and some political negotiations" (225). Dutch colonists adopted little indigenous material culture beyond the notas bag, a deerskin purse used to carry wampum for economic transactions (192–194).

Structurally, Dutch colonization of New York and Spanish colonization of San Francisco could not be more different. Whereas the Dutch wanted little to do with local indigenous peoples, the Spanish program for Alta California prescribed aggregation, religious conversion, and a program of directed acculturation that would transform Native Californians into proper subjects of the Spanish crown.

Dutch merchants and traders were European capitalists; the Presidio's military settlers were mixed-race, landless peasants. Dutch New York was integrated into a burgeoning web of global trade in raw materials and manufactured goods; Spanish-colonial San Francisco was economically isolated and dependent on financial subsidies and supplies from central New Spain. Yet both colonial communities pursued very similar material strategies that established and maintained firm distinctions between themselves and the local indigenous populations with whom they interacted.

This comparative perspective suggests two important insights into the archaeology and ethnohistory of colonization. The first is that the portrayal of the Spanish-colonial Americas as a cultural and biological cauldron of mestizaje may be an overgeneralization. Colonial San Francisco was governed by the same government and military policies as the rest of New Spain and deployed the same military and religious institutions that effected the Spanish colonization of its North and Central American territories. Yet, culturally, its military settlers forged a distinct historical path. Is the case of El Presidio de San Francisco a complete anomaly in the Spanish Americas? This is doubtful; rather, the contrast between the material strategies employed by the colonial residents of El Presidio de San Francisco and those used at many other Spanish-colonial settlements reveals that people defined social identities in colonial situations through a multitude of different practices and processes. It emphasizes the need for continued research on colonial settlements in a broad array of historical, political, and environmental settings to further explore the diversity of colonial strategies throughout the Spanish Americas.

The second implication is that the overt, structural conditions of colonization inform, but do not determine, the ways in which colonial identities are materialized and negotiated. This is perhaps most strongly illustrated by the similarities in the material strategies used by Dutch colonists in New York and the military settlers in San Francisco, participants in imperialist projects with radically different structural attributes. Likewise, it is clear that the tripartite settlement strategy of mission, presidio, and pueblo that was deployed by the Spanish crown throughout North America fostered very different local outcomes. The interface of global imperial systems with local contexts was unpredictable precisely because this interface afforded scope for meaningful actions among the individuals and social collectivities drawn into the web of colonization.

Implications for Investigations of Identity

The findings of this study have specific implications for historical, anthropological, and archaeological research on identity. As chapter 1 discusses, taking identity as the focus of one's research is epistemologically hazardous: there is the danger of reifying the very concepts one seeks to expose as culturally constructed. Nonetheless, identities are endemic to the modern world, a bundle of tactics and strategies through which social subjects negotiate the complex and ever-changing institutions and other structural conditions in which they find themselves. A focus on identity provides an important perspective on imperialism because colonization forces the restructuring of existing social relations of difference and similarity, as well as a concomitant repositioning of social subjects in new and changing political and economic orders.

This book's methodological approach highlights the importance of material practices in the ongoing negotiation and reformulation of social identity. It is often argued that archaeological evidence is needed to compensate for the political biases found in documentary sources and to fill in evidentiary gaps in the historical record (Andrén 1998; De Cunzo 1996; Deetz 1977, 1988; Little 1994; Scott 1994). This study, however, demonstrates that a methodological focus on material practices contributes much more than a simple additive or corrective to archival documents. Material practices constitute the interface between institutional systems of power and the agency of social subjects. They are the media through which people navigate, respond to, and precipitate the historical events that constitute their lives—what Michel de Certeau (1984:xiv) termed "the microphysics of power" in daily life. Because specific genres of material practice afford different possibilities for individual and collective actions and different scales of agency, it is important to research multiple genres of material practice along varying spatial and temporal scales of analysis. Such a multifaceted approach provides access to the complex interplay among local, regional, and global scales of social action.

A second general contribution of this study is its deconstruction of the historical production of colonial identities. Most archaeological research on colonization has taken colonial identities for granted, focusing more on the transformation of local colonized populations than on the ways that the colonizers themselves were affected. But it is clear that being "colonial" was an achieved and unstable identity, one that was continually destabilized by the heterogeneity within the colonial population and by the similarities between the military settlers and Native Californians. That the military settlers had to resort to material practices to stabilize and buttress their colonial status underscores just how fragile these colonial practices of identification actually were. In this regard, this book joins postcolonial deconstructions of imperial culture (Bhabha 2004; McClintock 1995; Said 1979; Stoler 2002) and critical studies of whiteness (Bell 2005; Hall 1989, 1996; Metz 1999) in calling attention to the contingency and historical construction of "dominant" identities.

A third general contribution relates to the persistent theme of the overdetermination of identity that circulates throughout this book. Research on colonial identities has generally viewed colonization as a conflict between different ethnic or racial groups, with less attention paid to the ways that colonization is always simultaneously sexualized and gendered. Californio ethnogenesis depended just as much on changes in gendered and sexual identifications and practices as it did on the transformation of ethnic and racial identities. Studies of social identity must not privilege one category of identification over others, but instead must ask how identities are formulated, articulated, and enunciated in historically contingent ways.

Finally, this study provides a valuable cautionary tale in the context of current scholarship that celebrates the fluidity and ambiguity of identities. Identities are never fully closed in their meaning or import; they are never self-contained and are always contingent on the specific historical social relations within which they are formed and enunciated. However, we must be careful not to suppose that identities are somehow flimsy, wispy, or easily changeable aspects of social life, nor should we assume that changes in identification practices are inherently liberatory. Colonial San Francisco was one historical case in which the transformation of social identities served to stabilize the overall structure of colonial power while improving the status of a small group of subordinated people who had been enlisted to serve as colonizing agents. Even within the community of military settlers, the emergence of Californio identity relied as much on new gendered systems of social inequality as it did on the repudiation of racialized hierarchies. In this regard, this study joins those of Robert Young (1995), Katharyne Mitchell (1997), Robbin Chatan (2003), and others who have pointed to the reactionary potential of hybridity and its limitations as a theory and practice of liberation.

Limits of Ethnogenesis

This book raises questions about the limits of ethnogenesis, both as a theoretical model of identity transformation and as a practical strategy. As discussed in chapter 1, researchers have increasingly argued that ethnogenesis is a form of subaltern resistance to external domination—a creative means of survival among people with few options. There is no question that ethnogenesis was one strategy that Presidio settlers used to challenge certain colonial systems of power and forge new lives for themselves in difficult circumstances. The findings detailed throughout this book suggest that this strategy of ethnogenesis was largely enacted by repudiating their connections to African and Mexican cultural heritage and ancestry, by privileging cultural homogeneity, by modifying and intensifying gendered hierarchies, and by asserting differences with and superiority over Native Californians.

This historical case of colonial ethnogenesis raises several challenging conceptual questions. Can practices of identification resist domination and subjugation without simultaneously relying on the politics of exclusion and separation from still other dominated and subjugated social subjects? Or do identities always rely on a "constitutive outside, premised on exclusion and otherness, [that] forms the corona of difference through which identities are enunciated" (Meskell 2002:280)? Is it possible, as Stuart Hall (1989) exhorts, to develop new theories of ethnicity that engage with, rather than suppress, the differences that are present both *within* and *between* ethnic groups?

If, as archaeologists, historians, and historical anthropologists, we hold that social subjects have the capacity and the agency to act in ways that "matter," then it follows that particular forms of social identification are not inevitable. Could the military settlers stationed at the Presidio have negotiated their social identities in a different manner? Could they have adopted practices of social identification that forged a sense of shared community but did not suppress internal difference and rely on subordination of indigenous peoples? The model of ethnogenesis used in this study is a powerful construct that illuminates the transformations in colonial identity at El Presidio de San Francisco specifically and in Alta California generally. But the concept of ethnogenesis should not be adopted unquestioningly, nor should it be used universally in studies of colonization and other moments of cultural change, since an emphasis on ethnic differentiation could obscure other social alliances, accommodations, and coexistences that depend less on hierarchical distinction.

The historical transformation of colonial identity at El Presidio de San Francisco and in Alta California also points to the limits of ethnogenesis as a practical strategy. Ethnogenesis provided the Californios with some relief from Spanish-colonial racial hierarchies, but in the end it did not afford much protection from stigmatization, discrimination, and subordination by Europeans and Anglo-Americans who followed the "one-drop" rule of hypodescent. With U.S. annexation, most Californios lost the land and livestock they had acquired during Alta California's years as a Mexican province. Many were reduced to poverty and forced into employment as manual laborers and domestic servants, sometimes alongside the very Native Californian populations they had formerly dominated (Chávez-García 2004; Haas 1995; Pitt 1971).

The limits of Californio ethnogenesis are also illustrated by the preliminary findings of an oral history program among people whose heritage is related to the Presidio's years as a Spanish-colonial and Mexican military outpost (Voss et al. 2004, 2005). To date, none of the interviewees who identify as Californios or descendants of Californios have been able to share oral histories or family documents that extend back to the Spanish-colonial and Mexican periods. Many have shared their frustration that, with the exception of the demographic records contained in extant mission and military records, they have little direct information about their families' histories prior to the 1860s and 1870s. This underscores the profound disruption that U.S. annexation caused to Californio families and communities.

Several present-day Californios have stated that during the mid- and late 1800s, birthrates in their ancestral families dropped precipitously, and entire branches of their family tree simply died out; they believe that late nineteenth-century Californios felt there was little future for their children in the new political order. Additionally, the strong pattern of intraethnic endogamy that had characterized Californio society throughout the Spanish-colonial and Mexican periods also eroded, with most Californios intermarrying with more recently arrived Mexican, Irish, Scotch, and German immigrants. These changes are evidenced in many family genealogies that have been meticulously researched by the study participants.[3]

I was initially surprised by how frequently those being interviewed would turn the conversation to concerns about present-day identities, including the ways in which the legacies of Spanish colonization have continued to affect their current social status, family structures, employment, class, and, especially, race. Publicly, many of today's Californios present a white or Hispanic racial identity and emphasize their unique heritage as descendants of the earliest Europeans in California. I learned that this is a matter of some controversy among descendants, some of whom strongly assert Mexican, Chicano, Latino, or Native American identities and dismiss others' claims to European heritage.

In private interviews, several study participants discussed how their status as people of ambiguous racial heritage creates ongoing difficulties and anxieties. One woman laughingly explained to me, "We're all things mixed up—in my family, when someone's pregnant, you never know what's going to come out." In a more serious tone, she then recounted how in her close-knit extended family, darker-skinned cousins were separated from their lighter-skinned relatives during California's century of court-sanctioned school segregation (1869–ca. 1960). Many interviewees mentioned that their children are repeatedly teased for not being clearly white, or Mexican, or black and that they themselves are frequently asked "what they are" by both strangers and acquaintances. Some did not learn of their African, Indian, or Mexican heritage until they were well into adulthood, when a Californio parent considered them old enough to know closely guarded family secrets.

For many, their participation in heritage organizations and genealogical and historical research provides an anchor in a society that affords little cultural and no legal recognition of Californio identity. The extent to which the oral history participants initiated conversations about their present-day concerns about race was a compelling reminder of the complicated legacy of Spanish colonization and Californio ethnogenesis. The transformation of "colonial" identities continues in this postcolonial epoch, as the descendants of the military settlers negotiate the ambiguous status accorded today to people of mixed racial and ethnic heritage in the United States.

This appendix, which supplements chapter 9, "Consuming Practices: Food-ways," describes the methods used to analyze animal bones, shells, and plant remains as well as the quantitative and qualitative evidence generated through those analyses.

Reconstructing past foodways from such archaeological evidence is a challenging endeavor. The durable skeletal elements and shells found in archaeological deposits are the discarded "hard parts" of animals that were harvested for their flesh. Plant remains decay rapidly in most environments, leaving few traces and requiring special excavation methods for recovery. Consequently, it is critical for archaeological interpretations to include rigorous attention to contexts of deposition, preservation issues, site formation processes, sampling, and analysis methods. That information is provided here to allow other archaeologists to independently evaluate the interpretive claims presented in chapter 9 and to facilitate comparison of the findings of this study with the results of research at other archaeological sites.

This research is the outcome of a collaborative process to which many specialists contributed their expertise. The first stage of zooarchaeological analysis was conducted at the University of California, Berkeley, Archaeological Research Facility, under the direction of the author in consultation with Cheryl Smith-Lintner. Smith-Lintner's recently completed dissertation (2007) includes further analysis of this and additional faunal collections from El Presidio de San Francisco and sheds even greater light on human-animal interactions and colonial foodways in Alta California. The second stage of zooarchaeological analysis was performed at labs in Marin County and Alameda County and at California State University, Bakersfield, by specialists in vertebrates (Valente 2002) and marine invertebrates (Melton 2000, 2002). Soil samples collected for archaeobotanical analysis were processed at the Presidio Archaeology Center field laboratory. Recovered flotation samples were analyzed under the direction of Virginia Popper at the Paleoethnobotany Laboratory at the Costen Institute of Archaeology, University of California, Los Angeles (Popper 2002; Popper and Martin 2000).

Zooarchaeology

Animal bone is one of the primary constituents of the Building 13 midden; the excavated sample, which totaled 4 cubic meters, yielded an estimated 22,000 bone specimens, weighing 26.6 kg. By both weight and estimated count, animal bone was the most abundant type of material recovered from the deposit (see table 5, in chapter 5). In comparison, the amount of shell recovered was miniscule—only 126 specimens weighing 16 g.

Sampling and Analysis Methods

The primary objectives of the zooarchaeological analysis were to develop a list of species represented by the bone and shell assemblages and to assess the extent to which these species were included in the colonial diet. Analyses of animal bones also sought to identify the anatomical parts represented by the specimens, to identify traces of butchering activity, and (whenever possible) to determine the ages of the represented animals. Together, these data sets contribute to a fine-grained understanding of meat procurement, distribution, and consumption at El Presidio de San Francisco.

Animal bone was analyzed in two stages. During the initial stage of artifact processing, all bone was separated from the recovered materials and inspected for traces of intentional modification or evidence of usewear. All the bones and shells in this assemblage appeared to be unmodified other than by butchering marks, confirming that they were generated and discarded as by-products of dietary practices rather than obtained to make tools and ornaments. A small fraction (3.6 percent) of the bone assemblage showed visible evidence of heat exposure (carbonization and calcination), most likely the result of being dropped or tossed into cooking hearths. The overwhelming majority of specimens (96.4 percent) were either unburned or incompletely oxidized, indicating that most food waste was collected and deposited directly into the midden rather than systematically incinerated to control odor, pests, and vermin.

The second stage of bone analysis prioritized identification of taxa, element, and butchering marks (Valente 2002; Voss 2002:462–472, 510–514). For this stage, I selected a sample consisting of all bone specimens recovered from three excavation units located at the edges and center of the Building 13 midden. This sample constituted 19.6 percent of the entire animal bone assemblage by weight and also represented 21.3 percent of the total volume of excavated soils.

In analysis, each bone specimen was identified to the most specific taxonomic unit possible. Any ambiguities were resolved by placing specimens in the next higher taxonomic category (for example, a bone not identifiable to species would be assigned to family, genus, or class). When possible, bones assigned only to class were additionally sorted by size category (for example, large mammal). In addition to taxonomic identification, each specimen was identified, to the extent possible, to anatomical element, side, size, and age or degree of fusion (Valente 2002). Analysis results were quantified using two measures: NISP (number of identified specimens) and MNI (minimum number of individuals). NISP provides a maximum number of taxonomic abundance, while MNI, in calculating the smallest possible number of animals represented by the assemblage, provides a minimum measure of abundance (Grayson 1984; Lyman 1994; Marshall and Pilgram 1993). These two measures, with additional consideration of animal body size, allow some assessment of the relative contribution of each taxon to the colonial diet.

In comparison with the vertebrate remains, shell remains of marine invertebrates were few and highly fragmented. Of the 126 specimens (16 g), none are complete shells, and only 6 could be identified to species (Melton 2000, 2002). Because of the small size of the assemblage, shell analysis was based entirely on NISP counts rather than MNI or weight-based quantification methods (Glassow 2000; Grayson 1984; Mason, Peterson, and Tiffany 1998).

Taxonomic, Element, and Butchery Analysis

Tables A-1 and A-2 show the results of taxonomic analysis for bone and shell, respectively. Like the ceramics discussed in chapter 8, bone and shell recovered from the Building 13 midden were highly fragmented, as would be expected of material deposited in an open-air refuse dump that had been subject to trampling and scavenging. For bone, the average mean weight per specimen was 1.81 g; shell was even more fragmented, with a mean weight of 0.13 g per specimen. Fragmentation adversely affects taxonomic identification: for bone, 1,374 specimens (nearly 48 percent) were identifiable only to Vertebrata; and for shell, 12 specimens (10 percent) were identifiable only to Molluska. It is likely that a large number of these minimally identifiable specimens are small fragments broken from larger, more identifiable shells and bones in the assemblage. The remaining 1,499 bone specimens were identifiable to class and,

Taxonomic list of vertebrate
faunal remains found in the Building 13 midden

Taxon	Common Name	NISP	MNI	% NISP	% MNI
Amphibia	Amphibians	1	1	0.03	4.55
Aves					
Anatidae	Duck/goose	3	1	0.10	4.55
Gallus gallus	Domestic chicken	25	2	0.87	9.09
cf. Gallus gallus	Domestic chicken	3	—	0.10	—
Passeriforme	Perching bird	1	1	0.03	4.55
Uria aalge	Common murre	1	1	0.03	4.55
Aves	Birds	155	—	5.40	—
	TOTAL AVES	188	5	6.54	22.73
Mammalia					
Artiodactyla	Even-toed ungulates	24	—	0.84	—
Bos taurus	Cattle	43	1	1.50	4.55
Canidae	Coyote/fox/dog/wolf	2	—	0.07	—
Canis sp.	Coyote/dog/wolf	1	1	0.03	4.55
Carnivora	Carnivores	4	—	0.14	—
Leporidae	Hare/rabbit	5	—	0.17	—
Mysticeti	Baleen whale	1	1	0.03	4.55
Odocoileus hemionus	Mule deer	1	1	0.03	4.55
Ovis/Capra	Sheep/goat	9	1	0.31	4.55
Rodentia	Rodents	1	1	0.03	4.55
Sylvilagus sp.	Brush/cottontail rabbit	12	2	0.42	9.09
Urocyon cinereoargenteus	Gray fox	12	1	0.42	4.55
Ursus arctos	Grizzly bear	2	1	0.07	4.55
Mammalia	Mammal	771	—	26.84	—
Mammalia, large[a]	Large mammal	215	—	7.48	—
Mammalia, medium[a]	Medium mammal	15	—	0.52	—
Mammalia, medium/large[a]	Medium/large mammal	25	—	0.87	—
Mammalia, small[a]	Small mammal	47	—	1.64	—
	TOTAL MAMMALIA	1,190	10	41.42	45.45

(continued)

Taxon	Common Name	NISP	MNI	% NISP	% MNI
Osteichthyes					
Clupeidae	Herring	9	1	0.31	4.55
Embiotocidae	Surf perch	54	1	1.88	4.55
Ophiodon elongarus	Lingcod	1	1	0.03	4.55
Porichthys notatus	Plainfin midshipman	1	1	0.03	4.55
Rhacochilus vaca	Pileperch	1	1	0.03	4.55
Osteichthyes	Fish	51	—	1.78	—
	TOTAL OSTEICHTHYES	117	5	4.07	22.73
Reptilia					
Clemmys marmorata	Western pond turtle	3	1	0.10	4.55
Vertebrata	Vertebrate (undetermined)	1,374	—	47.82	—
	TOTALS	2,873	22	100.00	100.00

SOURCE: Developed from data provided in Valente 2002.

[a] Large mammals include those animals that are deer size or greater; medium mammals are those smaller than a deer but larger than a jackrabbit; small mammals include rabbit-sized animals and smaller; medium/large refers to specimens that could belong to either category.

TABLE A-2.   Taxonomic list of invertebrate faunal remains found in the Building 13 midden

Taxon	NISP	% NISP
Bivalvia		
Mytilus sp. (California bay mussels)	80	63
Bivalvia	27	21
TOTAL BIVALVIA	107	84
Gastropoda		
Haliotis rufescens (red abalone)	6	5
Gastropoda	1	1
TOTAL GASTROPODA	7	6
Molluska	12	10
TOTAL	126	100

SOURCE: Developed from data provided in Melton 2000, 2002.

TABLE A-3. Age profile data for *Bos taurus* (cattle)

Element	Number of Elements	Portion	Fused/Unfused	Age of Fusion
Humerus	1	Distal	Fusion line visible	12–18 months
Scapula	1	Complete	Fused	7–10 months
Scapula	1	Proximal	Fused	7–10 months
Metacarpal	1	Complete	Fused	Proximal before birth; distal 2–2½ years
Tibia	1	Proximal	Unfused	3½–4 years
Metatarsal	1	Distal	Unfused	2¼–3 years
1st phalange	5	Complete	Fused	1½ years
2nd phalange	8	Complete	Fused	1½ years
3rd phalange	4	Complete	Fused	Before birth
1st upper premolar	2	Complete	Adult dentition	Erupts 24–30 months
2nd upper premolar	1	Complete	Adult dentition	Erupts 18–30 months
2nd upper molar	1	Complete	Adult dentition	Erupts 15–18 months
2nd lower molar	1	Complete	Adult dentition	Erupts 15–18 months

SOURCE: Developed from data provided in Valente 2002 (table 3).

in some cases, to family and species; together, this assemblage was calculated to represent 22 MNI.

Mammals were the most frequently identified class by both NISP (41.42 percent) and MNI (45.45 percent). Most of the mammalia specimens that were identifiable to either family, species, or size class were large mammals (deer size or greater). *Bos taurus* (cattle) was the most common large mammal species (43 NISP, 1 MNI). Analysis of the degree of epiphyseal fusion and tooth eruption (following guidelines outlined in Silver 1969) indicates that the age of the cattle represented in the assemblage ranged between seven to ten months and thirty months at time of death (table A-3). However, these age guidelines are for modern domestic animals, and there may be some variance between the cattle breeds herded in Spanish-colonial Alta California and those raised in present-day agriculture. If the ages are valid, they are typical of young steer populations raised for slaughter but not of cattle populations managed for dairy production. Because the sample of specimens whose age could be determined is small (30 NISP out of 43 NISP), this discussion of herd management should be taken as suggestive rather than definitive.

Other large mammal taxa included *Odocoileus hemionus* (mule deer), *Ursus arctos* (grizzly bear), and, surprisingly, Mysticeti (baleen whale); each of these was represented by only 1 or 2 NISP. Medium mammals (smaller than a deer but larger than a jackrabbit) were represented by thirty-nine specimens, including *Ovis/Capra* (sheep/goat), *Canis* sp. (coyote/dog/wolf), and *Urocyon cinereoargenteus* (gray fox) specimens. Small mammals (rabbit-sized and smaller) included Rodentia (rodents) and Leporidae (hare/rabbits), some of which were identifiable as *Sylvilagus* sp. (brush/cottontail rabbit).

Of the mammalia bone specimens, 342 were identifiable to anatomical element (table A-4). For all size classes, all parts of the animals were apparently deposited into the Building 13 midden. There is no indication that either elements with greater meat weight (such as upper limb bones and ribs) or elements with lower meat weight (such as the spine, lower limbs, and head) were being removed and disposed of in separate locations. Thirty-nine mammal bones had butchery marks (table A-5), and most of these were blade-cut marks evident on specimens from animals that were large to large/medium in size. The pattern of blade-cut marks on these specimens is characteristic of a well-documented Spanish-colonial style of butchering in which the carcass was subdivided and meat was manually stripped from the bones after muscle attachment points and tendons had been severed (Gust 1982; Walker and Davidson 1989). Thirteen bone specimens (including two with cut marks) are long bones that have spiral fractures, which may indicate marrow extraction or may have been the result of natural breakage (Behrensmeyer, Gordon, and Yanagi 1986).

Nonmammal vertebrates included birds, fish, amphibians, and reptiles. Birds were the most numerous of these, consisting primarily of *Gallus gallus* (domestic chicken). Other bird taxa included Anatidae (duck/goose), *Uria aalge* (common murre), and Passeriforme (perching bird). The element distribution for Aves is shown in table A-6; as with Mammalia, all major skeletal areas were represented in the assemblage with the exception of the skull. Fish remains consisted primarily of vertebrae, a common result of differential preservation; some cranial, jaw, fin, and ray bones were also present. The most abundant fish taxon was Embiotocidae (surf perch, 54 NISP, 1 MNI). *Rhachochilus vaca* (pileperch), Clupeidae (herring), *Ophiodon elongarus* (lingcod), and *Porichthys notatus* (plainfin

TABLE A-4. Element distribution analysis, Mammalia

	Large Mammal				Medium/Large Mammal			Medium Mammal					Small Mammal				Other		TOTAL
	Bos taurus	*Odocoileus hemionus*	Mysticeti	*Ursus arctos*	Large Mammal	Artiodactyla	Medium/Large Mammal	*Ovis/Capra*	Canidae	*Canis* sp.	*Urocyon cinereoargenteus*	Medium Mammal	Leporidae	*Sylvilagus* sp.	Rodentia	Small Mammal	Carnivora	Mammal	TOTAL
Axial skeleton																			
Skull																			
Skull	1	—	—	—	—	—	—	—	—	—	—	—	—	—	—	—	—	2	3
Maxilla	—	—	—	—	1	—	—	—	—	—	—	—	—	—	—	—	—	—	1
Mandible	—	—	—	—	—	2	—	—	—	—	—	—	—	1	—	—	1	1	5
Teeth	7	—	—	—	3	12	—	7	—	—	1	3	5	—	1	—	2	23	64
Axis, atlas, vertebrae, sacrum																			
Axis	—	—	—	—	—	2	—	—	—	—	—	—	—	—	—	—	—	—	2
Atlas	—	—	—	—	1	—	—	—	—	—	—	—	—	—	—	1	—	—	2
Vertebrae	—	—	1	—	22	—	8	—	—	—	—	9	—	—	—	14	—	5	59
Sacrum	—	—	—	—	1	—	—	—	—	—	—	—	—	—	—	—	—	—	1
Rib and sternum																			
Rib	—	—	—	—	64	—	10	—	—	—	—	2	—	—	—	17	—	1	94
Sternum	—	—	—	—	1	—	—	—	—	—	—	—	—	—	—	—	—	—	1

Appendicular skeleton														
Upper front limb														
Scapula	2	2	—	1	—	—	—	—	1	—	—	4	1	11
Humerus	1	—	—	—	—	—	3	—	—	1	—	2	—	7
Lower front limb														
Radius	—	—	1	—	1	—	—	—	—	—	—	—	—	3
Ulna	1	—	—	—	—	—	—	2	—	—	—	—	—	3
Metacarpal	1	—	—	1	—	—	—	—	—	—	—	—	—	2
Carpal	3	—	—	—	—	—	2	—	—	—	—	1	—	6
Upper rear limb														
Innominate	—	3	—	—	—	1	—	—	—	1	—	3	—	8
Femur	—	1	—	—	—	—	1	—	—	—	—	1	—	3
Patella	1	—	—	—	—	—	—	—	—	—	—	—	1	2
Lower rear limb														
Tibia	1	—	1	—	1	—	1	—	—	—	—	3	—	7
Astralagus	1	—	—	—	—	—	1	—	—	—	—	1	—	3
Calcaneous	—	—	—	—	1	—	—	—	—	2	—	—	—	3
Tarsals	—	—	1	2	—	—	—	—	—	—	—	—	—	3
Metatarsal	1	—	—	—	—	—	—	—	—	—	—	—	—	1
Lower limb (front or rear)														
Metapodials	—	—	1	—	—	2	2	—	—	4	—	—	1	10
Carpals/tarsals	—	—	—	—	—	—	—	—	—	—	—	—	2	2
Phalanges	17	—	2	2	—	—	—	—	—	—	—	1	5	27
Sesamoids	6	2	—	1	—	—	—	—	—	—	—	—	—	9

SOURCE: Developed from data provided in Valente 2002.

Table A-5.
Butchery marks on mammal bones

Taxon	Element/Part	Side	Number
Cut marks			
Artiodactyl	Innominate fragment	Right	1
Artiodactyl	Mandible fragment	Right	1
Bos taurus	Complete 3rd phalange	Unknown	1
Large mammal	Atlas fragment	Axial	1
Large mammal	Bone fragment	Unknown	2
Large mammal	Complete lumbar vertebra	Axial	1
Large mammal	Distal rib fragment	Unknown	1
Large mammal	Long bone shaft fragment	Unknown	1
Large mammal	Lumbar vertebra fragment	Axial	2
Large mammal	Proximal rib fragment	Left	1
Large mammal	Proximal scapula fragment	Left?	1
Large mammal	Rib shaft fragment	Unknown	9
Large mammal	Rib shaft fragment	Left?	1
Mammal	Bone fragment	Unknown	1
Medium/large mammal	Proximal scapula fragment	Right	1
Medium/large mammal	Rib shaft fragment	Unknown	1
Cut mark and spiral fracture			
Large mammal	Long bone shaft fragment	Unknown	2
Spiral fracture			
Odocoileus hemionus	Proximal radius fragment	Right	1
Large mammal	Femur shaft fragment?	Unknown	1
Large mammal	Long bone fragment	Unknown	9

SOURCE: Developed from data provided in Valente 2002 (table 2).

	Anatidae (Duck/Goose)	Gallus gallus[a] (Domestic Chicken)	Passeriformes (Perching Bird)	Uria aalge (Common Murre)	Aves (General)	TOTAL
Axial skeleton						
Head	—	—	—	—	—	0
Axis, atlas, vertebrae, sacrum						
Axis	—	1	—	—	—	1
Atlas	—	—	—	—	—	0
Vertebrae	—	—	—	—	28	28
Synsacrum	—	—	—	—	2	2
Rib and sternum						
Rib	—	—	—	—	1	1
Sternum	—	—	—	—	3	3
Appendicular skeleton						
Upper front limb						
Scapula	1	—	—	—	—	1
Coracoid	—	5	—	—	1	6
Furcula	—	—	—	1	2	3
Humerus	—	5	—	—	6	11
Lower front limb						
Radius	—	3	—	—	5	8
Ulna	1	2	1	—	4	8
Ulnare	—	2	—	—	1	3
Carpometacarpus	—	1	—	—	—	1
Phalanx	1	2	—	—	—	3
Upper rear limb						
Pelvis	—	—	—	—	—	0
Femur	—	1	—	—	2	3
Lower rear limb						
Fibula	—	—	—	—	2	2
Tibiotarsus	—	4	—	—	4	8
Tarsometatarsus	—	1	—	—	4	5
Rear phalanges	—	—	—	—	28	28
Lower limb (front or back)						
Phalanx	—	—	—	—	2	2

SOURCE: Developed from data provided in Valente 2002.

[a] Includes cf. *Gallus gallus*.

midshipman) were also present in smaller numbers. Amphibia (amphibians, such as frogs, salamanders, and toads) is represented by only one specimen. The class Reptilia is represented by three plastron/carapace fragments from a *Clemmys marmorata* (western pond turtle).

The invertebrate (shell) assemblage is dominated by bivalves, notably *Mytilus* sp. (mussels) (80 NISP, 63 percent). Also known as California and bay mussels, *Mytilus* sp. is found attached to rocks near the low tide line and is common to rocky littoral zones along both the ocean and bayshore near the Presidio. Six very small shell fragments were identified as *Haliotis rufescens* (red abalone), a gastropod that dwells in estuaries and bays at depths of 20 to 60 feet.

Archaeobotany

Interpreting botanical remains recovered from archaeological sites requires attention to both preservation issues and site formation processes. El Presidio de San Francisco is an open-air site in a Mediterranean climate with annual wet/dry cycles. Such conditions generally result in poor preservation of unburned organic material; carbonized (burned) organic materials are more likely to be preserved. Consequently, historical plant materials recovered through archaeological excavation usually consist of seeds and other plant parts that have been intentionally or unintentionally incinerated. As a rule, plant materials burned as fuel are differentially preserved. Plant materials collected for food, however, are usually burned only through accidents (for instance, wastage during roasting or when a pot is spilled into the fire) unless waste food is intentionally burned before disposal. The ways that specific plants are used influence the probability of archaeological preservation. Seeds that would have been discarded before cooking, seeds that were regularly ingested as part of a vegetable or fruit, and seeds from foods that were usually eaten raw are highly unlikely to be represented. In contrast, the preparation of whole seeds is more likely to leave archaeological traces.

For a deposit like the Building 13 midden, where household trash apparently was deposited incrementally over several years, carbonized plant remains probably entered the archaeological record through episodes of hearth-cleaning. There is no indication that household trash was intentionally burned; very few of the artifacts or bone fragments recovered from the midden appear heat-affected. Remains of food plants in the Building 13 midden most likely represent accidental spillage into fires during cooking. Because scavenging, trampling, and exposure to the elements accelerated the decomposition of plant remains dumped into the midden, we can assume that the low density of preserved seeds may be only a small fraction of the plants originally deposited there.

In contrast, the depositional processes that shaped the apartment floor deposits were exceedingly favorable to the preservation of botanical remains. Small plant seeds appear to have been easily lost in the dirt or matted floor, and the hearths themselves contain thousands of plant seeds that were probably charred during cooking spills. Because they were inside a roofed building, the apartment floor and hearths were sheltered from the elements; and archaeological stratigraphy suggests that once the building was abandoned, the deposits were rapidly covered by layers of adobe and clay tile rubble, further aiding preservation.

Interpretation of the archaeobotanical data must therefore take into account the differences between these two contexts of recovery. Both samples consist primarily of seeds burned in hearths, including plants used as fuel and plants used as food. The Building 13 midden, representing the cumulative waste deposited by the Presidio's colonial population in the 1780s and 1790s, is a lower-density assemblage. In contrast, botanicals recovered from the apartment floor deposits and hearth deposits came from a primary context, generated by a single household and preserved under more favorable conditions.

Sampling and Analysis Methods

Plant seeds were recovered from both the midden and apartment deposits through flotation sampling. Routine soil samples of 10 L were collected from each excavated stratum in each unit; the size of these samples was increased in contexts where it appeared that botanical remains might be particularly well preserved. The soil samples were processed at the field laboratory using a standard barrel-type flotation machine; recovered materials were analyzed at the Paleoethnobotany Laboratory at the UCLA Costen Institute of Archaeology (Popper 2002; Popper and Martin 2000).

Overall, 190 L of archaeobotanical soil samples were collected, processed, and analyzed from the Building 13 midden; this represented 4.8 percent of the total volume of soils excavated from the deposit. This sample yielded 629 seeds and seed fragments, for a density of 3.3 seeds/L. The apartment floor deposits yielded 170.25 L of archaeobotanical soil samples, constituting 27 percent of the total volume of excavated soil. Botanical remains were especially dense in these floor and hearth deposits, with the samples yielding 9,397 seeds and seed fragments, for a density of nearly 55.2 seeds/L (table A-7).

Seeds from both archaeological contexts were rarely identifiable to the species level. As with the bone and shell analyses, each botanical specimen was identified to the most specific taxonomic unit possible, so that seeds not identifiable to species were assigned to family, genus, or class. Both the midden and apartment floor archaeobotanical assemblages included small frequencies

TABLE A-7. Categorization of seed remains, Building 13 midden and apartment deposits

Taxon	Common Name	Building 13 Midden			Apartment Deposits		
		Count	Density (seeds/L)	%	Count	Density (seeds/L)	%
A. Edibles							
A.1 Cultivated cereals							
Hordeum	Cultivated barley	0	0.000	0.00	15	0.088	0.16
Triticum (a)	Wheat (rounded grain)	14	0.074	2.23	1,290	7.577	13.73
Triticum (b)	Wheat (elongated grain)	0	0.000	0.00	208	1.222	2.21
Unknown cereal	Probably emmer wheat	0	0.000	0.00	1	0.006	0.01
Zea mays[a]	Maize	3	0.016	0.48	0	0.000	0.00
Zea mays cf. fragment	Maize	17	0.089	2.70	6	0.035	0.06
Cereal fragment	Maize, wheat, or barley	24	0.126	3.82	1,222	7.177	13.00
TOTAL CULTIVATED CEREALS		58	0.305	9.22	2,742	16.105	29.18
A.2 Cultivated legumes							
Pulse fragment	Bean or pea	14	0.074	2.23	342	2.009	3.64
Pisum sp.	Pea	0	0.000	0.00	65	0.382	0.69
Vicia faba	Fava bean	0	0.000	0.00	65	0.382	0.69
Phaseolus sp. cf. fragment	Common bean	1	0.005	0.16	0	0.000	0.00
TOTAL CULTIVATED LEGUMES		15	0.079	2.38	472	2.773	5.02

A.3 Edible wild plants

Hordeum and H.

brachyantherum cf.	Wild barley	0	0.000	0.00	23	0.135	0.24
Lathyrus sp.	Wild pea	0	0.000	0.00	3	0.018	0.03
Fabacae cf.	Legume family	1	0.005	0.16	25	0.147	0.27
Corylus sp.	Hazelnut	2	0.011	0.32	1	0.006	0.01
Atriplex sp.	Saltbush	1	0.005	0.16	0	0.000	0.00
Carex sp.	Sedge	1	0.005	0.16	3	0.018	0.03
Juncus sp.	Rush	3	0.016	0.48	0	0.000	0.00
Rubus sp.	Blackberry, raspberry	2	0.011	0.32	0	0.000	0.00
Sambucus sp.	Elderberry	1	0.005	0.16	0	0.000	0.00
TOTAL EDIBLE WILD PLANTS		11	0.058	1.75	55	0.324	0.59
TOTAL EDIBLES		84	0.442	13.35	3,269	19.202	34.79
B. Mallow							
Malva sp.	Mallow	105	0.553	16.69	49	0.288	0.52
C. Bluegrass and other wild grasses							
Poa sp.	Bluegrass	335	1.763	53.26	5,617	32.993	59.77
Poaceae	Wild grass	4	0.021	0.64	64	0.376	0.68
TOTAL BLUEGRASS AND OTHER WILD GRASSES		339	1.784	53.90	5,681	33.369	60.46
D. Other wild plants							
Erodium sp.	Filaree	24	0.126	3.82	112	0.658	1.19
Cactaceae	Cactus family	0	0.000	0.00	1	0.006	0.01
Asteraceae	Sunflower family	3	0.016	0.48	2	0.012	0.02
Rosaceae	Rose family	0	0.000	0.00	1	0.006	0.01

(continued)

TABLE A-7 (continued)

Taxon	Common Name	Building 13 Midden			Apartment Deposits		
		Count	Density (seeds/L)	%	Count	Density (seeds/L)	%
Polygonaceae	Knotweed family	1	0.005	0.16	0	0.000	0.00
Solanaceae cf.	Nightshade family	0	0.000	0.00	1	0.006	0.01
Malvaceae cf.	Mallow family	1	0.005	0.16	0	0.000	0.00
Phacelia sp.	Phacelia	1	0.005	0.16	0	0.000	0.00
TOTAL OTHER WILD PLANTS		30	0.157	4.77	117	0.688	1.25
E. Weedy annuals, probably intrusive							
Silene sp.	Catchfly	2	0.011	0.32	82	0.482	0.87
Calandrinia sp.	Red maids	1	0.005	0.16	4	0.023	0.04
Oxalis sp.	Wood sorrel	6	0.032	0.95	0	0.000	0.00
TOTAL WEEDY ANNUALS		9	0.048	1.43	86	0.505	0.92
F. Unidentifiable							
Unidentifiable seeds		54	0.284	8.59	154	0.905	1.64
Unknown types		8	0.043	1.27	41	0.241	0.44
TOTAL UNIDENTIFIABLE		62	0.327	9.86	195	1.146	2.08
TOTAL SEED REMAINS		629	3.311	100.00	9,397	55.198	100.00

SOURCE: Popper 2002; Popper and Martin 2000.
[a] Includes one kernel, one cupule, and one scutellum with embryo.

of uncarbonized seeds from weed plants that grow on the surface of the present-day archaeological site (*Silene* sp., *Calandrinia* sp., and *Oxalis* sp.). These are almost certainly intrusive specimens that entered archaeological deposits through downward filtration and bioturbation and were excluded from further consideration.

NOTES

Chapter 1. Ethnogenesis
and the Archaeology of Identity

1. See statements on race issued by the American Anthropological Association (1998) and the American Association of Physical Anthropologists (1996).

2. See also Bhabha 2004; Butler 1999; Derrida 1973; and Hall 1996.

3. Bhabha 2004; Butler 1990, 1993a; Fanon 1967, 1977; Hall 1996; Haraway 1989, 1997; McClintock 1995; Ortner 1996; Said 1979; Stoler 1995; and Voss 2005a.

4. E.g., Dietler and Herbich 1998; Jones 1997; Lightfoot, Martinez, and Schiff 1998; Loren 1999, 2000; Mullins 1999; Orser 2004; Silliman 2001a; and Williams 1992.

5. But see Casella and Fowler 2005; Joyce 2000a, 2000b, 2000c, 2005; Meskell 2002; Meskell and Joyce 2003; and Voss 2005b, 2006a, 2006b for important exceptions.

6. For examples, see Alexander and Mohanty 1997; Anzaldua 1987; Behar 1993; Davis 1981; Hull, Smith, and Bell-Scott 1982; Mohanty 2003; Smith 2000; and Spivak 1988, 1996.

7. E.g., Hall 1989, 1996; Lucas 2006; Nagel 2003; Spivak 1988, 1996; Staats 1996; Stoler 2002; Verdery 1994; Wilkie 2000; and Young 1995.

8. The development of the archaeological culture concept is most generally credited to Franz Boas and V. Gordon Childe. For comprehensive overviews and critiques of this approach, see Jones 1997; Orser 2004; and Trigger 1989.

9. E.g., Anderson 1993; Anzaldua 1987; Bhabha 1990; Fischer 1986; Hall 1996; Lamont and Molnár 2002; Nagel 2003; and Wolf 1982.

10. Hodder's (1982) ethnoarchaeological study in the Baringo District of Kenya was a key turning point in moving beyond the archaeological culture model of ethnic identity. Congruent with Barth, Hodder found that intense interaction across tribal boundaries did not impede the maintenance of clear material distinctions, even as other materials flowed freely across such boundaries. "There is," Hodder concluded, "a continual tension between boundary maintenance and boundary disruption; the one exists in relation to the other" (1982:73). See also Cordell and Yannie 1991; Dietler and Herbich 1998; Franklin and Fesler 1999; Jones 1997; McGuire 1982; Orser 2004; and Stark 1998.

11. See Cohen 1978; Horning 1999; Horvath 1982; McGuire 1982; Sider 1994; and Williams 1992.

12. See Fesler and Franklin 1999:8; Leone, LaRoche, and Babiarz 2005; Orser 2004; and Williams 1992. See also Harrison 1995 for a more general critique of the relationship between ethnicity and race in anthropology as a whole.

13. For further discussion of the potentials and challenges in archaeological research on sexuality, see Voss 2000b, 2005b, 2006b; and Voss and Schmidt 2000.

14. See Butler 1993a, 1993b, 1994, 1999, 2004; Grosz 1989; Grosz and Probyn 1995; and Laqueur 1990.

15. See Enloe 1990; Manalansan 2002, 2003; McClintock 1995; Nagel 2003; Stoler 1995, 2002; and Young 1995.

16. My discussion focuses on ethnogenesis studies in ethnography, sociology, archaeology, and ethnohistory. The term "ethnogenesis" is also used in physical anthropology and cultural evolutionary studies, where it pertains to culture change that results from horizontal patterns of cross-cultural borrowing and transmission (Bellwood 2004; Moore 2004). There has been little intersection between ethnohistorical studies of ethnogenesis and those working within a cultural evolutionary framework, with evolutionists arguing that most ethnohistorical studies are too focused on short-term events and unique historical moments to be relevant to the study of human evolution.

17. For further discussion of Childe's engagement with ethnogenesis, see Levy and Holl 2002; Ordner 1985; and Trigger 1989.

18. Marxists agonized over the "national question": how could the socialist state adhere to the principle of self-determination for ethnic groups while pursuing its primary goal of forging class solidarity? The issue was "resolved" through the principle of voluntary union and the formation of ethnically identified semi-autonomous regions within Soviet nations. Ethnographers and archaeologists were instructed to trace the ethnogenetic origins of these different peoples and

provide data that could be used to establish and justify territorial and language policies (Dolitsky 1984; Kohl 1998:231–232; Michael 1962; Thompson 1965).

19. For studies of African American ethnogenesis, see Heath 1999; Leone, LaRoche, and Babiarz 2005; Parrillo 1994; Taylor 1979; and Williams 1992. Kolb (1984) and Ayubi (1991) apply Singer's model of African American ethnogenesis to Hispanic [sic] Americans; Hall (1989), Delle (2000), and Guss (1996) consider the development of black ethnic identities in Britain, Jamaica, and Venezuela, respectively; and Whitten (1976) traces the emergence of pan-indigenous identities in Ecuador.

20. For examples of such studies of North American tribal histories, see Albers 1996; Anderson 1999; Bateman 1992; Burch et al. 1999; Campisi and Starna 2004; Davis 2001; Galloway 1995; Haley and Wilcoxon 2005; Mullins and Paynter 2000; Roosens 1989; Sattler 1996; and Sider 1994. On Mexican Indians, see Wilson 1993; on Caribbean native groups, see González 1988 and Howard 2002; and on South American indigenous identities, see Hill 1996; Powers 1995; and Whitten 1976, 1996a.

21. For examples, see Bateman 1992; Bilby 1996; Brown 1993; Campisi and Starna 2004; Cordell and Yannie 1991; Davis 2001; Devine 2004; González 1988; Howard 2002; and Pérez 2000.

Chapter 2. Spanish-Colonial San Francisco

1. Petlenuc is a Yelamu Ohlone place-name that refers generally to the northwest tip of the San Francisco peninsula—a region encompassing approximately four miles of bay and ocean shoreline—and the coastal villages that once stood there. It also seems to have been used specifically to refer to the Yelamu bayshore village located at what today is Crissy Field in the Presidio of San Francisco and the adjacent Palace of Fine Arts lagoon. The historical indigenous village shifted locations over the centuries to accommodate changes in the bayshore and estuarine marshes. Archaeological investigations have located three shellmound sites (SFR-7, SFR-9, and SFR-129) along the bayshore in this region; the earliest archaeologically known occupation date for the area known as Petlenuc is AD 740, with the most recent location occupied from ca. AD 1350 until colonization (Clark 2001; Gambastiani and Fitzgerald 2001; Milliken 1995; Milliken, Shoup, and Ortiz 2005; Moratto 1984; Palóu 1926; Rudo 1982; Stewart 2003).

2. European explorers first encountered California in the 1530s, when Spanish ships made landfall on what is now known as the southern Baja California peninsula. The term "California" came to refer to the entire North American Pacific coastline, from present-day Cabo San Lucas to Alaska. Spain claimed the western North American coast in its entirety in 1542, in a maritime voyage headed by Juan Rodriguez Cabrillo. An expedition led by English explorer Sir

Francis Drake made landfall in California shortly afterward, in or near the San Francisco Bay.

3. Milliken observes that the Ssalson attack raises many unanswerable questions. The Ssalson may have attacked the Yelamu because of an ongoing intertribal dispute, or the violence might have been a response to the establishment of the mission and the Presidio. Perhaps, Milliken speculates, the Ssalson were removing an impediment to their own access to the colonial settlements, or they might have been trying to develop an alliance with the colonists by helping them to secure complete control of Yelamu lands (1995:63).

4. Much of what is known about precontact native cultures in California is based on "salvage ethnographies" conducted in the early 1900s by Alfred Kroeber (1925) and his colleagues, more than one hundred years after Spanish colonization. More recent scholarship (e.g., Lightfoot 2005; Milliken 1995) has challenged many of the assumptions of these early anthropological studies. This section draws heavily on Milliken's research as well as on archaeological studies, oral histories, colonial documents, indigenous scholarship and writings, and my own conversations with present-day Native Californians (Bean 1976, 1994; Bickel 1976; Blackburn and Anderson 1993; Castillo 1989, 1991; Chartkoff and Chartkoff 1984; Cook 1943, 1976; Costanso 1992; Field et al. 1992; Heizer 1978a, 1991; Heizer and Elsasser 1980; Hurtado 1988, 1992; Kroeber 1925; La Pérouse 1989; Levy 1978; Margolin 1978, 1981; Milliken, Shoup, and Ortiz 2005; Moratto 1984; Sandos 1998; Vancouver 1984; Yamane 2002).

5. *Costeños* (coast-dwellers, later anglicized as Costanoan) was the term used by Spanish explorers and colonists to refer to native communities living in and around the Monterey and San Francisco Bay regions. Most descendants prefer to be described as "Ohlone," and I use that term throughout this book.

6. For a synthesis of this debate, see Lightfoot 2005:44–48.

7. For more detailed accounts of the founding of Alta California and the related development of San Blas, see Bancroft 1886a; Barker, Allen, and Costello 1995; Brinkerhoff and Faulk 1965; Chapman 1916; Costello and Hornbeck 1989; Fireman 1977; Navarro García 1964, 1979; Thurman 1967; and Weber 1992.

8. Major historical and archaeological studies of the Spanish-colonial presidio military system include Bense 2004; Campbell 1977; Faulk 1969, 1971; Gerald 1968; Langellier and Peterson 1981; Moorhead 1969, 1975; Navarro García 1964; Naylor and Polzer 1986, 1988; Polzer and Sheridan 1997; and Williams 2004. See Barker, Allen, and Costello 1995; Dobyns 1980; Gilmore 1995; Jones 1979; Levine 1995; and Weber 1992 for more general accounts of the role of presidios in the colonization of New Spain's northern frontier. On the relationship of presidios to the colonial military, see Archer 1977 and Fireman 1977. For translations and historical analyses of the military regulations that governed the operation of frontier presidios, see Brinkerhoff and Faulk 1965; Croix 1941;

Gálvez 1951; Kinnaird 1958; Naylor and Polzer 1988; Oconór 1994; and Thomas 1941.

9. Allen 1998; Cook 1943; Hornbeck 1989; Hornbeck and Fuller 1983; Mason 1998; Milliken 1995; and Ríos-Bustamante 1993.

10. For reviews and new perspectives on mission research in Alta California, see Barker, Allen, and Costello 1995; Costello and Hornbeck 1989; Dartt-Newton and Erlandson 2006; Graham 1998; Lightfoot 2005; and Silliman 2001b.

11. Bouchard's ships, the *Argentina* and the *Santa Rosa*, entered Monterey Bay in October 1818 and launched a full-scale attack. His ships left the next day and sailed south; they attacked Mission San Juan Capistrano and a rancho near Santa Bárbara before leaving the coast (Bancroft 1886b:220–249; Osio 1996:44–53).

12. Russia was not the only country to take advantage of the economic opportunities afforded by the Mexican independence struggle, but it was the only foreign power to claim land in Alta California. British, French, and "Boston" traders regularly traversed Alta California's shores and frequently entered the San Francisco Bay. As it did with the Russians, El Presidio de San Francisco set aside military ideals of territorial defense in its desperate need for trading partners (Costello and Hornbeck 1989).

13. For accounts of Russian colonization of northern California and interactions between Colony Ross and El Presidio de San Francisco, see Blind et al. 2004; Farris 1989; Langellier and Rosen 1996:120–138; Lightfoot, Wake, and Schiff 1991; and Osborn 1997. After Mexico achieved independence from Spain, Russian fur hunting in Alta California's waters was legalized through a profit-sharing agreement. From that point forward, economic and social interchange between the two colonies flourished.

14. See Camarillo 1979; Chávez-García 2004; Haas 1995; Hughes 1975; McWilliams 1949; Pitt 1971; Ríos-Bustamante 1993; Sanchez 1984; and Sánchez 1995 for historical studies of the Californios during and shortly after the transition to U.S. rule.

Chapter 3. From Casta to Californio, I

1. Gifford-Gonzales (1993) calls attention to the prevalence of this "drudge-on-the-hide" motif in archaeological reconstructions. It is significant that this manner of hide preparation was not widely used in Spanish-colonial Alta California.

2. See Cook 1976; Costello and Hornbeck 1989; Hornbeck and Fuller 1983; and Ríos-Bustamante 1993.

3. Mission priests were responsible for enumerating Alta California's native populations and did so by counting the number of baptized Native Californians living under the jurisdiction of each mission and by estimating the number of people living at nonmission native villages.

4. In many parts of the Interior Provinces, such adoptions were a form of domestic enslavement or indentured servitude (Brooks 2002). The same may have been the case in Alta California.

5. It is especially difficult to reconstruct the villages, districts, and language group affiliations of the Presidio's Native Californian population. Milliken, Shoup, and Ortiz (2005) suggest that the Indian population living at Mission San Francisco de Asís and the Presidio initially came from the San Francisco peninsula, but by the early 1800s, this native population was dominated by Coast Miwok, Bay Miwok, and Patwin speakers. There are also archaeological indications that at least some of the Native Californians brought to the Presidio were likely to have been Yokuts speakers from the Central Valley (E. Blind and L. N. Clevenger, personal communication, 2006).

6. For historical and archaeological analyses and case studies related to the nonphysiological dimensions of racial and casta status in the Spanish-colonial Americas, see Althouse 2005; Boyer 1997; Carrera 2003; Chance 1979; Chávez-García 2004; Cope 1994; Deans-Smith 2005; Fisher 1992; Haas 1995; Jamieson 2004, 2005; Jones 1979; Katzew 2004; Loren 1999, 2001a; Mason 1998; Milton and Vinson 2002; Mörner 1970; Schwartz 1995; Seed 1988; Taylor 1979; and Twinam 1999.

7. For examples, see Boyer 1997; Carrera 2003; Chance 1979; Cope 1994; Forbes 1966; Haley and Wilcoxon 2005; Jamieson 2004, 2005; Mason 1998; Moorhead 1975; and Twinam 1999.

8. See Althouse 2005; Jamieson 2005; Johnson and Lipsett-Rivera 1998; Katzew 2004; Kuznesof 1995; and Schwartz 1995.

9. E.g., Gutiérrez 1993a, 1993b; Hurtado 1999; Seed 1988; Stern 1995; and Twinam 1999.

10. In 1760, a royal decree required members of the military to obtain permission to marry from their commanding officer, in order to prevent dishonorable marriages (Castañeda 1993a). In 1776, the Royal Pragmatic on Marriage sought to further deter marriages between high-ranking castas and blacks, mulatos, and other castas of African origin by requiring parental consent for marriages of people under age twenty-five. It exempted "negros, mulattoes, *coyotes,* and other such individuals" from the requirement for parental permission if the person seeking to marry served in an official capacity or was otherwise distinguished (Bouvier 2001:113–114; Castañeda 1993a:736).

11. Some of the more specific casta terms were often used interchangeably; for example, *pardo, moreno, morizco,* and *mulato* all appear to have been used more or less synonymously to denote people of African heritage.

12. See also Campbell 1972, 1977; Jones 1979; Langellier and Peterson 1981; Moorhead 1969; and Vigil 1983. However, some military companies, such as the Indian Auxiliaries throughout the Interior Provinces and the Free Colored

militia in southern New Spain, reinforced rather than destabilized racial identities (Jackson 1999; Vinson 2001).

13. Such methodological approaches reflect the very real spatial segregation of racialized populations that was typical of race relations in the United States from the eighteenth to the twentieth century (Ferguson 1992; Leone, LaRoche, and Babiarz 2005; Mullins 1999; Voss 2005a; Wilkie 2000).

14. Data for this analysis were gathered primarily from historical studies that used the 1776 Presidio roster, the 1782 census, and the 1790 Revillagigedo census (Forbes 1983; Langellier and Rosen 1996; Mason 1998). Of these, casta data were most complete for the 1790 census, with 100 percent of all listed adults identified by racial casta. The 1776 roster and the 1782 census were less complete: in the former, less than half of the Presidio's adult population was classified by casta; in the latter, a little over 10 percent of those listed were not identified by casta. In both 1776 and 1782, women were more likely than men to lack a recorded casta. It is unclear how the differences in sample completeness between the three documents affect this analysis. It may simply be that, unless pressed to do so, many colonial settlers felt it was either unimportant or disadvantageous to have their casta recorded. Forbes's study of the people listed in the 1776 and 1782 censuses indicates that those settlers whose casta was not listed had been recorded at birth as mestizo, mulato, or indio (Forbes 1983). If that is the case, then it is likely that the increase in español identity was even more dramatic than the available data show.

15. See Bouvier 2001:6–12; Engstrand 1998; Hurtado 1999:xxvi; and Polk 1991 for further discussion of Montalvo's novel.

16. See Bouvier 2001; Castañeda 1988, 1992, 1993a, 1998; and Chávez-García 2004.

17. I use terms such as "transgendered" and "heterosexual" very guardedly. Terms generally used today to describe gender and sexual identities are modern phenomena, linked to the development of sexology in the late nineteenth and early twentieth centuries. In Spanish-colonial North America, regulation of sexuality and gender focused on acts and behaviors rather than on classifying individuals according to their sexual proclivities. For further discussion of the difficulties inherent in sexual terminology in archaeology, see Voss 2000b, 2005b, 2006b; and Voss and Schmidt 2000.

18. The importance of honor and shame in Spanish-colonial North America has been discussed at great length in Castañeda 1993a, 1993b, 1998; Castillo 1994a; Chávez-García 2004; Gutiérrez 1991, 1993a, 1993b; Jackson and Castillo 1995; Monroy 1990a, 1990b; and Voss 2000a. This brief synopsis is drawn from these sources.

19. Men were sometimes socially condemned if their sexual affairs were disruptive to the well-being of the community; such actions showed poor judgment and a lack of consideration for other men of standing. Additionally, in-

cest, bestiality, and taking the receptive role in sexual relations with other men were also seen as dishonorable sexual conduct.

20. Arranged marriage affected sons as well as daughters and signified a general subordination of children to parents in the interest of forging honorable family connections (Castañeda 1993a; Gutiérrez 1993a). However, age disparities between brides and grooms at the time of marriage (on average, 18.4 years for women and 28.4 years for men) suggest that the practice was intended in part to safeguard the sexual virtue of adolescent girls (Garcia-Moro, Toja, and Walker 1997).

Chapter 4. From Casta to Californio, II

1. Haas 1995; Mason 1993:173; Monroy 1990b:136; Sánchez 1995:57.

2. Mason has identified rare exceptions: a select few Native Californians "who spoke Spanish, dressed and behaved as did the other non-Indian inhabitants were able to consider themselves [gente de razón]" (1998:61).

3. See Egan 1969; Mora 1949; Pitt 1971; and Sanchez 1929 for later works that have perpetuated Bancroft's rhetoric.

4. See Camarillo 1979; Chávez-García 2004; García 1975; Haas 1995; Hughes 1975; McWilliams 1949:88–94; Pitt 1971; and Sanchez 1984.

5. These recent works include Chávez-García 2004; Gutiérrez and Orsi 1998; Monroy 1990b, 1998; Sánchez 1995; and Thomas 1989. For historical and archaeological research focusing on Native American life in Mexican California, see Hurtado 1988; Jackson and Castillo 1995; Lightfoot 2005; Milliken 1995; and Silliman 2004a. For studies with a focus on gender, see Bouvier 1995, 2001; Castañeda 1988, 1990a, 1990b, 1992, 1993a, 1993b, 1993c, 1998; Chávez-García 2004; Hurtado 1999; and Lothrop 1994. These new "retellings" (Monroy 1998:177) of Californio history are accompanied by the published translations and new analyses of memoirs, correspondence, and other writings by the Californios themselves (Beebe and Senkewicz 2001, 2006; Mason 1998; Osio 1996; Sánchez 1995).

6. See also García 1975; Haas 1995; McWilliams 1949; Miranda 1988; Monroy 1990b; and Pitt 1971:6.

7. See Beebe and Senkewicz 1996, 2001; Haas 1995; Pitt 1971; Ríos-Bustamante 1993; and Sánchez 1995. Historians are divided about whether the political actions of Californios constituted an emerging nationalism. While this is perhaps the most pervasive interpretation (Haas 1995; Monroy 1990b; Sánchez 1995), others argue that the disputes between the Mexican Congress and the California territorial legislature were political differences among Mexicans about how Mexico should be governed (Beebe and Senkewicz 1996; Ríos-Bustamante 1993). These disputes were not unlike present-day debates about "states' rights" and federalism in the United States of America.

8. See Beebe and Senkewicz 2006; Bouvier 1995, 2001; Castañeda 1988, 1990a, 1990b, 1992, 1993a, 1993b, 1993c, 1998; Chávez-García 2004; Hurtado 1999; and Lothrop 1994.

9. Camarillo (1979) and Ríos-Bustamante (1993) assert that the association of Californio identity with "Spanish" ancestry was a myth perpetuated during the latter half of the nineteenth century by Anglo-Americans who wished to deny the important role played by Mexicans in the history of the western United States. By portraying Californios as Spanish, Anglo-Americans were able to posit continuity between themselves and their "Spanish" antecedents and portray Mexicans as recently arrived immigrants and "hyphenated Americans" in their own homeland.

10. Castañeda 1990b; Clark 1974; Gendzel 2001; Haas 1995; Hackel 1998; Sánchez 1995; and Weber 1979.

Chapter 5. From Artifacts to Ethnogenesis

1. For one of the earlier examples of attention to ambiguity, see Hodder 1976. My own approach to this concern has been most heavily informed by feminist engagement with science studies (Haraway 1988; Longino 1990; Schiebinger 2003) and archaeology (Conkey 2003; Conkey and Gero 1997; Wylie 1996a, 1996b, 1997, 2002).

2. Schiffer (1972) was among the first to highlight context as fundamental to archaeological epistemology; this concept was greatly expanded by Hodder (1982, 1985, 1987a, 1991). See also Conkey 1991; De Cunzo 1996; and Moore 1986.

3. See Lightfoot 1995; Lightfoot, Martinez, and Schiff 1998; Martinez 1998; Nassaney 1989; and Rothschild 2003 for other examples of diachronic comparative studies of ethnogenesis in colonial contexts.

4. Efforts to increase the visibility of the Spanish-colonial and Mexican history of the park are already underway, through interpretive programs and the development of permanent on-site exhibits of in situ archaeological remains (Presidio Archaeology Center 2004).

5. Some earlier predictive studies were developed from the 1920s to the 1940s with the specific goal of identifying the location of the historical Presidio's main quadrangle, but these were not oriented toward archaeological investigation (Daughters of the American Revolution 1928; Hendry and Bowman 1940; St. Croix 1939).

6. Presidio Trust and NPS archaeologists and historians coordinate historical preservation efforts through the N2 Process, a procedure that combines National Historic Preservation Act and National Environmental Policy Act reviews of proposed projects in the Presidio.

7. In 1997 and 1998, archaeologists from San Francisco State University con-

ducted additional geophysical surveys in regions of the main quadrangle and at El Polín Springs. These field exercises were organized primarily as an opportunity for student training.

8. See Lightfoot 1986, 1989; McManamon 1984; Nance and Ball 1986, 1989; and Shott 1986.

9. Household ceramics from the midden deposit consist almost entirely of wares and decorative types that were being produced before 1800. Only 6 of the 7,467 sherds recovered from the deposit (less than 0.1 percent) are ware-types that were clearly manufactured after 1800. The mean ceramic date for the deposit is 1777, only one year after the settlement was founded. This date seems unrealistically early, but it is another line of evidence supporting the interpretation that the deposit was formed primarily before 1800. Additionally, the glass bottles represented in the assemblage are also generally associated with eighteenth-century manufacture. Gunflints recovered from the deposit are primarily French honey-colored cherts, which were in greater widespread use in the eighteenth century. None of these chronological indicators are absolute, but they all point to 1776–1800 as a working chronological framework for the formation of the bulk of the deposit, with a small amount of materials continuing to be deposited between 1800 and ca. 1810. For interpretive purposes, this means that it is possible to view the contents of the midden as refuse generated primarily by the first generation of residents at El Presidio de San Francisco.

10. Laboratory methods used to process, inventory, catalog, analyze, and conserve materials recovered from the Building 13 midden deposit are described in detail in technical reports (Ramsay and Voss 2002; Voss, Ramsay, and Naruta 2000) and theses (Hirata 2001; Voss 2002). In brief, excavated soils were wet-screened through ⅛-inch mesh; the recovered materials were first broadly sorted and inventoried by material type and then cataloged before analysis. In addition, flotation samples were recovered from each excavated stratum of each unit. These were processed in the field in a barrel-style flotation chamber, with the light fraction drained through a tightly woven cloth to capture charred plant remains and a ¹⁄₃₂-inch mesh catchment basin for the heavy fraction. This provided a volume-controlled sample of the deposit's microconstituents.

Chapter 6. Sites of Identification

1. Historians have long argued that the east-west cordon—a strategy termed "as rational and geometrical as it was unrealistic" (Weber 1992:216)—was largely ineffective in containing indigenous resistance. Removing the presidios from close proximity to missions and pueblos exposed these civilian settlements to constant assault by raiding parties. In the 1780s, many of the measures stipulated in the 1772 Reglamento slowly unraveled under the leadership of Commander General Teodoro de Croix and Viceroy Bernardo de Gálvez. However,

the north-south cordon along the Pacific coast was comparatively more successful, and the spatial organization of colonial settlements in Alta California continued to follow the cordon strategy throughout the Spanish-colonial era.

2. Despite their coastal location, colonial communities in Alta California never developed a maritime culture or economy. Although each presidio had a landing for visiting ships, these facilities were not substantially developed into formal ports until the growth of the hide and tallow trade in the 1830s and 1840s. The colonial settlers did not construct ocean-going ships, nor did they harvest marine resources to any substantial extent. The terrestrial orientation of the Spanish-colonial settlements stands in sharp contrast to the colonial practices of British and Russian enterprises in the Pacific Northwest. For example, the Russian outpost of Colony Ross was entirely oriented toward sea mammal hunting and the fur trade, even to the point of developing an active shipyard.

3. Firsthand accounts of some of these tactical expeditions, and the violence intrinsic to them, can be found in the recently translated and published oral memoirs of José María Amador, who grew up at El Presidio de San Francisco and served as a soldier there from 1809 to 1827 (Mora-Torres 2005).

4. Brinkerhoff and Faulk 1965:49; Gerald 1968:14; Turpin and Eling 2004:100−101; Weber 1992:216−217; and Williams 2004.

5. Prior to the 1772 Reglamento, the architecture and layout of presidios varied widely. Some settlements were little more than nucleated clusters of residences and administration buildings; others contained small fortified compounds but left the rest of the settlement unguarded; and still others, especially those to the east, were constructed according to individual formal plans designed by military engineers. See Voss 2007 for a more detailed discussion of the architecture of pre-1772 presidios.

6. The master plan produced by Lafora has not been located in historical archives, but it is referenced in other historical documents, such as the *Real instrucción y plan para la construcción de los presidios* (Williams 2004:17). Williams notes that Commandant-Inspector Hugo Oconór's correspondence regarding the new presidio construction suggests that the plan called for the presidio quadrangles to be built 200 varas (524 feet) to a side and to be fully enclosed by a perimeter wall. The center of the presidio was to be an open plaza. The defense of the presidio quadrangle would be secured by guardhouses surrounding a single entrance to the quadrangle and by diamond-shaped bastions protruding from two opposing corners (Williams 2004:17). Gerald's plan (1968) of the archaeological remains of the Presidio of San Carlos is considered one of the best approximations of Lafora's plan.

7. This type of separate defensive wall is depicted in the 1776, 1795, and 1796 construction plans for El Presidio de San Francisco, but these plans were never realized. Historian Richard Whitehead states that presidio exterior walls were intended to create protected rear gardens behind the quadrangle build-

ings. If Native Californians attacked, they would first be exposed to fire from the top of the exterior wall and crossfire from the bastions; "if they were successful in climbing over the wall, they found themselves trapped in the back garden, exposed to fire from the rear windows and doors of the buildings" (Whitehead 1983:71).

8. In order to evaluate the possibility that this deposit could have formed from the mixing of a prehistoric deposit with later-period colonial materials, three obsidian projectile points from the deposit were submitted for XRF sourcing, hydration band analysis, and lithic reduction analysis (Hughes 2005; Origer 2005a, 2005b). The analyses found that all three specimens had been modified by intentional flaking and retouch two hundred to three hundred years ago, a range that certainly intersects with the Spanish-colonial occupation of El Presidio de San Francisco.

9. It is unusual that such a rich historical body of information regarding a colonial woman survives. However, Juana Briones was a prominent personality in 1840s San Francisco, and many people with whom she associated left written accounts of their interactions with her. Additionally, she was an astute businesswoman who engaged trusted advisors to transcribe her correspondence and legal documents. Jan Bowman was the first to compile a biographical account of Juana Briones's life (Bowman 1957); his files at the Bancroft Library also provide key sources and notes. Jeanne McDonnell has written the most recent, and comprehensive, account of Juana Briones's life (forthcoming). In addition, present-day descendants of the Briones have graciously shared their family histories with me.

10. In an experience common to most rancheros and rancheras, Juana Briones's land titles were challenged by newly arrived Anglo-American settlers during the 1850s and 1860s. She was unusually successful in defending her claims. The U.S. Land Commission approved her claim to Rancho La Purísima Concepción after hearing definitive testimony from her neighbors. Her title to property in Yerba Buena (San Francisco) was more difficult to retain; after twelve years of hearings, her case was eventually referred to the U.S. Supreme Court, which ruled in her favor.

11. Translated with assistance from Nicole Von Germeten.

Chapter 7. Structuring Structures

1. Vancouver's estimate of the quadrangle's size appears to be grossly inaccurate; he may have meant feet instead of yards, which would closely match the Sal plan dimensions.

2. See Ramsay and Voss 2002; Simpson-Smith and Edwards 2000; URS Greiner Woodward Clyde 1999; Voss and Benté 1996a; and Voss, Ramsay, and Naruta 2000.

3. For accounts of the Presidio quadrangle during the Mexican era, see Beechey 1941; Duhaut-Cilly 1929; Langellier and Rosen 1996:155–156; Robinson 1970; Vallejo 1878; Vischer 1878; and Zavalishin 1973.

4. These estimates are based on archaeologically known dimensions of the main quadrangle, along with some conservative assumptions about wall height and roof span. On average, the walls of the third quadrangle were 1.2 m thick; foundations extended to a depth of ca. 70 cm, tapering inward toward the base. Each wing had two parallel walls, those on the east and west wings measuring 163 m long and those on the north wing measuring 145 m. Wall height is estimated at a minimum 2.5 m, which is a conservative estimate in comparison with extant adobe buildings in Alta California. Roof span is presumed not only to cover the walls and the enclosed room but also to extend for a minimum of 1 vara on each side, as was customary to protect the mud brick walls from rain.

5. Ruiz and Sal provided estimates of materials and labor for eight tasks: master craftwork, quarrying and transporting stone for foundations, making adobe bricks, making floor tiles, making roof tiles, hauling rock for the manufacture of mortar and lime whitewash, hauling timber, and hauling barrels of water. Estimates of the number of workers required to manufacture adobe bricks are based on Ruiz's stipulation that 244,634 bricks were needed; he estimated that each worker could produce thirty per day, which over the course of a year would require a work gang of twenty-four laborers (Schuetz-Miller 1994:45). Ruiz and Sal did not include estimates of labor for obtaining mortar, whitewash, and timber; they simply noted that such materials had to be obtained from a great distance and that carts and mules were needed for transport. If they had identified the number of workers required for these tasks, no doubt the labor force estimate would have been much higher.

Chapter 8. Tradition and Taste

1. Sherd weights, sherd counts, and minimum vessel calculations are each influenced differently by the physical properties of each waretype and by taphonomic processes. When used in combination, the three measures indicate central trends in ceramic quantification.

2. A similar set of documents from El Presidio de Santa Bárbara (forty requisitions and twelve invoices) has been transcribed, translated, and published by a research team led by Giorgio Perissinotto (1998); these documents are generally consistent with those for El Presidio de San Francisco.

3. The term losa is translated by both Dado (2004) and Perissinotto (1998) as "earthen dinnerware," a term that implies use in food consumption; but losa has also been translated to refer to a more general category of household ceramics that includes cooking, storage, and personal use items (e.g., Katz 1977). This latter usage is supported by entries in requisitions and invoices in which

crates of *losa surtida* are described as including pots, skillets, water jugs, and chamber pots in addition to plates, bowls, and cups.

4. One unusual invoice for goods shipped from San Blas in 1796 included a special order of two crates of fine Chinese tableware; the entry lists particular forms such as serving plates of three sizes, salad bowls, fingerbowls, fish dishes, soup tureens with covers, and salt shakers, all in small quantities (two to six pieces each) along with seventeen dozen plates (Dado 2004:doc. 102).

5. Majolica has received the most descriptive and typological attention of any Spanish-colonial waretype in the Americas (e.g., Barnes and May 1972; Deagan 1987:53–96; Goggin 1968; Lister and Lister 1974; Marken 1994:214–239). For this analysis, I have relied primarily on the classification scheme articulated by May (1972), which focuses specifically on the majolicas commonly found at Alta California colonial sites.

6. The latter combination has been sometimes designated galera polychrome or occasionally, Tlaquepaque Polychrome, after a Jalisco town of the same name where these wares are still produced today (Gerald 1968:53).

7. In archaeological studies in the American Southeast, this ware has been included in ceramic categories referred to as Guadalajara Polychrome, Aztec IV Polychrome, and *bucaro* ware (Deagan 1987:44–46).

8. The glaze and paste attributes do not conform to black-glazed ceramic types found at other Spanish-colonial settlements in the Interior Provinces. The sherds do not match Barnes's description of Mexican Black Glazed Ware, which has a reddish-brown or yellowish-red paste (Barnes 1980:99); nor do they fit Deagan's description of Black Lead-Glazed Coarse Earthenware, which has a cream-colored to terra cotta–colored paste (Deagan 1987:52). The sherds also differ from the British-produced Jackfield Ware, which has a red paste, and from Basaltware, which has a very dark gray or black paste (Hughes and Hughes 1968).

9. In Alta California, locally produced earthenwares are referred to by a vague and diverse nomenclature, including brownwares, neophyte wares, mission wares, Tizon brown wares, Colono-Indian wares, and Hispanic unglazed wares. I prefer the more neutral description "locally produced earthenwares," because it does not imply the ethnicity or other social identities of the potters.

10. See, for example, Avery 1995; Barbolla 1992; Barnes 1984; Bense 2003; Deagan 1983b; and Di Peso 1953.

11. Paste color is influenced by many factors, including the source of the clay and the firing conditions (temperature, duration, and oxygen availability) (Rice 1987). For this study, sherd color was measured using the Munsell color system of hue, value, and chroma, with observations taken at the interior surface, interior margin, core, exterior margin, and exterior surface of each sherd or minimum vessel grouping (Hirata 2001; Voss 2002).

12. Manufacture technique could not be determined for five of the sixty-three minimum vessel groupings.

Chapter 9. Consuming Practices

1. E.g., Deetz 1963; Draper 1992; Greenwood 1989:455; Gust 1982:138; and Wallace, Desautels, and Kritwarm 1991.

2. Initially, I wondered whether the presence of fish in the Building 13 midden might be connected to Catholic restrictions on consumption of terrestrial meat and dairy during portions of Lent and Holy Week and on several other designated religious observances. However, all Presidio troops in the Interior Provinces, including Alta California, were exempt from these restrictions according to the "integral code." The integral code applied to all military personnel, regardless of rank, who were on active campaign or living under frontier conditions. The integral code recognized that normal fasting requirements would be too burdensome for these soldiers, officers, and their families "because of their low pay and because of the circumstances and distance of their posts and scarcity of food supplies which force them to choose for their necessary nutrition that which they encounter or are able to purchase at the lowest price" (Dobyns 1976:122–123).

3. Only two other objects related to food preparation were recovered: a forged, slightly curved ferrous metal fragment with a finished edge that may have been a fragment of an iron pot or skillet; and a fragment of a vesicular basalt *mano* typical of those mass-manufactured in Mexico for use in grinding grain.

4. Although rim diameters may underrepresent the maximum diameter of constricted mouth vessels, cooking vessels found at the Presidio are generally either open or only slightly constricted, and rim diameter is not an inappropriate proxy for overall volume.

5. The form of this vessel is similar to the "bean pots" described by Carrillo (1997) in his study of Hispanic pottery in New Mexico, but the specimens recovered from the Presidio lack handles and have a more sharply defined inflection point between the vessel orifice and the flared collar.

Chapter 10. Fashioning the Colonial Subject

The title of this chapter was inspired by Jean Comaroff's landmark 1996 article, "The Empire's Old Clothes: Fashioning the Colonial Subject."

1. Dress is a category that encompasses clothes, hair styles, skin modifications (tattoos, scarification, tanning, and so on), mannerisms, and postures as well as items that are attached to, suspended from, or wrapped around the body, such as clothes (Turner 1980).

2. See Fisher and Loren 2003; Joyce 2005; Meskell 1996; and Turner 1980, 1995.

3. Prosthesis provides a metaphor for understanding how certain material

objects and media become incorporated into or act as extensions of the body (Attfield 2000:245). The interface between the physiological body and its pros-thetics is inherently unstable, leading to what Haraway has termed a "leaky dis-tinction" between the organism and technology (1997:152). Proprioception is one of the sensory paths through which objects that are physically distinct from the physiological body are experientially incorporated into the lived body.

4. Boyer 1997; Carrera 2003; Dean 1999; Fisher 1992; Jackson 1999; Jamieson 2004, 2005; Katzew 2004; Loren 1999, 2000, 2001a, 2001b; and Scaramelli and Scaramelli 2005.

5. Royal pragmatics on matters of dress were issued in 1521, 1571, 1684, 1691, 1716, 1767, 1776, and 1782 (Carrera 2003:118–119; Earle 2003; Fisher 1992:62–71; Katzew 2004:68).

6. Cope 1994; Earle 2003; Fisher 1992:71–72; Jackson 1999:4; Jamieson 2004; Katzew 2004:68; Loren 1999; Love 1970; and Mörner 1967.

7. Carrera 2003:119; Cope 1994; Fisher 1992:40; Loren 1999; Love 1970; and Milton and Vinson 2002.

8. Since Saíz (1989) published the first catalog of casta paintings, the genre has received considerable attention from scholars interested in the relationship between race and material culture in Bourbon New Spain. Major studies include Carrera 2003; Deans-Smith 2005; Fisher 1992; Katzew 2004; and Loren 1999.

9. Archer 1977; Brinkerhoff and Faulk 1965; Faulk 1971; and Moorhead 1969, 1975.

10. Heizer 1978:493–494; Jackson and Castillo 1995:11; Kroeber 1925:467; Langellier and Rosen 1996:15; La Pérouse 1989:92; Milliken 1995:18–19; and Palóu 1926:121.

11. Hurtado 1999:10; Jackson and Castillo 1995:50; La Pérouse 1989:92; Mackey and Sooy 1932:9–10; and Milliken 1995:87.

12. Given differences in depositional processes, deposit attributions, and ex-cavation methods, the comparison of artifacts recovered from these two as-semblages proceeds best not as a quantitative analysis but rather as a holistic consideration of qualitative similarities and differences.

13. Flat-drilled wedge shank buttons are one type of eighteenth-century button that is clearly identifiable as Spanish, since they were not used by British or French troops. In the eastern regions of New Spain, these buttons are rare after 1760, with attached brass or copper wire eyes becoming more common (Deagan 2002:168). The single wire eye loop button compares favorably to Olsen's Type G, which dates to 1785–1800 (Olsen 1963), and also to Powell's Type K, which is also attributed to post-1780 (Deagan 2002:168).

14. Phoenix buttons are disk brass buttons that were minted by Bushby of London for Haitian troop uniforms during the reign of Christophe I (1811–1820). When Christophe I committed suicide in 1820, the buttons became sur-

plus and were traded to Hawaii and the North American west coast. Following the notation system outlined by Sprague (1998), this button can be classified as Type I159.

15. Beads were analyzed and classified following procedures established and used by Kidd and Kidd (1970), Karklins and Sprague (see Karklins 1982; Karklins and Sprague 1972; Sprague 1985), and Ross (1997).

Conclusion

1. Deagan 1983a, 1990a, 1990b, 1996, 1998, 2003; Ewen 2000; Loucks 1993; McEwan 1991a, 1991b, 1995; and Vernon and Cordell 1993.

2. El Presidio de San Francisco also stands in contrast to many other non-Spanish colonial settlements in which cultural mixing, rather than cultural separation, was the general pattern. See, for example, studies of Russian California (Lightfoot, Martinez, and Schiff 1998; Martinez 1994, 1998), British Fort Michilimackinac (Scott 1991), and South Africa (Lucas 2006).

3. Los Californianos, a nonprofit heritage association to which many interviewees belong, is a pedigreed organization, in that regular membership is available only to those who can demonstrate lineal descent "of an Hispanic person or Hispanic persons who arrived in Alta California prior to the Treaty of Guadalupe Hidalgo, February 2, 1848" (Los Californianos 2004). Ancestral lineage charts must be reviewed and approved by the organization's Genealogical Committee.

REFERENCES

Albers, P. C. 1996. "Changing Patterns of Ethnicity in the Northeastern Plains." In *History, Power, and Identity: Ethnogenesis in the Americas, 1492–1992*, ed. J. D. Hill, 90–118. Iowa City: University of Iowa Press.

Alexander, M. J., and C. T. Mohanty, eds. 1997. *Feminist Genealogies, Colonial Legacies, Democratic Futures*. New York: Routledge.

Allen, R. 1998. *Native Americans at Mission Santa Cruz, 1791–1834: Interpreting the Archaeological Record*. Perspectives in California Archaeology 5. Institute of Archaeology, University of California, Los Angeles.

Alley, P., L. R. Barker, G. Chappell, C. Feierabend, J. P. Langellier, D. Quitevis, and S. A. Dean. 1993. *Presidio of San Francisco National Register of Historic Places Registration Forms*. San Francisco: Golden Gate National Recreation Area, National Park Service.

Althouse, A. 2005. "Contested Mestizos, Alleged Mulattos: Racial Identity and Caste Hierarchy in Eighteenth-Century Pátzcuaro, Mexico." *The Americas* 62 (2): 151–175.

American Anthropological Association. 1998. "Statement on 'Race.'" Available online at www.aaanet.org/stmts/racepp.htm (accessed June 27, 2006).

American Association of Physical Anthropologists. 1996. "Statement on Biological Aspects of Race." *American Journal of Physical Anthropology* 101:569–570.

Americans for Peace Now. 2005. "Yossi Alpher's [sic] Analyses an Israeli Demographic Study of Palestinian Population." Arabic Media Internet Network.

Available online at www.peacenow.org/about/press.asp?cid=210 (accessed June 27, 2006).

Anderson, B. 1993. *Imagined Communities: Reflections on the Origin and Spread of Nationalism*. New York: Verso.

Anderson, G. C. 1999. *The Indian Southwest, 1580–1830: Ethnogenesis and Reinvention*. Norman: University of Oklahoma Press.

Anderson, M. K. 2005. *Tending the Wild: Native American Knowledge and Management of California's Natural Resources*. Berkeley: University of California Press.

Andrén, A. 1998. *Between Artifacts and Texts: Historical Archaeology in Global Perspective*. Trans. A. Crozier. New York: Plenum Press.

Anzaldúa, G. 1987. *Borderlands/La Frontera: The New Mestiza*. San Francisco: Spinsters/Aunt Lute.

Appadurai, A. 1986. "Introduction: Commodities and the Politics of Value." In *The Social Life of Things: Commodities in Cultural Perspective*, ed. A. Appadurai, 3–63. Cambridge: Cambridge University Press.

Archer, C. I. 1977. *The Army in Bourbon Mexico, 1760–1810*. Albuquerque: University of New Mexico Press.

Argüello, L. 1810. Filiación de Apolinario Miranda, July 1, 1810, M. G. Vallejo Documentos para la Historia de California. BANC MSS C-B 2, XV:47. Bancroft Library, University of California, Berkeley.

Attfield, J. 2000. *Wild Things: The Material Culture of Everyday Life*. Oxford: Berg Press.

Avery, G. 1995. "More Friend than Foe: Eighteenth Century Spanish, French, and Caddoan Interaction at Los Adaes, a Capital of Texas Located in Northwestern Louisiana." *Louisiana Archaeology* 22:163–193.

Ayubi, Y. 1991. "U.S. Hispanic Ethnogenesis and Sociopolitical Mobilization." PhD diss., Department of Urban Social Institutions, University of Wisconsin, Milwaukee.

Balls, E. K. 1962. *Early Uses of California Plants*. Berkeley: University of California Press.

Bancroft, H. H. 1886a. *History of California, Vol. 1: 1542–1800*. Vol. 18 of *The Works of Hubert Howe Bancroft*. San Francisco: History Company.

———. 1886b. *History of California, Vol. 2: 1801–1824*. Vol. 19 of *The Works of Hubert Howe Bancroft*. San Francisco: History Company.

———. 1886c. *History of California, Vol. 3: 1825–1840*. Vol. 20 of *The Works of Hubert Howe Bancroft*. San Francisco: History Company.

———. 1888. *California Pastoral*. Vol. 24 of *The Works of Hubert Howe Bancroft*. San Francisco: History Company.

Barbolla, D. E. 1992. "Alta California Troops: Acculturation and Material Wealth in a Presidio and Mission Context, 1769–1810." PhD diss., Department of Anthropology, University of California, Riverside.

Barker, L. R. 1992. "Presidio of San Francisco National Historic Landmark District Predicted Archaeological Features and Historic Forest Plantation [map]." San Francisco: National Park Service, Western Regional Office.

———. 2007. "Text-Based Reality: Material Culture at El Presidio de San Francisco." Paper presented at the annual meeting of the California Mission Studies Association, San Francisco, Calif.

Barker, L. R., R. Allen, and J. G. Costello. 1995. "The Archaeology of Spanish and Mexican Alta California." In *The Archaeology of Spanish and Mexican Colonialism in the American Southwest*, ed. J. E. Ayres, 3–51, vol. 3 of *Guides to the Archaeological Literature of the Immigrant Experience in America*, R. L. Michael, general editor. Ann Arbor: Society for Historical Archaeology.

Barker, L. R., C. Whatford, and V. Benté. 1997. "Unraveling the Archeological Structure of the Presidio of San Francisco." Paper presented at the thirty-first annual meeting of the Society for California Archaeology, Rohnert Park, Calif.

Barnaal, H. 2006. "Archaeological Assessment 2006 Elevation Change Model [map]." Presidio Archaeology Center, San Francisco, Presidio Trust and National Park Service.

Barnes, M. R. 1972. "Majolica of the Santa Cruz Valley, Arizona." In *Mexican Majolica in Northern New Spain*, ed. M. R. Barnes and R. V. May, 1–24. Occasional Paper no. 2. Costa Mesa, Calif.: Pacific Coast Archaeological Society.

———. 1980. "Mexican Lead-Glazed Earthenwares." In *Spanish Colonial Frontier Research*, ed. H. F. Dobyns, 92–110. Spanish Borderlands Research no. 1. Albuquerque: Center for Anthropological Studies.

———. 1983. "Tucson: Development of a Community." PhD diss., Catholic University of America.

———. 1984. "Hispanic Period Archaeology in the Tucson Basin: An Overview." *The Kiva* 49 (3–4): 213–223.

Barnes, M. R., and R. V. May, eds. 1972. *Mexican Majolica in Northern New Spain*. Occasional Paper no. 2. Costa Mesa, Calif.: Pacific Coast Archaeological Society.

Barth, F., ed. 1969. *Ethnic Groups and Boundaries: The Social Organization of Cultural Difference*. London: Allen and Unwin.

———. 1994. "Enduring and Emerging Issues in the Analysis of Ethnicity." In *The Anthropology of Ethnicity: Beyond "Ethnic Groups and Boundaries,"* ed. H. Vermeulen and C. Govers, 11–32. Amsterdam: Het Spinhuis.

Bateman, R. B. 1992. "Naming Patterns in Black Seminole Ethnogenesis." *Ethnohistory* 49 (2): 227–257.

Bean, L. J. 1976. "Social Organization in Native California." In *Native Califor-*

nians: *A Theoretical Perspective*, ed. L. J. Bean and T. C. Blackburn, 99–124. Ramona, Calif.: Ballena Press.

———. 1994. *The Ohlone Past and Present: Native Americans of the San Francisco Bay Region*. Menlo Park, Calif.: Ballena Press.

Beebe, R. M., and R. M. Senkewicz. 1996. Introduction to *The History of Alta California: A Memoir of Mexican California*, by Antonio María Osio, trans. R. M. Beebe and R. M. Senkewicz, 5–26. Madison: University of Wisconsin Press.

———, eds. 2001. *Lands of Promise and Despair: Chronicles of Early California, 1535–1846*. Santa Clara and Berkeley: Santa Clara University and Heyday Books.

———, eds. 2006. *Testimonios: Early California through the Eyes of Women, 1815–1848*. Berkeley: Heyday Books.

Beechey, F. W. 1941. *An Account of a Visit to California, 1826–1827, Reprinted from a Narrative of a Voyage to the Pacific and the Bering Strait*. San Francisco: Grabhorn Press.

Behar, R. 1993. *Translated Woman*. Boston: Beacon Press.

Behrensmeyer, A. K., K. Gordon, and G. T. Yanagi. 1986. "Trampling as a Cause of Bone Surface Damage and Pseudo-Cutmarks." *Nature* 319:768–771.

Beilharz, E. A. 1971. *Felipe de Neve: First Governor of California*. San Francisco: California Historical Society.

Bell, A. 2005. "White Ethnogenesis and Gradual Capitalism: Perspectives from Colonial Archaeological Sites in the Chesapeake." *American Anthropologist* 107 (3): 446–460.

Bellwood, P. 2004. "Cultural Evolution: Phylogeny versus Reticulation." In *International Encyclopedia of the Social and Behavioral Sciences*, ed. N. J. Smelser and P. B. Baltes, 3052–3057. Exeter, U.K.: Elsevier/Pergemon. Online edition, www.sciencedirect.com/science/referenceworks/0080430767 (accessed October 19, 2005).

Bense, J. A. 2003. *Presidio Santa María de Galve: A Struggle for Survival in Colonial Spanish Pensacola*. Gainesville: University Press of Florida.

———, ed. 2004. "Presidios of the Northern American Spanish Borderlands." Thematic issue, *Historical Archaeology* 38 (3).

Bentley, G. C. 1987. "Ethnicity and Practice." *Comparative Studies in Society and History* 29 (1): 24–55.

Bhabha, H. K. 1990. "DissemiNation: Time, Narrative, and the Margins of the Modern Nation." In *Nation and Narration*, ed. H. K. Bhabha, 291–322. London: Routledge.

———. 2004. *The Location of Culture*. London: Routledge.

Bickel, P. M. 1976. "Toward a Prehistory of the San Francisco Bay Area: The Archaeology of Sites Ala-328, Ala-13, and Ala-12." PhD diss., Department of Anthropology, Harvard University.

Bilby, K. 1996. "Ethnogenesis in the Guianas and Jamaica: Two Maroon Cases." In *History, Power, and Identity: Ethnogenesis in the Americas, 1492–1992*, ed. J. D. Hill, 119–141. Iowa City: University of Iowa Press.

Blackburn, T. C., and K. Anderson, eds. 1993. *Before the Wilderness: Environmental Management by Native Californians*. Menlo Park, Calif.: Ballena Press.

Bland, L., and L. Doan, eds. 1998a. *Sexology in Culture: Labeling Bodies and Desires*. Chicago: University of Chicago Press.

———, eds. 1998b. *Sexology Uncensored: The Documents of Sexual Science*. Chicago: University of Chicago Press.

Blind, E. B. 2005. "Officers' Club Structural History." Manuscript on file at Presidio Archaeology Center, Presidio Trust, Presidio of San Francisco.

Blind, E. B., and B. Blakely. 1999a. *Early Drawings and Photographs of the Spanish and American Presidio*. Compilation of archival images, report on file at Presidio Archaeology Center, Presidio Trust, Presidio of San Francisco.

———. 1999b. *Historical Context Maps for Funston Avenue*. Compilation of archival images, report on file at Presidio Archaeology Center, Presidio Trust, Presidio of San Francisco.

Blind, E. B., B. L. Voss, S. K. Osborn, and L. R. Barker. 2004. "El Presidio de San Francisco: At the Edge of Empire." *Historical Archaeology* 38 (3): 135–149.

Blind, H., and K. Bartoy. 2006. *Archaeological Investigations of the Mesa Room, Building 50 of the Officers' Club, El Presidio de San Francisco, San Francisco, California*. Report submitted by Pacific Legacy, Berkeley, to Presidio Trust, Presidio of San Francisco.

Bourdieu, P. 1977. *Outline of a Theory of Practice*. Trans. R. Nice. Cambridge: Cambridge University Press.

———. 1980. *The Logic of Practice*. Trans. R. Nice. Stanford, Calif.: Stanford University Press.

———. 1984. *Distinction: A Social Critique of the Judgment of Taste*. Trans. R. Nice. Cambridge, Mass.: Harvard University Press.

Bouvier, V. M. 1995. "Women, Conquest, and the Production of History: Hispanic California, 1542–1840." PhD diss., Department of History, University of California, Berkeley.

———. 2001. *Women and the Conquest of California, 1542–1840: Codes of Silence*. Tucson: University of Arizona Press.

Bowman, J. N. 1957. "Juana Briones de Miranda." *Historical Society of Southern California Quarterly* 39 (3): 227–241.

Boyer, R. 1997. "Negotiating Calidad: The Everyday Struggle for Status in Mexico." *Historical Archaeology* 31 (1): 64–72.

Breen, M. S., and W. J. Blumenfeld, comps., with S. Baer, R. A. Brookey, L. Hall,

V. Kirby, D. H. Miller, R. Shail, and N. Wilson. 2001. "'There Is a Person Here': An Interview with Judith Butler." *International Journal of Sexuality and Gender Studies* 6 (1/2): 7–23.

Brillat-Savarin, J. A. 1999. *The Physiology of Taste, or, Meditations on Transcendental Gastronomy*. Trans. M. F. K. Fisher. New York: Counterpoint Press.

Brinkerhoff, S. B., and O. B. Faulk. 1965. *Lancers for the King: A Study of the Frontier Military System of Northern New Spain, with a Translation of the Royal Regulations of 1772*. Phoenix: Arizona Historical Foundation.

Briones, J. 1844. Juana Briones to Señor don Francisco García y Moreno, Most Honorable Bishop of the Californias, July 10, 1844. Archives of the Archdiocese of Los Angeles, Mission Hills, Calif.

Brooks, J. F. 2002. *Captives and Cousins: Slavery, Kinship, and Community in the Southwest Borderlands*. Chapel Hill: University of North Carolina Press.

Brown, J. S. H. 1993. "Métis, Halfbreeds, and Other Real People: Challenging Cultures and Categories." *History Teacher* 27 (1): 19–26.

Brumfiel, E. M. 1991. "Weaving and Cooking: Women's Production in Aztec Mexico." In *Engendering Archaeology: Women and Prehistory*, ed. J. M. Gero and M. W. Conkey, 224–254. Cambridge, Mass.: Basil Blackwell.

Buchli, V. 2000. *An Archaeology of Socialism*. Oxford: Berg Press.

Burch, E. S., Jr., E. Jones, H. P. Loon, and L. Kaplan. 1999. "The Ethnogenesis of the Kuuvaum Kangiagmiut." *Ethnohistory* 46 (2): 291–327.

Butler, J. 1990. *Gender Trouble: Feminism and the Subversion of Identity*. New York: Routledge.

———. 1993a. *Bodies That Matter: On the Discursive Limits of "Sex."* New York: Routledge.

———. 1993b. "Imitation and Gender Insubordination." In *The Lesbian and Gay Studies Reader*, ed. H. Abelove, M. A. Barale, and D. Halpern, 307–320. New York: Routledge.

———. 1994. "Against Proper Objects." *differences* 6 (2–3): 1–26.

———. 1999. *Gender Trouble: Feminism and the Subversion of Identity*. Rev. 10th anniversary ed. New York: Routledge.

———. 2004. *Undoing Gender*. New York: Routledge.

Calhoun, C. 1993. "Nationalism and Ethnicity." *Annual Review of Sociology* 19: 211–39.

Camarillo, A. 1979. *Chicanos in a Changing Society*. Cambridge, Mass.: Harvard University Press.

Campbell, L. G. 1972. "The First Californians: Presidial Society in Spanish California, 1769–1822." *Journal of the West* 11 (4): 582–595.

————. 1977. "The Spanish Presidio in Alta California during the Mission Period, 1769–1784." *Journal of the West* 16 (4): 63–77.

Campisi, J., and W. A. Starna. 2004. "Another View on 'Ethnogenesis of the New Houma Indians.'" *Ethnohistory* 51 (4): 779–791.

Carby, H. V. 1987. *Reconstructing Womanhood: The Emergence of the Afro-American Woman Novelist.* Oxford: Oxford University Press.

Carrera, M. M. 2003. *Imagining Identity in New Spain: Race, Lineage, and the Colonial Body in Portraiture and Casta Paintings.* Austin: University of Texas Press.

Carrillo, C. M. 1997. *Hispanic New Mexican Pottery: Evidence of Craft Specialization, 1790–1890.* Albuquerque: LPD Press.

Casella, E. C., and C. Fowler. 2005. "Beyond Identification: An Introduction." In *The Archaeology of Plural and Changing Identities: Beyond Identification,* ed. E. C. Casella and C. Fowler, 1–8. New York: Kulwer Academic/Plenum Publishers.

Castañeda, A. I. 1988. "Comparative Frontiers: The Migration of Women to Alta California and New Zealand." In *Western Women: Their Land, Their Lives,* ed. L. Schliessel, V. Ruiz, and J. Monk, 283–300. Albuquerque: University of New Mexico Press.

————. 1990a. "Gender, Race, and Culture: Spanish-Mexican Women in the Historiography of Frontier California." *Frontiers* 11 (1): 8–20.

————. 1990b. "The Political Economy of Nineteenth Century Stereotypes of Californianas." In *Between Borders: Essays on Mexicana/Chicana History,* ed. A. R. Del Castillo, 213–236. Encino, Calif.: Floricanto Press.

————. 1992. "Presidarias y Pobladoras: The Journey North and Life in Frontier California." Renato Rosaldo Lecture Series Monograph 8:25–54. Mexican American Studies and Research Center, University of Arizona, Tucson.

————. 1993a. "Marriage: The Spanish Borderlands." In *Encyclopedia of the North American Colonies,* ed. J. E. Cook, 2:727–738. New York: Maxwell Macmillan International.

————. 1993b. "The Political Economy of Nineteenth Century Stereotypes of Californianas." In *Region of La Raza: Changing Interpretations of Mexican American Regional History and Culture,* ed. A. Ríos-Bustamante, 189–211. Encino, Calif.: Floricanto Press.

————. 1993c. "Sexual Violence in the Politics and Policies of Conquest: Amerindian Women and the Spanish Conquest of Alta California." In *Building with Our Hands: New Directions in Chicana Studies,* ed. A. de la Torre and B. M. Pesquera, 15–33. Berkeley: University of California Press.

————. 1998. "Engendering the History of Alta California, 1769–1848." In *Contested Eden: California before the Gold Rush,* ed. R. A. Gutiérrez and R. J. Orsi, 230–259. Berkeley: University of California Press.

Castillo, E. D. 1989. "The Native Response to the Colonization of Alta California." In *Columbian Consequences*, vol. 1, *Archaeological and Historical Perspectives on the Spanish-Colonial Borderlands West*, ed. D. H. Thomas, 377–393. Washington, D.C.: Smithsonian Institution Press.

————, ed. 1991. *Native American Perspectives on the Hispanic Colonization of Alta California*. New York: Garland.

————. 1994a. "Gender Status Decline, Resistance, and Accommodation among Female Neophytes in the Missions of California: A San Gabriel Case Study." *American Indian Culture and Research Journal* 18 (1): 67–93.

————. 1994b. "The Language of Race Hatred." In *The Ohlone Past and Present: Native Americans of the San Francisco Bay Region*, ed. L. J. Bean, 271–295. Menlo Park, Calif.: Ballena Press.

Caywood, L. R. 1950. "Hispanic Pottery as a Guide in Historical Studies." In *For the Dean: Essays in Anthropology in Honor of Byron Cummings on His Eighty-Ninth Birthday, September 20, 1950*, ed. E. K. Read and D. S. King, 77–98. Tucson and Santa Fe: Hohokam Museums Association and Southwestern Monuments Association.

Chace, P. G. 1969. "The Archaeology of 'Cienaga,' the Oldest Historic Structure on the Irvine Ranch." *Pacific Coast Archaeological Society Quarterly* 5 (3): 39–55.

Chance, J. K. 1979. "On the Mexican Mestizo." *Latin America Research Review* 14 (3): 153–168.

Chapman, C. E. 1916. *The Founding of Spanish California: The Northwest Expansion of New Spain, 1687–1783*. New York: Macmillan.

Chappell, G., ed. 1976. *The Presidio of San Francisco, 1776—1976: A Collection of Historical Source Materials*. San Francisco: National Park Service, Western Regional Office.

Charlton, T. H., and R. Katz. 1979. "Tonalá Bruñida Ware: Past and Present." *Archaeology* 32 (January-February): 44–53.

Chartkoff, J. L., and K. K. Chartkoff. 1984. *The Archaeology of California*. Stanford, Calif.: Stanford University Press.

Chatan, R. 2003. "The Governor's *vale levu*: Architecture and Hybridity at Nasova House, Levuka, Fiji Islands." *International Journal of Historical Archaeology* 7 (4): 267–292.

Chávez-García, M. 2004. *Negotiating Conquest: Gender and Power in California, 1770s to 1880s*. Tucson: University of Arizona Press.

Childe, V. G. 1926. *The Aryans: A Study of Indo-European Origins*. London: Kegan Paul.

Clark, H. 1974. "Their Pride, Their Manners, and Their Voices: Sources of the Traditional Portrait of the Early Californians." *California Historical Quarterly* 53:71–82.

Clark, M. R. 2001. *Crissy Field Restoration Project Final Report of Archaeological Investigations at the Crissy Field Prehistoric Site, CA-SFR-129, Presidio of San Francisco, Golden Gate National Recreation Area.* Submitted by Holman and Associates, San Francisco, to Division of Resource Management and Planning, Golden Gate National Recreation Area, National Park Service.

Clevenger, L. N. 2006. "Deconstructing the Presidio Officers' Club." Paper presented at the annual meeting of the Society for Historical Archaeology, Sacramento, Calif.

Cohen, A., ed. 1974. *Urban Ethnicity.* London: Tavistock.

Cohen, R. 1978. "Ethnicity: Problem and Focus in Anthropology." *Annual Review of Anthropology* 7:379–403.

Cohen-Williams, A. G., and J. S. Williams. 2001. "Tried and Tested! Medical Care and Malpractice in the Healing Arts among the Settlers of Monterey: 1770–1835." *California Mission Studies Association Newsletter* 18 (1): 3–11.

Cohn, B. S. 1996. *Colonialism and Its Forms of Knowledge.* Princeton, N.J.: Princeton University Press.

Collins, P. H. 2000. *Black Feminist Thought.* Rev. 10th anniversary ed. New York: Routledge.

Comaroff, J. 1996. "The Empire's Old Clothes: Fashioning the Colonial Subject." In *Cross-Cultural Consumption,* ed. D. Howes, 19–38. London: Routledge.

Conkey, M. W. 1991. "Contexts of Action, Contexts for Power: Material Culture and Gender in the Magdalenian." In *Engendering Archaeology: Women and Prehistory,* ed. J. M. Gero and M. W. Conkey, 57–92. Cambridge, Mass.: Basil Blackwell.

———. 2003. "Has Feminism Changed Archaeology?" *Signs: Journal of Women in Culture and Society* 28 (3): 867–880.

Conkey, M. W., and J. M. Gero. 1997. "From Programme to Practice: Gender and Feminism in Archaeology." *Annual Review of Anthropology* 26:411–437.

Cook, S. F. 1943. *The Conflict between the California Indian and White Civilization.* Berkeley: University of California Press.

———. 1976. *The Population of the California Indians, 1769–1970.* Berkeley: University of California Press.

Cook, S. F., and W. Borah. 1979. *Essays in Population History.* Vol. 3, *Mexico and California.* Berkeley: University of California Press.

Cope, R. D. 1994. *The Limits of Racial Domination: Plebeian Society in Colonial Mexico City, 1660–1720.* Madison: University of Wisconsin Press.

Cordell, L. S., and V. J. Yannie. 1991. "Ethnicity, Ethnogenesis, and the Individual: A Processual Approach toward Dialogue." In *Processual and Postprocessual Archaeologies: Multiple Ways of Knowing the Past,* ed. R. W. Preucel, 96–107.

Occasional Paper no. 10. Center for Archaeological Investigations, Southern Illinois University, Carbondale.

Costanso, M. 1992. *The Discovery of San Francisco Bay: The Portolá Expedition of 1769–1770* [Diario del viage de tierra hecho al norte de la California]. Ed. and trans. Peter Browning. Lafayette, Calif.: Great West Books.

Costello, J. G. 1989a. *Santa Ines Mission Excavations: 1986–1988*. California Historical Archaeology no. 1. Salinas, Calif.: Coyote Press.

———. 1989b. "Variability among the Alta California Missions: The Economics of Agricultural Production." In *Columbian Consequences*, vol. 1, *Archaeological and Historical Perspectives on the Spanish Borderlands West*, ed. D. H. Thomas, 435–449. Washington, D.C.: Smithsonian Institution Press.

Costello, J. G., and D. Hornbeck. 1989. "Alta California: An Overview." In *Columbian Consequences*, vol. 1, *Archaeological and Historical Perspectives of the Spanish Borderlands West*, ed. D. H. Thomas, 303–331. Washington, D.C.: Smithsonian Institution Press.

Croix, T. de. 1941. *Teodoro de Croix and the Northern Frontier of New Spain, 1776–1783, from the Original Document in the Archives of the Indies, Seville.* Trans. and ed. A. B. Thomas. Norman: University of Oklahoma Press.

Crosby, A., S. K. Osborn, V. Benté, L. Barker, M. Wilkinson, and E. B. Blind. 2004. "Preliminary Condition Assessment, Bldg 50, Presidio of San Francisco, California." *Society for California Archaeology Newsletter* 38 (1):25–28.

Crosby, A. W. 1972. *The Columbian Exchange, Biological and Cultural Consequences of 1492.* Westport, Conn.: Greenwood Press.

Cross, G. M., and R. L. Burk. 1995. *Report on Geophysical Investigation of the Spanish Colonial Presidio de San Francisco.* Submitted by Woodward-Clyde Consultants, Oakland, to U.S. Army Corps of Engineers, Sacramento District.

Cross, G. M., and B. L. Voss. 1996. "Geophysical Remote Sensing of Spanish-Colonial Archaeological Remains: Presidio de San Francisco." *Proceedings of the Society for California Archaeology* 9:330–336.

Crown, P. L. 2000. "Women's Role in Changing Cuisine." In *Women and Men in the Prehispanic Southwest: Labor, Power, and Prestige*, ed. P. L. Crown, 221–266. Santa Fe: School of American Research Press.

Cutter, D. C. 1990. *California in 1792: A Spanish Naval Visit.* Norman: University of Oklahoma Press.

Dado, V. 2003. *El Presidio de San Francisco: Spanish Colonial Documentation Translation Project.* Report on file at Presidio Archaeology Center, Presidio of San Francisco. Presidio Trust and National Park Service, Golden Gate National Recreation Area.

———. 2004. *El Presidio de San Francisco: Spanish Colonial Documentation Translation*

Project. Report on file at Presidio Archaeology Center, Presidio of San Francisco. Presidio Trust and National Park Service, Golden Gate National Recreation Area.

———. 2006. "From Urban Manila to Frontier California: Asian Goods and California Presidios." *Mains'l Haul: A Journal of Pacific Maritime History* 41/42 (Fall/Winter): 48–53.

Dames and Moore. 1995. *Report: Geotechnical Investigation, Preliminary Design Services for Rehabilitating Funston Avenue Houses, National Park Service Task Order No. 34, Presidio of San Francisco.* Dames and Moore, Architectural Resources Group, San Francisco.

Dartt-Newton, D., and J. M. Erlandson. 2006. "Little Choice for the Chumash: Colonialism, Cattle, and Coercion in Mission Period California." *American Indian Quarterly* 30 (3–4): 416–430.

Daughters of the American Revolution. 1928. Commemorative plaques erected to mark the northwest and northeast corners of the historical Presidio de San Francisco. Located in the Main Post region of the Presidio of San Francisco.

Davin, A. 1978. "Imperialism and Motherhood." *History Workshop Journal* (Spring): 10–65.

Davis, A. Y. 1981. *Women, Race, and Class.* New York: Vintage Books.

Davis, D. D. 2001. "A Case of Identity: Ethnogenesis and the New Houma Indians." *Ethnohistory* 48 (3): 473–494.

Davis, W. H. 1889. *Sixty Years in California.* San Francisco: A. J. Leary.

Deagan, K. 1973. "Mestizaje in Colonial St. Augustine." *Ethnohistory* 20 (1): 55–65.

———. 1975. "Sex, Status, and Role in the Mestizaje of Spanish Colonial Florida." PhD diss., Department of Anthropology, University of Florida.

———. 1983a. "The Mestizo Minority: Archaeological Patterns of Intermarriage." In *Spanish St. Augustine: The Archaeology of a Colonial Creole Community,* ed. K. Deagan, 99–124. New York: Academic Press.

———, ed. 1983b. *Spanish St. Augustine: The Archaeology of a Colonial Creole Community.* New York: Academic Press.

———. 1987. *Artifacts of the Spanish Colonies of Florida and the Caribbean, 1500–1800.* Vol. 1, *Ceramics, Glassware, and Beads.* Washington, D.C.: Smithsonian Institution Press.

———. 1990a. "Accommodation and Resistance: The Process and Impact of Spanish Colonization in the Southeast." In *Columbian Consequences,* vol. 2, *Archaeological and Historical Perspectives on the Spanish Borderlands East,* ed. D. H. Thomas, 297–314. Washington, D.C.: Smithsonian Institution Press.

———. 1990b. "Sixteenth-Century Spanish-American Colonization in the Southeastern United States and the Caribbean." In *Columbian Consequences,* vol. 2, *Ar-*

chaeological and Historical Perspectives on the Spanish Borderlands East, ed. D. H. Thomas, 225–250. Washington, D.C.: Smithsonian Institution Press.

———. 1996. "Colonial Transformation: Euro-American Cultural Genesis in the Early Spanish-American Colonies." Journal of Anthropological Research 52: 135–160.

———. 1998. "Transculturation and Spanish American Ethnogenesis: The Archaeological Legacy of the Quincentenary." In Studies in Culture Contact: Interaction, Culture Change, and Archaeology, ed. J. G. Cusick, 126–145. Occasional Paper no. 25. Center for Archaeological Investigations, Southern Illinois University, Carbondale.

———. 2002. Artifacts of the Spanish Colonies of Florida and the Caribbean, 1500–1800. Vol. 2, Portable Personal Possessions. Washington, D.C.: Smithsonian Institution Press.

———. 2003. "Colonial Origins and Colonial Transformations in Spanish America." Historical Archaeology 27 (4): 3–13.

Dean, C. 1999. Inka Bodies and the Body of Christ: Corpus Christi in Colonial Cuzco, Peru. Durham, N.C.: Duke University Press.

Deans-Smith, S. 2005. "Creating the Colonial Subject: Casta Paintings, Collectors, and Critics in Eighteenth-Century Mexico and Spain." Colonial Latin American Review 14 (2): 169–204.

de Certeau, M. 1984. The Practice of Everyday Life. Trans. S. F. Rendall. Berkeley: University of California Press.

De Cunzo, L. A. 1996. "Introduction: People, Material Culture, Context, and Culture in Historical Archaeology." In Historical Archaeology and the Study of American Culture, ed. L. A. De Cunzo and B. L. Herman, 1–18. Winterthur, Del.: Henry Francis du Pont Winterthur Museum.

de Erauso, C. 1996. Lieutenant Nun: Memoir of a Basque Transvestite in the New World. Trans. M. Stepto and G. Stepto. Boston: Beacon Press.

Deetz, J. F. 1963. "Archaeological Investigations at La Purisima Mission." UCLA Archaeological Survey Annual Report 5:165–191.

———. 1977. In Small Things Forgotten. New York: Doubleday.

———. 1988. "American Historical Archaeology: Methods and Results." Science 239 (January 22): 362–367.

———. 1993. Flowerdew Hundred: The Archaeology of a Virginia Plantation, 1619–1864. Charlottesville: University Press of Virginia.

Delle, J. A. 2000. "The Material and Cognitive Dimensions of Creolization in Nineteenth-Century Jamaica." Historical Archaeology 34 (3): 56–72.

Derrida, J. 1973. "Différance." In Speech and Phenomena and Other Essays on Husserl's Theory of Signs, 129–160. Evanston, Ill.: Northwestern University Press.

Devine, H. 2004. *The People Who Own Themselves: Aboriginal Ethnogenesis in a Canadian Family, 1660–1900.* Calgary, Alberta: University of Calgary Press.

Diaz, M. N. 1966. *Tonalá: Conservatism, Responsibility, and Authority in a Mexican Town.* Berkeley: University of California Press.

Dietler, M. 2006. "Culinary Encounters: Food, Identity, and Colonialism." In *The Archaeology of Food and Identity,* ed. K. C. Twiss, 218–242. Occasional Paper no. 34. Center for Archaeological Investigations, Southern Illinois University, Carbondale.

Dietler, M., and I. Herbich. 1998. "Habitus, Techniques, Style: An Integrated Approach to the Social Understanding of Material Culture and Boundaries." In *The Archaeology of Social Boundaries,* ed. M. T. Stark, 232–263. Washington, D.C.: Smithsonian Institution Press.

Di Peso, C. C. 1953. *The Sobaipuri Indians of the Upper San Pedro River Valley, Southeastern Arizona.* Dragoon, Ariz.: Amerind Foundation.

Dobyns, H. F. 1976. *Spanish Colonial Tucson: A Demographic History.* Tucson: University of Arizona Press.

———. 1980. "The Study of Spanish Colonial Frontier Institutions." In *Spanish Borderlands Frontier Research,* ed. H. F. Dobyns, 5–26. Spanish Borderlands Research no. 1. Albuquerque: Center for Anthropological Studies.

Dolitsky, A. B. 1984. "Soviet Studies of Northern Peoples." *Current Anthropology* 24 (4): 502–503.

Draper, C. 1992. "Faunal Remains at the San Diego Presidio. Abstract." In *Approaches to Historical Archaeology: The Case of the Royal Presidio de San Diego,* ed. S. A. Colston, 2. San Diego: San Diego History Research Center, San Diego State University.

Driesbach, J. 2000. "A Vision for the West: Judge Crocker's Art Gallery and California Paintings Collection—Edwin Bryant Crocker." *Magazine Antiques,* November. Available online at www.findarticles.com/p/articles/mi_m1026/is_5_158/ai_67161987 (accessed November 28, 2005).

Duggan, L. 1995. "The Discipline Problem: Queer Theory Meets Lesbian and Gay History." *GLQ: A Journal of Lesbian and Gay Studies* 2 (3): 179–192.

Duhaut-Cilly, A. 1929. "Duhaut-Cilly's Account of California in the Years 1827–1828." Trans. C. F. Carter. *California Historical Society Quarterly* 8, no. 2 (June): 130–166; no. 3 (September): 214–250; no. 4 (December): 306–336.

Durkheim, E. 1982. "What Is a Social Fact?" In *The Rules of Sociological Method,* ed. S. Lukes, trans. W. D. Halls, 50–59. New York: Free Press.

Earle, R. 2003. "Luxury, Clothing, and Race in Colonial Spanish America." In *Luxury in the Eighteenth Century: Debates, Desires, and Delectable Goods,* ed. M. Berg and E. Eger, 219–227. Basingstoke, England: Palgrave MacMillan.

Egan, F. 1969. "Twilight of the Californios." *American West* 6 (2): 34–42.

El Guindi, F. 1999. *Veil: Modesty, Privacy, and Resistance*. Oxford: Oxford University Press.

Engstrand, I. H. W. 1998. "Seekers of the 'Northern Mystery': European Exploration of California and the Pacific." In *Contested Eden: California before the Gold Rush*, ed. R. A. Gutiérrez and R. J. Orsi, 78–110. Berkeley: University of California Press.

Enloe, C. 1990. *Bananas, Beaches, and Bases: Making Feminist Sense of International Politics*. Berkeley: University of California Press.

Ericksen, T. H. 1993. *Ethnicity and Nationalism*. London: Pluto Press.

Etlin, R. 1995. *Symbolic Space: French Enlightenment Architecture and Its Legacy*. Chicago: University of Chicago Press.

Ewen, C. R. 2000. "From Colonist to Creole: Archaeological Patterns of Spanish Colonization in the New World." *Historical Archaeology* 34 (3): 36–45.

Fairbanks, C. H. 1973. "The Cultural Significance of Spanish Ceramics." In *Ceramics in America*, ed. I. M. G. Quimby, 141–174. Winterthur Conference Report 1972. Charlottesville: University Press of Virginia.

Fanon, F. 1967. *Black Skin, White Masks*. Trans. C. L. Markmann. New York: Grove Press.

———. 1977. *The Wretched of the Earth*. New York: Grove Press.

Farris, G. 1989. "The Russian Imprint on the Colonization of California." In *Columbian Consequences*, vol. 1, *Archaeological and Historical Perspectives on the Spanish Borderlands West*, ed. D. H. Thomas, 481–497. Washington, D.C.: Smithsonian Institution Press.

Faulk, O. B. 1969. "The Presidio: Fortress or Farce?" *Journal of the West* 49 (January): 22–28.

———. 1971. *The Leather Jacket Soldier: Spanish Military Equipment and Institutions of the Late 18th Century*. Pasadena, Calif.: Socio-Technical Press.

Federal Writers' Project. 1976. Excerpt from files of "American Guide," Federal Writers' Project, W.P.A., San Francisco Headquarters Research District. In *The Presidio of San Francisco, 1776—1976: A Collection of Historical Source Materials*, ed. G. Chappell, 50–60. San Francisco: National Park Service, Western Regional Office.

Felton, D. L., and P. D. Schulz. 1983. *The Diaz Collection: Material Culture and Social Change in Mid-Nineteenth-Century Monterey*. California Archaeological Reports no. 23. Cultural Resource Management Unit, Resource Protection Division, State of California Department of Parks and Recreation, Sacramento.

Ferguson, L. 1992. *Uncommon Ground: Archaeology and Early African America, 1650–1800*. Washington, D.C.: Smithsonian Institution Press.

Fesler, G., and M. Franklin. 1999. "The Exploration of Ethnicity and the Historical Archaeological Record." In *Historical Archaeology, Identity Formation, and the Interpretation of Ethnicity*, ed. M. Franklin and G. Fesler, 1–10. Richmond, Va.: Colonial Williamsburg Research Publications/Dietz Press.

Field, L., A. Leventhal, D. Sanchez, and R. Cambra. 1992. "A Contemporary Ohlone Tribal Revitalization Movement: A Perspective from the Muwekma Costanoan/Ohlone Indians of the San Francisco Bay Area." *California History* 71 (3): 412–432.

Fink, A. 1972. *Monterey County: The Dramatic Story of Its Past—Monterey Bay, Big Sur, Carmel, Salinas Valley*. Santa Cruz, Calif.: Western Tanager Press/Valley Publishers.

Fireman, J. 1977. *The Spanish Royal Corps of Engineers in the Western Borderlands: Instrument of Bourbon Reform, 1764 to 1815*. Glendale, Calif.: Arthur H. Clark.

Fischer, M. M. J. 1986. "Ethnicity and the Post-Modern Arts of Memory." In *Writing Culture: The Poetics and Politics of Ethnography*, ed. J. Clifford and G. E. Marcus, 194–233. Berkeley: University of California Press.

Fisher, A. S. 1992. "Mestizaje and the Cuadros de Castas: Visual Representations of Race, Status, and Dress in Eighteenth Century Mexico." PhD diss., University of Minnesota.

Fisher, G., and D. D. Loren. 2003. "Embodying Identity in Archaeology: Introduction." *Cambridge Archaeological Journal* 13 (2): 225–230.

Fitts, R. K. 2001. "The Rhetoric of Reform: The Five Points Missions and the Cult of Domesticity." *Historical Archaeology* 35 (3): 115–132.

Forbes, J. D. 1965. *Warriors of the Colorado: The Yumas of the Quechan Nation and Their Neighbors*. Norman: University of Oklahoma Press.

———. 1966. "Black Pioneers: The Spanish-Speaking Afroamericans of the Southwest." *Phylon* 27:233–246.

———. 1983. "Hispano-Mexican Pioneers of the San Francisco Bay Region: An Analysis of Racial Origins." *Aztlan* 14:175–189.

Foucault, M. 1975. *Discipline and Punish: The Birth of the Prison*. New York: Vintage Books.

———. 1978. *The History of Sexuality*. Vol. 1, *An Introduction*. Trans. R. Hurley. New York: Pantheon.

———. 1980. *Power/Knowledge: Selected Interviews and Other Writings, 1972–1977*. London: Harvester.

Fowler, C. 2004. *The Archaeology of Personhood: An Anthropological Approach*. London: Routledge.

Franklin, M. 2001. "The Archaeological Dimensions of Soul Food: Interpreting Race, Culture, and Afro-Virginian Identity." In *Race and the Archaeology of Identity*, ed. C. E. Orser Jr., 88–107. Salt Lake City: University of Utah Press.

Franklin, M., and G. Fesler, eds. 1999. *Historical Archaeology, Identity Formation, and the Interpretation of Ethnicity.* Richmond, Va.: Colonial Williamsburg Research Publications/Dietz Press.

Frierman, J. D., ed. 1982. *The Ontiveros Adobe: Early Rancho Life in Alta California.* Pacific Palisades, Calif.: Greenwood and Associates.

———. 1992. "The Pastoral Period in Los Angeles: Life on the Ranchos and in the Pueblo, 1800–1850." In *Historical Archaeology of Nineteenth-Century California,* 1–52. Los Angeles: William Andrews Clark Memorial Library, University of California, Los Angeles.

Galloway, P. 1995. *Choctaw Genesis, 1500–1700.* Lincoln: University of Nebraska Press.

Gálvez, B. de. 1951. *Instructions for Governing the Interior Provinces of New Spain, 1786.* Trans. and ed. Donald E. Worcester. Berkeley: Quivira Society.

Gambastiani, M. A., and R. Fitzgerald. 2001. "The Rediscovery of Presidio Mound (CA-SFR-6)." *Society for California Archaeology Newsletter* 35 (4): 12, 14.

García, M. T. 1975. "The Californios of San Diego and the Politics of Accommodation, 1846–1860." *AZTLAN—International Journal of Chicano Studies Research* 6 (1): 69–85.

Garcia-Moro, C., D. I. Toja, and P. Walker. 1997. "Marriage Patterns of California's Early Spanish-Mexican Colonists (1742–1876)." *Journal of Biosocial Science* 29:205–217.

Geertz, C. 1977. *The Interpretation of Cultures.* New York: Basic Books.

Gendzel, G. 2001. "Pioneers and Padres: Competing Mythologies in Northern and Southern California, 1850–1930." *Western Historical Quarterly* 32 (1): 55–82.

Gerald, R. E. 1968. *Spanish Presidios of the Late Eighteenth Century in Northern New Spain.* Museum of New Mexico Research Records no. 7. Santa Fe: Museum of New Mexico Press.

Giddens, A. 1984. *The Constitution of Society: Outline of the Theory of Structuration.* Berkeley: University of California Press.

Gifford-Gonzales, D. 1993. "You Can Hide, But You Can't Run: Representations of Women's Work in Illustrations of Paleolithic Life." *Visual Anthropology Review* 9 (1): 23–41.

Gilchrist, R. 1994. *Gender and Material Culture: The Archaeology of Religious Women.* New York: Routledge.

Gilmore, K. 1995. "The Archaeology of Spanish and Mexican Colonialism in Texas." In *The Archaeology of Spanish and Mexican Colonialism in the American Southwest,* ed. J. E. Ayres, 105–133. Ann Arbor: Society for Historical Archaeology.

Ginn, S. 2005. "Investigating Culture Contact through 'Missionwares.'" Paper presented at the seventieth annual meeting of the Society for American Archaeology, Salt Lake City.

Glassow, M. A. 2000. "Weighing vs. Counting Shellfish Remains: A Comment on Mason, Peterson, and Tiffany." *American Antiquity* 65 (2): 407–414.

Goggin, J. M. 1968. *Spanish Majolica in the New World: Types of the Sixteenth to Eighteenth Centuries.* Yale University Publications in Anthropology no. 72, Department of Anthropology, Yale University, New Haven, Conn.

Goldberg, P. 2005. *Thin Section Observation of Samples Collected from Officer's Club, Presidio, California, February, 2005.* Submitted by Boston University Micromorphology Laboratory to Presidio Archaeology Center, Presidio of San Francisco.

González, M. J. 1998. "'The Child of the Wilderness Weeps for the Father of Our Country': The Indian and the Politics of Church and State in Provincial California." In *Contested Eden: California before the Gold Rush,* ed. R. A. Gutiérrez and R. J. Orsi, 147–172. Berkeley: University of California Press.

Graham, E. 1998. "Mission Archaeology." *Annual Review of Anthropology* 27:25–62.

Grayson, D. K. 1984. *Quantitative Zooarchaeology: Topics in the Analysis of Archaeological Faunas.* New York: Academic Press.

Greenwood, R. S. 1989. "The California Ranchos: Fact and Fancy." In *Columbian Consequences,* vol. 1, *Archaeological and Historical Perspectives on the Spanish Borderlands West,* ed. D. H. Thomas, 451–465. Washington, D.C.: Smithsonian Institution Press.

Greenwood, R. S., J. M. Foster, and A. Q. Duffield. 1988. *Historical and Archaeological Study of the Yorba-Slaughter Adobe, San Bernardino County.* Report prepared by Infotec Research and Greenwood Associates, Pacific Palisades, Calif., for the U.S. Army Corps of Engineers, Los Angeles.

Grosz, E. A. 1989. *Sexual Subversions: Three French Feminists.* Sydney: Allen and Unwin Academic.

Grosz, E., and E. Probyn, eds. 1995. *Sexy Bodies: The Strange Carnalities of Feminism.* London: Routledge.

Guest, F. F. 1996. *Hispanic California Revisited: Essays by Francis F. Guest, O.F.M.* Ed. D. B. Nunis Jr. Mission Archive Library, Santa Barbara, Calif.

Guss, D. M. 1996. "Cimarrones, Theater, and the State." In *History, Power, and Identity: Ethnogenesis in the Americas, 1492–1992,* ed. J. D. Hill, 180–192. Iowa City: University of Iowa Press.

Gust, S. M. 1982. "Faunal Analysis and Butchering." In *The Ontiveros Adobe: Early Rancho Life in Alta California,* ed. J. D. Frierman, 101–144. Pacific Palisades, Calif.: Greenwood and Associates.

Gutiérrez, R. A. 1991. *When Jesus Came, the Corn Mothers Went Away: Marriage, Sexuality, and Power in New Mexico, 1500–1846. Stanford, Calif.: Stanford University Press.

————. 1993a. "Family Structures: The Spanish Borderlands." In Encyclopedia of the North American Colonies, vol. 2, ed. J. E. Cook, 672–682. New York: Maxwell Macmillan International.

————. 1993b. "Sexual Mores and Behavior: The Spanish Borderlands." In Encyclopedia of the North American Colonies, vol. 2, ed. J. E. Cook, 700–710. New York: Maxwell Macmillan International.

Gutiérrez, R. A., and R. J. Orsi, eds. 1998. Contested Eden: California before the Gold Rush. Berkeley: University of California Press.

Haas, L. 1995. Conquest and Historical Identities in California, 1769–1936. Berkeley: University of California Press.

Hackel, S. W. 1998. "Land, Labor, and Production: The Colonial Economy of Spanish and Mexican California." In Contested Eden: California before the Gold Rush, ed. R. A. Gutiérrez and R. J. Orsi, 111–146. Berkeley: University of California Press.

Hale, M. R., and R. Bevill. 1997. Report: Archaeological Monitoring Services, Task Order 53, Building 10 Funston Avenue, Presidio of San Francisco, Golden Gate National Recreation Area, San Francisco, San Francisco County, California, Job No. 02050–242–019. San Francisco: Dames and Moore.

Haley, B. D., and L. R. Wilcoxon. 2005. "How Spaniards Became Chumash and Other Tales of Ethnogenesis." American Anthropologist 107 (3): 432–445.

Hall, M. 2000. Archaeology and the Modern World: Colonial Transcripts in South Africa and the Chesapeake. London: Routledge.

Hall, S. 1989. "New Ethnicities." In Black Film, British Cinema, 27–31. ICA Documents 7. London: Institute of Contemporary Arts.

————. 1996. "Introduction: Who Needs 'Identity'?" In Questions of Cultural Identity, ed. S. Hall and P. Du Gay, 1–17. London: Sage.

Haraway, D. 1988. "Situated Knowledge: The Science Question and the Privilege of Partial Perspective." Feminist Studies 14 (3): 575–599.

————. 1989. Primate Visions: Gender, Race, and Nature in the World of Modern Science. New York: Routledge.

————. 1997. Simians, Cyborgs, and Women: The Reinvention of Nature. New York: Routledge.

Harlow, N. 1982. California Conquered: The Annexation of a Mexican Province, 1846–1850. Berkeley: University of California Press.

Harris, E. C. 1989. Principles of Archaeological Stratigraphy. 2nd ed. San Diego: Academic Press.

Harris, E. C., M. Brown, and G. Brown. 1993. Practices of Archaeological Stratigraphy. Orlando: Academic Press.

Harris, J. E. 1979. "Eighteenth-Century French Blue-Green Bottles from the Fortress of Louisbourg, Nova Scotia." In *History and Archaeology*, no. 29, 83–149. Ottawa: Parks Canada.

Harrison, F. V. 1995. "The Persistent Power of 'Race' in the Cultural and Political Economy of Racism." *Annual Review of Anthropology* 24:47–74.

Harrison, R. 2002. "Archaeology and the Colonial Encounter: Kimberley Spearpoints, Cultural Identity, and Masculinity in the North of Australia." *Journal of Social Archaeology* 2 (3): 352–277.

Heath, B. J. 1999. "Buttons, Beads, and Buckles: Contextualizing Adornment within the Bounds of Slavery." In *Historical Archaeology, Identity Formation, and the Interpretation of Ethnicity*, ed. M. Franklin and G. Fesler, 47–70. Richmond, Va.: Colonial Williamsburg Research Publications/Dietz Press.

Heizer, R. F., ed. 1978. *California*. Vol. 8 of *Handbook of North American Indians*, W. C. Sturtevant, general editor. Washington, D.C.: Smithsonian Institution.

———. 1991. "Impact of Colonization on Native California Societies." First published 1978. Reprinted in *Native American Perspectives on the Hispanic Colonization of Alta California*, ed. E. D. Castillo, 155–173, vol. 26 of *Spanish Borderlands Sourcebooks*, D. H. Thomas, general editor. New York: Garland.

Heizer, R. F., and A. B. Elsasser. 1980. *The Natural World of the California Indians*. California Natural History Guides 46. Berkeley: University of California Press.

Hendry, G. W. 1931. "The Adobe Brick as a Historical Source." *Agricultural History* 5:110–127.

Hendry, G. W., and J. N. Bowman. 1940. *The Spanish and Mexican Adobe and Other Buildings in the Nine San Francisco Bay Counties, 1776 to about 1850*. mF868.S156 .H4. Bancroft Library, University of California, Berkeley.

Hickerson, N. P. 1996. "Ethnogenesis in the South Plains." In *History, Power, and Identity: Ethnogenesis in the Americas, 1492–1992*, ed. J. D. Hill, 70–89. Iowa City: University of Iowa Press.

Hill, J. D., ed. 1996. *History, Power, and Identity: Ethnogenesis in the Americas, 1492–1992*. Iowa City: University of Iowa Press.

Hirata, R. 2001. "Bits and Pieces: An Analysis of Unglazed Ceramics from 1999 Archaeological Excavations at El Presidio de San Francisco from an Artist's Perspective." Undergraduate senior honors thesis, Department of Anthropology, University of California, Berkeley.

Hitt, J. 2005. "The Newest Indians." *New York Times Magazine*, August 21, 2005, 36–41.

Hobsbawm, E., and T. Ranger, eds. 1983. *The Invention of Tradition*. Cambridge: Cambridge University Press.

Hodder, I. 1982. *Symbols in Action*. Cambridge: Cambridge University Press.

————. 1985. "Postprocessual Archaeology." In *Advances in Archaeological Method and Theory*, ed. M. B. Shiffer, 8:1–25. Orlando: Academic Press.

————, ed. 1987a. *Archaeology of Contextual Meanings*. Cambridge: Cambridge University Press.

————. 1987b. "The Meaning of Discard: Ash and Domestic Space in Baringo." In *Method and Theory for Activity Area Research: An Ethnoarchaeological Approach*, ed. S. Kent, 424–448. New York: Columbia University Press.

————. 1991. *Reading the Past*. 2nd ed. Cambridge: Cambridge University Press.

Hodder, I., and C. Orton. 1976. *Spatial Analysis in Archaeology*. Cambridge: Cambridge University Press.

Hornbeck, D. 1989. "Economic Growth and Change at the Missions of Alta California, 1769–1846." In *Columbian Consequences*, vol. 1, *Archaeological and Historical Perspectives on the Spanish Borderlands West*, ed. D. H. Thomas, 423–433. Washington, D.C.: Smithsonian Institution Press.

Hornbeck, D., and D. L. Fuller. 1983. *California Patterns: A Geographical and Historical Atlas*. Palo Alto, Calif.: Mayfield.

Horning, A. J. 1999. "In Search of a 'Hollow Ethnicity': Archaeological Explorations of Rural Mountain Settlement." In *Historical Archaeology, Identity Formation, and the Interpretation of Ethnicity*, ed. M. Franklin and G. Fesler, 121–138. Richmond, Va.: Colonial Williamsburg Research Publications/Dietz Press.

Horowitz, D. L. 1985. *Ethnic Groups in Conflict*. Berkeley: University of California Press.

Horvath, S. J. 1982. "Forgotten Places and Things: Archaeological Perspectives on American History." In *Forgotten Places and Things: Archaeological Perspectives on American History*, ed. A. E. Ward, 23–26. Albuquerque: Center for Anthropological Studies.

Howard, R. 2002. *Black Seminoles in the Bahamas*. Gainesville: University Press of Florida.

Howes, D. 1996. "Introduction: Commodities and Cultural Borders." In *Cross-Cultural Consumption*, ed. D. Howes, 1–16. London: Routledge.

Hughes, B., and T. Hughes. 1968. *The Collector's Encyclopaedia of English Ceramics*. London: Murray's Sales and Service.

Hughes, C. 1975. "The Decline of the Californios: The Case of San Diego, 1846–1856." *Journal of San Diego History* 21 (3): 1–31.

Hughes, R. E. 2005. *Geochemical Research Laboratory Letter Report 2005–11*. Submitted by Geochemical Research Laboratory, Portola Valley, Calif., to Presidio Archaeology Center, Presidio Trust, San Francisco.

Hull, G. T., B. Smith, and P. Bell-Scott, eds. 1982. *But Some of Us Are Brave: All the Women Are White, All the Blacks Are Men: Black Women's Studies*. Old Westbury, N.Y.: Feminist Press.

Hurtado, A. L. 1988. *Indian Survival on the California Frontier*. New Haven, Conn.: Yale University Press.

———. 1992. "Sexuality in California's Franciscan Missions: Central Perceptions and Sad Realities." *California History* 71 (3): 370–386.

———. 1999. *Intimate Frontiers: Sex, Gender, and Culture in Old California*. Albuquerque: University of New Mexico Press.

Ivey, J. 1991. *Inventory of Potential Archaeological Resources of Presido [sic] San Francisco*. San Francisco: Golden Gate National Recreation Area, National Park Service.

Jackson, H. H. 1970. *Ramona*. New York: Avon. First published 1884.

Jackson, R. H. 1999. *Race, Caste, and Status: Indians in Colonial Spanish America*. Albuquerque: University of New Mexico Press.

Jackson, R. H., and E. Castillo. 1995. *Indians, Franciscans, and Spanish Colonization*. Albuquerque: University of New Mexico Press.

Jamieson, R. W. 2000. "Doña Luisa and Her Two Houses." In *Lines That Divide: Historical Archaeologies of Race, Class, and Gender*, ed. J. A. Delle, S. A. Mrozowski, and R. Paynter, 142–167. Knoxville: University of Tennessee Press.

———. 2004. "Bolts of Cloth and Sherds of Pottery: Impressions of Caste in the Material Culture of the Seventeenth Century Audiencia of Quito." *The Americas* 60 (3): 431–446.

———. 2005. "Caste in Cuenca: Colonial Identity in the Seventeenth Century Andes." In *The Archaeology of Plural and Changing Identities: Beyond Identification*, ed. E. C. Casella and C. Fowler, 211–232. New York: Kulwer Academic/Plenum Publishers.

Johnson, L. L., and S. Lipsett-Rivera, eds. 1998. *The Faces of Honor: Sex, Shame, and Violence in Colonial Latin America*. Albuquerque: University of New Mexico Press.

Jones, O., and C. Sullivan. 1989. *The Parks Canada Glass Glossary for the Description of Containers, Tableware, Flat Glass, and Closures*. Rev. ed. Quebec: Canadian Government Publishing Centre, National Historic Parks and Sites, Canadian Parks Service.

Jones, O. L., Jr. 1979. *Los Paisanos: Spanish Settlers on the Northern Frontier of New Spain*. Norman: University of Oklahoma Press.

Jones, S. 1997. *The Archaeology of Ethnicity: Constructing Identities in the Past and Present*. London: Routledge.

Joyce, R. A. 2000a. *Gender and Power in Prehispanic Mesoamerica*. Austin: University of Texas Press.

———. 2000b. "Girling the Girl and Boying the Boy: The Production of Adulthood in Ancient Mesoamerica." *World Archaeology* 31 (3): 473–483.

———. 2000c. "A Precolumbian Gaze: Male Sexuality among the Ancient

Maya." In *Archaeologies of Sexuality*, ed. R. A. Schmidt and B. L. Voss, 263–283. London: Routledge.

———. 2005. "Archaeology of the Body." *Annual Review of Anthropology* 34: 139–158.

Karklins, K. 1982. "Guide to the Description and Classification of Glass Beads." In *Glass Beads*, 59:83–117. Ottawa: National Historic Parks and Sites Branch, Parks Canada and Environment Canada.

Karklins, K., and R. Sprague. 1972. "Glass Trade Beads in North America: An Annotated Bibliography." *Historical Archaeology* 6 (1): 87–101.

Katz, R. 1977. "The Potters and Pottery of Tonalá, Jalisco, Mexico: A Study in Aesthetic Anthropology." PhD diss., Department of Anthropology, Columbia University.

Katzew, I. 2004. *Casta Painting: Images of Race in Eighteenth-Century Mexico*. New Haven, Conn.: Yale University Press.

Kidd, K. E., and M. A. Kidd. 1970. "A Classification System for Glass Beads for the Use of Field Archaeologists." *Canadian Historic Sites*, Occasional Papers in Archaeological History no. 1, 45–89.

Kidder, T. R. 2004. "Plazas as Architecture: An Example from the Raffman Site, Northeast Louisiana." *American Antiquity* 69 (3): 514–532.

King, C. 1994. "Central Ohlone Ethnohistory." In *The Ohlone Past and Present: Native Americans of the San Francisco Bay Region*, ed. L. J. Bean, 203–228. Menlo Park, Calif.: Ballena Press.

Kinnaird, L., ed. 1958. *The Frontiers of New Spain: Nicolas de Lafora's Description, 1766–1768*. Berkeley: Quivira Society.

Kipling, R. 1996. *Just So Stories*. New York: Books of Wonder. First published in 1902.

Kohl, P. L. 1998. "Nationalism and Archaeology: On the Constructions of Nations and the Reconstructions of the Remote Past." *Annual Review of Anthropology* 27:223–246.

Kolb, P. J. 1984. "Ethnogenesis: The Development of an Ethnic Group." PhD diss., Department of Political and Social Science, New School for Social Research, New York.

Kotzebue, O. von. 1830. *A New Voyage Round the World in the Years 1823, 24, 25, and 26*. London: H. Colburn and R. Bentley.

Kroeber, A. L. 1925. *Handbook of the Indians of California*. Smithsonian Institution Bureau of American Ethnology Bulletin 78. Washington, D.C.: Government Printing Office.

———. 1955. "Nature of the Landholding Group." *Ethnohistory* 2 (4): 303–314.

Kurien, P. 1994. "Colonialism and Ethnogenesis: A Study of Kerala, India." *Theory and Society* 23:385–417.

Kuznesof, E. A. 1995. "Ethnic and Gender Influences on 'Spanish' Creole Society in Colonial Spanish America." *Colonial Latin American Review* 4 (1): 153–176.

Lamont, M., and V. Molnár. 2002. "The Study of Boundaries in the Social Sciences." *Annual Review of Sociology* 28:167–195.

Langellier, J. P., and K. M. Peterson. 1981. "Lances and Leather Jackets: Presidial Forces in Spanish Alta California." *Journal of the West* 20 (4): 3–11.

Langellier, J. P., and D. B. Rosen. 1992. *Historic Resource Study: El Presidio de San Francisco—A History under Spain and Mexico, 1776–1846.* Presidio of San Francisco, Golden Gate National Recreation Area, and U.S. Department of the Interior, National Park Service, Denver Service Center.

———. 1996. *El Presidio de San Francisco: A History under Spain and Mexico, 1776–1846.* Spokane, Wash.: Arthur H. Clark.

Langsdorff, G. H. von. 1927. *Langsdorff's Narrative of the Rezanov Voyage to Nueva California in 1806.* San Francisco: Private Press of T. C. Russell.

Langum, D. J. 1987. "Sin, Sex, and Separation in Mexican California: Her Domestic Relations Law." *Californians* 5 (3): 44–50.

La Pérouse, J. F. de. 1989. *Monterey in 1786: The Journals of Jean François de La Pérouse.* Berkeley: Heyday Books.

Laqueur, T. 1990. *Making Sex: Body and Gender from the Greeks to Freud.* Cambridge, Mass.: Harvard University Press.

Larick, R. 1991. "Warriors and Blacksmiths: Mediating Ethnicity in East African Spears." *Journal of Anthropological Archaeology* 10 (4): 299–331.

Larson, P. M. 1996. "Desperately Seeking 'the Merina' (Central Madagascar): Reading Ethnonyms and Their Semantic Fields in African Identity Histories." *Journal of Southern African Studies* 22 (4): 541–560.

Leone, M. P., C. J. LaRoche, and J. J. Babiarz. 2005. "The Archaeology of Black Americans in Recent Times." *Annual Review of Anthropology* 34:575–598.

Levine, F. 1995. "The Archaeology of Spanish and Mexican Colonialism in New Mexico." In *The Archaeology of Spanish and Mexican Colonialism in the American Southwest*, ed. J. E. Ayres, 53–104. Ann Arbor: Society for Historical Archaeology.

Levy, R. 1978. "Costanoan." In *California*, ed. R. F. Heizer, 485–495, vol. 8 of *Handbook of North American Indians*, W. C. Sturtevant, general editor. Washington, D.C.: Smithsonian Institution.

Levy, T. E., and A. F. C. Holl. 2002. "Migrations, Ethnogenesis, and Settlement Dynamics: Israelites in Iron Age Canaan and Shuwa-Arabs in the Chad Basin." *Journal of Anthropological Archaeology* 21 (1): 83–118.

Lightfoot, K. G. 1986. "Regional Surveys in the Eastern United States: The

Strengths and Weaknesses of Implementing Subsurface Testing Programs." *American Antiquity* 51 (3): 484–504.

————. 1989. "A Defense of Shovel-Test Sampling: A Reply to Shott." *American Antiquity* 54 (2): 413–416.

————. 1995. "Culture Contact Studies: Redefining the Relationship between Prehistoric and Historical Archaeology." *American Antiquity* 60 (2): 119–217.

————. 2005. *Indians, Missionaries, and Merchants: The Legacy of Colonial Encounters on the California Frontiers.* Berkeley: University of California Press.

Lightfoot, K. G., A. Martinez, and A. M. Schiff. 1998. "Daily Practice and Material Culture in Pluralistic Social Settings: An Archaeological Study of Culture Change and Persistence from Fort Ross, California." *American Antiquity* 63 (2): 199–222.

Lightfoot, K. G., and W. S. Simmons. 1998. "Culture Contact in Protohistoric California: Social Contexts of Native and European Encounters." *Journal of California and Great Basin Anthropology* 20 (2): 138–170.

Lightfoot, K. G., T. Wake, and A. Schiff, eds. 1991. *The Archaeology and Ethnohistory of Fort Ross, California.* Vol. 1, *Introduction.* Contributions of the University of California Archaeological Research Facility no. 49. Berkeley: Archaeological Research Facility.

Lister, F. C., and R. H. Lister. 1974. "Maiolica in Colonial Spanish America." *Historical Archaeology* 8 (1): 17–52.

Little, B. J. 1994. "People with History: An Update on Historical Archaeology in the United States." *Journal of Archaeological Method and Theory* 1 (1): 5–40.

Longino, H. E. 1990. *Science as Social Knowledge: Values and Objectivity in Scientific Inquiry.* Princeton, N.J.: Princeton University Press.

Loren, D. D. 1999. "Creating Social Distinction: Articulating Colonial Policies and Practices along the 18th Century Louisiana/Texas Frontier." PhD diss., Department of Anthropology, State University of New York, Binghamton.

————. 2000. "The Intersections of Colonial Policy and Colonial Practice: Creolization on the Eighteenth-Century Louisiana/Texas Frontier." *Historical Archaeology* 34 (3): 85–98.

————. 2001a. "Manipulating Bodies and Emerging Traditions at the Los Adaes Presidio." In *The Archaeology of Traditions: Agency and History before and after Columbus,* ed. T. R. Pauketat, 58–76. Gainesville: University Press of Florida.

————. 2001b. "Social Skins: Orthodoxies and Practices of Dressing in the Early Colonial Lower Mississippi Valley." *Journal of Social Archaeology* 1 (2): 172–189.

Los Californianos. 2004. Membership Information (updated October 1, 2004). Available online at www.loscalifornianos.org/membership.htm (accessed June 26, 2005).

Lothrop, G. R. 1994. "Rancheras and the Land: Women and Property Rights in Hispanic California." *Southern California Quarterly* 76 (1): 59–84.

Loucks, L. J. 1993. "Spanish-Indian Interaction on the Florida Missions: The Archaeology of Baptizing Spring." In *The Spanish Missions of La Florida*, ed. B. G. McEwan, 193–216. Gainesville: University Press of Florida.

Love, E. F. 1970. "Legal Restrictions on Afro-Indian Relations in Colonial Mexico." *Journal of Negro History* 55 (2): 131–139.

Lucas, G. 2006. *An Archaeology of Colonial Identity: Power and Material Culture in the Dwars Valley, South Africa*. New York: Springer.

Luthin, H. W., ed. 2002. *Surviving through the Days: Translations of Native California Stories and Songs*. Berkeley: University of California Press.

Lyman, R. L. 1994. "Quantitative Units and Terminology in Zooarchaeology." *American Antiquity* 59 (1): 36–71.

Mackey, M. G., and L. P. Sooy. 1932. *Early California Costumes, 1769–1850*. Stanford, Calif.: Stanford University Press.

Mahr, A. C. 1932. *The Visit of the "Rurik" to San Francisco in 1816*. Stanford, Calif.: Stanford University Press.

Majewski, T., and M. J. O'Brien. 1987. "The Use and Misuse of Nineteenth-Century English and American Ceramics in Archaeological Analysis." *Advances in Archaeological Method and Theory* 11:97–209.

Manalansan, M. F., VI. 2002. "A Queer Itinerary: Deviant Excursions into Modernities." In *Out in Theory*, ed. E. Lewin and W. L. Leap, 246–263. Urbana: University of Illinois Press.

———. 2003. *Global Divas: Filipino Gay Men in the Diaspora*. Durham, N.C.: Duke University Press.

Margolin, M. 1978. *The Ohlone Way: Indian Life in the San Francisco–Monterey Bay Area*. Berkeley: Heyday Books.

———. 1981. *The Way We Lived*. Berkeley: Heyday Books.

Marken, M. W. 1994. *Pottery from Spanish Shipwrecks, 1500–1800*. Gainesville: University Press of Florida.

Markus, T. A. 1993. *Buildings and Power: Freedom and Control in the Origin of Modern Building Types*. London: Routledge.

Marshall, F., and T. Pilgram. 1993. "NISP vs. MNI in Quantification of Body-Part Representation." *American Antiquity* 58 (2): 261–269.

Martinez, A. 1994. "Native California Women as Cultural Mediators." *Proceedings of the Society for California Archaeology* 7:41–46.

———. 1998. "An Archaeological Study of Change and Continuity in the Material Remains, Practices, and Cultural Identities of Native Californian Women in a Nineteenth Century Pluralistic Context." PhD diss., Department of Anthropology, University of California, Berkeley.

Mason, B. 1978. "The Garrisons of San Diego Presidio: 1770–1794." *Journal of San Diego History* 24 (4): 399–424.

Mason, R., M. L. Peterson, and J. A. Tiffany. 1998. "Weighing vs. Counting: Measurement Reliability and the California School of Midden Analysis." *American Antiquity* 63 (2): 303–324.

Mason, W. M. 1993. "Alta California's Colonial and Early Mexican Era Population, 1769–1846." In *Region of La Raza: Changing Interpretations of Mexican American Regional History and Culture*, ed. A. Ríos-Bustamante, 169–188. Encino, Calif.: Floricanto Press.

———. 1998. *The Census of 1790: A Demographic History of Colonial California*. Menlo Park, Calif.: Ballena Press.

Massey, D. 1994. "Double Articulation: A Place in the World." In *Displacements: Cultural Identities in Question*, ed. A. Bammer, 110–121. Bloomington: Indiana University Press.

Matsuda, M. 2004. "Ethnogenesis in Anthropology." In *International Encyclopedia of the Social and Behavioral Sciences*, ed. N. J. Smelser and P. B. Baltes, 4854–4857. Exeter, U.K.: Elsevier/Pergemon. Online edition at www.sciencedirect.com/science/referenceworks/0080430767 (accessed October 19, 2005).

Mauss, M. 1990. *The Gift: The Form and Reason for Exchange in Archaic Societies*. Trans. D. D. Halls. New York: Norton. First published in 1925.

May, R. V. 1972. "An Evaluation of Mexican Majolica in Alta California." In *Mexican Majolica in Northern New Spain*, ed. M. R. Barnes and R. V. May, 25–50. Occasional Paper no. 2. Costa Mesa, Calif.: Pacific Coast Archaeological Society.

———. 1975. "Mexican Majolica in Northern New Spain: A Model for Interpreting Ceramic Change." M.A. thesis, Department of Anthropology, San Diego State University.

McClintock, A. 1995. *Imperial Leather: Race, Gender, and Sexuality in the Colonial Conquest*. New York: Routledge.

McDonnell, J. Forthcoming. *Juana Briones of Nineteenth-Century California: A Biography*. Tucson: University of Arizona Press.

McEwan, B. G. 1991a. "The Archaeology of Women in the Spanish New World." *Historical Archaeology* 25 (4): 33–41.

———. 1991b. "San Luis de Talimali: The Archaeology of Spanish-Indian Relations at a Florida Mission." *Historical Archaeology* 25 (3): 36–60.

———. 1995. "Spanish Precedents and Domestic Life at Puerto Real: The Archaeology of Two Spanish Homesites." In *Puerto Real: The Archaeology of a Sixteenth-Century Spanish Town in Hispaniola*, ed. K. Deagan, 197–229. Gainesville: University Press of Florida.

McGuire, R. H. 1982. "The Study of Ethnicity in Historical Archaeology." *Journal of Anthropological Archaeology* 1 (2): 159–178.

McManamon, F. P. 1984. "Discovering Sites Unseen." *Advances in Archaeological Method and Theory* 7:223–292.

McWilliams, C. 1949. *North from Mexico: The Spanish-Speaking People of the United States.* Philadelphia: Lippincott.

Melton, L. J. 2000. "Section C.7: Shell." In *Final Report, Funston Avenue Archaeological Research Project, Presidio of San Francisco,* 1999, by B. L. Voss, A. Ramsay, and A. Naruta. Submitted by Archaeological Research Facility, University of California, Berkeley, to Presidio Trust and National Park Service, Golden Gate National Recreation Area.

———. 2002. "Appendix G: Shell." In *Final Report, Funston Avenue Archaeological Research Project, Presidio of San Francisco,* 2000, by A. Ramsay and B. L. Voss. Submitted by Archaeological Research Facility, University of California, Berkeley, to Presidio Trust and National Park Service, Golden Gate National Recreation Area.

Menzies, A. 1924. "Archibald Menzies' Journal of the Vancouver Expedition." Ed. A. Eastwood. *California Historical Society Quarterly* 2 (4): 265–340.

Mesa, T. D. 1937. T. D. Mesa to J. N. Bowman, August 13, 1937; file 11, "Notes on Juana Briones," J. N. Bowman Papers Regarding California History. BANC MSS C-R 18. Bancroft Library, University of California, Berkeley.

Meskell, L. 1996. "The Somatization of Archaeology: Institutions, Discourses, Corporeality." *Norwegian Archaeological Review* 29 (1): 2–16.

———. 2002. "The Intersections of Identity and Politics in Archaeology." *Annual Review of Anthropology* 31:279–301.

Meskell, L., and R. A. Joyce. 2003. *Embodied Lives: Figuring Ancient Maya and Egyptian Experience.* London: Routledge.

Metz, J. 1999. "Industrial Transition and the Rise of a 'Creole' Society in the Chesapeake, 1600–1725." In *Historical Archaeology, Identity Formation, and the Interpretation of Ethnicity,* ed. M. Franklin and G. Fesler, 11–30. Richmond, Va.: Colonial Williamsburg Research Publications/Dietz Press.

Meyer, J. 2005. "Appendix D: A Geoarchaeological Study for the Tennessee Hollow Project, Presidio, City and County of San Francisco, California." In *Tennessee Hollow Watershed Archaeology Project, 2004–2005 Annual Progress Report, Excavations at El Polín Springs,* by B. L. Voss et al. Submitted by Department of Cultural and Social Anthropology and Stanford Archaeology Center, Stanford University, to Presidio Trust and National Park Service, Golden Gate National Recreation Area.

Michael, H. N., ed. 1962. *Studies in Siberian Ethnogenesis.* Toronto: Arctic Institute of North America/University of Toronto Press.

Miller, D. 1987. *Material Culture and Mass Consumption*. Oxford: Basil Blackwell.

———. 2001. "Behind Closed Doors." In *Home Possessions*, ed. D. Miller, 1–19. Oxford: Berg Press.

Milliken, R. 1995. *A Time of Little Choice*. Menlo Park, Calif.: Ballena Press.

Milliken, R., L. E. Shoup, and B. Ortiz. 2005. *The Historic Indian People of California's San Francisco Peninsula—Draft Report*. Submitted by Archaeological Consulting Services, Oakland, to National Park Service, Golden Gate Recreation Area, San Francisco.

Milton, C., and B. I. Vinson. 2002. "Counting Heads: Race and Non-Native Tribute Policy in Colonial Spanish America." *Journal of Colonialism and Colonial History* 3 (3): 1–18.

Miranda, G. E. 1981. "*Gente de Razón* Marriage Patterns in Spanish and Mexican California: A Case Study of Santa Barbara and Los Angeles." *Southern California Quarterly* 63 (1): 1–21.

———. 1988. "Racial and Cultural Dimensions of *Gente de Razón* Status in Spanish and Mexican California." *Southern California Quarterly* 70 (3): 265–278.

Mitchell, K. 1997. "Different Diasporas and the Hype of Hybridity." *Environment and Planning D: Society and Space* 15:533–553.

Mohanty, C. T. 1997. "Under Western Eyes: Feminist Scholarship and Colonial Discourses." In *Dangerous Liaisons: Gender, Nations, and Postcolonial Perspectives*, ed. A. McClintock, A. Mufti, and E. Shohat, 255–277. Minneapolis: Minnesota University Press.

———. 2003. *Feminism without Borders: Decolonizing Theory, Practicing Solidarity*. Durham, N.C.: Duke University Press.

Monroy, D. 1990a. "'They Didn't Call Them "Padre" for Nothing': Patriarchy in Hispanic California." In *Between Borders: Essays on Mexicana/Chicana History*, ed. A. R. Del Castillo, 433–445. Encino, Calif.: Floricanto Press.

———. 1990b. *Thrown among Strangers: The Making of Mexican Culture in Frontier California*. Berkeley: University of California Press.

———. 1998. "The Creation and Re-creation of Californio Society." In *Contested Eden: California before the Gold Rush*, ed. R. A. Gutiérrez and R. J. Orsi, 173–195. Berkeley: University of California Press.

Moore, H. L. 1986. *Space, Text, and Gender*. Cambridge: Cambridge University Press.

Moore, J. H. 1994. "Putting Anthropology Back Together Again: The Ethnogenetic Critique of Cladistic Theory." *American Anthropologist* 94 (4): 925–948.

———. 2004. "Cultural Evolution: Ethnogenesis." In *International Encyclopedia of the Social and Behavioral Sciences*, ed. N. J. Smelser and P. B. Baltes, 3045–3049. Exeter, U.K.: Elsevier/Pergemon. Online edition at www.sciencedirect.com/science/referenceworks/0080430767 (accessed October 19, 2005).

Moorhead, M. L. 1969. "The Soldado de Cuera: Stalwart of the Spanish Borderlands." *Journal of the West* 49 (January): 38–55.

———. 1975. *The Presidio: Bastion of the Spanish Borderlands*. Norman: University of Oklahoma Press.

Mora, J. 1949. *Californios*. Garden City, N.Y.: Country Life Press.

Mora-Torres, G., ed. and trans. 2005. *Californio Voices: The Oral Memoirs of José María Amador and Lorenzo Asisara*. Denton: University of North Texas Press.

Moratto, M. J. 1984. *California Archaeology*. Orlando: Academic Press.

Mörner, M. 1967. *Race Mixture in the History of Latin America*. Boston: Little, Brown.

———, ed. 1970. *Race and Class in Latin America*. New York: Columbia University Press.

Moser, S., and C. Gamble. 1997. "Revolutionary Images: The Iconic Vocabulary for Representing Human Antiquity." In *The Cultural Life of Images: Visual Representation in Archaeology*, 184–211. London: Routledge.

Mullins, P. 1999. *Race and Affluence: An Archaeology of African American and Consumer Culture*. New York: Kulwer Academic/Plenum Publishers.

Mullins, P., and R. Paynter. 2000. "Representing Colonizers: An Archaeology of Creolization, Ethnogenesis, and Indigenous Material Culture among the Haida." *Historical Archaeology* 34 (3): 73–84.

Nagel, J. 2000. "Ethnicity and Sexuality." *Annual Review of Sociology* 26:107–133.

———. 2003. *Race, Ethnicity, and Sexuality: Intimate Intersections, Forbidden Frontiers*. Oxford: Oxford University Press.

Nance, J. D., and B. F. Ball. 1986. "No Surprises? The Reliability and Validity of Test Pit Sampling." *American Antiquity* 51 (3): 457–483.

———. 1989. "A Shot in the Dark: Shott's Comments on Nance and Ball." *American Antiquity* 54 (2): 405–412.

Naruta, A. 2000. "Section 4.0: In-field Geophysical Survey"; "Section 6.0: Post-field Geophysical Survey Study"; and "Appendix D: Geophysical Survey Data." In *Final Report, Funston Avenue Archaeological Research Project, Presidio of San Francisco, 1999*, by B. L. Voss, A. Ramsay, and A. Naruta. Submitted by Archaeological Research Facility, University of California, Berkeley, to Presidio Trust and National Park Service, Golden Gate National Recreation Area.

Nassaney, M. S. 1989. "An Epistemological Enquiry into Some Archaeological and Historical Interpretations of 17th Century Native American–European Relations." In *Archaeological Approaches to Cultural Identity*, ed. S. J. Shennan, 76–93. London: Unwin Hyman.

Navarro García, L. 1964. *Don José de Gálvez y la Comandancia General de las Provincias Internas del Norte de Nueva España*. Seville, Spain: Escuela de Estudios Hispano-Americanos.

———. 1979. "The North of New Spain as a Political Problem in the Eighteenth Century." In New Spain's Far Northern Frontier, ed. D. J. Weber, 201–214. Trans. E. Gard and D. J. Weber. Albuquerque: University of New Mexico Press. First published in Spanish in 1960.

Naylor, T. H., and C. W. Polzer. 1986. The Presidio and Militia on the Northern Frontier of New Spain: A Documentary History, Volume 1, 1570–1700. Civil/Military Series of the Documentary Relations of the Southwest. Tucson: University of Arizona Press.

———. 1988. Pedro de Rivera and the Military Regulations for Northern New Spain, 1724–1729. Civil/Military Series of the Documentary Relations of the Southwest. Tucson: University of Arizona Press.

Neiman, F. D. 1999. "Dimensions of Ethnicity." In Historical Archaeology, Identity Formation, and the Interpretation of Ethnicity, ed. M. Franklin and G. Fesler, 139–149. Richmond, Va.: Colonial Williamsburg Research Publications/Dietz Press.

Newell, Q. D. 2004. "Transforming Mission: Catholic Rites of Passage and Changing Family Structures among Central California Indians at Mission San Francisco de Asis, 1776–1821." PhD diss., Department of Religious Studies, University of North Carolina, Chapel Hill.

Oconór, H. 1994. The Defenses of Northern New Spain: Hugo O'Conor's Report to Teodoro de Croix, July 22, 1777. Trans. and ed. D. C. Cutter. Dallas: Southern Methodist University Press and DeGolyer Library.

Olsen, S. J. 1963. "Dating Early Plain Buttons by Their Form." American Antiquity 28 (4): 551–554.

Ordner, K. 1985. "Saamis (Lapps), Finns, and Scandinavians in History and Prehistory." Norwegian Archaeological Review 18:1–12.

Origer, T. M. 2005a. Letter Report, Results of Obsidian Hydration Band Analysis. Submitted by Origer's Obsidian Laboratory, Rohnert Park, Calif., to Presidio Archaeology Center, Presidio Trust, San Francisco.

———. 2005b. Lithic Reduction Analysis of Three Specimens from the El Presidio Site, San Francisco, California. Submitted by Origer's Obsidian Laboratory, Rohnert Park, Calif., to Presidio Archaeology Center, Presidio Trust, San Francisco.

Orser, C. E., Jr. 1998. "The Challenge of Race to American Historical Archaeology." American Anthropologist 100 (3): 1–14.

———. 2004. Race and Practice in Archaeological Interpretation. Philadelphia: University of Pennsylvania Press.

Ortiz, B. R. 1994. "Chochenyo and Rumsen Narratives: A Comparison." In The Ohlone Past and Present: Native Americans of the San Francisco Bay Region, ed. L. J. Bean, 99–163. Menlo Park, Calif.: Ballena Press.

Ortner, S. B. 1996. Making Gender: The Politics and Erotics of Culture. Boston: Beacon Press.

Ortner, S. B., and H. Whitehead, eds. 1981. *Sexual Meanings: The Cultural Construction of Gender and Sexuality*. Cambridge: Cambridge University Press.

Osborn, S. K. 1997. "Death in the Daily Life of the Ross Colony: Mortuary Behavior in Frontier Russian America." PhD diss., Department of Anthropology, University of Wisconsin, Milwaukee.

————. 2006. "Chiles and Chocolates." Paper presented at the fortieth annual meeting of the Society for California Archaeology, Ventura, Calif.

Osio, A. M. 1996. *The History of Alta California: A Memoir of Mexican California*. Trans. R. M. Beebe and R. M. Senkewicz. Madison: University of Wisconsin Press.

Palóu, F. 1926. *Historical Memoirs of New California*, vol. 4. Trans. H. E. Bolton. Berkeley: University of California Press.

Parr, R. E. 2005. *Protein Residue Analysis of an Obsidian Projectile Point from Presidio de San Francisco, San Francisco, California*. Submitted by Laboratory of Archaeological Sciences, California State University, Bakersfield, to Presidio Archaeology Center, Presidio Trust, San Francisco.

Parrillo, V. N. 1994. "Diversity in America: A Sociohistorical Analysis." *Sociological Forum* 9 (4): 523–545.

Pels, P. 1997. "The Anthropology of Colonialism: Culture, History, and the Emergence of Western Governmentality." *Annual Review of Anthropology* 26: 163–83.

Pérez, B. E. 2000. "The Journey to Freedom: Maroon Forebears in Southern Venezuela." *Ethnohistory* 47 (3–4): 611–634.

Pérez, E. 1993. "Speaking from the Margin: Uninvited Discourse on Sexuality and Power." In *Building with Our Hands: New Directions in Chicana Studies*, ed. A. de la Torre and B. M. Pesquera, 57–72. Berkeley: University of California Press.

————. 1999. *Decolonial Imaginary: Writing Chicanas into History*. Bloomington: Indiana University Press.

Perissinotto, G. 1998. *Documenting Everyday Life in Early Spanish California: The Santa Barbara Presidio Memorias y Facturas, 1779–1810*. Santa Barbara Trust for Historic Preservation, Santa Barbara, Calif.

Perry, E. M., and R. A. Joyce. 2001. "Providing a Past for 'Bodies that Matter': Judith Butler's Impact on the Archaeology of Gender." *International Journal of Sexuality and Gender Studies* 6 (1/2): 63–76.

Phillips, G. H. 1993. *Indians and Intruders in Central California, 1769–1849*. Norman: University of Oklahoma Press.

Pitt, L. 1971. *The Decline of the Californios: A Social History of the Spanish-Speaking Californians, 1846–1890*. Berkeley: University of California Press.

Polk, D. B. 1991. *The Island of California: A History of the Myth*. Lincoln: University of Nebraska Press.

Polzer, C. W., and T. E. Sheridan. 1997. *The Presidio and Militia on the Northern Frontier of New Spain: A Documentary History; The Californias and Sinaloa-Sonora, 1700–1765*. Civil/Military Series of the Documentary Relations of the Southwest 2, pt. 1. Tucson: University of Arizona Press.

Poovey, M. 1988. *Uneven Developments: The Ideological Work of Gender in Mid-Victorian England*. Chicago: University of Chicago Press.

Popper, V. 2002. "Appendix H: Macrobotanical Analysis of Soil Samples from El Presidio de San Francisco, San Francisco County, California." In *Final Report, Funston Avenue Archaeological Research Project, Presidio of San Francisco*, 2000, by A. Ramsay and B. L. Voss. Submitted by Archaeological Research Facility, University of California, Berkeley, to Presidio Trust and National Park Service, Golden Gate National Recreation Area.

———. 2005. "Appendix E: Macrobotanical Analysis of Soil Samples from the 2004 Excavation at El Polín Springs, El Presidio de San Francisco, San Francisco County, California." In *Tennessee Hollow Watershed Archaeology Project, 2004–2005 Annual Progress Report, Excavations at El Polín Springs*, by B. L. Voss et al. Submitted by Department of Cultural and Social Anthropology and Stanford Archaeology Center, Stanford University, to Presidio Trust and National Park Service, Golden Gate National Recreation Area.

Popper, V., and S. L. Martin. 2000. "Section C.8.1: Macrobotanical Analysis of Soil Samples from El Presidio de San Francisco, San Francisco County, California." In *Final Report, Funston Avenue Archaeological Research Project, Presidio of San Francisco, 1999*, by B. L. Voss, A. Ramsay, and A. Naruta. Submitted by Archaeological Research Facility, University of California, Berkeley, to Presidio Trust and National Park Service, Golden Gate National Recreation Area.

Powers, K. V. 1995. *Andean Journeys: Migration, Ethnogenesis, and the State in Colonial Quito*. Albuquerque: University of New Mexico Press.

Pred, A. 1990. *Making Histories and Constructing Human Geographies: The Local Transformation of Practice, Power Relations, and Consciousness*. Boulder, Colo.: Westview Press.

Presidio Archaeology Center. 2004. *Levantar: The Presidio of San Francisco Management Strategy* [draft]. Presidio Trust and National Park Service, San Francisco.

Preston, W. 1998. "Serpent in the Garden: Environmental Change in Colonial California." In *Contested Eden: California before the Gold Rush*, ed. R. A. Gutiérrez and R. J. Orsi, 260–298. Berkeley: University of California Press.

Ramamurthy, P. 2003. "Material Consumers, Fabricating Subjects: Perplexity, Global Connectivity Discourses, and Transnational Feminist Research." *Cultural Anthropology* 18 (4): 524–550.

Ramsay, A., and B. L. Voss. 2002. *Final Report, Funston Avenue Archaeological Research Project, Presidio of San Francisco, 2000*. Submitted by Archaeological Research Facility, University of California, Berkeley, to Presidio Trust and National Park Service, Golden Gate National Recreation Area.

Rathje, W., and C. Murphy. 2001. *Rubbish! The Archaeology of Garbage.* Tucson: University of Arizona Press.

Reader, P. 1997. "Branciforte History." *Santa Cruz County History Journal* 3:17–28.

Rezanov, N. P. 1926. *The Rezanov Voyage to Nueva California in 1806.* San Francisco: Private Press of T. C. Russell.

Rice, P. 1987. *Pottery Analysis: A Sourcebook.* Chicago: University of Chicago Press.

Rico, M. T. 2006. "Laser Scanning as a Conservation Tool: An Experiment at the Presidio Officers' Club." Paper presented at the annual meeting of the Society for Historical Archaeology, Sacramento, Calif.

Ríos-Bustamante, A. 1993. "Nineteenth Century Mexican Californians a Conquered Race: From Landowners to Laborers and 'Tenants At Will.'" In *Region of La Raza: Changing Interpretations of Mexican American Regional History and Culture,* ed. A. Ríos-Bustamante, 237–269. Encino, Calif.: Floricanto Press.

Robinson, A. 1970. *Life in California, 1806–1896.* Santa Barbara, Calif.: Peregrine Press.

Roos-Collins, M. 1990. *The Flavors of Home: A Guide to Wild Edible Plants of the San Francisco Bay Area.* Berkeley: Heyday Books.

Roosens, E. E. 1989. *Creating Ethnicity: The Process of Ethnogenesis.* Newbury Park, Calif.: Sage.

Rosaldo, R. 1989. "Imperialist Nostalgia." *Representations* 26:107–22.

Roscoe, W. 1998. *Changing Ones: Third and Fourth Genders in Native North America.* New York: Saint Martin's Press.

Ross, L. A. 1997. "Glass and Ceramic Trade Beads from the Native Alaskan Neighborhood." In *The Archaeology and Ethnohistory of Fort Ross,* vol. 2, *The Native Alaskan Neighborhood: A Multiethnic Community at Colony Ross,* ed. K. G. Lightfoot, A. M. Schiff, and T. A. Wake, 179–212. Archaeological Research Facility, University of California, Berkeley.

Rothschild, N. A. 2003. *Colonial Encounters in a Native American Landscape: The Spanish and Dutch in North America.* Washington, D.C.: Smithsonian Books.

Rubin, G. 1975. "The Traffic in Women: Notes on the 'Political Economy' of Sex." In *Toward an Anthropology of Women,* ed. R. R. Reiter, 157–210. New York: Monthly Review Press.

———. 1984. "Thinking Sex: Notes for a Radical Theory of the Politics of Sexuality." In *Pleasure and Danger: Exploring Female Sexuality,* ed. C. S. Vance, 267–319. London: Pandora Books.

Rudo, M. O. 1982. "The Prehistory of San Francisco." Master's thesis, Department of Anthropology, San Francisco State University.

Ruiz de Burton, M. A. 1997. *The Squatter and the Don*. Houston: Arte Público Press. First published in 1885.

Sabbagh, S., ed. 1998. *Palestinian Women of Gaza and the West Bank*. Bloomington: Indiana University Press.

Said, E. W. 1979. *Orientalism*. New York: Vintage Books.

Saíz, M. C. G. 1989. *The Castes: A Genre of Mexican Painting/Las Castas Mexicanas: Un Género Pictórico Americano*. Milan: Olivetti and Grafiche Milani, Segrate.

Sal, H. 1792. Escala que demuestra las habitaciones que tiene el Presidio de San Francisco. California Archives 6, Provincial State Papers, Tomo XI:234. Bancroft Library, University of California, Berkeley.

———. 1976. "Hermenegildo Sal to Romero—Information about the Presidio of San Francisco." Trans. Mother Dolores Sarre. First published in 1792. In *The Presidio of San Francisco, 1776—1976: A Collection of Historical Source Materials*, ed. G. Chappell, 47–49. San Francisco: National Park Service, Western Regional Office.

Sánchez, F. 1993. "Rancho Life in Alta California." In *Region of La Raza: Changing Interpretations of Mexican American Regional History and Culture*, ed. A. Ríos-Bustamante, 213–235. Encino, Calif.: Floricanto Press.

Sanchez, G. J. 1984. "Adaptation to Conquest: The Mexican Community of San José, 1845–1880." Stanford Center for Chicano Research, Working Paper Series no. 4, Stanford University.

Sánchez, J. P. 1990. *Spanish Bluecoats: The Catalonian Volunteers in Northwestern New Spain, 1767–1810*. Albuquerque: University of New Mexico Press.

Sanchez, N. V. G. 1929. *Spanish Arcadia*. San Francisco: Powell.

Sánchez, R. 1995. *Telling Identities: The Californio Testimonios*. Minneapolis: University of Minnesota Press.

Sandos, J. A. 1998. "Between Crucifix and Lance: Indian-White Relations in California, 1769–1848." In *Contested Eden: California before the Gold Rush*, ed. R. A. Gutiérrez and R. J. Orsi, 196–229. Berkeley: University of California Press.

San Francisco State University. 1997a. *Ground Penetrating Radar, Magnetic, and Resistivity Survey, Officer's Quarters (Backyard #1), Presidio of San Francisco*. Department of Anthropology, San Francisco State University.

———. 1997b. *Ground Penetrating Radar Survey, El Polín Springs, Presidio of San Francisco*. Department of Anthropology, San Francisco State University.

———. 1997c. *Ground Penetrating Radar Survey, Officer's Quarters (Frontyards), Presidio of San Francisco*. Department of Anthropology, San Francisco State University.

———. 1997d. *Magnetic Survey, Officer's Quarters (Backyard #2), Presidio of San Francisco*. Department of Anthropology, San Francisco State University.

————. 1998. *Ground Penetrating Radar, Magnetic, and Resistivity Survey, El Polín Springs, Presidio of San Francisco.* Department of Anthropology, San Francisco State University.

Sattler, R. A. 1996. "Remnants, Renegades, and Runaways: Seminole Ethnogenesis Reconsidered." In *History, Power, and Identity: Ethnogenesis in the Americas, 1492–1992*, ed. J. D. Hill, 36–69. Iowa City: University of Iowa Press.

Scaramelli, F., and K. T. Scaramelli. 2005. "The Roles of Material Culture in the Colonization of the Orinoco, Venezuela." *Journal of Social Archaeology* 5 (1): 135–168.

Schiebinger, L. 2003. "Introduction: Feminism inside the Sciences." *Signs: Journal of Women in Culture and Society* 28 (3): 859–866.

Schiffer, M. B. 1972. "Archaeological Context and Systematic Context." *American Antiquity* 37 (2): 156–165.

Schuetz-Miller, M. K. 1994. *Buildings and Builders in Hispanic California.* Tucson and Santa Barbara, Calif.: Southwest Mission Research Center and Santa Barbara Trust for Historic Preservation.

Schwartz, S. B. 1995. "Colonial Identities and the *Sociedad de Castas*." *Colonial Latin American Review* 4 (1): 185–201.

Scott, E. M. 1991. "A Feminist Approach to Historical Archaeology: Eighteenth-Century Fur Trade Society at Michilimackinac." *Historical Archaeology* 25 (4): 42–53.

————. 1994. *Those of Little Note: Gender, Race, and Class in Historical Archaeology.* Tucson: University of Arizona Press.

Scott, J. W. 1986. "Gender: A Useful Category of Historical Analysis." *American Historical Review* 91 (5): 1035–1075.

————. 1988. *Gender and the Politics of History.* New York: Columbia University Press.

Seed, P. 1988. *To Love, Honor, and Obey in Colonial Mexico: Conflicts over Marriage Choice, 1574–1824.* Stanford, Calif.: Stanford University Press.

Servín, M. P. 1970. "Costanso's 1794 Report on Strengthening New California's Presidios." *California Historical Society Quarterly* 49 (September): 221–232.

Shennan, S. J. 1989. "Introduction: Archaeological Approaches to Cultural Identity." In *Archaeological Approaches to Cultural Identity*, ed. S. J. Shennan, 1–32. One World Archaeology 10. London: Unwin Hyman.

Shipley, W. F. 1978. "Native Languages of California." In *California*, ed. R. F. Heizer, 6–15. Vol. 8 of *Handbook of North American Indians*, W. C. Sturtevant, general editor. Washington, D.C.: Smithsonian Institution.

Shirazi, F. 2001. *The Veil Unveiled: The Hijab in Modern Culture.* Tallahassee: University Press of Florida.

Shott, M. J. 1986. "Shovel-Test Sampling in Archaeological Survey: Comments on Nance and Ball, and Lightfoot." *American Antiquity* 54 (2): 396–404.

Sider, G. 1994. "Identity as History: Ethnohistory, Ethnogenesis, and Ethnocide in the Southeastern United States." *Identities* 1 (1): 109–122.

Silliman, S. W. 1999. *Beneath Historic Floors: Archaeological Investigations of the Petaluma Adobe Seismic Retrofit Project.* Submitted by Archaeological Research Facility, University of California, Berkeley, to California Department of Parks and Recreation, State Archaeological Collections Facility, West Sacramento, Calif.

———. 2000. "Colonial Worlds, Indigenous Practices: The Archaeology of Labor on a 19th-Century California Rancho." PhD diss., Department of Anthropology, University of California, Berkeley.

———. 2001a. "Agency, Practical Politics, and the Archaeology of Culture Contact." *Journal of Social Archaeology* 1 (2): 190–209.

———. 2001b. "Theoretical Perspectives on Labor and Colonialism: Reconsidering the California Missions." *Journal of Anthropological Archaeology* 20 (4): 379–407.

———. 2004a. *Lost Laborers in Colonial California: Native Americans and the Archaeology of Rancho Petaluma.* Tucson: University of Arizona Press.

———. 2004b. "Missions Aborted: California Indian Life on Nineteenth-Century Ranchos, 1834–1848." *Boletín: Journal of the California Mission Studies Association* 21 (1): 3–22.

Silver, I. A. 1969. "The Aging of Domestic Animals." In *Science in Archaeology*, ed. D. Brothwell and E. Higgs, 283–302. New York: Praeger.

Simmons, E. K. 2006. "A Geoarchaeological Analysis of Adobe from the Presidio, San Francisco." Undergraduate honors thesis, Interdisciplinary Program in Archaeology, Stanford University.

Simpson-Smith, C., and R. Edwards. 2000. *San Francisco Spanish Colonial Presidio: Field and Laboratory Report for 1996, 1997, 1998, and 1999, with Stratigraphic Discussion.* Submitted by Archaeological Technology Program, Cabrillo College, Aptos, Calif., to Presidio Trust and National Park Service, Golden Gate National Recreation Area.

Simpson-Smith, C., R. Edwards, and L. Barker. 1997. *Cabrillo College Archaeological Technology Program: Excavation Procedures for El Presidio de San Francisco.* Submitted by Archaeological Technology Program, Cabrillo College, Aptos, Calif., to Presidio Trust and National Park Service, Golden Gate National Recreation Area.

Singer, L. 1962. "Ethnogenesis and Negro Americans Today." *Social Research* 29:419–432.

Skowronek, R. K., R. L. Bishop, M. J. Blackman, S. Ginn, and M. G. Heras. 2003.

"Chemical Characterization of Earthenware on the Alta California Frontier." *Proceedings of the Society for California Archaeology* 16:209–219.

Skowronek, R. K., M. J. Blackman, and R. L. Bishop. 2007. "To Produce and Consume: Ceramic Composition Variation in the San Francisco Presidio District." Manuscript.

Skowronek, R. K., M. J. Blackman, R. L. Bishop, S. Ginn, and M. G. Heras. 2001. "Chemical Characterization of Earthenware on the Alta California Frontier." Paper presented at the third International Symposium on Nuclear and Related Techniques, Havana, Cuba.

Skowronek, R. K., M. J. Blackman, R. L. Bishop, S. Riggins, and E. Johnson. 2005. "Mission San Francisco de Asís (PMK) and the Presidio of San Francisco (PME): Report on Neutron Activation Analysis of Earthenwares." Manuscript on file, Santa Clara University Archaeology Research Lab and Santa Clara University Archives, Santa Clara, Calif.; and Department of Anthropology, National Museum of Natural History, Smithsonian Institution, Washington, D.C.

Smith, B. 2000. *The Truth That Never Hurts: Writings on Race, Gender, and Freedom.* New Brunswick, N.J.: Rutgers University Press.

Smith-Lintner, C. A. 2007. "Becoming *Californio*: Archaeology of Communities, Animals, and Identity in Colonial California." PhD diss., Department of Anthropology, University of California, Berkeley.

Smith-Rosenberg, C. 1985. *Disorderly Conduct: Visions of Gender in Victorian America.* New York: Oxford University Press.

Sollors, W. 1986. *Beyond Ethnicity: Consent and Descent in American Culture.* Oxford: Oxford University Press.

Spector, J. D. 1993. *What This Awl Means: Feminist Archaeology at a Wahpeton Dakota Village.* St. Paul: Minnesota Historical Society Press.

Spillers, H. 1987. "Mamma's Baby, Papa's Maybe: An American Grammar Book." *Diacritics* (Summer): 65–81.

Spivak, G. C. 1988. "Can the Subaltern Speak?" In *Marxism and the Interpretation of Culture,* ed. C. Nelson and L. Grossberg, 271–313. Basingstoke, England: Macmillan Education.

———. 1996. "Diasporas Old and New: Women in the Transnational World." *Textual Practice* 10 (2): 245–269.

Sprague, R. 1985. "Glass Trade Beads: A Progress Report." *Historical Archaeology* 19 (2): 87–105.

———. 1998. "The Literature and Locations of the Phoenix Button." *Historical Archaeology* 32 (2): 56–77.

St. Croix, C. 1939. "Original Presidio Boundary (Most Probable Location in 1792)." Unpublished map. Bancroft Library, University of California, Berkeley.

Staats, S. K. 1996. "Fighting in a Different Way: Indigenous Resistance through the Alleluia Religion of Guayana." In History, Power, and Identity: Ethnogenesis in the Americas, 1492–1992, ed. J. D. Hill, 161–179. Iowa City: University of Iowa Press.

Stallaert, C. 1998. "'Biological' Christianity and Ethnicity: Spain's Construct from Past Centuries." In The Dynamics of Emerging Ethnicities: Immigrant and Indigenous Ethnogenesis in Confrontation, ed. J. Leman, 115–147. Frankfurt: Peter Lang.

Staniforth, M., and M. Nash. 1998. Chinese Export Porcelain from the Wreck of the Sydney Cove (1797). Australian Institute for Maritime Archaeology, Special Publication no. 12. Canberra: Brolga Press.

Stark, M. T., ed. 1998. The Archaeology of Social Boundaries. Washington, D.C.: Smithsonian Institution Press.

Stern, S. J. 1995. The Secret History of Gender: Women, Men, and Power in Late Colonial Mexico. Chapel Hill: University of North Carolina Press.

Stewart, S. B. 2003. An Overview of Research Issues for Indigenous Archaeology: Archaeological Research Issues for the Point Reyes National Seashore–Golden Gate National Recreation Area. Submitted by Anthropological Studies Center, Sonoma State University, Rohnert Park, Calif., to Golden Gate National Recreation Area, National Park Service, San Francisco. Available online at www.sonoma.edu/asc/projects/pointreyes/overview2.pdf (accessed May 16, 2006).

Stoler, A. L. 1995. Race and the Education of Desire: Foucault's History of Sexuality and the Colonial Order of Things. Durham, N.C.: Duke University Press.

———. 2002. Carnal Knowledge and Imperial Power: Race and the Intimate in Colonial Rule. Berkeley: University of California Press.

Strathern, M. 1990. The Gender of the Gift. Berkeley: University of California Press.

Sturtevant, W. C. 1971. "Creek into Seminole." In North American Indians in Historical Perspective, ed. E. Leacock and N. O. Lurie, 92–128. New York: Random House.

Taylor, R. L. 1979. "Black Ethnicity and the Persistence of Ethnogenesis." American Journal of Sociology 84 (6): 1401–1423.

Taylor, W. B. 1979. Drinking, Homicide, and Rebellion in Colonial Mexican Villages. Stanford, Calif.: Stanford University Press.

Thomas, A. B. 1941. "Historical Introduction." In Teodoro de Croix and the Northern Frontier of New Spain, 1776–1783, from the Original Document in the Archives of the Indies, Seville, trans. and ed. A. B. Thomas, 3–68. Norman: University of Oklahoma Press.

Thomas, D. H., ed. 1989. Columbian Consequences. Vol. 1, Archaeological and Historical Perspectives of the Spanish Borderlands West. Washington, D.C.: Smithsonian Institution Press.

Thomas, N. 1991. *Entangled Objects: Exchange, Material Culture, and Colonialism in the Pacific*. Cambridge, Mass.: Harvard University Press.

Thompson, E. N., and S. B. Woodbridge. 1992. *Special History Study: Presidio of San Francisco, An Outline of Its Evolution as a U.S. Army Post, 1847–1990*. Presidio of San Francisco, Golden Gate National Recreation Area, National Park Service.

Thompson, M. W. 1965. "Marxism and Culture." *Antiquity* 39 (154): 108–116.

Thurman, M. E. 1967. *The Naval Department of San Blas: New Spain's Bastion for Alta California and Nootka, 1769–1798*. Glendale, Calif.: Arthur H. Clark.

Treganza, A. E. 1958. *Archaeological Investigation of the Vallejo Adobe, Petaluma Adobe State Park Historical Monument*. California Department of Parks and Recreation, Sacramento.

Trigger, B. G. 1989. *A History of Archaeological Thought*. Cambridge: Cambridge University Press.

Tsing, A. L. 1994. "From the Margins." *Cultural Anthropology* 9 (3): 279–297.

Tunnell, C. D. 1966. *A Description of Enameled Earthenware from an Archaeological Excavation at Mission San Antonio de Valero (The Alamo)*. Texas State Building Commission Archaeological Program, Austin.

Tunnell, C. D., and J. R. Ambler. 1967. *Archaeological Excavations at Presidio San Agustín de Ahumada*. Report no. 6. Texas State Building Commission Archaeological Program, Austin.

Turner, T. S. 1980. "The Social Skin." In *Not Work Alone: A Cross-Cultural View of Activities Superfluous to Survival*, ed. J. Cherfas and R. Lewin, 112–140. Beverly Hills: Sage.

———. 1995. "Social Body and Embodied Subject: Bodiliness, Subjectivity, and Sociality among the Kayapo." *Cultural Anthropology* 10 (2): 143–170.

Turpin, S. A., and H. H. J. Eling. 2004. "Augaverde: A Forgotten Presidio of the Line, 1773–1781." *Journal of Big Bend Studies* 16:83–138.

Twinam, A. 1999. *Public Lives, Private Secrets: Gender, Honor, Sexuality, and Illegitimacy in Colonial Spanish America*. Stanford, Calif.: Stanford University Press.

Upton, D. 1996. "Ethnicity, Authenticity, and Invented Traditions." *Historical Archaeology* 30 (2): 1–7.

URS Greiner Woodward Clyde. 1999. *Archaeological Ground Truthing of a Ground Penetration Radar Study at the Presidio de San Francisco*. Submitted by URS Greiner Woodward Clyde, Oakland, to U.S. Army Corps of Engineers, Sacramento District, and National Park Service.

Valente, N. 2002. "Appendix F: The Vertebrate Assemblage from the Funston Avenue Project, Presidio of San Francisco, PSF FAARP 2000." In *Final Report, Funston Avenue Archaeological Research Project, Presidio of San Francisco, 2000*, by A. Ramsay and B. L. Voss. Submitted by Archaeological Research Facility, University of California, Berkeley, to Presidio Trust and National Park Service, Golden Gate National Recreation Area.

Vallejo, G. 1890. "Ranch and Mission Days in Alta California." *Century Magazine* 41 (2): 186–187.

Vallejo, M. G. 1878. Handwritten note on reverse of drawing, "Presidio of San Francisco, 1920." Edward Vischer Papers. BANC MSS 77/37 c. Bancroft Library, University of California, Berkeley.

Van Buren, M. 1999. "Tarapaya: An Elite Spanish Residence near Colonial Potosí in Comparative Perspective." *Historical Archaeology* 33 (2): 101–115.

Vancouver, G. 1984. *A Voyage of Discovery to the North Pacific and Round the World, 1791–1795.* 3 vols. Cambridge: Hakluyt Society.

Venegas, Y. 2004. "The Erotics of Racialization: Gender and Sexuality in the Making of California." *Frontiers* 25 (3): 63–89.

Verdery, K. 1994. "Ethnicity, Nationalism, and State-Making—*Ethnic Groups and Boundaries: Past and Future.*" In *The Anthropology of Ethnicity: Beyond 'Ethnic Groups and Boundaries,'* ed. H. Vermeulen and C. Govers, 33–58. Amsterdam: Het Spinhuis.

Vermeulen, H., and C. Govers. 1994. "Introduction." In *The Anthropology of Ethnicity: Beyond 'Ethnic Groups and Boundaries,'* ed. H. Vermeulen and C. Govers, 1–10. Amsterdam: Het Spinhuis.

Vernon, R., and A. S. Cordell. 1993. "A Distributional and Technological Study of Apalachee Colono-Ware from San Luis de Talimali." In *The Spanish Missions of La Florida,* ed. B. G. McEwan, 418–441. Gainesville: University Press of Florida.

Vidler, A. 1987. *The Writing of the Walls: Architectural Theory in the Late Enlightenment.* Princeton, N.J.: Princeton Architectural Press.

Vigil, R. H. 1983. "Colonial Institutions." In *Borderlands Sourcebook: A Guide to the Literature on Northern Mexico and the American Southwest,* ed. E. R. Stoddard, R. L. Nostrand, and J. P. West, 36–41. Norman: University of Oklahoma Press.

Vinson, B. I. 2001. *Bearing Arms for His Majesty: The Free-Colored Militia in Colonial Mexico.* Stanford, Calif.: Stanford University Press.

Vischer, E. 1878. "Military Mementos. Presidios, Fortifications under Spain, 1820." Edward Vischer Papers. BANC MSS 77/37 c. Bancroft Library, University of California, Berkeley.

Voss, B. L. 1996. "From Presidio to Post: Recent Archaeological Discoveries of the Spanish, Mexican, and American Periods at the Presidio of San Francisco." *Proceedings of the Society for California Archaeology* 9:278–283.

———. 1999. *Report on Archaeological Shovel Probe Survey at the Presidio of San Francisco, 1997–1998.* Submitted by Archaeological Research Facility, University of California, Berkeley, to National Park Service, Golden Gate National Recreation Area.

————. 2000a. "Colonial Sex: Archaeology, Structured Space, and Sexuality in Alta California's Spanish-Colonial Missions." In *Archaeologies of Sexuality*, ed. R. A. Schmidt and B. L. Voss, 35–61. London: Routledge.

————. 2000b. "Feminisms, Queer Theories, and the Archaeological Study of Past Sexualities." *World Archaeology* 32 (2): 180–192.

————. 2000c. "History, the Family, and Household Archaeologies." In *The Entangled Past: Integrating History and Archaeology—Proceedings of the 30th Annual Chacmool Archaeological Conference, Calgary, Alberta*, ed. M. Boyd, J. C. Erwin, and M. Hendrickson, 292–301. Calgary: Archaeological Association of the University of Calgary, Alberta.

————. 2001a. *Report on Test Excavations at El Polín Springs, Presidio of San Francisco, San Francisco, California*. Submitted by Archaeological Research Facility, University of California, Berkeley, to National Park Service, Golden Gate National Recreation Area, and Presidio Trust.

————. 2001b. *Report on Test Excavations at the Lovers' Lane Bridge Deposit, Presidio of San Francisco, San Francisco, California*. Submitted by Archaeological Research Facility, University of California, Berkeley, to National Park Service, Golden Gate National Recreation Area, and Presidio Trust.

————. 2001c. "Thinking about Galera: The Interpretive Potential of Spanish-Colonial Lead-Glazed Earthenware." Paper presented at the annual meeting of the Society for California Archaeology, Modesto, Calif.

————. 2002. "The Archaeology of El Presidio de San Francisco: Culture Contact, Gender, and Ethnicity in a Spanish-Colonial Military Community." PhD diss., Department of Anthropology, University of California, Berkeley.

————. 2005a. "The Archaeology of Overseas Chinese Communities." *World Archaeology* 37 (3): 424–439.

————. 2005b. "From *Casta* to *Californio*: Social Identity and the Archaeology of Culture Contact." *American Anthropologist* 107 (3): 461–474.

————. 2005c. "Sexual Subjects: Identity and Taxonomy in Archaeological Research." In *The Archaeology of Plural and Changing Identities: Beyond Identification*, ed. E. C. Casella and C. Fowler, 55–78. New York: Kulwer Academic/Plenum Publishers.

————. 2006a. "Engendered Archaeology: Men, Women, and Others." In *Historical Archaeology: Studies in Global Archaeology*, ed. M. Hall and S. Silliman, 107–127. London: Blackwell.

————. 2006b. "Sexuality in Archaeology." In *The Handbook of Gender in Archaeology*, ed. S. M. Nelson, 365–400. Walnut Creek, Calif.: AltaMira Press.

————. 2007. "Image, Text, Object: Interpreting Documents and Artifacts as 'Labors of Representation.'" *Historical Archaeology* 41 (4):144–168.

Voss, B. L., and V. G. Benté. 1995. *Wayside Exhibit Field Investigation, Presidio of San Francisco, California*. Submitted by Woodward-Clyde Consultants, Oakland, to U.S. Army Corps of Engineers, Sacramento District.

————. 1996a. *Archaeological Discovery and Investigation of the Historic Presidio de San Francisco*. Submitted by Woodward-Clyde Consultants, Oakland, to U.S. Army Corps of Engineers, Sacramento District.

————. 1996b. *Archaeological Investigation Reports, Presidio of San Francisco, California*. Vol. 1. Submitted by Woodward-Clyde Consultants, Oakland, to U.S. Army Corps of Engineers, Sacramento District.

————. 1996c. *Archaeological Investigation Reports, Presidio of San Francisco, California*. Vol. 2. Submitted by Woodward-Clyde Consultants, Oakland, to U.S. Army Corps of Engineers, Sacramento District.

————. 1996d. *Archaeological Investigation Reports, Presidio of San Francisco, California*. Vol. 3. Submitted by Woodward-Clyde Consultants, Oakland, to U.S. Army Corps of Engineers, Sacramento District.

————. 1996e. *Report on Recordation of Six Archaeological Features Discovered during Fiber Optic Cable Installation, Presidio of San Francisco, San Francisco, California*. Submitted by Woodward-Clyde Consultants, Oakland, to U.S. Army Corps of Engineers, Sacramento District.

Voss, B. L., with contributions by H. Blind, S. Camp, E. Clevenger, J. McCann, B. Cox, J. Meyer, I. Newquist, V. Popper, J. Sidlovsky, E. Simmons, and M. Touton. 2005. *Tennessee Hollow Watershed Archaeology Project, 2004–2005 Annual Progress Report, Excavations at El Polín Springs*. Submitted by Department of Cultural and Social Anthropology and Stanford Archaeology Center, Stanford University, to Presidio Trust and National Park Service, Golden Gate National Recreation Area.

Voss, B. L., with contributions by H. Blind, E. Clevenger, K. Eklund, I. Newquist, V. Popper, C. A. Smith, M. St. Clair, and B. Williams. 2004. *Tennessee Hollow Watershed Archaeology Project, 2003–2004 Annual Progress Report, Test Excavation at El Polín Springs*. Submitted by Stanford Archaeology Center, Stanford University, to Presidio Trust and National Park Service, Golden Gate National Recreation Area.

Voss, B. L., A. Ramsay, and A. Naruta. 2000. *Final Report, Funston Avenue Archaeological Research Project, Presidio of San Francisco, 1999*. Submitted by Archaeological Research Facility, University of California, Berkeley, to Presidio Trust and National Park Service, Golden Gate National Recreation Area.

Voss, B. L., and R. A. Schmidt. 2000. "Archaeologies of Sexuality: An Introduction." In *Archaeologies of Sexuality*, ed. R. A. Schmidt and B. L. Voss, 1–32. London: Routledge.

Walker, P. L., and K. D. Davidson. 1989. "Analysis of Faunal Remains from Santa Ines Mission." In *Santa Ines Mission Excavations, 1986–1988,* ed. J. G. Costello, 162–176. California Historical Archaeology 1. Salinas, Calif.: Coyote Press.

Walker, P. L., P. Lambert, and M. J. DeNiro. 1989. "The Effects of European Contact on the Health of Alta California Indians." In *Columbian Consequences,* vol. 1, *Archaeological and Historical Perspectives on the Spanish Borderlands West,* ed. D. H. Thomas, 349–364. Washington, D.C.: Smithsonian Institution Press.

Wall, D. de. 1994. *The Archaeology of Gender: Separating the Spheres in Urban America.* New York: Plenum Press.

———. 1999. "Examining Gender, Class, and Ethnicity in Nineteenth-Century New York City." *Historical Archaeology* 33 (1): 102–117.

Wallace, W. J., R. J. Desautels, and G. Kritwarm. 1991. "The House of the Scot Paisano: Archaeological Investigations at the Hugo Reid Adobe, Arcadia, California." In *The Archaeology of Alta California,* ed. L. R. Barker and J. Costello, 126–137, vol. 15 of *Spanish Borderlands Sourcebooks,* D. H. Thomas, general editor. New York: Garland.

Webb, E. B. 1952. *Indian Life in the Old Missions.* Los Angeles: Warren F. Lewis.

Weber, D. J. 1979. "Here Rests Juan Espinosa: Toward a Clearer Look at the Image of the 'Indolent' Californios." *Western Historical Quarterly* 10 (1): 61–69.

———. 1992. *The Spanish Frontier in North America.* New Haven, Conn.: Yale University Press.

Weber, M. 1978. *Economy and Society: An Outline of Interpretive Sociology.* Trans. G. Roth and C. Wittich. Berkeley: University of California Press.

West, G. J. 1989. "Early Historic Vegetation Change in Alta California: The Fossil Evidence." In *Columbian Consequences,* vol. 1, *Archaeological and Historical Perspectives on the Spanish Borderlands West,* ed. D. H. Thomas, 333–348. Washington, D.C.: Smithsonian Institution Press.

Weston, K. 1995. "Forever Is a Long Time: Romancing the Real in Gay Kinship Ideologies." In *Naturalizing Power: Essays in Feminist Cultural Analysis,* ed. S. J. Yanagisako and C. Delaney, 69–86. New York: Routledge.

Whitehead, N. L. 1996. "Ethnogenesis and Ethnocide in the European Occupation of Native Surinam, 1499–1681." In *History, Power, and Identity: Ethnogenesis in the Americas, 1492–1992,* ed. J. D. Hill, 20–35. Iowa City: University of Iowa Press.

Whitehead, N. L., and R. B. Ferguson. 1992. *War in the Tribal Zone: Expanding States and Indigenous Warfare.* Santa Fe: SAR Press.

Whitehead, R. S. 1983. "Alta California's Four Fortresses." *Southern California Quarterly* 65 (1): 67–94.

———. 1996. *Citadel on the Channel: The Royal Presidio of Santa Barbara, Its Founding* and Construction, 1782–1798. Santa Barbara, Calif., and Spokane, Wash.: Santa Barbara Trust for Historic Preservation and Arthur H. Clark.

Whitten, N. E., Jr. 1976. *Ecuadorian Ethnocide and Indigenous Ethnogenesis: Amazonian Resurgence amidst Andean Colonialism*. Copenhagen: International Work Group for Indigenous Affairs.

———. 1996a. "The Ecuadorian Levantamiento Indígena of 1990 and the Epitomizing Symbol of 1992: Reflections on Nationalism, Ethnic-Bloc Formation, and Racialist Ideologies." In *History, Power, and Identity: Ethnogenesis in the Americas, 1492–1992*, ed. J. D. Hill, 193–217. Iowa City: University of Iowa Press.

———. 1996b. "Ethnogenesis." In *Encyclopedia of Cultural Anthropology*, ed. D. Levinson and M. Ember, 407–411. New York: Henry Holt.

Wilkie, L. A. 2000. *Creating Freedom: Material Culture and African American Identity at Oakley Plantation*. Baton Rouge: Louisiana State University Press.

———. 2003. *The Archaeology of Mothering: An African-American Midwife's Tale*. New York: Routledge.

Williams, B. F. 1992. "Of Straightening Combs, Sodium Hydroxide, and Potassium Hydroxide in Archaeological and Cultural-Anthropological Analyses of Ethnogenesis." *American Antiquity* 57 (4): 608–612.

Williams, J. S. 2004. "The Evolution of the Presidio in Northern New Spain." *Historical Archaeology* 38 (3): 6–23.

Williams, W. L. 1986. *The Spirit and the Flesh: Sexual Diversity in American Indian Culture*. Boston: Beacon Press.

Wilson, R. 1993. "Anchored Communities: Identity and History of the Maya-Q'eqchi'." *Man* N.S. 28 (1): 121–138.

Wolf, E. R. 1982. *Europe and the People without History*. Berkeley: University of California Press.

Woodward-Clyde Consultants. 1994. *Report on Archaeological Monitoring, Underground Storage Tank Removal Project, Presidio of San Francisco*. Submitted by Woodward-Clyde Consultants, Oakland, to Army Corps of Engineers, Sacramento District.

Worthington, M. 2006. "The Dendrochronological Study of the Timbers from the Officers' Club." Paper presented at the annual meeting of the Society for Historical Archaeology, Sacramento, Calif.

Wurst, L. 1999. "Internalizing Class in Historical Archaeology." *Historical Archaeology* 33 (1):7–21.

Wylie, A. 1986. "Bootstrapping in Un-natural Sciences: Archaeological Theory Testing." *Philosophy of Science Association* 1:314–321.

———. 1992a. "The Interplay of Evidential Constraints and Political Interests: Recent Archaeological Research on Gender." *American Antiquity* 57 (1): 15–35.

————. 1992b. "Reasoning about Ourselves: Feminist Methodology in the Social Sciences." In *Women and Reason*, ed. E. Harvey and K. Okruhlik, 225–244. Ann Arbor: University of Michigan Press.

————. 1996a. "Alternative Histories: Epistemic Disunity and Political Integrity." In *Making Alternative Histories: The Practice of Archaeology and History in Non-Western Settings*, ed. P. R. Schmidt and T. C. Patterson, 255–272. Santa Fe: School of American Research Press.

————. 1996b. "The Constitution of Archaeological Evidence: Gender Politics and Science." In *The Disunity of Science: Boundaries, Contexts, Power*, ed. P. Galison and D. J. Stump, 311–343. Stanford, Calif.: Stanford University Press.

————. 1997. "The Engendering of Archaeology: Refiguring Feminist Science Studies." *OSIRIS* 12:80–99.

————. 2002. *Thinking from Things: Essays in the Philosophy of Archaeology.* Berkeley: University of California Press.

Yamane, L., ed. 2002. *A Gathering of Voices: The Native Peoples of the Central California Coast.* (*Santa Cruz County History Journal*, no. 5.) Santa Cruz, Calif.: Museum of Art and History.

Yanagisako, S. J. 1983. "Feminism and Kinship Theory." *Current Anthropology* 24 (4): 511–516.

Yanagisako, S. J., and C. Delaney, eds. 1995. *Naturalizing Power: Essays in Feminist Cultural Analysis.* New York: Routledge.

Yelvington, K. A. 1991. "Ethnicity as Practice? A Comment on Bentley." *Comparative Studies in Society and History* 33 (1): 158–168.

Yentsch, A. 1991. "Engendering Visible and Invisible Ceramic Artifacts, Especially Dairy Vessels." *Historical Archaeology* 25 (4): 132–155.

Young, R. J. C. 1995. *Colonial Desire: Hybridity in Theory, Culture, and Race.* New York: Routledge.

Yuval-Davis, N. 1996. "Women and the Biological Reproduction of 'The Nation.'" *Women's Studies International Forum* 19 (1/2): 17–24.

Zavalishin, D. 1973. "California in 1824." Trans., with annotation, James R. Gibson. *Southern California Quarterly* (Winter): 369–412.

INDEX

Italic page numbers refer to figures, maps, and tables.

adobe: bricks, 58, 122, 124, 140, 158, 185, 191, 193, 337n5; manufacture of, 58, 124; in Officers' Club, 122, *125*, 137, 181, 185, 186; and quadrangle construction, 175, *177*, 178, 180, 181, 185, 186, 188–89, 190, 191, 193, 200

African heritage: of Californios, 1, 11, 71, 83, 102, 114, 170, 305; and clothing styles, 256, 258, 259, 265, 298; and cuisine, 249–50, 291; and sistema de castas, 85, 86–88, 99; women of, 258, 265, 274, 298

agency, social, 12, 16–19, 21, 63, 94, 97, 254, 286, 288, 302, 304

agriculture, 58, 59, 61, 234; Briones family's practice of, 165–68, 170; and rancho culture, 106, 108–9, 110

Alberni, Pedro di, *44*

Alta California: as Mexican province, 66–68, 103, 107, 114–15; as

Spanish-colonial province, 47, 54–66, 83, 113–14, 150–52; U.S. acquisition of, 62, 68, 115, 304–5

Amador, José María, 235, 274–75, 335n3

Amador, Pedro, 78–79

Anderson, Benedict, 28

Anza, Juan Bautista de, 42–43, 45, 54, 59, 64, 89, 93, 254

Anza: expedition, 41–46, *42*, 52, 67, 69, 72, 75, 76, 89, 165, 234, 287; Trail, *42*, 42–45, 54, 63–64

Anzaldua, Gloria, 14

Appadurai, Arjun, 22

archaeobotany, 139, 166, *167*, 239–40, *241*, 242–43, *318–19*, *320–22*, 323

architecture of El Presidio de San Francisco: and ethnogenesis of Californio identity, 174, 196–97, 293–94; expansion of, 190, 195–96; heterogeneity vs. homogeneity of, 190–91; master plan for, 152–

architecture of El Presidio de San Francisco (continued)
    55, 173–74; Sal plan for, *179*, 181, *182*, 184, 198, 199, 336n1; social aspects of, 196–202. *See also* El Presidio de San Francisco, main quadrangle of
Argüello, José Darío, *44*, 76
Argüello, Luis Antonio, *44*, 66, 187, 188, 192
Army, U.S., 118–19, 122, 159, 175; Corps of Engineers, *127–29*, 133
Arrillaga, José Joaquín de, 65
Augustine Pattern, 299

Baja California, 1, 54, 57, 92, 109, 327n2
Bancroft, Hubert Howe, 104
Barker, Leo, 118, 205
Barnes, Mark, 300
Barth, Frederick, 26–27
bastions, 58, 152–55, 157, 335n6, 336n7
La Batería de San José, 58, 65, 157, *158*, 182, 293
Bay Miwok language group, 11, 48, *49*, 50, 330n5
beads, 43, 52, 132, *253*, 276, 280–83, *282*
beans, as dietary staple, 61, 234, 235, 242, 245
Bear Flag Revolt, 68
Beebe, Rose Marie, 187
beef, 235, 237–39, 245, 250, 291
Bell, Alison, 37
Benté, Vance, 118
Bhabha, Homi, 13, 14
Borica, Diego de, 182, *183*, 184, 193
borrow pits, 58, 124, 139–40, 158
Bos taurus. See cattle bone
botanical specimens. *See* plant specimens
Bouchard, Hipólito, 66, 76, 329n11
Bourbon Reforms, 149
Bourbon styles of clothing, 256–58, *257*, 261, 265, 273, 277, 291
Bourdieu, Pierre, 17–20, 29, 219
Bouvier, Virginia M., 45
Bowman, Jan, 336n9

bricks, adobe, 58, 122, 124, 140, 158, 185, 191, 193, 337n5
Brillat-Savarin, Jean Anthelme, 233
Briones, Juana, 163, *164*, 165–71, 336nn9–10
Briones-Miramontes family, 159, *166*
British activity on Pacific coast, 54, 65, 180–81, 201, 327–28n2, 329n12, 335n2
British whiteware, 167, *168*, 186, *205*, *210*, 216–18, *218*
Brumfiel, Elizabeth, 249
Bruñida de Tonalá, *205*, *215*, 215–16, *218*
Buchli, Victor, 17
buckles, *252*, 278, *279*
Building 12 Field Investigation, *127*, *134*
Building 13 midden: archaeological dating of, 137, 140, 186; archaeological excavation of, 140–42, *141–42*; clothes-related items in, *253*, 262, 276–83, *279*, *282*; food deposits in, 237, 238, 239, 240, *241*, 242, 243, 293, 307–9, *310–12*, 312–13, *314–17*, 318–19, *320–22*, 323
—, ceramics in, 186, *205*, *210*, 212–15, *212–18*, *217–18*, 334nn9–10; compositional analysis of, 223, 226, 228; decorative attributes of, *210*, 212–19, *217*, *218*, *219*; and depositional processes, 204, 207–8; food-preparation practices indicated by, 245–49, *247*, *248*; functions of, *208*, 208–10, *210*, 245–49, *248*; imported, 204, *206*, 206–7; locally produced, 204, 220–23, *224*, *225*, 225–26, 227, 229, 231
Building 15 Excavation, *127*, *134*
Building 39: Excavation, *127*, *134*; midden, 161
Building 49 seismic retrofit, *128*, *134*
Butler, Judith, 19–20
buttons, *252*, *253*, 256, *257*, 261, 262, *263*, *264*, 273, 276–78, *279*, *280*, 340nn13–14

Cabrillo, Juan Rodríguez, 327n2
Californios: aristocratic aspirations
of, 106–7; disenfranchisement of,
68, 115, 304–5; family histories
of, 11–12, 305, 341n3; family
relations of, 106, 107; historical
studies of, 100–101, 103–13,
115–16, 288; and landownership,
105–10, 336n10; Mexican identity
asserted by, 109; mixed heritage
of, 1, 11, 71, 83, 102, 114, 115,
170, 298, 304, 305; political relations of, 107; present-day identity
of, 2, 7, 305–6; racial categories
manipulated by, 71, 83, 91, 101,
107, 113–14, 115; and rancho
culture, 105–12, 289; romantic
representations of, 98–99, 103–4,
111; social relations of, 106, 115,
305; "Spanish" identity ascribed
to, 333n9. See also ethnogenesis of
Californio identity
Camarillo, Albert, 109, 333n9
Cambon, Pedro, 43
Campbell, Leon, 84
Cañizares, José de, 46
Carlos III (king of Spain), 149
Castañeda, Antonia, 107
castas. See sistema de castas
El Castillo de San Joaquín, 58, 65, 76,
157, 158, 182, 192, 293
Catalonian Volunteers, 65, 73, 75–76,
84, 264
Catholic Church, 93, 95, 101, 276
cattle, 41, 67, 79, 80, 105, 110, 166,
234, 239, 313
cattle bone (Bos taurus), 161, 238, 310,
312, 312
ceramics: classification of, 208–9, 212,
225; compositional analysis of,
222–23, 226, 228; decorative
attributes of, 210, 212–19, 217,
218, 219; documentary record of,
204–6, 211–12; importation of,
204–7, 206, 210, 211, 220, 221,
230, 233; local production of, 58,
140, 204, 211, 220–23, 224, 225,

225–26, 227, 228–32, 229; production methods for, 225–26, 228–
29; and rancho culture, 110; social
relations indicated by, 210–11,
220–22, 230–32, 290, 291. See also
waretypes
cereals, 234, 239, 240, 242–46, 249,
250, 291, 321
Chamisso, Adelbert von, 186–87
chapel area, clothing-related artifacts in,
276, 278, 279, 280, 280, 281, 282,
282, 283, 285
Chapel Investigations, 128, 134, 135,
160, 181, 276
Chatan, Robbin, 303
Chávez-García, Miroslava, 112
Childe, V. Gordon, 34
children: clothing of, 254, 255, 257;
at El Presidio de San Francisco,
70, 72, 74, 89–90, 99, 194; and
sistema de castas, 89–90
Chinese porcelain, 204, 206, 207, 210,
211, 212, 216
Choris, Louis, 187, 272
Chutchui, 44, 48
clothing: for Anza expedition, 254, 255,
265–67, 273; Bourbon styles of,
256–58, 257, 261, 265, 273, 277;
and Building 13 midden artifacts,
253, 262, 276–83, 279, 282; documentary record of, 267–69, 270–
71, 272–75; and military uniforms,
262, 262–65, 263, 264, 273–74,
278, 279, 280; Native Californian,
51, 266–67, 267, 292; and racial
passing, 256; and sistema de castas,
258–59, 260, 261–62, 265, 274,
277; social identity indicated by,
252–54, 272, 283–86, 291–92;
and sumptuary laws, 258–59, 265,
274, 298
Coast Miwok language group, 11, 48,
49, 50, 330n5
colonization: of Alta California, 2–3, 54,
57, 63, 93, 113–14, 149; comparative perspectives on, 299–301. See
also identity: colonial

Colony Ross, 56, 59, 66, 186, 200–201, 275, 335n2
Comaroff, Jean, 272, 274, 339
Congress, U.S., 119
cordons, defensive, 150–52, 151, 155, 289, 292, 334–35n1
corn, 43, 78, 235, 242, 244, 245, 250, 291
Cortés, Hernán, 92
Cox, Bea, 10
criollo, as casta category, 85, 87
Crosby, Alfred, 244
Cross, Guy, 131

Dado, Veronica, 205, 337n3
Darek, Francis, 328n2
Deagan, Kathleen, 211, 299
de Certeau, Michel, 16, 17, 21, 302
diachronic model, 113–15, 121, 292–94
diet, 43, 48, 235–40, 241, 242–45, 291
domestic sphere, 209, 211
dress. See clothing
Durkheim, Emile, 15
Dutch activity on Pacific coast, 54, 201
Dutch colonization of New York, 300–301

earthenware: local production of, 204, 211, 220–23, 224, 225, 225–26, 227, 228–30, 229, 338n9; ware-types of, 168, 204, 205, 206, 210, 211–12, 214, 216–18. See also ceramics
earthquakes, 175, 185, 186, 196
Eastern Miwok language group, 48, 49
economic relations, 66, 67, 204, 207, 217, 218; women's participation in, 96–97, 108–9, 167–68, 170, 171. See also trade
Enlightenment, 13, 107, 149, 152, 258
epidemics, 60
español, as casta category, 85–89, 90, 91, 99, 101, 102, 113, 331n14
ethnogenesis: archaeological investigation of, 12, 121; concept of, 1, 33–37; and social identity, 13, 15,

27; theoretical and practical limits of, 303–6
ethnogenesis of Californio identity: archaeological investigation of, 111–12, 121, 142, 286, 287–88; and architectural design, 174, 196–97, 293–94; and aristocratic ideology, 106–7; and clothing, 274, 284–86, 292; and colonial appropriation of territory, 289, 292; diachronic model of, 113–15, 292–94; dietary aspects of, 244, 245, 250–51, 291, 293, 294; and differential masculinities, 6, 296–97; and distinction from Native Californians, 6, 287, 294, 296; and gender relations, 297–99, 303; and gente de razón status, 91, 101–2, 112; and immigration to Alta California, 108; and inadequacy of documentary records, 111–13; and isolation from New Spain, 63, 91, 114, 293; and liberalism, 107, 114; as multigenerational process, 100, 292; multiple factors in, 105, 108, 110, 112, 288, 292; and noncasta identification strategies, 91, 101–3, 113, 293; overdetermination of, 110, 288, 295; practical limits of, 304–6; and rancho culture, 105–12, 289, 292; and sistema de castas, 2, 7, 11, 71, 91, 101–2, 112, 113–14, 142, 197, 274, 292, 293; and social homogenization, 115, 294; and within-group identification, 295; women's role in, 297–99
Europe: and competition for control of Alta California, 54, 64–65; and immigration to Alta California, 108

Fages, Pedro, 43
faience, 205, 210, 217–18
Fairbanks, Charles, 211
family relations: in missions, 60; at El Presidio de San Francisco, 72, 73, 74; and rancho culture, 106, 107

feminism, 16, 17, 24, 30, 31, 104, 108, 111

Fernández, José Pérez, 44

Fiber Optic Cable Installation Investigation, *128*, *134*

fire damage, 175, 176, 178

firewood, 43, 52, 58, 159

fish, consumption of, 236, 238–39, *311*, *313*, 339n2

Fisher, Abby Sue, 261, 277

Font, Pedro, 42, 43, 59

food: archaeologically significant deposits of, 158, 237–40, *241*, 242–49, *247*, *248*, 293, 307–9, *310–12*, 312–13, *314–17*, 318–19, *320–22*, 323; Californio ethnogenesis indicated by, 244, 245, 250–51, 291, 293, 294; consumption of, 43, 48, 204, 209–10, 233–45, 291; preparation of, 158, 204, 209–10, 235–36, 245–51, 290–91, 293

Forbes, Jack D., 331n14

Foucault, Michel, 17, 21, 22, 148

Frémont, John C., 68

French activity on Pacific coast, 54, 65, 201, 329n12

Fuller, David, 234

Funston Avenue Archaeological Research Project, *129*, *134*, *135–37*, *136*, *138*, *160*

galera, 204, *205*, *210*, *214*, 214–15, 218, 222, *223*

Gálvez, José de, 54, 58–59

Gamble, Clive, 70

Geertz, Clifford, 21, 22

gender relations: ceramics as indicators of, 211; and cordon strategy, 152, 289; and ethnogenesis of Californio identity, 297–99, 303; and food-related activities, 235–36, 290–91, 297; and honor/shame complex, 95–96, 97, 197; and Native Californian laborers, 82, 244; and patriarchal ideology, 94–97; at El Presidio de San Francisco,

97, 174, 194, 197, 297–99; and rancho culture, 109, 110; and sistema de castas, 87, 197, 298. *See also* identity: gender

gente de razón status, 2, 91, 101–2, 112, 113, 114

Gerald, Rex, 222, 335n6

Giddens, Anthony, 17, 21, 148

Ginn, Sarah, 222

glass: beads, 43, 52, 132, *253*; vessels, 132, 142, *142*, 161, 210, 218, 237, 245, 334n9

Golden Gate National Recreation Area (GGNRA), 119

gold rush, 68

González, Diego, 44

Grijalva, Juan, 52–53

Haas, Lisbeth, 107, 112

Haley, Brian, 11–12

Hall, Stuart, 13, 14, 37, 304

Harris Matrix system, 133, *138*

Hernández, Santiago, 44

Hidalgo Revolt, 66, 175, 185

hide and tallow trade, 62, 67, 106, 108, 110, 170, 335n2

hijos del país, 2, 101, 102, 114

Hirata, Rita, 223

honor/shame complex, 87, 95–96, 97, 106, 174, 197, 198, 200, 297

Hornbeck, David, 234

Horning, Audrey, 29

Huchiun, 45, 50

Huimen, 45, 50

huipil, 257, *257*, 258, 274

Hull, Kathleen, 161

Hurtado, Albert, 109

hybridity, 14–15, 32, 33, 289, 303

hypodescent, 85, 115, 304

identity: and agency, 16–19, 21, 254, 286; alterity vs. similarity in, 14; Bourdieu on, 17–20, 29; Butler on, 19–20; class, 29, 30; clothing as indicator of, 252–54, 272, 283–86, 291–92; colonial, 11, 46, 102, 103, 113, 115, 142, 171, 245, 287,

mestizo, as casta category, 87–89, 90, 91, 98, 101, 259, 331n14
Metz, John, 37
Mexico: Alta California as province of, 66–68, 103–12, 114–15; Californios' identification with, 109, 292; ceramics made in, 204, 206, 211, 212–15; independence of, 47, 66–67, 76, 83, 114, 175, 185, 292, 329n13
midden deposits, 122, 124, 130, 131, 139–40, 141, 158. See also Building 13 midden
Milliken, Randall, 61, 328n3
Miranda, Apolinario, 165–66, 169
missions, 54, 55, 56, 58–61; secularization of, 61, 67, 103, 105, 114, 292
Mission San Francisco de Asís (Mission Dolores): agriculture at, 234; chapel at, 277; establishment of, 43–45, 59; Native Californians in, 52, 53, 79, 267, 330n5; pottery produced at, 220, 222, 230; and roadway to El Presidio, 157, 159; troops stationed at, 45, 59, 73
Mission San Francisco Solano, 56, 59, 68
Mission San José, 56, 59, 65, 76, 102
Mission San Juan Capistrano, 329n11
Mission San Rafael, 56, 59, 66
Mission Santa Clara, 56, 59, 73, 79, 168, 169, 222, 234
Mission Santa Cruz, 56, 59, 67, 222
Mitchell, Katharyne, 303
Miwok language groups. See Bay Miwok; Coast Miwok; Eastern Miwok
Montalvo, Garcí Ordóñez de, 92–93
Moraga, José Joaquín, 42, 43, 44, 45, 46, 77–78, 82, 176, 177
Moser, Stephanie, 70
mulato, as casta category, 87–89, 90, 98, 258, 331n14

Nahl, Charles Christian, 97–99, 98
Naruta, Anna, 131

National Park Service, 68, 70, 119, 126, 205, 333n6; field investigations led by, 127–29
Native Californians: artifacts of, 160, 160–61, 162, 163; Californio identity distinguished from, 6, 287, 294, 296; clothing of, 51, 266–67, 267, 292; diet of, 43, 48, 244, 291; gender relations of, 92; and gente de razón status, 101–2, 114; as hunter-gatherers, 48, 51; intertribal conflict among, 45, 155, 328n3; as laborers, 61, 72, 77–79, 80–81, 82–83, 105–6, 156, 163, 182, 184–85, 188–89, 192–95, 244, 290, 293, 294, 297; language groups of, 48, 49; material culture of, 160, 160–61, 162, 163; as mission neophytes, 52, 59, 60, 79, 82, 102, 107, 151, 222, 266, 293; political organization of, 48, 50, 51–52; population of, 72; and pottery production, 221, 222; at El Presidio de San Francisco, 10–11, 61, 72, 77–79, 80–81, 82–83, 156, 161, 163, 172, 182, 184–85, 188–89, 192–95, 290, 293, 294, 330n5; sexual practices of, 51; sexual violence against, 93, 152, 155, 289, 297; social relations of, 47–49, 51, 52; Spanish-colonial expeditions' encounters with, 43, 52; Spanish-colonial impact on, 51–52, 53–54, 61; Spanish-colonial military conflicts with, 52–53, 60–61, 65–66, 79, 80–81, 82, 155–56, 289, 290, 297; Spanish-colonial military's recruitment of, 82; trading by, 48, 51, 151. See also names of specific Native Californian districts and language groups
Neiman, Fraser, 25–26
neophytes, 52, 59, 60, 79, 82, 102, 107, 151, 222, 266, 293
Neve, Felipe de, 176

New Spain: Bourbon fashions in, 256–58, 277; colonization of Alta California by, 54, 62–63, 83, 93; map of, *42*; presidios in, 57, 149. *See also* Interior Provinces
Nootka Convention, 64–65

Oconór, Hugo, 335n6
Officers' Club: Adobe Initiative, 122, *129*, 137; adobe walls in, *3*, 122, *125*, 137, 181, 185, 186; Mesa Room investigation, *129, 134*
Officers' Quarters: excavation of, *127, 134*; rehabilitation of, 135
Ohlone language group, 11, 48, *49*, 50, 327n1, 328n5
El Ojo de Agua de Figueroa, *164*, 166–67, 171
ollas de aceite, *205*, 209, 237, *248*
Orser, Charles, 29
Osborn, Sannie, 118
Osio, Antonio María, 187–88, 189, 192, 194
overdetermination, 5, 24–25, 110, 288, 295

Palóu, Francisco, 43, 44, 45, 52
patriarchy, 94–97, 106, 108
Patwin language group, 11, 48, *49*, 50, 330n5
Peña, Joaquín, *44*
Pérez Fernández, José, *44*
Perissinotto, Giorgio, 337nn2–3
Pershing Square Field Investigation, *127, 134*
Petlenuc, 41, 48, 327n1
plant specimens: in Building 13 midden, 239–40, *241*, 242–43, 318–19, *320–22*, 323; at El Polín Springs, 166, *167*; in residential apartment, 139
El Polín Springs, 132, *158*, 159, 161, *162*, 165–66, *166*, 334n7
Pomo language group, 48, *49*, 50
porcelain, 204, *206*, 207, *210*, 211, 212, 216, 218
Portolá, Gaspar de, 43

Port Rumiantsev, 56
pottery. *See* ceramics
Prado Mesa, Juan, *44*
Pred, Allan, 148
Presidio Archaeology Center, 9, 119, 122, 126, 205
El Presidio de Los Adaes, 191, 300
El Presidio de Monterey, 41, 42, 55, 66, 67, 76, 196
El Presidio de San Carlos, *153*, 335n6
El Presidio de San Diego, 55, 196
El Presidio de San Francisco: artists' depictions of, 70–71, *71*, 187, *187*, 272, *272*; children at, 70, 72, 74, 89–90, 99, 194; civilian personnel at, 76; commanders of, *44*; compared to other colonial settlements, 299–301, 341n2; craft production and manufacture at, 57, 158, 184, 220, 222, 230–32, 290, 293; establishment of, 41–46, *42*, 176; European visitors to, 66, 180, 200–201; family relations at, 72, 73, *74*; food-related activities at, 158, 209–10, 218–20, 233–36, 249–51; gender relations at, 97, 174, 194, 197, 297–99; labor relations at, 61, 72, 76, 77–79, *80–81*, 82–83, 156, 163, 172, 182, 184–85, 188–89, 192–95, 244, 297; and links to neighboring settlements, 157–59, *158*; military importance of, 57, 64–66, 67–68, 293; Native Californians at, 10–11, 61, 72, 77–79, *80–81*, 82–83, 156, 161, 163, 172, 182, 184–85, 188–89, 192–95, 290, 293, 297, 330n5; natural resources at, 58, 159, 188, 293; population of, 72–73, *73–75*, *75*–76, 82; royal reserve and ranchlands of, 58; sistema de castas at, 88–91, *90*, 265; social relations at, 196–202, 272–76, 283–86; troop strength at, 72–73, *75*, *75*–76, 84; U.S. takeover of, 68, 118, 122; women at, 72, *74*, 89,

90, 94, 99, 194, 197, 249–51, 265, 290, 293–94
—, archaeological investigation of: and archaeological monitoring, 117–18, 126, *127–29*, 130, 137, 158, 161, 185; and excavation methods, 132–33; and excavation of midden deposits, 139–41, *141–42*; and excavation of quadrangle architecture, 133, *134*, 135–37, *136*, *138*, 139, 174–75, 181, 185–86; and excavation of residential space, 133, *134*, 135–37, *136*, *138*, 139; and food-related deposits, 158, 237–40, *241*, 242–50, 247, *248*; history of, 126, *127–29*; and pedestrian surveys, 131–32; project area of, 121–22, *123–24*, 124, 126; and remote sensing, 131, 135, 137, 181, 185; and shovel test surveys, 132, 158, 161
—, main quadrangle of, 122, *123–24*, 157, 173–74; architectural homogeneity of, 190–91; and architectural indicators of social relations, 196–202; architectural master plan for, 152–55, 173–74; building materials used in, 176, 184, 190–91, 290, 293; centralized construction of, 189, 190, 192–95; decline of, 175, 176, 178, 180, 185, 189, 196; defensive attributes of, 153–55, 289, 335n6, 336n7; documentary record of, 174, 175, 176, *177*, 178, *179*, 180–81, *183–84*, 186–88, 192, 193; excavation of, 133, *134*, 135–37, *136*, *138*, 139, 174–75, 181, 185–86; expansion of, 190, *195*, 195–96, 290; first quadrangle, 46, 176, *177*, 178, 190, 195; second quadrangle, 176, 178, *179*, 180–85, *182–84*, 195; third quadrangle, 176, 185–89, *187*, 192–93, 195, 199–200, 290
—, main quadrangle structures: bas-

tions, 58, 152–55, 157, 335n6, 336n7; chapel, 46, 57, 135, 152, 176, 181–83, 185–89 passim, 191, 192, 277, 280; comandancia, 46, 57, 176, 178, 189, 190, 191, 198; defensive structures, 65, 153–55; guardhouses, 46, 152, 176, 191, 335n6; prison, 57, 76, 180, 189; residences, 133, 135–37, 139, 198–200, 290, 293; storehouses, 46, 57, 176, 178, 180, 184, 190, 191, 230
—, waterworks, 58, 159, 293
El Presidio de Santa Bárbara, 55, 196, 205, 337n2
El Presidio de Tucson, 300
presidios, 54, 55, 55, 57–58, 112, 149–50, 152–53
Presidio Trust, 119, 135, 333n6
primordialism, 27, 36, 295
private sphere, 96, 197, 198, 211
projectile points, 160, *160*, 161, 163, 336n8
public sphere, 96, 290
pueblos, 54–55, 56, 112

racial categories. *See* sistema de castas
rancho culture, 105–12, 289, 292
Rancho La Purísima Concepción, *164*, 167, 170, 336n10
rape, 152, 155, 297
refuse disposal. *See* midden deposits; waste disposal
regionalization, 148, 156
Reglamento (regulations) of 1772 for presidios, 57, 58, 149–50, 152, *153*, 154, 171, 273, 335n5
religious charms, 252, 280–81, *281*
remote sensing, 131, 135, 137, 181, 185
Ríos-Bustamante, Antonio, 109, 333n9
Rivera y Moncada, Fernando Xavier de, 43
roasting pits, 158
Rodríguez, Dámaso, *44*
Rodríguez, Manuel, *44*
Romeu, José Antonio, 178

roof tile, 58, 118, 122, 161, 184,
186, 190, 193, 194, 222, 293,
337n5
Rosaldo, Renato, 104
Ross. *See* Colony Ross
Rothschild, Nan, 299, 300
Rudolph, Catherine, 205
Ruiz de Burton, María Amparo, 104
Russian activity on Pacific coast, 54, 56,
59, 65, 66, 68, 186, 200–201,
329nn12–13, 335n2

St. Augustine, colonial settlement at,
299
Sal, Hermenegildo, *44*, 65, 79, 178,
179, 180–82, *182–83*, 193; and
Sal plan, *179*, 181, *182*, 184, 198,
199, 336n1
Salinan language group, 11, *49*
San Blas: craftworkers from, 222; supplies from, 54, 201, 204–5, 207,
220, 231, 234, 236–37, 245, 267,
269, 292, 338n4; troops from, 66,
75, 76, 84
Sánchez, Francisco, *44*
Sánchez, José Antonio, *44*
Sánchez, Rosaura, 107, 112
Sánchez family, in Tennessee Hollow,
159
Sandos, James A., 61
San Francisco, city of, 62. *See also* Mission San Francisco de Asís; Yerba
Buena
San Francisco, Presidio of (post-1848):
acquired from Mexico, 68, 118,
122; federal administration of,
119; as U.S. Army post, 68, 118–
19, 122, 124, 126, 175. *See also*
El Presidio de San Francisco
San Francisco State University, *128*,
333–34n7
San José, pueblo of, 56, 61, 62, 73, 76,
234, 244
Santa Barbara Presidio History Center,
205
Senkewicz, Robert, 187
sexuality: Catholic precepts of, 95;

and honor/shame complex, 95–
96, 197; and Nahl's artwork,
98; Native Californian, 51, 92;
and politics of identity, 5–6;
and sexual violence, 93, 152,
197, 289, 297; social iteration
of, 19; Spanish-colonial, 92, 95,
197. *See also* gender relations;
identity; rape
sherds. *See* ceramics
Sheridan Avenue Field Investigation,
128, 134
shovel test surveys, 132, 158, 161
Sider, Gerald, 16, 21–22
Singer, Leslie, 35, 36
sistema de castas: abolition of, 102; and
casta paintings, 259, *260*, 261, 277,
340n8; and clothing, 258–59, *260*,
261–62, 265, 274, 277; and ethnogenesis of Californios, 2, 7, 11, 71,
91, 101–2, 112, 113–14, 142,
197, 274, 292, 293; and gender
relations, 87, 197; legal codifica-
tion of, 85; mobility within, 83,
84–87
Smith-Lintner, Cheryl, 307
Solá, Pablo Vicente de, 187, 188
Soler, Nicolás, 64
Sonoma Barracks, 68, *73*, 189
Sonora, 1, 45, 54, 64, 109, 300
space, social aspects of, 147–49,
197–200
Spain: colonization of Alta California
by, 54, 57, 63, 93, 113–14, 149,
327n2; and European rivals in
Alta California, 54, 64–65; Mexican independence from, 47,
66–67; and war against Great
Britain, 65
Ssalson, 45–46, 50, 328n3
Stern, Steve, 97
Sturtevant, William, 35, 36
sumptuary laws, 258–59, 265, 274,
298
supply ships, 45, 58, 64, 158, 176,
204–5, 234, 237, 245
survey, archaeological, 131–32

women, Spanish-colonial (*continued*) ship, 109, 167–68, 336n10; in missions, 60; as necessary to colonial project, 93–94, 298; patriarchal domination of, 94–97; at El Presidio de San Francisco, 72, *74*, 89, *90*, 94, 194, 197, 249–51, 265, 290, 293–94; sexual surveillance of, 197, 290, 293–94; underrepresented in documentary records, 111, 112

women of African heritage, 258, 265, 274, 298

Woodward-Clyde Consultants, 117, *127–28, 160*

Wylie, Alison, 120

Yelamu, 41, 43, 44, 45, 48, *50*, 52–53, 327n1, 328n3

Yerba Buena, pueblo of, 56, 62, *158*, *164*, 167, 171, 189

Yokuts language group, 11, 48, *49*

Young, Robert, 303

Yuma, 47, 64, 77

zooarchaeology, 237–39, 307–9, *310–12*, 312–13, *314–17*, 318

Text:	10/13 Joanna
Display:	Syntax, Joanna
Compositor:	Integrated Composition Systems
Indexer:	Andrew Joron
Cartographer:	Landis Bennett
Printer/Binder:	Thomson-Shore, Inc.